MEETINGS, EXPOSITIONS, EVENTS, AND CONVENTIONS

An Introduction
to the Industry

George G. Fenich, Ph.D.

PEARSON

Boston   Columbus   Indianapolis   New York   San Francisco   Upper Saddle River
Amsterdam   Cape Town   Dubai   London   Madrid   Milan   Munich   Paris   Montreal   Toronto
Delhi   Mexico City   Sao Paulo   Sydney   Hong Kong   Seoul   Singapore   Taipei   Tokyo

Editorial Director: Vernon Anthony
Senior Acquisitions Editor: William Lawrensen
Editorial Assistant: Lara Dimmick
Director of Marketing: David Gesell
Senior Marketing Manager: Leigh Ann Sims
Senior Marketing Coordinator: Alicia Wozniak
Marketing Assistant: Les Roberts
Project Manager: Holly Shufeldt
Senior Art Director: Jodi Notowitz
Manager, Visual Research: Karen Sanatar
Full-Service Project Management/Composition: Jogender Taneja/Aptara®, Inc.
Printer/Binder: Edwards Brothers
Cover Printer: Lehigh-Phoenix Color
Text Font: 10/12 Minion

10 9 8 7 6 5 4 3 2 1

Prentice Hall
is an imprint of

ISBN 10:   0-13-271991-6
ISBN 13: 978-0-13-271991-9

Dedicated to Breast Cancer Survivors
Notably my wife Kathryn

BRIEF CONTENTS

CONTENTS

PART 3   Important Elements in Meeting, Exposition, Event, and Convention Planning

PREFACE

The meetings, expositions, events, and conventions (MEEC, pronounced like *geese*) industry continues to grow and garner increasing attention from the hospitality industry, colleges and universities, and communities. This book gives a broad overview of this industry and is thus an introduction. It is not meant to provide a hands-on or step-by-step method for handling gatherings in the MEEC industry.

This book is being produced at this time for a number of reasons. One is the continued growth of this industry; in spite of the ebbs and flows of the economy and disasters such as 9/11 and Hurricane Katrina, the MEEC segment of the hospitality industry remains resilient. Communities continue to build or expand MEEC venues unabated, and the private sector has also become a player in convention center construction and operation. People still find a need for face-to-face meetings. The MEEC industry appears to be on a growth curve and is of interest to many people (not unlike the casino industry was in the early 1990s).

Also, college faculties have indicated a need for a book such as this. The author has been teaching an introductory MEEC course for many years and has found himself having to continually supplement the existing books to make them both current and more complete in addressing the various segments of the MEEC industry. Therefore, he began to contemplate the development of a book on the subject. Then, at a meeting of the Convention Special Interest Group at the Council on Hotel, Restaurant, and Institutional Education (CHRIE) Convention in 2001, the need for a new text was discussed. The members of this group all noted the need, and the author/editor volunteered to spearhead an effort to put together a new book using faculty and industry experts to write various chapters. This book is a culmination of that effort. The result is a text in which some of the best and most notable people in the MEEC industry have made contributions; as you will see, there is a fairly even balance between educators and practitioners among the chapter contributors.

The approach to deciding on topics was unusual. Rather than have a list of topics or chapters based on people's willingness to contribute, a more scientific method was used. The author/editor reviewed existing books, both theoretical and practical, to ascertain which topics to cover. Topics that appeared in more than one text were compiled into a list. Then a number of meetings were held with educators, and the relative importance of topics was discussed, which led to the development of a comprehensive list of topics. This list was sent to educators and practitioners, who were asked to rank the importance of each topic as critically important, important, or not important. Results were used to pare down the list, and this iterative voting procedure (Delphi technique) was used to reach the decision as to the topics to include in the book. This third edition not only has updated material and statistics but has relied on feedback from adopters and reviewers to make improvements to the previous edition.

It should be noted that this industry is referred to in many ways: "Meetings and Events," "Events," "Meeting Planning," and others. A very common acronym, and one used extensively in Asia is "MICE," which stands for "Meetings, Incentives, Conventions, Events" and is pronounced as the plural of mouse. That acronym was purposely *not* chosen for the title of this text. The reason is that most programs of study deal with the Incentives or Incentive Travel very little, if at all. Furthermore, the Incentive Travel segment has evolved significantly in the past few years moving away from trips that were strictly for pleasure (as a reward for performance) and much more into trips that have notable education and training components. Thus, they are now much more like sales training meetings, but on a more grandiose scale. Thus, this book deals with Meetings, Expositions, Events, and Conventions.

Meetings, Expositions, Events, and Conventions should be of interest to practitioners, educators, students, and the general public. It is the most up-to-date book on the MEEC industry and will provide users with an overview of the industry; it is also comprehensive and covers a wider range of MEEC topics than any other book available. It can easily serve as the basis for an introductory college course on the subject or for orientation sessions for new employees in the industry. It should meet the needs of anyone interested in knowing more about the MEEC industry.

NEW TO THIS EDITION

This third edition of the book has undergone major revisions. All current events as well as statistical material have been updated to reflect the "state of the art". Furthermore, all the chapters have been extensively revised and additional supplemental material added.

- New material supplied by Meeting Planners International has been added to multiple chapters.
- A new chapter on "green meetings" has been added.
- The chapters on planning and producing meetings and events gatherings have been consolidated into a single chapter.
- A supplemental compendium of over 30 case studies in meetings and events has been developed.
- A supplemental compendium of hundreds of current events articles, each relating to a specific chapter has been developed.
- Over two-thirds of the chapters have new contributors.

George G. Fenich, Ph.D.

ACKNOWLEDGMENTS

I would like to thank Kathryn Hashimoto for her unabated support, patience, and encouragement; the chapter contributors for their work and insights; and students everywhere for their interest in the MEEC industry. Also, thank you to the educators in the MEEC field for helping develop the concept for this book and for continuing support through adoptions of this text.

The following reviewers of this edition also deserve a special thank you. They are Jen Colman, Champlain College; Nicole Davis, SIUC; Jamal Feerasta, Summit College; Stephen Fries, Gateway Community College; Julianna Frisch, Monroe Community College; William Host, Roosevelt University; Carl Lindblade, University of NH; Eric Lund, Grossmont College; Laurel Marshall, CUNY Kingsborough Community College; Rich Patterson, Western Kentucky University; Dr. Kate Sullivan, San Jose State University; Erin Tierney, University of Massachusetts; and John Wolper, The University of Findlay—College of Business.

ABOUT THE AUTHOR

George G. Fenich, Ph.D., is a professor in the Hospitality Management Department at East Carolina University. Dr. Fenich worked in the hospitality industry for 15 years before joining academe in 1985. He teaches and researches in the area of conventions and meetings, has written over 30 academic articles, and has presented at over 100 conferences—including the Council on Hotel Restaurant and Institutional Education, the Destination Marketing Association International, the Association for Convention Operations Management, the International Association of Assembly Managers, and the Professional Convention Management Association. He is on the editorial board of five academic journals—including associate editor for conventions and meetings for *HTL Science* and the *Journal of Convention and Exhibition Management.* He is also the principal of the consulting firm Fenich & Associates LLC.

MEETINGS, EXPOSITIONS, EVENTS, AND CONVENTIONS

CHAPTER 1

Introduction to the Meetings, Expositions, Events, and Conventions Industry

The Olympic Games are but one of the many aspects of the meetings, expositions, events, and conventions industry. *Courtesy of Dreamstime LLC—Royalty Free.*

Chapter Objectives

This chapter provides the reader with an understanding of the following:

- The history of the Meetings, Expositions, Events, and Conventions (MEEC) industry
- Where MEEC fits in relation to the hospitality industry
- The magnitude and impact of MEEC
- Careers in MEEC
- Different types of gatherings

Prologue

The vignette that follows is meant to provide an example and insights into the field of meetings, expositions, events, and conventions (MEEC). The chapter concludes with the second half of this vignette "The End of the Big Day." Readers are directed to the glossary at the end of this book and to the Convention Industry Council online glossary at http://glossary.conventionindustry.org for the definitions of any words or terms that they are not familiar with.

The Big Day

Picture this: The sun rises above the horizon, releasing rays of blue and pink light that whisk across the ocean and spill onto the beautifully manicured greens of the resort hotel's championship golf course. Against the backdrop of the crashing surf and pleas of hungry gulls, you can also hear the sounds of morning stirring at the resort hotel. Car doors slamming, muffled voices sharing greetings and farewells, china and silver clashing, and the squeaking wheels of fully laden carts, each heading off to its appointed area under the guiding hand of one of many hotel staff who have arrived before most guests are awake.

Today is a big day. The Association of Amalgamated Professionals (AAP) will open its 35th Annual Congress with an evening reception, and before the day is done, 1,900 guests and hundreds of vendors will have descended on this resort hotel. Since there are growing concerns about the image conveyed by using apparently "glitzy" venues, the venue eliminated the word "resort" from its name. This was done *after* the contract was signed.

A fully laden pastry cart ready to head to its appointed destination.   *Courtesy of Wayne Sorce.*

Todd Cliver, Convention Services Manager (**CSM**) for the hotel, convenes a last-minute meeting for the hotel's team that is handling the Annual Congress. Todd has worked tirelessly for nearly nine months, when the account was turned over from the Sales and Marketing department of the hotel, coordinating all of the plans, wants, and needs of his client, the association's Senior Meeting Manager, Barbara Tain. Today represents the culmination of hundreds of e-mails, phone calls, videoconferences, and personal meetings between Todd and Barbara. Todd interacted with every department in the hotel. Barbara worked closely with AAP staff and volunteers, worked with other vendors, and supervised AAP support staff for the AAP's 35th Annual Congress.

Donna Miller, Director of **Sales and Marketing**, whose department was responsible for contracting this—the largest meeting the hotel will have ever managed—reports on her client's last-minute changes and concerns, all meticulously logged since her client, Barbara Tain, arrived two days ago. David Stern, Front Desk Manager, recaps the latest report on expected room occupancy and on the timing and numbers of anticipated arrivals. Throughout the day, he will continue to check with his staff to ensure that there will be adequate (and contracted!) numbers of front desk clerks to support the check-in flow, bell staff to manage the deluge of luggage and golf clubs, and doorstaff, valet parkers, concierge and guest services staff, and housekeeping services.

David Fenner, Director of Catering, provides his final status report, commenting on the readiness of the kitchen and banquet staff to serve over the next three days the equivalent of almost 12,000 meals and untold gallons of juice, milk, coffee, tea, soda, and alcoholic beverages. In addition, the hotel's **outlets** (restaurants and lounges) expect a much higher than average volume and have planned for supplies and personnel accordingly.

Other hotel staff members report to the Director of Sales and the CSM. These include those involved with recreation (golf, tennis, health club, and pool), maintenance, security, and accounting. Even the animal handlers who work with the parrots, an attraction for guests as they enter the property, want to ensure there are only healthy, well-behaved birds to greet the guests!

This one **convention** has already impacted and will impact every area of the hotel's operations. Armed with all this information, Todd leaves for his final preconference meeting (pre-con) with Barbara Tain, his client.

Meanwhile, on the other side of the country, Jane Lever steps onto Concourse B of the Philadelphia International Airport, her airline boarding pass, e-ticket receipt with its special "meeting discount" price, and government issued photo ID firmly in her grasp. She has checked her luggage, making sure it is locked with only TSA-approved locks for a possible security search. She scans the bank of monitors for her flight information. Before her day ends, she will have touched down at two other airports, eaten one airline snack, grabbed a candy bar on her way through a change of planes at another airport, made numerous mobile phone calls, bought a newspaper and a few magazines, and paid for a taxi to the hotel. Around the country, 1,899 other professionals just like Jane will do the same thing and travel to the same place for the same purpose—a **meeting**.

In the hotel's **destination** (city), Kathy Sykes, the owner and president of Skylark Destination Management Company **(DMC)**, is already at her office reviewing final arrangements for ground transportation for VIPs and off-site events, event theme preparations, and entertainment for the AAP meeting. Kathy has already received two complaints from the manager of the headliner rock star booked for tonight's reception: The entertainer wants only chilled glasses for his orange juice—which he expects to be freshly squeezed in his suite—and can only get dressed if he is provided with navy blue towels for his after-shower rubdown. Kathy, of course, will ensure compliance with these requests; she wants to avoid any problems before tonight's event.

With a thunderstorm threatening for tomorrow afternoon, Kathy's mind is also already racing about alternatives for the golf tournament. She knows the golfers can play in the rain, but a thunderstorm would endanger their safety.

Jack Ardulosky, a senior technical engineer for an audiovisual company, pulls into the hotel's delivery area while completing his mental checklist for final site review, satellite link integrity, picture clarity, and sound quality. With three global broadcasts and webcasts, he will have little room for error. He sees the florist unloading the last of the fresh floral arrangements and makes a note to himself that leaves and petals can cause just as much of a viewing obstruction as meeting room columns. He scans the area around him for a parking spot since not much is available with all the trucks and vans unloading the trade show booths. Jack notices the rising **ambient** temperature and expects a long, hot day. He will feel better as long as he can find parking in the shade, even if he has to walk a greater distance.

Barbara Tain, the Senior Meeting Manager for the association, wipes the beginning of fatigue from her eyes—she has already been on site for two days, and her constant checking of details has not allowed her to sleep as well as she would have liked—and continues her walk-through of the registration area, information center, and cyber café, ensuring the meeting space will be appropriately set for delivery of the education critical to the meeting's objectives—en route to a meeting with Todd Cliver and David Fenner. Having eaten just a few bites of her breakfast during a meeting with association executives and key committee members, she will still be late to her meeting with Cliver and Fenner because of last-minute details and concerns from the meeting with association staff and volunteers.

Only half glancing at the space around her, she again reviews her lengthy checklists: speaker and trainer arrivals and needs, banquet event orders **(BEOs)**, transportation schedules, badges, staffing, centerpiece design and delivery, phone and data lines, computers and printers, exhibitor booth setup, VIP procedures, concerns about tomorrow's weather, special check-in process, audiovisual equipment, opening production rehearsal times and needs, PowerPoint™ files, handouts, arrangements for participants with disabilities including those who have specified food allergies, amenities for VIPs . . . her mind is crowded with details.

With all this and more going through her mind, her most dominant thought is, "What could go wrong over the next three days—weather? Delayed arrivals? Delayed departures? The illness, or worse, death, of a participant, vendor or speaker? How prepared am I, and is the hotel and our vendors and off-site venues ready to respond quickly and effectively?" The fact is, although it is almost never apparent to a meeting participant, some things may not proceed as planned. The meeting planner and CSM are never more important than at that moment when a crisis must be anticipated and then averted.

It is opening day at last, and everything is in motion.

INTRODUCTION

What a Difference a Day Makes

Planning for AAP's 35th Annual Congress began long before the previous year's program ended and before nine months ago when the file was turned over to Convention Services. The scenario in the opening of this chapter is only a brief glimpse of the multitude of complexities that support planning and management, and of the jobs that employ those who work in and around the **MEEC** industry, all of which contribute to a meeting's success.

By the time the AAP program is over, roughly 1,900 people (participants and exhibitors) will have flown on approximately 9 major airlines and regional carriers on 200 different flights, covered 4 million air miles, consumed 1,000 airline snacks, thousands of bags of candy or snacks grabbed on runs through airports; participated in 60,000 people hours of presentations, education, and social events; played 4,000 person hours of golf; and eaten approximately 12,000 catered meals. They will have made about 80,000 telephone calls, purchased and read 5,700 newspapers (both in hard copy and virtually), transmitted and received more than 10,000 emails, and injected about $5,000,000 into the local economy. Their presence will generate about $500,000 in taxes toward state and local coffers. Countless local business owners will make sales in everything from clothing to artwork to souvenirs. Dry cleaners, cab drivers, restaurateurs, sports facilities, attractions, and hotels will all see jumps in their average weekly revenue. There may also be a significant boost to the local underground, cash-only economy, with contributions from the seamier side of this phenomenon such as gambling, drugs, and prostitution. In total, the convention-related activities for this single event will touch more than 250 local jobs.

Performing poorly at any of the hundreds of potential failure points of planning and executing a meeting or event, and especially not achieving the objectives and meeting the needs of the participants and vendors, can cause a dramatic immediate financial loss to the geographic area. In addition, the financial impact could result in positive or negative impacts for years to come: A good experience by each attendee will result in praise to many others; a negative experience will result in even more people hearing the results of the stay in that destination. Each of these people can bring or deny more business to the destination and the resort.

ACCEPTED PRACTICES EXCHANGE (APEX)

Throughout this book, you will hear about the Convention Industry Council (**CIC**) and its Accepted Practices Exchange (APEX). The following is from http://www.conventionindustry.org/apex/FAQ_File.htm and is meant to provide early insight into this initiative.

The CIC is at the forefront of efforts to advance the meeting, convention, and exhibition industry. It represents a broad cross-section with 34 member organizations representing more than 103,500 individuals as well as more than 17,300 firms and properties involved in the meetings, conventions, and exhibitions industry. Formed in 1949 to provide a forum for member organizations seeking to enhance the industry, the CIC facilitates the exchange of information and develops programs to promote professionalism within the industry and educates the public on its profound economic impact. By its nature, the CIC provides an impartial and inclusive forum for APEX and the development of accepted practices for the industry.

APEX is an initiative of the CIC that has brought together all stakeholders in the development and implementation of industry-wide accepted practices to create and enhance efficiencies throughout the meetings, conventions, and exhibitions industry.

Some of the results of accepted practices implementation will be:

- Time & Cost Savings
- Eased Communication and Sharing of Data
- Enhanced Customer Service
- Streamlined Systems and Processes
- Less Duplication of Effort and Increased Operational Efficiencies
- Better Educated, More Professional Employees

The APEX Commission and panels addressing key areas have completed most of their reports on accepted practices. Still in process as we go to print is the Green Meetings and Event

Standards. Each panel was charged to develop work in its specific areas: A download from the APEX site indicates the following:

Apex Industry Glossary: The definitive source of terms and definitions for the meetings, conventions, and exhibitions industry. (*Produced by the Terminology Panel.*)

APEX Event Specifications Guide: This template is the industry's official format for delivering information clearly and accurately to appropriate venue(s) and/or suppliers regarding all requirements for an event. (*Produced by the Resumes and Work Orders Panel.*)

APEX Request For Proposal (RFPs) Forms: These accepted practices forms are used to create consistent and thorough Requests for Proposals (RFPs) that address core information and unique needs.

APEX Housing & Registration Accepted Practices: These accepted practices are for the collecting, reporting, and retrieving of complete housing and registration data for meetings, conventions, and other events; and for housing issues such as housing providers, internet issues, international housing, and disclosure.

APEX Contracts Accepted Practices: The original purpose of the APEX Contracts Panel was to review all aspects of industry contracts and develop contract guidelines and, where appropriate, acceptable contract language guidelines. Additionally, the panel was to develop an outline to format industry contracts. The panel determined that for legal and practical reasons "acceptable contract language" should not be created.

APEX Post-Event Report: A report of the details and activities of an event is called a "Post-Event Report" or PER. A collection of PERs over time will provide the complete history for an event. This template is the industry's accepted format. (*Produced by the History/Post-Event Reports Panel.*)

APEX Meeting and Site Profile Report: The report of the Meeting and Site Profiles panel contains consistent and thorough profile formats for sites. It includes five primary location and facility types: hotels, resorts, convention centers, conference centers, and cities.

Source: http://www.conventionindustry.org/apex/apex.htm

WHAT IS A MEETING?

What are these things called "meetings," "exhibitions," "symposia," "congresses," "events," and "conventions?" In what ways do meetings contribute to furthering skills and knowledge for those who attend and participate? Why are they so important to the economy? Will virtual events take the place of face-to-face gatherings in the years ahead? Why hold meetings at all? In what ways can our specific meetings be designed better to meet our audience's needs? How do we differentiate what we do versus what the competition does so that we can market share? All of these questions are addressed in this chapter. Welcome to the fast-paced, tense, yet ultimately fulfilling world of MEEC.

The **APEX** initiative proposes the generic definition of *meeting:* A gathering for business, educational, or social purposes. Associations often use the term to refer to a combination of educational sessions and exhibits. This can include seminars, forums, symposia conferences, workshops, clinics, and so on.

In various online tools, synonyms for "meeting" include the following:

Entry:	meeting
Function:	noun
Definition:	gathering
Synonyms:	affair, assemblage, assembly, assignation, audience, bunch, buzz session, call, cattle call, clambake, company, competition, conclave, concourse, concursion, confab, **conference**, conflict, confrontation, congregation, congress, contest, convention, convocation, date, encounter, engagement, gang, get-together, gig, huddle, introduction, meet, nooner, parley, powwow, quickie, rally, rap session, rendezvous, reunion, session, showdown, sit-in, talk, tryst, turnout
Concept:	business action

Source: Roget's Interactive Thesaurus, First Edition (v 1.0.0)

Industry Terminology and Practice

We have always, generically, referred to gatherings of two or more people as "meetings." This term clearly could encompass meetings that are also called "conventions," "congresses," "symposia," and so on, some of which could have tens of thousands of people in attendance. If one adds displays of materials or products to a meeting, the meeting then has a trade show or **exposition** or **exhibition** component. When sporting, social, or life cycle activities are added, then a generic term that encompasses them all is *events*. Even broader and more generic is the term "gathering." One has to be conscious of how your stakeholders or target audience will interpret the name that you apply to your gathering.

The following list of terms is important for anyone involved in the MEEC industry to know. The terms were developed by the terminology panel of APEX and are a small sample of the thousands of words that apply to this industry. The complete glossary of terms used in the MEEC industry can be found online at http://glossary.conventionindustry.org.

- *Meeting:* An event where the primary activity of the attendees is to attend educational sessions, participate in meetings/discussions, socialize, or attend other organized events. There is no exhibit component to this event. See also Convention, Exhibition, Trade Show, Consumer Show.
- *Exposition:* See Exhibition.
- *Exhibition:* (1) An event at which the primary activity of the attendees is to visit exhibits on the show floor. These events focus primarily on business-to-business (B2B) relationships. (2) A display of products or promotional material for the purposes of public relations, sales and/or marketing. Same as Exposition or Trade Show. See Trade Show, Consumer Show, Gate Show, Public Show.
- *Event:* An organized occasion such as a meeting, convention, exhibition, special event, gala dinner, etc. An event is often composed of several different yet related FUNCTIONS.
- *Convention:* An event where the primary activity of the attendees is to attend educational sessions, participate in meetings/discussions, socialize, or attend other organized events. There is a secondary exhibit component. Compare with Meeting, Exhibition, Trade Show, Consumer Show.
- *Trade Show:* An exhibit of products and services targeted to a specific clientele and not open to the public.
- *Seminar:* (1) A lecture and dialogue allowing participants to share experiences in a particular field under the guidance of an expert discussion leader. (2) A meeting or series of meetings of ten to fifty specialists who have different specific skills but have a specific common interest and come together for training or learning purposes. The work schedule of a seminar has the specific object of enriching the skills of the participants.
- *Workshop:* (1) A meeting of several persons for intensive discussion. The workshop concept has been developed to compensate for diverging views in a particular discipline or on a particular subject. (2) An informal and public session of free discussion organized to take place between formal plenary sessions or commissions of a congress or of a conference, either on a subject chosen by the participants themselves or else on a special problem suggested by the organizers. (3) A training session in which participants, often through exercises, develop skills and knowledge in a given field.
- *Conference:* (1) A participatory meeting designed for discussion, fact-finding, problem solving, and consultation. (2) An event used by any organization to meet and exchange views, convey a message, open a debate, or give publicity to some area of opinion on a specific issue. No tradition, continuity, or periodicity is required to convene a conference. Although not generally limited in time, conferences are usually of short duration with specific objectives. Conferences are generally on a smaller scale than congresses. See also Congress, Convention.
- *Clinic:* A workshop-type educational experience where attendees learn by doing.
- *Break-Out Sessions:* Small group sessions, panels, workshops, or presentations offered concurrently within the event, formed to focus on specific subjects. Break-Out sessions are separate from the general session, but within the meeting format, and formed to focus on specific subjects. These sessions can be arranged by basic, intermediate, or advanced information, or divided by interest areas or industry segment.

- *Assembly:* (1) The process of erecting display component parts into a complete exhibit. (2) A general or formal meeting of an organization attended by representatives of its membership for the purpose of deciding legislative direction, policy matters, the election of internal committees, and approval of balance sheets, budgets, and so on. Consequently, an assembly usually observes certain rules of procedure for its meetings, mostly prescribed in its articles and bylaws.
- *Congress:* (1) The regular coming together of large groups of individuals, generally to discuss a particular subject. A congress will often last several days and have several simultaneous sessions. The length of time between congresses is usually established in advance of the implementation stage and can be either semiannual or annual. Most international or world congresses are of the former type, whereas national congresses are more frequently held annually. (2) A meeting of an association of delegates or representatives from constituent organizations. (3) A European term for convention. See also Conference, Convention.
- *Forum:* (1) An open discussion with an audience, panel, and moderator. (2) A meeting or part of a meeting set aside for an open discussion by recognized participants on subjects of public interest. Also for legal purposes, as part of the proceedings of a tribunal, court, or similar body.
- *Symposium:* A meeting of a number of experts in a particular field, at which papers are presented and discussed by specialists on particular subjects with a view to making recommendations concerning the problems under discussion.
- *Institute:* An in-depth instructional meeting providing intensive education on a particular subject.
- *Lecture:* An informative and instructional speech.
- *Panel Discussion:* Instructional technique using a group of people chosen to discuss a topic in the presence of an audience.
- *Incentive Travel:* A travel reward given by companies to employees to stimulate productivity. Also known as an incentive trip; sometimes simply incentive.

THE ORGANIZATIONAL STRUCTURE OF THE HOSPITALITY INDUSTRY: HOW MEEC FITS IN

MEEC is a part of and encompasses many elements of the hospitality and tourism industry. In order to understand how MEEC is related to the hospitality and service industry, one must understand the organization and structure of the tourism and hospitality industry itself.

There are six major divisions, or segments, of the tourism and hospitality industry: lodging, food and beverage, transportation, attractions, entertainment, and shopping.

1. *Lodging:* The lodging segment consists of all types of places where travelers may spend the night. These can include hotels, conference centers, resorts, motels, bed-and-breakfasts, cruise ships, trailer parks or campsites, condominiums, and college dormitories. The important characteristics of this segment are that they are available to the public and charge a fee for usage.
2. *Food and Beverage:* Obviously, this segment actually contains two sub-segments: food service operations and beverage operations. Food service operations can include the following: table service facilities that can be further broken down by price—high, medium, and low; by type of service—luxury, quick service, and so on; or by cuisine—American, East Asian, Italian, and others. Food service also embraces other types of operations, including catering, chains, and institutional feeding. Beverage operations can also be broken down by price or type of service, and even whether they serve alcoholic beverages or not.
3. *Transportation:* This segment includes any means, or modality that people use to get from one place to another, including walking. The better-known elements include air, water, and ground transportation.

   Air transportation: This sub-segment includes regularly scheduled carriers such as Delta or Southwest and charter air service that can involve jets, propeller aircraft, and helicopters.

   Water transportation: This sub-segment includes cruise ships and paddle wheelers, charter operations, ferries, and water taxis.

   Ground transportation: This sub-segment includes private automobiles, taxis, limousines, jitneys, buses, trains, cog railways, cable cars, monorails, horse drawn vehicles, and even elephants and camels.

4. *Attractions:* This segment of the hospitality and tourism industry is anything that attracts people to a destination and can be further divided into natural and person-made attractions.

   Natural attractions: This sub-segment includes mountains, seashores, lakes, forests, swamps, climate, and rivers.

   Person-made attractions: This sub-segment consists of things made or constructed by human beings, including buildings such as monuments, museums, theme parks, zoos, aquariums, and some restaurants and shopping venues.

5. *Entertainment:* This includes anything that provides entertainment value for a guest such as movie theaters, playhouses, orchestras, bands, and festivals.

6. *Shopping:* This is an important segment of the hospitality and tourism industry, and an area in which people may spend considerable sums of money, contributing to the local economy. Many attractions have developed products that carry their theme or logo and result in significant revenue streams for the operator. Probably the best known is Disney, whose products are sold not only at its attractions, but also in stand-alone retail centers.

As you can see, the hospitality and tourism industry is multifaceted. Furthermore, the framework offered in the preceding list is meant to help provide an understanding of the industry, and is not intended to be a well-delineated typology. There are many overlaps between the categories: A hotel may be an attraction in itself, such as the MGM Mirage CityCenter in Las Vegas; the same is true of some stores, such as FAO Schwarz in New York City or the Mall of America in Minneapolis. Hotels often have food and beverage outlets, retail stores, and even entertainment. Furthermore, some of the businesses mentioned above cater to both the tourist, meeting-goer and local resident, making it difficult to determine how much business is derived from each constituency.

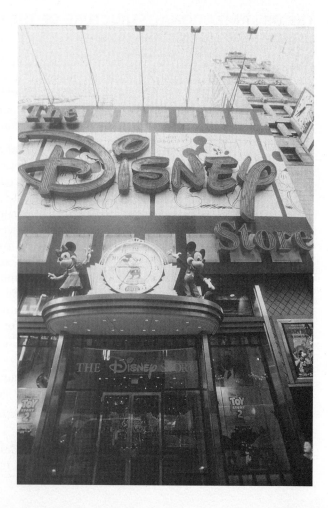

Shopping, such as in a Disney store, is an important segment of the hospitality and tourism industry. *Courtesy of Brent Stirton/Liaison/Getty Images, Inc. Disney characters © Disney Enterprises, Inc. Used by permission from Disney Enterprises, Inc.*

It would seem then, that the MEEC industry is involved with all segments of the hospitality and tourism industry. Understanding the interactions and complexities of the hospitality and tourism industry, along with MEEC, helps explain why it is difficult to determine the size and scope of these industries. Until the late 1990s, the U.S. government, using its Standard Industry Classification (SIC) codes, did not even track many elements of these industries. For example, the government did not even list "meeting planner" as a recognized profession until the late 1980s.

Background of the Industry

Gatherings, meetings, events, and conventions (of sorts) have been a part of people's lives since the earliest recorded history. Archeologists have found primitive ruins from ancient cultures that were used as meeting areas where citizens would gather to discuss common interests, such as government, war, hunting, or tribal celebrations. Once humans developed permanent settlements, each town or village had a public meeting area, often called a town square, where residents could meet, talk, and celebrate. Under the leadership of Alexander the Great, over half a million people traveled to what was then Ephesus (now Turkey) to see exhibitions that included acrobats, magicians, animal trainers, and jugglers. Andrew Young, the former U.S. ambassador to the United Nations, said at a Meeting Professionals International (MPI) meeting in Atlanta in the middle 1990s that he was sure there would have been a meeting planner for the Last Supper and certainly for the first Olympics. In Rome, the Forum was a type of organized meeting to discuss politics and decide the fate of the country. Ancient Rome had the Coliseum, which was the site of major sporting events such as gladiatorial contests—someone had to organize them! Through the use of excellent roadways, the Romans were able to establish trade markets to entice people to visit their cities. In Old England, there are stories of King Arthur's Round Table, another example of a meeting to discuss the trials and tribulations of the day. Religious gatherings of various faiths and pilgrimages to Mecca are examples of ancient religious meetings and festivals. The Olympics began as an ancient sporting event that was organized as similar events are today. World's fairs and expositions are still another piece of the MEEC industry.

The MEEC industry has also been a part of American culture and development. The white steeples surrounded by snow-covered ground seen in Currier and Ives prints actually depicted the town square of New England cities. In one of the oldest communities in North America, Santa Fe, the square not only houses the seat of government but also has been traditionally used as a festival marketplace. Even today, Native Americans can be seen around the perimeter of the square displaying their handicrafts for sale.

The First Continental Congress in Philadelphia is an example of a "formal meeting," in this case to decide the governance of the thirteen colonies. Political conventions have a long history in

Native Americans have held their festival marketplace in Santa Fe for centuries.   © *Danny Lehman/ CORBIS*

the United States, and are part of the MEEC industry. Americans have also made festivals and celebrations of every sort, such as Mardi Gras in New Orleans, a part of their lives since the early days of this country, and events like these can also be part of the MEEC industry.

Today, structures supporting the MEEC industry are integral parts of major cities. It is a well-known fact that in order to be considered a "world class city," a community must have a convention center and a stadium or arena for sports and events. All the largest cities have them, including New York, Washington, DC, Los Angeles, Chicago, London, Moscow, Pretoria, and Hong Kong. The hope is that these public facilities will attract out-of-town attendees for conventions and events who will spend money in the community.

In spite of its long history, meeting planning as a recognized profession did not develop until 1972, when **MPI** was founded. Only 120 planners and suppliers attended its first convention. The first board of directors was headed by "Buzz" Bartow and led to the development of the first academic meeting planning program. This program, approved by the state of Colorado in September of 1976, was implemented by Metropolitan State College in Denver. This initiative was closely followed by the meeting planning program at Northeastern Oklahoma University in Tahlequah. In 1979, Patti Shock started the convention service management (hotel perspective) and meeting planning classes at Georgia State University (GSU). In 1983, trade show classes were added with the financial support of the National Association of Exposition Managers (NAEM) (now the International Association of Exposition Managers, or IAEM) and IAFE (International Association of Fairs and Expositions). GSU was the first to implement trade show classes, and therefore the first to cover the whole convention industry. MPI recently received a Global Certificate in Meetings and Business Events (GCMBE).

There were two factors that contributed to the rapid development of both industry workshops and academic programs during the 1980s. The first was the development and implementation of the Certified Meeting Professional (CMP) examination and designation by the Convention Liaison Council (CLC now CIC). This certification gives both status and credence to the person who achieves it. Additional certificate programs have followed, including CMM, CDEM, and others.

Since its founding in New York in 1949 by four organizations—the American Society of Association Executives (ASAE), American Hotel and Motel Association (AH&MA, now the American Hotel Lodging Association), Hospitality (then Hotel) Sales and Marketing Association International (HSMAI), and International Association of Convention and Visitor Bureaus (IACVB) (now Destination Marketing Association International or **DMAI**)—the CIC (then, the Convention Liaison Council) has traditionally followed the lead of its constituent organizations, which now number 37 (http://www.conventionindustry.org).

In 1895, "[t]he roots of present-day convention & visitor bureaus (CVBs) [were] planted when journalist Milton Carmichael suggest[ed] in *The Detroit Journal* that local businessmen band together to promote the city as a convention destination, as well as represent the city and its many hotels to bid for business. Two weeks later, what [became] the Detroit Convention and Businessmen's League form[ed] to do just that. Carmichael head[ed] the group, which . . . later evolve[d] into the Detroit Metro CVB." (*EXPO Magazine* at http://www.expoweb.com/expomag/BackIssues/2001/Apr/feature2.htm).

The role of CVB's (now referred to as Destination Marketing Organizations or DMO's) has changed over time. As in Detroit, most began by trying to attract only conventions and business meetings to their community. Later, they realized leisure visitors were an important source of business and added the "V" for visitors to their name. Today, virtually every city in the United States and Canada, and many cities throughout the world, has a DMO or convention and visitors association (CVA). The DMO (CVB, CVA) is a membership organization that helps promote tourism, meetings, and related business for their cities. Most recently, the term "DMO" is being used in place of CVB. In this text, the terms are synonymous and interchangeable.

Economic Impact

The MEEC industry is diverse. As a result, it is hard to estimate the size, magnitude, and impact of MEEC. According to the CIC in Mclean Virginia, the meetings, conventions, exhibitions, and incentive travel industry supports 1.7 million jobs in the United States alone. It is estimated that 1 in every 86 individuals is employed in some aspect of the industry. These numbers are estimated to grow every year as many individuals, corporations, and many countries start to understand the importance of the MEEC industry. "As a whole, meetings, conventions, exhibitors and incentive travel generated $122.31 billion in total direct spending in 2004" (CIC, 2004). This made the MEEC industry the 29th largest contributor to the gross national product. This gives me great hope for my career in the MEEC industry because I see that my industry is very important to the economy and jobs will always be needed. Not only is the MEEC industry the 29th largest contributor but 1,710,000 full-time equivalent jobs are supported by the industry's direct spending. Spending for the industry is broken down by two-thirds or $81.94 billion going toward association-sponsored events and corporate-sponsored events accounting for the remaining third or $40.37 billion. The hotel segment of the industry actually generates more than 36% of the industry's $109.3 billion in operating income while air transportation accounts for almost 17% of the industry's operating income.

Source: Convention Industry Council. (2004). CIC 2004 Economic Industry Impact Study. www.conventionindustry.org

One of the most comprehensive accounts of the impact of the MEEC industry is published biannually in the "Meetings Market Report" in *Meetings & Conventions Magazine.* The August 2008 issue reports that both the number of meetings and the number of attendees were up compared to two years before, while the total expenditures on events declined slightly. Nearly $103 billion was spent last year, down about 4% from 2005. Corporate meetings accounted for $30.2 billion, down 5% from two years ago. Quite a bit less was spent on association meetings other than conventions, which fell 9% to $38.1 billion in 2007. Convention spending was the bright spot, rising 3% to $34.6 billion in 2007. Readers are reminded that these figures are for direct spending and do not include the "multiplier effect." This is a term from economics and refers to the indirect effect of spending when the money circulates through the regional economy. When the latter is considered, the amounts listed above are doubled. Thus, the "total impact" of the MEEC industry sector studied is extremely significant. (The preceding data is the most recent available, and the study is not being replicated in 2010). Detailed information on specific types of meetings is found in Chapter 2.

According to the Professional Convention Management Association (PCMA), meetings and events are responsible for 15% of all travel-related spending; create nearly $40 billion in tax revenue at the federal, state, and local level; and generate more than one million jobs. Without the jobs generated by meetings, events and incentive travel, the current unemployment rate of 7.6% would rise to 8.2% and cost the average American household additional annual taxes.

Source: PCMA, 2009 at http://www.pcma.org/Resources/Meetings_Industry_Advocacy.htm

Scenario Planning

Smart industry professionals, regardless of the industry segment in which they work, plan for contingencies and their impact. This awareness is heightened by disasters such as acts of terrorism, hurricanes (most recently Katrina and Rita), or the economic crisis that began in 2008. How can the industry plan for such events? What can be done far in advance to anticipate and plan for potential devastating events that can affect people and their businesses over which they have seemingly little control? How can they address the sense of uncertainty from communities such as New Orleans and the U.S. Gulf Coast or in Thailand and Haiti or anywhere in the world where there has been a significant impact on the MEEC industry? How can the future of booking those destinations be addressed? A July 2006 article by Sarah Torrence in the PCMA journal *Convene* addresses these questions by suggesting that meeting planners use scenario planning, "a dynamic strategic planning concept." The complete article is available at http://www.pcma.org/resources/convene/archives/displayArticle.asp?ARTICLE_ID=5359, and is excerpted here:

> For the past five years, the uncertainty of our times has certainly been played out in the meetings industry—with the after-effects of Sept. 11, the SARS scare, and raging hurricanes, such as Katrina, disrupting the normal flow of business.
>
> While new to many planners, scenario planning can help them assist their organizations as a whole—in addition to looking at their meetings in a new way. As Laura Jelinek, associate executive director, American Association of Oral and Maxillofacial Surgeons said, "We are in business to provide benefits to our membership."

Brad Kent, vice president, sales, AVW-TELAV, noted, "Our industry, in many ways, became a victim after Sept. 11. Scenario planning gives you a 35,000-foot view before getting consumed with the emotion of the situation. You can plan for the unexpected, rather than be a victim."

"Scenario planning is best used for strategic planning in a world of uncertainty," explained Roch Parayre, Ph.D., senior fellow at the Mack Center for Technological Innovation at the Wharton School, and managing director and scenario planning expert with Decision Strategies Inc. (DSI), "The world for most industries is becoming increasingly unpredictable today. Many are beginning to 'twist in the wind.' This is certainly true of the travel and hospitality industry, especially after Sept. 11," he emphasized.

Indeed, the meetings industry seems to possess many conditions under which scenario planning should be used, as outlined by Dr. Parayre:

- uncertainty is high, relative to one's ability to adjust
- too many costly surprises have occurred in the past
- insufficient new opportunities are perceived
- the quality of thinking is deemed to be low
- a common language is desired, without stifling diversity
- major differences of opinion exist, each having merit
- your competitors use scenario planning.

When implementing scenario planning, planners and executives alike should consider the forces that are shaping the future of their organization or industry, and then build a scenario matrix relative to these forces. "There could be hundreds of forces facing an organization or industry," Dr. Parayre said. "Scenario planning is a systematic way of taking those forces into account when you plan."

Dr. Parayre provided a six-step process for formulating strategies in uncertain conditions. Planners can easily use these steps to strategize for their meetings, as well as the direction of their department and association.

1. Consider general scenarios. As an example, Dr. Parayre said, if a group is planning a meeting in a certain destination, think about what political or other scenarios might play out there.
2. Examine the organization's market. "One size does not fit all," he said. "There are individual strategic market segments. Conduct market research and detailed needs assessments to understand each group," he advised.
3. Assess the organization's internal core capabilities. "It's better to stick to what you do well, and look to a partner or third party to do the rest," he gave as an example. Too many planners try to do it all, so this is sound advice.
4. Put the pieces together. Looking at your information in the first three steps, analyze how different outcomes will be influenced by different scenarios.
5. Identify tactical initiatives to support strategic directives. "For example, if you want to enhance certain capabilities, such as data mining, how will you make that happen? Through partnering?" asked Dr. Parayre.
6. Implement. Be sure to measure the initiation of strategies against pre-set developmental milestones, budgets, and time frames.

So, scenario planning may be helpful for the meeting professionals in preparing ways to address an uncertain environment. Today, the economic uncertainty in the United States and throughout the world, the reality of civil wars, the possibility of international war, and the disarray and financial woes of the airline industry have made the traveling public skittish about leisure and business travel. Hotel occupancy rates in all cities have fallen—more dramatically in what the industry calls "first-tier" cities, which are those that host large conventions and trade shows. Cities continue to build convention centers and new hotel projects that were planned before the economic downturn, and hope to be able to fill them with meetings that will in turn bolster the local economy.

Why Have Meetings and Events?

In the early to mid-1980s, there were discussions, (as there was immediately after September 11, 2001) and again during the economic crisis that begin in 2008, that face-to-face meetings would be things of the past—that virtual meetings (teleconferencing, webinars, etc.) would supplant face-to-face gatherings. The Foundation of MPI conducted studies in the mid-1990s that focused on what made meetings work for associations and corporations (http://www.mpiweb.org). These

Shaking hands is a form of nonverbal communication.
© *Dorling Kindersley*

studies showed that people preferred meeting face-to-face, and that one of the most important values of gatherings is the ability to meet with and learn from peers. "Virtual" meetings in all forms (audio and video conferences, webinars, podcasts, online learning and exchanges) do not yet create the desired effect, although various companies such as CISCO (http://www.cisco.com/en/US/products/sw/ps5664/ps5669/index.html) and other platforms are working to improve the future of virtual meetings. The debate rages on, with articles such as one in *BusinessWeek* (http://www.businessweek.com/debateroom/archives/2009/01/virtual_meeting.html) that gives some of the pros and cons of virtual vs. face-to-face meetings.

Face-to-face meetings have the benefit of including all forms of communication, including verbal and nonverbal. For example, what does the strength and style of a handshake tell you about people in some cultures? How do their facial expressions support their words, or are they sending mixed messages? How do you feel if the people to whom you are speaking never look you "straight in the eye?" Nonverbal communication is a very important part of meeting with people. Others cite the importance of face-to-face vs. virtual meetings in "closing deals." See http://www.thestandard.com/news/2009/09/17/survey-conferencing-technologies-cant-replace-face-face-meetings.

When we meet, we build "communities of practice." Today, we use social media to develop communities of practice, which then often want to meet face to face. What we more often see is "blended learning" that is often used to define blending the use of technology and face-to-face interactions to deliver content and build communities of practice. (CIC's APEX has yet to define the term.)

Virtually or face to face, through these communities of practice, we are able to strengthen skills (at sales or association educational meetings, or symposia), impact change (at political conventions or governance meetings), observe accomplishments (at incentive meetings and celebrations), renew acquaintances (at reunions), and learn about new products in our field (at exhibitions and trade shows).

Today, we participate, virtually, in many events and interactions: attending classes; viewing live streaming of sporting events and meetings; and even attending community, religious, or spiritual events. In 1999, *High Tech-High Touch*, written by John Naisbitt and others, was first published. In this book (http://www.amazon.com/High-Tech-Touch-Technology-Meaning/dp/1857882601/ref=sr_1_1?ie=UTF8&s=books&qid=1265642215&sr=8-1), the authors look at the impact of a technological society and the need for "unplugging" now and then. The need for **experiential learning and participation**, noted in Pine and Gilmore's *The Experience Economy* (http://www.amazon.com/Experience-Economy-Theater-Every-Business/dp/0875848192) continues to drive meetings and events: One attends the SuperBowl to participate in the excitement of the crowd and the **experience** of being there. One attends a wedding face to face to experience the joy of those gathered and to taste the cake and drink the champagne! Although there are sites, including islands in SecondLife ™ (such as Virtualis ™) that even offer virtual weddings, they are not yet in the mainstream.

Our jobs are to follow the trends and to find methods by which we can meet our objectives for meetings and events using the best methods possible for delivery for our demographic. In some cases, that will be face to face, and in others, virtual. In more cases, it will be blended.

EMPLOYMENT IN AND AROUND THE MEEC INDUSTRY

The MEEC industry is a sub-segment of the hospitality industry, which itself is part of the larger services industry. It encompasses many areas of the hospitality industry. Thus, readers are challenged to conceptualize their personal ideal job and then determine how and where in the MEEC industry they could be employed doing what they dream of.

Some of the careers in MEEC include the following:

- *Event Planner:* Puts together special events like the Olympics, the SuperBowl in football, the Final Four in basketball, festivals, and celebrations.
- *Meeting Planner:* Organizes meetings and other gatherings for companies, corporations, and associations. These gatherings can include a small board of directors meeting, a stockholders meeting, new product introductions and training, educational seminars, and regional or national conventions.
- *Wedding Planner:* A wedding planner assists the parties in selecting the site, décor, photographer, and other needed vendors, and is often there on the day of the event to ensure smooth operations.
- *Hotel or Conference Center Sales:* The majority of sales and convention or catering services positions in hotels and conference centers deal with groups, and MEEC covers most of those groups.
- *Restaurant Sales:* While most people think of restaurants attracting walk-in clientele, many rely heavily on the MEEC industry for business. Food and beverage (F&B) venues employ significant numbers of people on their group sales staff. In New Orleans, Arnaud's and Emeril's, for example, have group or convention sales teams.
- *Entertainment/Sporting Venue Sales & Services:* Although these places primarily attract individual patrons, most also devote much time and effort to selling, providing space for, and producing events for groups. These off-site venues are often good alternatives for experiential learning.
- *Destination Management:* Destination Management Companies (DMCs) function as the "local experts" for companies and associations in organizing gatherings and events, arranging and supervising transportation, and securing entertainers. People employed for DMCs usually work in either sales or production.
- *Hotels:* Hotels are one of the primary locations where MEEC events are held, using ballrooms, meeting rooms, break-out rooms, etc., for their gatherings along with sleeping rooms and F&B for their attendees. The hotel departments that deal with the MEEC industry are sales, catering, and convention services.
- *Convention Centers:* These venues include dedicated facilities such as McCormick Place in Chicago, the Jacob K. Javits Convention Center in New York, and the Mandalay Bay Hotel and Convention Center in Las Vegas. Also included in this category are multipurpose venues like the Superdome in New Orleans or the Astrodome in Houston. With these venues, careers are found in either sales or operations.
- *Exposition Services Contractors:* If you like to build things or have thought about being an engineer or architect, you should consider being an exposition services contractor (ESC). ESCs design and erect the booths, backdrops, staging, etc. for meetings and conventions. The decorations and backdrops for your school prom may have been done by an

ESC. Again, career paths exist in sales and production, and increasingly in design of sustainable/"green" products and services.

• **Destination Marketing Organizations (Convention and Visitor Bureaus):** DMOs serve to represent a wide range of MEEC companies and to market the destination to business and leisure travelers. DMOs have many departments and careers, including convention sales, tourism sales, housing bureaus, convention services, marketing, research, and member services.

As you can see, the MEEC industry is a vibrant, dynamic, and exciting part of the hospitality industry. Many careers in MEEC involve multiple aspects of the hospitality industry. For example, someone who works in convention or group sales in a facility must interface with, be knowledgeable about, and manage people who work with guest rooms, front desk, food and beverage, catering, and all of the meeting facilities. Some of the most important aspects of working in MEEC are business acumen (financial and people management, legalities and risk management, sales and marketing, ethical practices), visioning (what can be) and execution of ideas into concepts, and knowledge of adult learning techniques. In addition to knowledge and ability for preparing and delivering virtual and face-to-face meetings, industry professionals must know more about sustainability and "green" for meetings and events.

It is often said that MEEC is a "relationship industry," that is, one built on who you know and with whom you do business. As in many industries, we depend on those we know to help us learn and grow and to provide accurate information. These relationships are built over time and always with the understanding that first and foremost, ethical business practices will be the most important aspect of how we relate.

Think for just a moment about all the lives and jobs that could impact one of the meeting participants and the meeting organizers involved in the scenario for the Association of Amalgamated Professionals. They include the following:

The Meeting Sponsor

The Association of Amalgamated Professionals

Meeting planner

Executive director or chief executive officer (CEO)

Staff specialists in departments that include marketing, governance and government affairs, education/professional development/training, membership, information technology, and accreditation

Others who staff call centers, copy materials, process registrations, manage human resources, control purchasing, and more

Board of directors

Committees

Sponsors

The Facility

Owners

Executive staff, including but not limited to: general manager, revenue manager, resident or hotel manager, directors of sales, marketing, convention services, catering, housekeeping, engineering, maintenance, purchasing, human resources, food and beverage, front office operations, social responsibility, and security.

The thousands of other full- and part-time, year-round, and seasonal staff: groundskeepers, animal handlers, housekeepers, food servers (for banquets, room service, and the outlets), maintenance, security, and engineering

The Destination

DMO/CVB (president, directors of sales, marketing, convention services, membership, registration, social responsibility, and all support staff)

Restaurants

Attractions

Off-site venues

Theaters (movie and legitimate)

Copy and printing companies

Transportation (buses, airport shuttles, taxicabs, limousines)

Airport concessions

Doctors, medical personnel, emergency workers

Pharmacies

Florists

Department and other stores

Destination management companies

Audiovisual suppliers

General services contractors

Specialty services contractors

Dry cleaners and tailors

City, county, and state employees

IT division and telecommunications department

All Others Who Provide Services for Meetings

Talent (entertainers, disc jockeys, bands, magicians)

Education (speakers, trainers, facilitators)

Sound and lighting

Transportation (air, rail, car, boat, and travel agencies)

Printing

Shipping

Promotional products

Off-property food and beverage

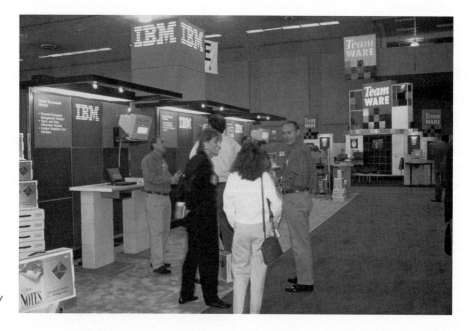

An industry trade show. *Courtesy of Cindy Charles, PhotoEdit, Inc.*

Translators for those who speak American Sign Language and other languages

Americans with Disabilities Act (ADA) equipment

Carpentry

National sales (hotels, conference centers)

"Third-party" or independent meeting planners

Is there anyone who does not have some influence on the MEEC industry? A case can be made that every person has an impact, in some way, on each and every meeting—even those meetings of two or three that take place in an office or restaurant. Take a few minutes and add to the jobs or functions above that might affect a meeting. Then think again. Even the president of the United States and Congress impact our industry by determining trade regulations, security issues, and whether or not our country goes to war.

What Does a Meeting or Event Planner Do?

When asked about a "typical day," there are few if any meeting professionals, whether they work in an organization or operate an external planning company, who could say that any day is "typical." The job of a planner is ideal for those who love to multitask, who have broad interests, who enjoy problem solving, and who care passionately about building community through meetings.

Doug Heath, Certified Association Executive (CAE) and Certified Meeting Professional (CMP), who was the second executive director of MPI, said many years ago, "Meeting planners have to be more than coffee-cup counters." When Heath said that, it was a time when most meeting planners were concerned only with logistics—ensuring room sets, coffee and refreshment breaks, meals, and audiovisual setup.

Today, the jobs of a planner are strategic. Planners are charged with supporting the work toward an organization's bottom line. To do that, and in the course of planning a meeting or event, a planner may do any or all of the following, and more:

- Define meeting/event goals and objectives and develop session content and design.
- Develop a request for proposal (RFP) based on the meeting/event objectives, audience profile, budget, and program (see Appendix A of this book for examples).
- Send the RFP to national sales offices of hotel and conference center companies, to DMOs, and to external meeting planning companies.
- Prepare and manage a budget and expenditures that can range from a few hundred dollars into the hundreds of millions.
- Negotiate contracts with a facility or multiple facilities, transportation providers, decorators, speakers, entertainers, and all the vendors and venues that will support a meeting/event.
- Market the meeting/event electronically and in print, and track results.
- Invite and manage needs (travel, lodging, registration, room setup, and audiovisual) for all speakers, trainers, and facilitators involved in delivery of information and knowledge for the meeting/event.
- Invite and manage contracts and needs for entertainers.
- Design food and beverage events, and negotiate contracts for these events. To do so, a planner must know the audience (age of participants, gender, abilities, allergies, geographic location, and more) and timing for the programs, and the budget and prices including labor costs and taxes.
- Prepare a crisis management plan in conjunction with other staff, facilities, vendors, and emergency personnel.
- Register participants, or manage a registration company, ensuring data are accurately entered and processed securely.
- Manage the multitude of changes that happen from first conceptualizing a meeting/event to the execution and follow-up.
- Monitor industry and business publications for changes in hotel ownership or management company, hotel foreclosures, facility and other strikes, and other issues.
- Calm others' nerves and remain calm.

The following are some of the questions you might ask yourself to determine if this may be the right profession for you:

- Do you like to plan parties, work schedules, your day, and ensure that the details are locked in?
- Do you have and regularly update a date book or personal digital assistant (PDA) or smart phone that includes everything you need to do for weeks or months into the future?
- Have you discovered your strengths (via "Strengths 2.0" by Tom Rath), and do you see how those strengths fit into this profession?
- Do you ask good questions, rarely taken anything as a given? If you answered "yes" to at least three-fourths of those questions, you may just have the aptitude to be a good meeting professional.

To be prepared for short- and long-term change, *meeting professionals*—a term that encompasses those who plan and execute meetings/events, those who work for and in facilities in which meetings are held, and the many vendors who supply services for meetings—must begin to anticipate changes that will occur as the nature of meetings changes. In the scenario at the beginning of the chapter, there is a designated vendor to work with satellite and other e-communication tools. Still, the meeting professional needs to know enough to contract with and manage that vendor.

FUTURE TRENDS

The future for the MEEC industry is put forth each year by MPI and its "FutureWatch." The findings are synopsized below:

- Meeting planners and suppliers generally predict a steady market for meetings and events over the next year, with little or no change in overall volume.
- Planners foresee healthy year over year increases in average meeting attendance—by 11% for corporate meetings, 18.3% for association events, and 19% across all conferences.
- Budgets and workloads are important in-house issues facing meeting professionals. A large proportion of respondents also expect to be involved with shifting goals and strategies within their organizations. Economic issues, fuel costs, and changing technologies lead the list of external issues and trends.
- A growing number of meeting professionals—19% overall, 31% in Europe, and 29% in Canada—list conservation and environmental concerns among the top three external trends affecting their work. Six percent overall, 12% in Europe, and 10% in Canada list these concerns as their leading external trend.
- Labor shortages are roughly twice as important for suppliers and independent planners as they are for corporate and association planners, suggesting that concern over the ability to hire and retain qualified employees is gradually permeating the industry.
- Meeting planners predict an 11% increase in their budgets over the next year, although expectations vary across sectors—while corporate planners anticipate a 27% increase and association.
- Although meeting professionals will make use of a wide variety of on-site technologies in 2008, they are not always satisfied with the adequacy, availability, accessibility, or affordability of those technologies.

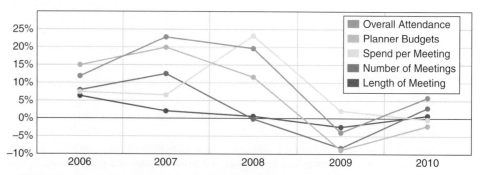

FIGURE 1-1   Year-to-Year Trend in Projected Meetings Statistics. *Source:* FutureWatch 2010 used with permission of Meeting Professionals International.

- Two in five meeting planners, and nearly half of corporate planners, expect their use of webcasts to increase in the next year. Three in 10 planners expect webcasts to be a more frequent feature of live meetings, leading to an overall increase in attendance at meetings that combine live and virtual audiences.
- The meetings and events industry is globalizing rapidly. Although the majority of *FutureWatch 2008* respondents work for organizations with operations in only one country, 20% expect their global reach to expand over the next year. And companies with the widest spheres of operation are most likely to expand—57% respondents in organizations with offices in six or more countries expect expansion in 2008.

For meeting professionals, meetings never truly end. No matter how we define a "meeting," each meeting is a matter of intense planning and execution, evaluation, follow-up, and starting over. Our role is critical in ensuring outcomes, and from those outcomes, we contribute to a sound economy.

The success of the industry to individuals who currently work in or who choose to work in MEEC depends on what we do now and how we anticipate and plan for the future. Those who choose to stay in or join this industry must have critical thinking skills and the willingness to consider the impact of all local and worldwide events on one's own meetings and events. Meeting professionals will need to know more about changing demographics in order to accommodate the needs of broader audiences; adult learning techniques to incorporate experiential learning and technology into face-to-face or virtual presentations or for blended learning; nutrition and food allergies to ensure healthy and safe participants; climate change to understand its impact on sustainability and availability of food and water and the bottom line; current events and projections about world population shifts; and the worldwide economy and its impact on availability of products and services, including safety and security. The list is even lengthier than those stated; additions and further explanations would be a chapter in itself.

Those who succeed will look beyond the jobs of yesterday and today to jobs that use many of the skills for which you are preparing today: jobs in eldercare, community organizing, music and arts, politics, and more. Those who succeed in the future will begin now to impact how people learn at meetings by remembering the lessons from Pine and Gilmore and "The Experience Economy." They will change how spaces are used in facilities; how content is derived and delivered; how participants are engaged. Those who succeed will enhance what they learn in classes and sessions by looking outside the industry for information. (Highly

End of the First Day

It is the end of the first day of the AAP's 35th Annual Congress, which Barbara Tain, the AAP Meeting Planner, refers to as the "Annual" or "Annual Meeting," and so far all has gone well.

Barbara will have had formal, prescheduled meetings with Todd Cliver, the hotel's CSM. Barbara will also have spoken with Todd and many others who work for the hotel via radio (sometimes referred to as a "walkie-talkie") and/or mobile phone, and through chance and scheduled meetings. These talks include a review of banquet checks with various departments, one of which will include accounting. Barbara will have talked with those on the AAP staff and in volunteer leadership and with outside vendors. She will also check the weather many times on her smart phone, television, radio, and, if there is one, the newspaper. Barbara will have eaten on the run, tried to find a few minutes to check office voice mail and e-mail, and, through it all, kept a smile on her face, even while her feet hurt!

At the end of the day, she will review her notes and check room sets for the next morning's sessions and crawl into bed for a few hours of sleep before it all begins again.

When the final curtain closes on the AAP's 35th Annual Congress, Barbara Tain will be one of the last to leave the hotel. Before leaving for the airport to fly home, she will review all the master account charges, conduct a postconvention ("post-con") meeting with the property staff and her vendors, and make notes for next year's meeting. Once back in the office, she'll work with the vendor companies that conducted the evaluations, review all the bills and ensure timely payment, and write thank you notes.

recommended is a membership in the World Future Society [www.wfs.org] and reading of *The Futurist* either in print or electronically, and engaging in discussions about the impact of what is read.)

Face-to-face meetings will continue because there is a need for human interaction. These meetings and events will succeed because they are enhanced by virtual audiences who add to the energy and diversity prior to, during, and after the meeting or event. (Think Twitter and the hashtags being used now for meetings; envision even greater involvement in the future.)

You've thus far decided to read this text and to learn about this dynamic industry. YOU are the future; you bring to it your experiences and insights. Observe, learn, and take action to keep MEEC moving forward.

Summary

In this chapter, you have been introduced to the world of MEEC. As we have seen, MEEC is multifaceted and exciting, and offers diverse career opportunities. MEEC is also very large and incorporates many facets of the hospitality industry. It has tremendous economic impact. You are now prepared to continue with the remaining chapters in this book. They expand on and provide more details about the concepts and practices of MEEC that this first chapter only touches on.

Key Words and Terms

For definitions, see GLOSSARY, or http://glossary.conventionindustry.org

APEX	Convention	Exhibition	MPI
BEO	CSM	Exposition	Meeting
CIC	Destination	DMAI	Outlet
Conference	DMC	MEEC	Sales and Marketing

Review and Discussion Questions

1. What are meetings?
2. Describe some events from the past that were "meetings."
3. Describe some current aspects of MEEC industry jobs.
4. Who attends meetings?
5. What can be accomplished by convening or attending a meeting?
6. What are five key jobs in a facility (hotel, resort, conference center) that contribute to the successful outcome of a meeting?
7. What is the CIC?
8. What is APEX, and what is its impact?
9. What is the impact of meetings on the U.S. economy?
10. What is the future of electronic meetings?

About the Chapter Contributor

Joan L. Eisenstodt, a facilitator, trainer, and meeting manager with 30+ years' experience, is president of Washington, DC-based Eisenstodt Associates, LLC, a company she founded in 1981. Eisenstodt is moderator of the "MiForum listserv," an international online community. In her community, she serves on the Executive Board of the Newton-Marasco Foundation. She has been recognized by hospitality industry organizations as Planner of the Year (MPI), Teacher of the Year (PCMA), and a "Pacesetter" (HSMAI). Joan has been regularly included in the *"One of the 25 Most Influential People in the Meetings Industry"* list. She has also been recognized as one of the "Power Players" ("10 Women who are Changing the Industry") and appears in "The 'A' List: 10 Women Meeting Industry Leaders." Joan is the recipient of the Pyramid Award from the International Association of Conference Centers, was recognized for Lifetime Achievement as an Educator by the PCMA Foundation, and was inducted into the CIC Hall of Leaders.

Additional information was provided by MPI.

About MPI

Meeting Professionals International (MPI), the meeting and event industry's largest and most vibrant global community, helps our members thrive by providing human connections to knowledge and ideas, relationships and marketplaces. MPI membership is comprised of more than 24,000 members belonging to 71 chapters and clubs worldwide.

For additional information, visit mpiweb.org.

**Meeting Professionals
International Headquarters**
3030 LBJ Freeway, Suite 1700
Dallas, TX 75234-2759
tel +1-972-702-3000
fax +1-972-702-3089

EMEA
Europe/Africa
28, Rue Henri VII
L1725 Luxembourg
tel +352-2687-6141
fax +352-2687-6343

Middle East
PC5 Offices,
Education City,
Doha, Qatar
tel +974-454-8000
fax +974-454-8047

Canada
6519-B Mississauga Road
Mississauga, Ontario
L5N 1A6
Canada
tel +905-286-4807
fax +905-567-7191

Asia Pacific
73, Bukit Timah Rd
#04-01 Rex House
Singapore 229832
tel +65-6496-5504
fax +65-6336-2263

Editorial Support
Bill Voegeli, President, Association Insights
Mitchell Beer, CMM, President and CEO,
The Conference Publishers Inc.

Special Thanks
American Express,
sponsor of MPI's *FutureWatch 2010*

FutureWatch 2010 is an official supplement to the January 2010 issue of *One+*, the official publication of Meeting Professionals International.

Printed by RR Donnelley & Sons Company

© 2010, Meeting Professionals International
All Rights Reserved

FIGURE 1-2 Meeting Professionals International (MPI) *Courtesy of MPI*

CHAPTER 2

Meeting, Exhibition, Event, and Convention Organizers and Sponsors

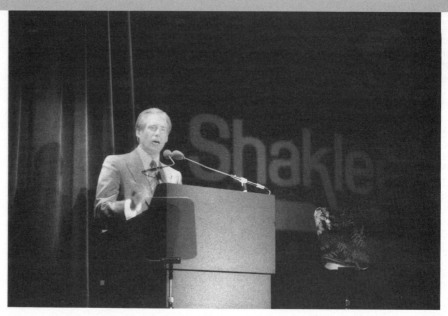

Corporations organize a significant number of MEEC events, such as this Shaklee company meeting. *Courtesy of Teri Leigh Stratford, Pearson Education/PH College*

Chapter Objectives

This chapter provides the reader with an understanding of the following:

- Major types of organizations that hold gatherings
- Types of meetings held by the different categories of organizations
- Typical lead times for planning the various types of gatherings
- Differences between the marketing strategies used to build attendance
- Associations that support the professional development of those responsible for producing gatherings

PURPOSE OF THIS CHAPTER

This chapter focuses on gaining an understanding of the entities that organize and sponsor different types of gatherings. Each segment of these entities creates gatherings to satisfy its unique needs and its constituent populations. Whether the organization is a nonprofit association or a corporation, a government agency, or a private company that produces exhibitions, it has goals that may require an MEEC gathering to commemorate an event. Our purpose here is to identify who these organizing/sponsoring organizations are, the types of gatherings they hold, how much time they have to plan the event, who their attendees are, and how they build attendance. The people who play a major role in producing the gatherings are identified, as are the professional associations who provide them with support and professional development.

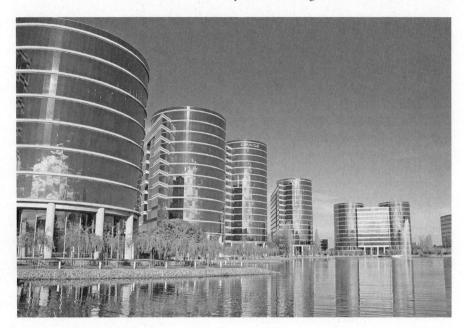

Corporate Headquarters of
Oracle Corp.   *Courtesy of
Dreamstime LLC—Royalty Free.*

WHO HOLDS THE GATHERINGS

The three most significant entities that organize and sponsor MEEC gatherings are (1) corporations, (2) associations, and (3) the government.

Corporations

Virtually all businesses have needs that require them to plan and execute gatherings. Publicly held companies have a legal requirement to hold an annual meeting of shareholders. All companies have varying needs to hold a press conference or a ribbon cutting ceremony. They also have continuing needs to train key personnel in matters of company policy and procedures, or to develop new policies and procedures and to improve their effectiveness. Client groups may be brought together to capture their opinions in a focus group or to introduce them to a new product or service. Executive retreats may be held to improve communication or to develop long-term business plans. Gatherings are also held to honor employees (for promotion or retirement), to celebrate holidays, and to build overall morale within the organization. Companies may also be involved with a sporting event or entertaining clients in VIP areas at major sporting events, such as the U.S. Open or Super Bowl.

DEFINITION   Although there are numerous kinds of **corporations**, for the purposes of this chapter the term "corporations" will refer to legally chartered enterprises that conduct business on behalf of their owners with the purpose of making a profit and increasing its value. These include public corporations that sell stock on the open market and have a board of directors who oversee the affairs of the corporation on behalf of the shareholders (or owners) who elected them. Private corporations have the same fundamental purposes as public corporations, but their stock is not sold on the open market.

NUMBER AND VALUE OF CORPORATE MEETINGS   When a corporation decides to hold a gathering, it determines what the budget will be, where the gathering will be held, and who will attend. Since the corporation typically pays for all expenses associated with attending the meeting, the corporation is in control. Attendance by corporate personnel is usually mandatory. Many corporate meetings are booked as needed, typically less than six months before the meeting will be held.

DECISION MAKERS   The decision to hold a corporate meeting is typically made by persons in positions of key responsibility within the corporate hierarchy. Officers and senior managers in the sales and marketing area may call for a meeting of their regional sales managers to develop sales strategies for new product lines, or senior financial managers and controllers may call a meeting of their dispersed staffs to discuss budgets for next year.

TYPES OF CORPORATE GATHERINGS AND EVENTS—THEIR PURPOSES AND OBJECTIVES

Corporations have a variety of needs that can be satisfied by scheduling a gathering. What follows should not be viewed as a comprehensive list, but rather as an indication of the types of gatherings sponsored by corporations.

- *Stockholders Meeting:* Voting shareholders of a corporation are invited to attend the company's annual stockholders meeting. Attendees are presented with reports on the state of the corporation and have the opportunity to vote on issues of significance. While most stockholders do not attend this meeting, they do participate in the governance of the corporation by filing a proxy statement in which they identify how they want their shares voted. This is an annual meeting that is usually held in the city where the company is headquartered, although there is an emerging trend to move it to different locations to be more accessible to the stockholders.
- *Board Meeting:* The board of directors is the governing body of a corporation that typically meets several times a year, usually in the city where the corporation is located. While a **board meeting** may be held in the corporate headquarters, lodging, dinners, and related activities are often held at local hotels.
- *Management Meetings:* There are numerous reasons for a company to hold management meetings. Every major division of a corporation may have a need to bring its decision makers and other important personnel together to develop plans, review performance, or improve their processes. While some of these meetings may occur on a scheduled basis, others may be called spontaneously to solve problems and address situations that require immediate attention.
- *Training Meetings:* As companies undergo change, it may be necessary to hold training meetings to bring their managers and key employees up-to-date on improved methods of job performance or to gain skills needed to operate new systems and equipment. Also, companies may use the training meeting to introduce new managers to corporate procedures and culture. Some of these meetings may be held on a regularly scheduled basis, while others may be held when conditions dictate it.
- *Incentive Trips:* Many corporations offer **incentive trips** to reward their top performers based on certain criteria. Those winning these trips may be employees, distributors, and/or customers. While these trips are often too exciting and glamorous destinations, an emerging trend is to schedule a number of activities for the participants to provide an added value to

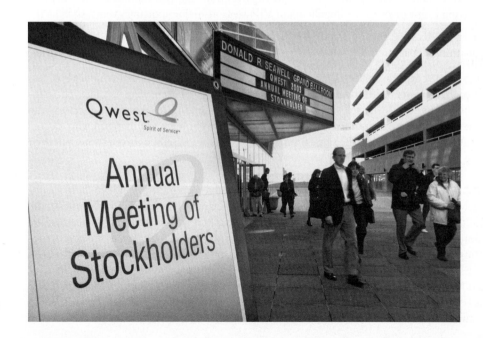

Qwest stockholders meeting.
Courtesy of Jack Dempsey, AP Wide World Photos

the sponsoring corporation. Companies may bring together these top performers with their corporate leadership to create a more synergistic organization.

- *Sales training and product launches:* These events are often held to upgrade the performance of the sales staff, distributors, and retailers, and to introduce new products and services to distribution networks and the general public. These events are designed to educate and motivate those who have a significant impact on the success of the corporation.
- *Professional and technical training:* These meetings may be held to bring managers and others up-to-date on issues relevant to their role within the company and to enhance the knowledge of their service providers. For example, a company may have a meeting of its unit and regional controllers to discuss changes in tax law and company policies.

ATTENDEES Most of the attendees of a corporate gathering or event are members of the corporate family and persons who have a close business relationship with the company. In the United States, almost 1.1 million events are held annually with a total attendance of 84 million. The total direct spending is over $30 billion per year with the average corporate event generating almost $550,000.

Source: 2008 Meetings Market Report produced by *Meetings & Conventions* Magazine, August 2008.

NEED FOR MARKETING TO BUILD ATTENDANCE While the purposes of corporate meetings should be carefully crafted, attendance at these meetings is mandatory for the majority of the attendees. Therefore, sending invitations or notices to those who will attend constitutes the majority of promotional activity. That it may be a command performance does not lessen the need to make the meeting informative, productive, and enjoyable for those attending.

DEPARTMENT AND/OR INDIVIDUAL RESPONSIBLE FOR ORGANIZING AND PLANNING Corporate planners are really a hybrid group. The majority of people who plan corporate meetings have responsibilities beyond or in addition to the planning of meetings. According to *Meeting & Conventions* 2008 Meetings Market Report, in 2008 corporate planners spent about 53% of their time planning meeetings. While about 30% of these meeting planners had meeting planner/convention management titles, the remaining majority had job titles that did not identify their meeting planning responsibilities (executive or management, 24%; general administration or management, 17%; sales and marketing, 11%; and other, 18%).

Therefore, since the typical meeting planners' job title does not specifically indicate "meetings" as part of their responsibilities, it should be no surprise that the majority do not work in a meeting planning department. They tend to work in the departments that hold the meetings (sales and marketing, finance) and have assumed meeting planning responsibility at the request of their supervisors. Of the corporate meeting planners who have earned profession certifications, 19% were Certified Meeting Professionals (CMP) and 4% were Certified Meeting Managers (CMM). According to Mary Jo Blythe of Masterplan, a company that provides meeting planning services for several major corporations, "most large corporations have internal meeting planning departments." However, they do also "utilize outside meeting planning firms for specific projects, overflow, or on an as needed basis."

PROFESSIONAL ASSOCIATIONS SUPPORTING THE CORPORATE MEEC INDUSTRY Many corporate meeting planners join associations to support their professional development. The associations that they most often join include Meeting Professionals International, 28% (http://www.mpiweb.org); the Society for Incentive & Travel Executives, 5% (http://www.siteglobal.org); the Society of Government Meeting Professionals, 3% (http://www.sgmp.org); and the Association of Insurance and Financial Services Conference Planners, 3% (http://www.icpanet.com), according to the 2008 Meetings Market Report. About 60% of corporate planners did not indicate membership in any meeting industry association.

The following are some links to resources about corporate meetings.

- http://www.meetingsnet.com/corporatemeetingsincentives/
- http://office.microsoft.com/en-us/products/FX011595271033.aspx
- http://www.businessballs.com/meetings.htm
- http://www.pointsebago.com/groups/groupscorpmeetings.html
- http://www.exhibitoronline.com/exhibitorshow/ExhibitorLearningEvents.asp

Corporate Meeting Planning
Mary Jo Blythe, CMP
President, Masterplan, Inc.

Corporate meetings range from small VIP board of directors meetings to large sales meetings, customer incentive meetings, and lower tiered staff training meetings. One common thread between them is that they are always paid for (hosted) by the corporation. The funds come from a department or individual budget, thus creating a VIP(s) "host(s)" at the meeting. This VIP(s) usually expects special treatment, and it is the planner's job to ensure that the VIP(s) is well taken care of.

The planner must also embrace the corporate culture and ensure that it is depicted in all aspects of the meeting, from hotel selection to airport transportation, to menu choices and social activities. Flashy companies will have flashy meetings, and conservative companies will have conservative meetings. The planner is the ultimate controller of this element.

The meeting objectives will typically include motivation, camaraderie, brainstorming, and reviewing goals. There is also quite often an emphasis on the social events at a meeting. Although perceived as recreation, the opportunity for sidebar conversations at non-meeting functions often will impact future corporate decisions. Social events should be strategically planned to ensure that the proper people are sitting together at dinner or assigned to the same foursome at the golf outing.

Corporate meetings, although a category of their own, can be as diverse as corporations themselves. Paying special attention to your VIPs, embracing the corporate culture, and knowing your objectives get the corporate meeting off to a successful start.

Associations

The name "association" implies the act of being associated for certain common purposes, whether for professional, industrial, educational, scientific, or social reasons. Gatherings such as annual **conventions**, topical conferences, world congresses, and topical workshops and seminars are held for the benefit of the association's membership. Other gatherings need to be held for the betterment of the organization. Examples of these include board of directors meetings, committee meetings, and leadership development workshops. Many **associations** have an affiliated exhibition held in conjunction with their convention at which products or services of interest to the attendees are displayed. Besides providing value to the members of the association and potential recognition for the association, these gatherings also generate a significant revenue stream for the organization. According to *PCMA Convene Magazine's* 18th Annual Meetings Market Survey (March, 2009), associations derive 32% of their organization's income from conventions, exhibits, and meetings.

NUMBER AND VALUE OF ASSOCIATION MEETINGS   A major difference between association and corporate gatherings is that attendance at association meetings is voluntary, not mandatory. Another difference is that the attendees are personally responsible for their registration, transportation, hotel, and related expenses. In some instances, employers may fund the attendance of employees at industry and professional association events that are work related.

Association meetings, especially conventions, tend to be very large, ranging from several hundred to tens of thousands of attendees. This issue of size can eliminate many smaller cities and venues from hosting these events, and can also create increased demand by larger associations for prime locations for their gatherings. It also creates increased competition among the larger destinations to capture the major association gatherings.

To adjust to these supply and demand factors, larger associations book their major gatherings five to ten or more years ahead of the scheduled date to ensure that they have the space needed for their event. Small associations have a broader selection of locations that can accommodate their gatherings and therefore require less lead time to secure needed accommodations and facilities.

The booths at the Global Gaming Expo (G2E) reflect gambling products.

The top cities hosting meetings in 2007, as reported in the *Meetings & Conventions'* 2008 Meetings Market Report include

1. Chicago
2. Las Vegas
3. Orlando
4. Atlanta
5. San Francisco/Oakland
6. Washington, DC
7. San Diego
8. Dallas/Fort Worth
9. Miami
10. Phoenix/Scottsdale & Boston

DECISION MAKERS   The decision-making process for association meetings is rather complex and goes through several distinct stages. Once it is decided that a meeting will be held (usually by the board of directors or as stated in the association's constitution or bylaws), the location needs to be decided. Some organizations rotate their meetings through their geographic regions, thereby dispersing hosting opportunities and responsibilities throughout their total membership. The specific city to host the meeting is decided by the board, based on the report of site visitations by the association's own meeting planner or by a contract meeting management provider.

Once the choice has been narrowed to a specific city, the meeting planner, based on site visits and inspections, will locate a venue (e.g., hotel and/or convention center) that is both available on the desired dates and well suited to the needs of the meeting. Typically, the meeting planner makes the recommendation to the association's board and, if approved, negotiates the financial and meeting details with the facility, which results in a contract that is eventually signed by both the venue and the association's senior staff person (usually the meeting planner's boss).

Types of Associations

Local: Most members are located in the metropolitan area where the organization is located.

State: Most members are located within the state where the organization is located.

Regional: Most members are located within the region (e.g., New England) where the organization is located.

National: Most members are located with the same country as where the organization is located.

International: Membership is comprised of people from different nations.

Professional: Membership is comprised of persons from the same industry.

Not-for-profits or Nonprofits: These organizations have a special tax-exempt status granted by the Internal Revenue Service. Although they do not have a profit motive, these associations need to be run efficiently and must have their revenues exceed expenses. Since all revenues are used to support the mission of the organization, excess funds (similar to profits in the corporate world) are allowed to stay with the organization, tax-free.

SMERFs: These are not the little blue people from Saturday morning television. This term refers to small associations with members who join for **S**ocial, **M**ilitary, **E**ducational, **R**eligious, and **F**raternal reasons. Persons attending these meetings tend to pay their own expenses; accordingly, this category tends to be very price sensitive.

Types of Association Gatherings and Events—Their Purposes and Objectives

Conventions: These are assemblies of people for a common purpose. Depending on the type of association sponsoring the convention, it may attract attendees from state, regional, national, or international markets. Many conventions have an exhibition (or trade show) as an added feature. The exhibition may be a major source of revenue for the association. Exhibitors participate in these events because these events offer them an opportunity to show their products and services to a well-targeted group of potential buyers.

Board Meetings: The association's board of directors typically meets several times a year to provide collective advice and direction to the association. This meeting is usually the smallest association meeting held.

Committee Meetings: Many association committees will hold smaller meetings to discuss the affairs related to their purpose (e.g., government relations, convention host committee, national conference program committee, and publications committee).

Regional Conferences: Organizations with a regional structure often schedule one or more events each year to bring together members who are in the same geographic area.

Training Meetings: Associations often offer their members opportunities to upgrade their professional skills and knowledge through meetings targeted to specific topics. Many professions require continuing education (e.g., continuing medical education for different medical specialties). Some associations offer training meetings to develop the leadership potential of the association's elected national and regional officers.

Educational Seminars: Association meetings led by an expert and allowing the participants to share their views and experiences.

ATTENDEES   Since attendance at association meetings is voluntary, the meetings must offer appealing programs to draw members to the events. In the United States, 227,000 association meetings and events occur each year that are attended by 37.5 million people who spend a total of $38 billion. The average annual expenditure for an association event is just over $300,000, which is down from $465,000 two years earlier. There is optimism that spending will return to those higher levels in the near future.

Source: 2008 Meetings Market Report, *Meetings & Conventions* Magazine, August 2008.

NEED FOR MARKETING TO BUILD ATTENDANCE   The marketing of association meetings is critical to the success of the gathering. All good association marketing should begin with an understanding of who the members are and their needs. This focus should be brought into the development of all meetings.

If the meeting provides genuine opportunities for the members to satisfy their needs, the promotional aspect of marketing the meeting becomes much less intense. Since the primary group of attendees is members of the association, the key elements of the meeting promotion

Association Meeting Planning

Susan Reichbart, CMP
Director, Conferences and Meetings College and University Professional
Association for Human Resources

Associations offer their members opportunities to enhance their professional development at conferences, seminars, and workshops. These events may combine structured educational sessions of several hours or days with informal networking events, such as receptions, golf tournaments, and dinners. These activities encourage collegiality and allow members to exchange information in a relaxed social setting.

Associations encourage their members to become involved so that meetings *for* members are planned with input *from* members. The meeting planner works with the member committees from the initial planning stage through the final production of the event. Committee members can suggest program topics and speakers that their colleagues will find appealing and, at best, compelling. Local committee members may suggest local venues for social events, tourist attractions and tours, entertainment options, and golf courses for a conference tournament. One particularly enterprising volunteer researched local options and put together a comprehensive notebook rivaling those found at hotel concierge desks. Working under the supervision of the meeting planner, volunteers perform a myriad of duties during the event, such as giving out badges at registration, monitoring recreational events, and hosting social events—all duties that save the association the cost of hiring temporary staff. Member assistance is a value-added and integral part of the planning that helps ensure an event's appeal and success.

Association events are a source of revenue for associations. The greater the number of paid attendees, the greater the revenue, and the more lucrative the event is to the association. However, since members must pay registration fees and spend additional funds for travel and lodging, the association must provide programs that its members will find too valuable to miss. The meeting planner develops a marketing strategy that promotes benefits to entice members and prospects. The marketing plan may feature keynote speakers, concurrent session programs, an appealing location, and exciting social and recreational events. This information may be posted on the association's Web site, highlighted in newsletters, mailed in comprehensive preliminary programs, and sent by fax and e-mail "blasts." In addition to promoting all facets of the event to all members and prospects, additional marketing emphasis may be directed at targeted groups, such as past attendees.

Association meeting planners work with their member committees to develop worthwhile programs and then design effective marketing plans to maximize participation. The combined focus results in events that are beneficial to members and the association.

include providing advance notification of the date and location of the upcoming meeting along with information about the planned content, speakers, and special activities. Later, detailed registration information and a preliminary program will need to be provided.

The vehicle for communicating this information to the members has traditionally been through direct mail and notices or advertisements in the association newsletter and magazine. Technology and cost considerations have moved many associations toward the use of electronic media to communicate with their members. There has been a rapid growth in the use of broadcast fax and e-mails, which emphasizes that recipients visit the association Web site to seek out the details.

To expand the number of attendees at the gathering, many associations send promotional materials and notices to nonmembers who have been targeted as sharing an interest in the meeting's purpose. Since the nonmember fee is usually higher than the member fee, this effort, if successful, could result in attracting new members to the organization.

DEPARTMENT AND/OR INDIVIDUAL RESPONSIBLE FOR ORGANIZING AND PLANNING

According to the *Meetings and Conventions* 2008 Meetings Market Report, about 30% of the association planners who responded to their survey had the word "planner," "coordinator," "manager," or "director of events, conventions, meetings, or conferences" in their job titles, while 20% were presidents, executive directors, or executive vice presidents. Another 14% were program or project directors, coordinators, or managers, and 8% were executive assistants. Other titles identified included director of education, 3%; marketing director, 3%; and member services manager, 2%.

The respondents spent an average of 60% of their workday planning. Some associations, usually smaller ones, contract out some or all of their meetings to independent planners and association management companies.

In the 2009 Meetings Market Report, 26% of the planners surveyed possessed an industry certification (16% were CMP, 5% were Certified Association Executives, and 2% were CMM).

Source: 2008 Meetings Market Report, *Meetings & Conventions* Magazine, August 2008.

PROFESSIONAL ASSOCIATIONS SUPPORTING THE ASSOCIATION MEEC INDUSTRY

Association meeting planners join professional associations in greater numbers than their corporate counterparts. Those associations include the American Society of Association Executives, the Center for Association Leadership (http://www.asaecenter.org/), the Meeting Professionals International (http://www.mpiweb.org), the Professional Convention Management Association (http://www.pcma.org), the Society of Government Meeting Planners (http://www.sgmp.org), and the Religious Conference Management Association (http://www.rcmaweb.org). There are also many local organizations of meeting planners that provide support and professional development opportunities for them.

The following are Web sites with examples of association meetings:

- http://www.pcma2010.org
- http://www.mpine.org/
- http://show.restaurant.org/

You can find sample programs from association meetings by going to any of the above Web sites.

Government

Governmental entities at all levels have continuing needs to hold gatherings, since they have continuing needs to communicate and interact with many constituent bodies. These meetings may involve the attendance of world leaders, with large groups of protestors and supporters, or a small group of elected local officials holding a legislative retreat. Government meetings are subject to many rules. The federal government and many state governments establish **per diem rates** that set limits on expenditures for lodging and meals. Facilities where federal meetings are held must be able to accommodate persons with certain physical limitations, as per the Americans with Disabilities Act (ADA) and they must meet fire safety certifications.

Canadian Government Building.
Courtesy of Surpasspro, Dreamstime LLC—Royalty Free.

Since the list of per diem rate tables is so extensive, it is recommended that those in need of the current federal domestic per diem rates visit the General Services Administration Web site at http://www.gsa.gov/.

DECISION MAKERS Managers at government agencies are typically those who identify the need to hold a meeting and have the responsibility to provide funding through their departmental budget process or to locate other sources of funding. Meetings, like other parts of an agency's budget, are very dependent on funding provided through the legislative process. Accordingly, as political interest in an agency's mission grows or diminishes, the budget will increase or decrease, as will its ability to sponsor gatherings.

TYPES OF GOVERNMENT GATHERINGS AND EVENTS AND THEIR PURPOSES AND OBJECTIVES
The purpose of many government meetings is the training of government workers. On the federal level, many of these meetings will be replicated in several areas of the country to minimize travel expenses for the employees of an agency's branch offices.

Other government meetings may involve both agency employees and those in the general public who may have an interest in the topic of the meeting. Meetings such as those to discuss prescription drug proposals or the future of social security are likely to go on the road to gather input from the public.

ATTENDEES Attendance by employees at government meetings would generally be mandatory, while attendance by the general public would be voluntary.

SECURITY There is no segment of the MEEC industry more attuned to safety and security than government. They work on a regular basis with the Department of Homeland Security since many of their attendees are high-profile leaders. The PCMA held a forum entitled "Security Door to Door" where the following suggestions were made for implementing security:

- Plan and prepare
- Refine the pre-convention meeting to emphasize security issues
- Be sure that there is coordination of all parties involved
- Establish a security team and its decision makers
- Provide education on security for attendees
- Be proactive rather than reactive
- Stay informed and alert to incidents

Source: Sara Torrence. (2004). "Security Door to Door." *Convene:* 22

NEED FOR MARKETING TO BUILD ATTENDANCE Government meetings have characteristics typical of both corporate and association meetings. Mandatory attendance by government employees requires only that sufficient notice be provided so that participants can adjust their schedules in order to attend. Attracting voluntary attendees may require additional promotion.

DEPARTMENT AND/OR INDIVIDUAL RESPONSIBLE FOR ORGANIZING AND PLANNING
Government meeting planners resemble their corporate counterparts, as they are located throughout their agencies. While some government meeting planners devote all their work time to planning meetings, others handle meetings as one of their extra assigned duties.

Many government agencies hire meeting management companies or independent meeting planners to handle meetings that fall beyond their internal capabilities. In the Washington, DC, area, there are several meeting planning companies that specialize in managing government meetings.

PROFESSIONAL ASSOCIATIONS SUPPORTING THE GOVERNMENT MEEC INDUSTRY
Meeting planners who work for the government and/or independent meeting management companies are likely to join associations to support their professional development. These associations include the Society of Government Meeting Planners (http://www.sgmp.org) and its local or regional chapters, the Professional Convention Management Association (http://www.pcma.org), and Meeting Professionals International (http://www.mpiweb.org). Those who have responsibility for organizing exhibitions are likely to join the International Association for Exhibition Management (http://www.iaem.org).

The following are Web sites providing examples of government meetings:

- http://en.wikipedia.org/wiki/2008_Republican_National_Convention
- http://en.wikipedia.org/wiki/2008_Democratic_National_Convention
- http://www.expo.gsa.gov/
- http://www.fbcinc.com/event.aspx?eventid=Q6UJ9A00LT7G

Government Meetings Are Unique

Sara Torrence
President, Sara Torrence & Associates
Gaithersburg, Maryland

(Prior to her recent retirement, Sara planned special meetings for the federal government)

Meetings for the government are unique. They are different from any other type of conference. Why is this so? Because these meetings are bound by government regulations and operating policies that do not apply to other types of meetings.

First, consider rates for sleeping rooms. In an effort to save the government money, the General Services Administration (GSA) Office of Government-wide Policy sets *per diem* rates for lodging, meals, and incidental expenses for individual travelers for all locations in the continental United States (CONUS). In most cities, these rates are below those charged to conference groups, which take up a larger amount of a hotel's inventory of rooms than transient travelers. To offset this problem, GSA allows government meeting organizers to negotiate a rate up to 25% above the lodging allowance. Also, GSA's Federal Premier Lodging Program offers government travelers guaranteed rooms at guaranteed rates—right where the federal traveler needs to be—and enters into contractual relationships with hotels in the top seventy U.S. travel markets. Additionally, meetings may only be held in properties that comply with the Hotel Motel Fire Safety Act of 1990. Government regulations regarding travel are located at http://www.policyworks.gov on the Web.

Federal procurement policies also distinguish the government meeting. Bids for meeting supplies and services must be obtained from *at least* three vendors for all but the smallest purchases. Additionally, government meeting planners usually are not the people who commit federal funds. All purchases must be approved and contracted for by a federal procurement official. In some cases, meeting planners have been trained by their agencies in procurement practices, so they are able to commit a limited amount of money ($2,500, $10,000, or $25,000, for example). But private sector meeting suppliers should be forewarned to determine who has the authority to commit funds and sign contracts.

Hotel contracts are not considered "official" by the government. A hotel contract may be attached to the paperwork submitted to the procurement official, but in all cases, the government contract—not that of private sector—is the prevailing authority. This applies to all procurements for meeting services. Funds *must* be approved before the service is rendered, not after. In addition, the government *must* be able to cancel a contract without liquidated damages if funding for an event is withdrawn, if there are furloughs or closures of government facilities, or if other government actions make it inadvisable to hold the meeting. The government cannot pay for services not received. And, the government cannot indemnify or hold harmless anyone who is not a government employee conducting official business.

Other characteristics that make government meetings unique include the following:

- ***There is a short turnaround time for planning government meetings.*** While associations plan their conferences with many years of lead time, most government meetings are planned only months—or even weeks—before the event. This is true for large, multifaceted meetings as well as small gatherings.
- ***Government meetings do not fit a particular mold.*** They may be elaborate international conferences for high-ranking dignitaries or small scientific conclaves for eight to twelve researchers. Some meetings may be held only once and therefore have no history.
- ***Government meetings often require a disproportionately large amount of function space relative to the number of sleeping room nights booked.*** This may be because only a small percentage of attendees are coming from out of town.
- ***Policies for meetings can vary from agency to agency.*** Some agencies collect registration fees to cover expenses.

Others will not allow appropriated fees to pay for lunches; collections often have to be made on-site from attendees. In addition, as GSA allows each agency to implement the "up to 25%" allowance as it sees fit, government lodging allowances may vary from agency to agency.

- *Government meetings frequently bring together representatives from the Uniformed Services and non-Department of Defense agencies.* Often, these groups share software applications designed for their *own* purposes, such as encrypted messaging and global directory systems that list only those with a "need to know" the information. Frequently, such meetings are classified and are required to be held in a "secure" facility, whether a government building or a public facility secured by trained personnel.

Government-sponsored meetings are far more complicated than most private-sector conferences that are often planned by people who are not full-time meeting planners. They may be budget analysts, public affairs officers, scientists, secretaries, or administrative officers. And as government meetings are perceived to provide less revenue for a hotel, they may be assigned to junior members of the hotel sales staff.

All government meeting organizers are bound by a code of ethics that prohibits them from accepting anything from a vendor that is valued at more than $20. Those who work with the government should realize this and not put the planner in a compromising position.

Thankfully, there is an organization that specializes in providing education and resources to government planners and suppliers—the Society of Government Meeting Professionals (SGMP).

ENTITIES THAT HELP ORGANIZE GATHERINGS

There are a number of categories of organizations that are key players in aiding corporations, associations, and government in producing their meetings and events. They include exhibition management companies and meeting management companies.

Exhibition Management Companies

There are a number of companies that are in the business of owning and managing trade shows and expositions. These companies both develop and produce shows that profit their companies as well as produce events for a sponsoring corporation, association, or government client. While trade shows and expositions are both events at which products and services are displayed for potential buyers, the **trade show** is generally not open to the public, while **expositions** are usually open to the public. The companies that operate these exhibitions are profit-making enterprises that have found areas of economic interest that attract, according to the purpose of the exhibition, either the general public (e.g., an auto, boat, home, or garden show) or members of a specific industry (e.g., high-technology communications networking). Exhibitions provide the opportunity for face-to-face marketing. Some associations hire **exhibition management companies** to manage all or part of their exhibitions. For their efforts, the companies are paid for the services they provide.

Among the largest exhibition management companies are Reed Exhibitions (http://www.reedexpo.com), which organizes more than 470 events in 37 countries, and George Little Management (http://www.glmshows.com), which markets and produces 17 shows. Their shows serve a wide variety of industries, domestically and globally, including aerospace, art and entertainment, electronics, hospitality, security, sport and health, and travel. Other exhibition management companies include International Gem and Jewelry Inc., Cygnus Expositions, National Event Management Inc., and SmithBucklin Corp.

DECISION MAKERS The owners and senior managers of company-owned shows decide where, when, and how often they will produce their shows. The decision is driven by the profit motive—offering too many shows could lead to a cannibalization of the market. Offering too few shows creates an opportunity for the competition to enter the market with their own show.

TYPES OF GATHERINGS—THEIR PURPOSES AND OBJECTIVES

Trade shows: Exhibits of products and services that are not open to the general public. Trade shows may be part of a convention or may stand alone.

Public shows: Exhibits of products and services that are open to the public and usually charge an admission fee.

ATTENDEES   Depending on the nature of the exhibition, the attendees vary greatly. For trade shows, the market is well defined by the trade or profession. For **public shows**, the attendees are basically defined by their interests and geographic proximity to the show location.

NEED FOR MARKETING TO BUILD ATTENDANCE   The exhibition management companies have a need to market to two distinctly different yet inexorably linked publics. One group that has to be targeted is exhibitors who need to reach potential buyers of their products and services. The others are members of the trade or general public who have a need or desire to view, discuss, and purchase the products and services presented by the exhibitors.

The trade group only needs to be informed of the dates and location of the trade show. Direct mail and e-mail may be all that is needed for an established show. Shows appealing to the general public require extensive media advertising (newspaper, radio, and television) to communicate the specifics within the geographic region. Promotional efforts like the distribution of discount coupons are common. In both cases, it is essential that the marketing effort results in a high volume of traffic at the exhibition to satisfy the needs of the exhibitors.

The exhibition management company really is a marketing company, since it is creating the environment in which need-satisfying exchanges can occur. Their focus is on selling exhibit space and building buyer attendance.

DEPARTMENT AND/OR INDIVIDUAL RESPONSIBLE FOR ORGANIZING AND PLANNING   In this case, the entire exhibition management company is dedicated to the organizing and planning of the exhibition.

PROFESSIONAL ASSOCIATIONS SUPPORTING THE EXPOSITION MANAGEMENT INDUSTRY
The associations that support the exhibition management industry include the International Association of Exhibitions and Events (http://www.iaee.com) for the production side of the business, and The Association for Exhibition and Event Professionals (http://www.tsea.org) for exhibit and event marketers. Other related associations include the Exhibit Designers and Producers Association (http://www.edpa.com), the Exposition Service Contractors Association (http://www.esca.org), and the Healthcare Convention and Exhibitor Association (http://www.hcea.org).

Corporations plan and execute production of gatherings that often include a keynote speaker, such as this one. Management companies are often used to secure keynote speakers.   *Used by permission of Paradise Light & Sound, Orlando, Florida*

Association Management Companies

As the name of this category implies, this type of company is contracted by an association to assume full or partial responsibility for the management of the association, based on its needs. A designated person in the association management company is identified as the main contact for the association and interacts with the board of directors and members to fulfill the association's mission. If the association is small and has limited financial resources, that contact person may serve in this capacity for two or more associations. Since they managed more than one association, association management companies were formerly known as multimanagement companies. Confusion as to who they targeted their services to necessitated this change.

Other employees of the association management company support the main contact and provide services as contracted (such as membership, finance, publications, government relations, and meeting management services). With this type of arrangement, the association office is typically located within the offices of the association management company. Examples of these types of companies include SmithBucklin & Associates of Chicago, Illinois, and the Association Management Group of McLean, Virginia.

Meeting Management Companies

These companies operate on a contractual basis, like the association management company, but limit their services to providing either selected or comprehensive meeting management services. They may manage all aspects of the meeting or may be focused on on-site research, hotel negotiations, exhibit sales, on-site management, handling registration and housing, or any combination of these. The meeting may be held at the association's own location, or the function may be located elsewhere. Examples of meeting management companies include ConferenceDirect of Los Angeles, California; Meeting Management Group of McLean, Virginia; and Conferon Inc. of Twinsburg, Ohio.

Independent Meeting Managers

Experienced meeting professionals often use their expertise and contacts to set up their own business of managing meetings, or parts of meetings, for an association or several associations. An independent meeting manager may be called in to run a golf tournament that is an integral part of a gathering, or to provide on-site management. In some instances, an independent is called in to handle crises in the meetings department. Personnel changes in the meetings department shortly before a meeting may require hiring a competent professional to pull the meeting together and bring it to a successful conclusion.

Event Management Companies

Within the context of the meetings industry, these companies are usually brought in to manage a specific aspect of a larger gathering. They may be hired to plan, script, and supervise all aspects of the awards ceremony or the closing gala. Depending on their market and location, some of these companies may provide local event management (including the grand opening of a building or business), handle the arrangement for a parade, and do wedding and other party planning.

Professional Congress Organizers (PCO)

Outside the United States, the term "professional congress organizer" is used to designate a meeting management company or meeting planner. In international destinations, a congress is defined as a conference or convention. According to the Convention Industry Council (CIC) APEX Glossary, it is a local supplier who can arrange, manage and/or plan any function or service for an event.

When sponsoring organizations from North America hold international events, they often engage the services of a PCO from the host region to assist them with local logistics. Some countries actually require that a domestic company be contracted to handle the meeting.

Professional Associations Supporting Independent Planners

The type of company that individuals are associated with will dictate the type of association that they would likely join to support their professional development. Many of them will join the

Professional Convention Management Association (http://www.pcma.org) or Meeting Professionals International (http://www.mpiweb.org). Others will choose to join organizations like the International Special Event Society (http://www.ises.com), the National Association of Catering Executives (http://www.nace.net), the American Rental Association (http://www.ararental.org), or the Association of Bridal Consultants (http://www.bridalassn.com).

Other Organizations Arranging Gatherings

There are a number of other entities that organize or sponsor gatherings or events. They include the following:

- Political Organizations
  - Republican or Democratic national parties
  - Local political organizations
- Labor Unions
  - The Teamsters
  - Service Employees International Union (SEIU)
  - Pipe Fitters Union
- Fraternal Groups
  - Kiwanis
  - Elks
  - University fraternities and sororities
- Military Reunion Groups
- Educational Groups
  - Universities
  - For-profit education groups
  - Common interest groups
  - High schools

FUTURE TRENDS

The year 2010 finds the world in the midst of a global economic recession. Thus, it is uncertain whether emerging patterns are temporary responses to tight budgets or are evolutionary in nature. Besides budgetary reasons, meetings are also being influenced by emerging technologies and by changing business needs. Some of those changing patterns are as follows:

- ***Shortening Meetings:*** Some sponsoring organizations have clipped off a day or half day from their meetings to reduce lodging and meal expenses for their participants.
- ***Changing Frequency of Annual Meetings:*** Some associations are considering holding their major meeting every other year, and focusing on regional gatherings so that attendees can drive with the result of lowering cost.
- ***Creating More Value for Their Members:*** Some associations are streaming live video of keynote speakers to non-attending members, who in turn will see the enhanced value of their memberships.
- ***Increasing the Interactivity of Meeting Sessions:*** Social media has been introduced to encourage greater involvement of attendees.
- ***Merging of Sponsoring Organizations:*** Organizations with compatible missions and, sometimes, overlapping members and supporters are combining their strengths into a single entity.
- ***Cyber Conferences:*** Technology has evolved to allow meetings of all sizes to occur via the Internet, thereby eliminating the need for participants to get on a plane and check into a hotel. This type of event, often with limited objectives, will serve to complement more traditional face-to-face gatherings.
- ***Virtual Trade Shows:*** A wider range of potential buyers can view innovations in their fields. They can also complement a live trade show where attendees and non-attendees can view the displays and communicate with representatives working the show.
- ***Outsourcing:*** Some organizations have downsized, or even eliminated their meeting planning departments as a cost-saving measure. The responsibilities are transferred to independent

meeting planners or meeting management companies: entities to which the sponsor or organizer has no long-term commitment.

- *Focus on ROI:* Many organizations, whether they are corporations or associations, are increasingly concerned about the return-on-investment (ROI) of their meetings and events. They are taking a hard look at costs and benefits with the goal of decreasing the former and increasing the latter. Post-event evaluations are more and more important.

Summary

The types of organizations that sponsor gatherings are as diverse as the types of gatherings held and the people who attend them. Most of the U.S. population will participate in these gatherings at least once in their lives. For many of them, attending a meeting, convention, exhibition, or other event will be a regular occurrence. The gatherings they attend reflect the personal and professional interests of the attendees.

People seeking career opportunities with sponsoring organizations will have to use targeting techniques to locate them, although these positions do exist throughout the nation. The greatest number of these positions can be found in locations where the organizations are headquartered. The metropolitan Washington, DC, area is considered to be the "meetings capital" of the world, with several thousand associations located there. Many national and international organizations are located in and around Washington, as is the federal government. State capitals are home to many state and regional associations, in addition to agencies of state government.

Major corporations tend to be located in large cities, although many may be located in smaller cities and towns. Their meetings are typically planned at corporate headquarters.

Employment opportunities with organizations and facilities that host gatherings are located in both major cities and small towns. The organization will select a location for its proximity to access by the attendees (near a major airport or the interstate highway) or for the purpose of the gathering.

With baby boomers (the largest age group in the U.S. population) approaching retirement age, it is anticipated that there will be an increasing number of employment opportunities in the coming years on both sides of the meeting, event, exhibition, and convention industry.

Key Words and Terms

For definitions, see the GLOSSARY, http://glossary.conventionindustry.org, or http://www.exhibitoronline.com/glossary/index.asp

Associations	Exhibition management	Not-for-profits and nonprofits	SMERFs
Conventions	companies	Per Diem rates	Trade shows
Expositions	Incentive trips	Public Shows	

Review and Discussion Questions

1. Identify the type of sponsoring organization that holds the greatest number of gatherings and the type that generates the greatest economic benefit.
2. Which type or types of sponsoring organizations have the greatest marketing challenges to ensure the success of their gatherings?
3. What changes are occurring with incentive trips to provide more value for the corporation sponsoring the gathering?
4. How do not-for-profit associations differ from for-profit organizations?
5. What type of organizations comprises the category of associations known as "SMERFs," and what similarities do they share with each other?
6. How do government procurement officers view meeting contracts from their hotel suppliers?
7. Distinguish between the trade show and the exposition.
8. What efficiencies do association management companies bring to the management and operation of small associations?

About the Chapter Contributor

Howard E. Reichbart is an associate professor in the Hospitality Management and Meeting, Event & Exhibition Management Department at Northern Virginia Community College in Annandale, Virginia. Professor Reichbart developed his interests in the hotel and meetings industry as a youngster working in the family hotel business. These interests led him to earn a degree in hotel administration from the University of New Hampshire. He then worked in hotel management for Hotel Corporation of America/Sonesta International Hotels in Hartford, Connecticut, and Washington, DC. He served in the U.S. Army as the club officer of the Ft. McPherson Officers Club in Atlanta, Georgia. Professor Reichbart has been a faculty member at Northern Virginia Community College for forty years, including almost twenty years as the program head. During his time as program head, he developed one of the first degree programs in meeting, event, and exhibition management in the United States. He has also taught at the University of Nevada–Las Vegas, the University of Maryland, and George Washington University.

Destination Marketing Organizations (DMOs)

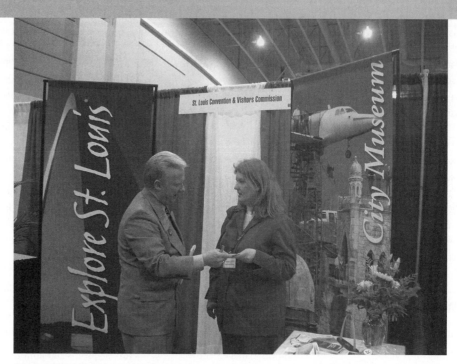

DMOs attend industry trade shows to promote their city.   *Photo by George G. Fenich, Ph.D.*

Chapter Objectives

This chapter provides the reader with an understanding of the following:

- The role and functions of DMOs
- The history of DMOs
- How DMOs can be organized and funded
- The activities of DMOs relative to convention marketing and sales
- An overview and definition of DMO services for meeting professionals
- The Destination Marketing Association International (DMAI) and its services to member DMOs and meeting professionals

INTRODUCTION

"If a destination were merely a place, a dot on a map, a bump in the road or just another stop along the way, then the destination would not matter—nor would this guide be meaningful."

Destinations matter. They are called destinations for a reason: People want or need to go there and visit. In many instances, people go to great lengths to get there. They are drawn to them. For a few, they may be the realization of some lifelong dream.

By boat, car, plane, or train, they go. Why? Because contrary to the wise old proverb, it is not about the journey, but about the destination. And the reasons for making the journey are as varied as the people traveling. Whether for business or leisure, they come because of the expectation of an enjoyable experience.

A desire for local flavor and fulfilling experiences is the force that centrifugally pulls visitors to destinations. This is the lure of a locale, and what a DMO is uniquely able to provide: an authentic exploration into the true heart of a destination.

Source: By Michael Gehrisch, President of DMAI.

THE ROLE AND FUNCTION OF DESTINATION MARKETING ORGANIZATIONS (DMOs)

What Is a Destination Marketing Organization?

Destination marketing organizations (DMOs), often called convention and visitor bureaus (CVBs), are not-for-profit organizations charged with representing a specific destination and helping the long-term development of communities through a travel and tourism strategy. The DMO in each city, county, or region has three prime responsibilities. The first is to encourage groups to hold meetings, conventions, and trade shows in the city or area it represents. The second is to assist those groups with their meetings and meeting preparations. The third is to encourage tourists to visit and enjoy the historic, cultural, and recreational opportunities that the destination offers.

A DMO does not organize meetings, events, and conventions. However, it assists planners and visitors in learning about the destination and area attractions, in order to make the best possible use of all the services and facilities the destination has to offer. The roots of present-day DMOs stretch back to 1895 when a group of businessmen in Detroit put a full-time salesman on the road to invite conventions to their city. His function expanded and the organization for which he worked was called a Convention Bureau. Today, DMOs operate throughout the world.

Initially, DMOs existed to sell and service conventions. As the years passed, more and more of these organizations became involved in the promotion of tourism. What were originally called Convention Bureaus expanded their scope to include tourism and were called CVBs. This evolution and expansion of roles and functions continues today. Many "bureaus" are changing their names to Destination Marketing Organizations or DMOs to better reflect their activities in selling and promoting their destinations to a wide range of customers. DMOs are synonymous with CVBs. In fact, the use of the term DMO began outside the United States but has now evolved to be commonly used worldwide.

The Purpose of a DMO

DMOs are primarily not-for-profit organizations charged with representing a specific destination helping the long-term economic development of communities throughout the travel and tourism business. DMOs are usually membership organizations bringing together local businesses that rely on tourism and meetings for revenue. DMOs serve as the "official" contact point for their destination. Some DMOs are departments of local government, not unlike the library or highway department. This structure is most common outside the United States where DMOs may be quasi-autonomous non-government organizations (QUANGO) or may function as an authority. Many fall under the government tax structure of a not-for-profit organization and are classified as either "501-C-3" or "501-C-6."

For visitors, DMOs are like a key to the city. As an unbiased resource, DMOs can serve as a broker or an official point of contact for convention, meeting, and event planners; tour operators; and tourists. They assist planners with meeting preparation and encourage business travelers and tourists alike to visit local historic, cultural, and recreational sites. For conventions, they are often the intermediary between the sponsoring organization and hospitality businesses. As such, the DMO may coordinate site visits, the dissemination and collection of requests for proposals (RFPs), and development of collateral material. Some DMOs will also find funding to help attract large conventions.

There are a number of reasons why a DMO is valuable to a meeting planner. DMOs offer unbiased information about a destination's services and facilities. They are a one-stop shop for local tourism interests and save meeting professionals' time and energy. DMOs provide a full range of information about a destination, and they do not charge for most of their services.

Chicago Convention and Tourism Bureau

CCTB Vision

Chicago will be the top global destination.

CCTB Mission

The Chicago Convention & Tourism Bureau is the premier sales and marketing organization that promotes Chicago's world-class assets to global leisure travel and convention business to ensure the economic vitality of the City and its member business community.

CCTB History

Chicago has a long and illustrious history as a convention and meeting site. The area's first recorded convention dates back to 1847, when the U.S. River and Harbor convention met to discuss the St. Lawrence River. By 1907, the city was beginning to establish itself as a world-class attraction, and the Chicago Association of Commerce moved to establish a local business committee charged with the responsibility of attracting conventions to the growing downtown area.

In 1943, the Chicago Convention and Visitors Bureau was founded to serve as Chicago's primary sales agent for conventions and trade shows of all types and sizes.

In 1970, the Bureau merged with the Tourism Council of Greater Chicago to form the Chicago Convention and Tourism Bureau.

In 1980, the Metropolitan Fair and Exposition Authority—owners and managers of McCormick Place—determined that the CCTB was the best qualified organization to serve as the principal sales agent for McCormick Place. The Bureau moved its offices to McCormick Place at the end of 1980.

In 1989, under the leadership of Governor James Thompson, the Metropolitan Fair and Exposition Authority assumed total responsibility for Navy Pier, thus the Authority was renamed the Metropolitan Pier and Exposition Authority (MPEA).

Acting under the agreement still in effect today, the Bureau plays a crucial role in enhancing the economic fabric of the Chicagoland community by selling and promoting the city and its facilities as the ideal destination for visitors of all types.

CCTB Impact

Visitors spend billions of dollars each year in metropolitan Chicago. This income spurs new business, which means new jobs for the area and economic growth for the region, benefiting everyone.

Located in the center of the United States, Chicago's size, transportation options, lively hospitality industry, and unparalleled meeting and exhibition facilities make Chicago the premier choice for group meetings of any type or size.

Funding

The CCTB is neither a branch of any government nor a charitable foundation. It is an independent not-for-profit organization, which receives its funding from several sources, including:

- A percentage of Chicago's hotel/motel tax
- State of Illinois grant monies for development of local conventions and tourism
- Membership dues from local hospitality-related businesses
- Grant money from the MPEA

Membership

The CCTB considers its members to be its greatest asset. The Bureau's membership provides products, services, and expertise vital to the Bureau's role as a liaison to the convention and tourism industries.

The CCTB boasts one of the largest membership bases (1,200) of any convention bureau in the nation. Membership in the CCTB provides a recognizable endorsement sought by meeting planners and also provides direct marketing opportunities to key buyers and decision makers.

Source: http://www.choosechicago.com/Pages/about_us.aspx

If DMOs Do Not Charge for Their Services, How Do They Make Money?

DMOs do not charge their clients—the leisure visitor, the business traveler, and the meeting planner—for services rendered. Instead, most DMOs are funded through a combination of hotel occupancy taxes and membership dues. If the DMO is a government agency, then funding comes from local government.

Jacob K. Javits Convention
Center. *Courtesy of Dave King*
© *Dorling Kindersley.*

Why Are Meetings and Tourism Important?

Travel and tourism enhances the quality of life for a local community by providing jobs; bringing in tax dollars for the improvement of services and infrastructure; and attracting facilities, such as restaurants, shops, festivals, and cultural and sporting venues that cater to both tourists and locals.

WHAT A DMO CAN DO FOR MEETING PROFESSIONALS

What Meeting Planners Need to Know about DMOs

Many people are not aware of the existence of DMOs, and therefore they do not realize the wealth of information and resources they provide.

Most DMOs are not-for-profit organizations representing a specific destination. Most are membership organizations bringing together businesses that rely on tourism and meetings for their livelihoods. A DMO has many responsibilities. Most important, it serves as *the* official point of contact for convention and meeting planners. It encourages groups to hold meetings in the city and assists groups with meeting preparations. DMOs also provide promotional materials to encourage attendance and establish room blocks, among other things.

Meeting planners can access a range of services, packages, and value-added extras through a DMO. Before going into the specifics of what a DMO can do for a meeting planner, let us examine a few common misconceptions about DMOs.

Misconception 1: DMOs solely book hotel rooms and convention space.

Fact: DMOs represent the gamut of visitor-related businesses, from restaurants and retail to rental cars and racetracks. Therefore, they are responsible for introducing planners to the range of meeting-related products and services the city has to offer.

Misconception 2: DMOs only work with large groups.

Fact: More than half of the average DMOs' efforts are devoted to meetings of fewer than 200 people. In fact, larger DMOs often have staff members specifically dedicated to small meetings, group tours, leisure tourists, and transient business travel.

Misconception 3: DMOs own and/or run the convention center.

Fact: Only 5% DMOs run the convention center in their locations. The Las Vegas Convention and Visitor Authority is one of them. Nevertheless, DMOs work closely with local convention centers and can assist planners in getting what they need from convention center staff.

Misconception 4: Planners have to pay DMOs for their services.

Fact: In truth, most services of a DMO are free. Michael D. Gehrisch, president and CEO of DMAI, points out, "DMOs are a hotel's best friend and a meeting planner's best friend. We don't charge either one. We book business for the hotel without a fee and we provide the same service, for free, to the planner." How is it that a DMO can work for free? Because most DMOs are funded through a combination of hotel occupancy taxes and membership fees.

Some may question the need to work through a DMO when planning a meeting, particularly in cases where the bulk of an event takes place at one hotel or at the convention center. However, the DMO can help a planner work with those entities and can help fill out the convention schedule (including spouse tours and pre- and post-tours) with off-site activities. Since the DMO is an objective resource, it can direct planners to the products and services that will work best to accommodate the needs and budgets of their client.

WHY USE A DMO?

DMOs make planning and implementing a meeting less time-consuming and more streamlined. They give meeting planners access to a range of services, packages, and value-added extras. Before a meeting begins, DMO sales managers can help locate meeting space, check hotel availability, and arrange for site inspections. DMOs can also link planners with suppliers, from motor coach companies and caterers, to off-site entertainment venues that can help meet the prerequisites of any event.

 Destination Marketing Association International   **2009 Profile of Destination Marketing Organizations**

The following is a profile of destination marketing organizations, as represented by a sample of 241 DMOs that participated in DMAI's *2009 DMO Organizational & Financial Profile Study. Note: Data were collected in mid-2009 and do not reflect any subsequent changes in DMO operations.*

DESTINATION PROFILE

Average Tax Rates

- **Total** Tax on a Hotel Room (incl. hotel room tax, sales taxes, etc.): 12.2%

- Special Restaurant Tax (excl. sales tax): 2.5%

- **Total** Tax on a Car Rental: (incl. rental tax, sales tax, etc.): 11.4%

How the Hotel Room Tax is Used
Hotel room/occupancy taxes are often allocated for tourism-related purposes. The chart below shows the various allocations of these taxes. DMO funding is the most prominent use.

Note: The above averages are for those DMOs that reported the specific allocation. For example, for those destinations where a percentage of the room tax was allocated to DMO funding, that average allocation was 55%. As a result, the figures in the chart above do not add to 100%.

Changes in Hotel Room Tax Rate and Allocation

More than one in ten report a recent/anticipated change in their destination's hotel room/occupancy tax with the average change being a one to two percentage point increase. While slightly more than half of the DMOs are receiving a portion of the increase, more than one-third of municipalities are also keeping a significant percentage to close budget shortfalls.

52%	44%	37%	11%	7%
DMO Funding	Other Visitor/ Non-Visitor Purposes	Municipal Fund	Arts Organizations	Convention Center

How the Special Restaurant Tax is Used: For destinations that have this tax (16%), the two common uses are convention center operations/construction/debt service and DMO funding.

How the Car Rental Tax is Used: Seven percent of destinations that have this tax use a portion of the revenues for facilities including convention centers, arenas and stadiums.

DMO PROFILE

Structure: The majority are independent, not-for-profits: 61% are 501(c)(6) and 4% are 501(c)(3). 21% are government agencies (city, county, state/province, authority) and 5% are a chamber of commerce or a division of a chamber. Almost one-quarter have an additional/affiliated corporation, the majority of which are 501(c)(3), or *foundation*.

Peripheral Operations: One in ten has non-traditional DMO operations. Almost half manage the destination's convention center, 17% a museum/cultural institution and 14% a parking facility.

Membership: Slightly fewer than half are membership organizations, averaging 535 members. The typical membership composition: 22% accommodations, 17% attractions/cultural institutions, 17% restaurants, 16% event services/suppliers, 11% retail and 17% other.

Contract with Primary Funding Source: 54% have a contract. Ten percent are awarded through an RFP process. Slightly less than half (47%) are annual; the remainder are multi-year terms, averaging eight years.

Quantifiable Goals in the Contract: 30% room nights booked, 22% ROI, 16% visitor spending generated by the DMOs efforts. Half have no quantifiable goals in their contract.

Staff Size: The average DMO has 13 full-time and two regular part-time employees. Almost one-quarter have employees who telecommute and 18% have satellite offices.

Funding/Finances

- *Average DMO revenue:* US$5.0 million in FY2009, down 2% over FY2008 (excl. Las Vegas). Larger DMOs reported larger decreases (4%–6%), due in part to a greater dependence on the long-haul, overnight visitor market (more susceptible to economic downturns) which, in turn, resulted in depressed hotel activity and reduced hotel tax collections – a key DMO funding mechanism.
- *Public funding* decreased 5%–6% among large DMOs, compared with 2% for those with smaller budgets. *Private funding* fell 16% for DMOs with budgets from $5 million to $10 million, while it was down 8% for DMOs with budgets more than $10 million. DMOs with budgets less than $500,000 reported no change.

Note: Revenue declines do not necessarily reflect the full impact of the recession because many DMO hotel tax funding are based on the previous year's hotel room tax collections. FY10 budgets are expected to include further declines.

- The vast majority (91%) receive hotel tax funding, averaging 77% of all revenue. In terms of *private* funding, 44% receive membership dues. Other top private sources include: print advertising, co-op promotional and advertising programs and visitor centers.
- Slightly more than one-quarter (27%) have separate bank accounts for public and private funds.
- More than half (54%) have a *formal reserve policy* while 41% have a *formal investment policy.*

Expenses

- DMOs spend almost half (47%) of their budget on sales and marketing efforts, with media advertising the top activity (18% of total expenses). The remainder is spent on personnel (41%) and administrative (13%).
- DMOs typically spend 35% of their sales and marketing budget on consumer leisure marketing efforts; 24% is allocated to convention sales and marketing. An additional 9% is directed towards the travel trade sector. Communications/PR efforts comprise 11% of budget and Visitor Services (incl. visitor centers), 5%.

For further information on this study and DMAI's research program, please contact research@destinationmarketing.org.

FIGURE 3-1 Organizational chart for a CVB

Advantages of Using a DMO to Plan a Meeting

There are many things a DMO can do to help an organizer, sponsor, or planner put together a meeting or event. A DMO can assist planners in all areas of meeting preparation, and provide planners with detailed reference material. It can also establish room blocks at local hotels and will market the destination to attendees via promotional material, thereby encouraging attendance. A DMO can act as a liaison between the planner and community officials, thus clearing the way for special permits, street closures, etc. The DMO can offer suggestions about ways meeting attendees can maximize free time, along with helping to develop companion programs and pre- and post-convention tours. A DMO can be an invaluable resource when putting together meetings, expositions, events, and conventions.

Activities of DMOs Relative to Convention Marketing and Sales

Professionals who work in a DMO serve as the sales representative for their destination. The membership base of DMOs includes: hotels, restaurants, attractions, convention centers, and many other entities. DMOs represent these businesses to meeting professionals who need their products and services. There is an entire process that a DMO undertakes with a meeting professional to bring a meeting to its destination.

Site Review and Leads Process

Determining if a site or location can accommodate a meeting's requirements is critical. The DMO is the central information source for advice on site selection, transportation, and available local services, all with no cost or obligation to the meeting or event manager. DMO representatives have the knowledge and information to provide up-to-date data about the area as well as planned future developments.

Regardless of the meeting size, the DMO can serve as the first stop in the site review process. When a meeting manager contacts a DMO, a DMO sales manager will be assigned to assist in securing the necessary information and facts to produce a successful meeting. The sales manager can gather information about preferred dates for the event and find out what facilities are available, if there are adequate sleeping rooms and meeting rooms, and whether convention facilities are available for the entire time period, including time for exhibitors to move in and out.

In order to represent all their members, most DMOs have a "leads" process, wherein the sales manager circulates meeting specifications to facilities and lodging entities that can accommodate the requirements. Basic information required by the DMO is indicated on the convention lead sheet. Many DMOs now distribute this information electronically.

The sales manager distributes the lead to all member-lodging properties capable of handling the meeting. However, the lead distribution may also be limited by establishing certain parameters, such as specifying a location downtown or near the airport. In cases as this, the lead would be forwarded only to properties that meet the requirements identified. If a meeting manager is familiar with the destination's properties, he or she may express interest in certain facilities by name. Then, only those facilities receive the lead.

The DMO sales manager will request that the receiving property send the information directly to the meeting manager, or the sales manager may gather the information, compile it into a package, and send it to the meeting professional. In the United States, federal antitrust laws prohibit DMOs from discussing pricing policies with hotels under consideration. All pricing discussions must take place between the meeting manager and the prospective property. A DMO salesperson may relate to a property that a meeting manager is looking for a specific price range of room rates but cannot negotiate on the meeting manager's behalf.

Convention Lead Sheet

The convention lead sheet used by DMOs will usually contain the following information:

- Name of the sales representative or account manager
- Date of the sheet distribution
- File number
- Name of the primary contact for the inquiring group
  - Person's title
- Name of the group or organization
  - Address
  - City
  - State
  - Zip code
- Telephone number, fax number, and cell phone number of the primary contact
- Total number of room nights anticipated
  - Peak room nights and date of peak
- Dates for the event or meeting
- Decision date
- Total anticipated attendance
- Occupancy pattern
  - Day
  - Date
  - Rooms
- Sequential order
- Meeting space requirements
  - Exhibit space
  - Food functions
  - History
  - Competing cities
- Additional information
- Name of person who prepared the sheet and date of preparation

Source: Adapted from *Professional Meeting Management,* 4th Edition. Chicago (IL): Education Foundation Professional Convention Management Association: 89–90.

The DMO sales manager will communicate with the meeting manager and the facilities to ensure that all information is disseminated, received, and understood. Any additional questions will be answered, and the meeting manager will be encouraged to visit the city to personally review the properties being considered. The DMO can be of significant assistance during a personal site review by arranging site inspections. If there are several facilities to review, the DMO sales manager will develop a complete itinerary and schedule appointments with a salesperson at each property. If other facilities must be reviewed during the visit, the DMO will contact the necessary parties and include them on the itinerary. In most cases, the sales manager will accompany the meeting manager on the site reviews and respond to any questions that may arise.

The DMO can also make a meeting manager aware of any local laws and regulations that may impact the meeting. A meeting manager should ask about issues, such as unions, taxes, alcohol serving laws, and any other peculiarities during the information-gathering process. For example, in Las Vegas and New Orleans, bars can stay open 24/7, while in Amsterdam it is legal to sell and consume marijuana in certain "coffee shops." A DMO representative can also discuss the condition of the local economy and local economic trends that could have an impact on the meeting. The DMO sales manager should be able to answer most of these questions or find out the answers.

The "lead process" takes place far in advance of the event. For an Association, the average "horizon" or time between looking at a destination and the event taking place is about three years. However, with large groups and large cities, the horizon can be twenty-five years or longer. Think about the typical age of a sales manager: What will he be doing in twenty-five years?

Albuquerque Convention and Visitors Bureau

The mission of the Albuquerque Convention & Visitors Bureau is to stimulate economic growth by marketing Albuquerque as a convention and visitor destination.

Accredited Destination Marketing Organization
The Albuquerque CVB is proud to be accredited by the **Destination Marketing Accreditation Program (DMAP)** of the **Destination Marketing Association International**.
- See **Accreditation News Release**

Vision

To be recognized and respected as a leading tourism marketing organization and to achieve economic vitality and success through integrity, enthusiasm, and creative involvement for the promotion of Albuquerque as a world-class destination.

ACVB Is

- A private, not-for-profit organization (501c6).
- Selling and marketing Albuquerque as a destination.

- Focused on conventions, meetings, leisure travelers, and travel professionals.
- Funded by lodgers tax through a contract with the City of Albuquerque.
- Supported by a partnership of almost 1,000 organizations.
- A Board of Directors of approximately 30.
- A full-time staff of 40 and over 100 volunteers.
- An equal opportunity employer.
- Funded with ~$7M (~$6M from lodgers tax and ~$1M from private sector **activities**).

ACVB Values

- We are goal-oriented and results-directed.
- We look for opportunities, and we build on them.
- We are responsible and accountable.
- We value quality in our service, work, and ourselves.
- We strive for excellence, honesty, and integrity.
- We encourage teamwork while expecting high levels of individual performance.
- We treat our customers, members, and staff with courtesy, respect, and fairness.
- We honor our promises and commitments.

- We maximize communication to minimize misunderstanding.
- We encourage feedback, so we can continually improve.

Albuquerque Convention & Visitors Bureau

Mailing Address: P.O. Box 26866, Albuquerque, NM 87125-6866

Physical Address: 20 First Plaza NW Ste. 601; Albuquerque, New Mexico 87102

Our business office is located at 20 First Plaza on the 6th floor, just south of the **Convention Center** in downtown Albuquerque.

Visitor Information: 1-800-284-2282
info@itsatrip.org
Business Office: 1-800-733-9918; 505-842-9918
Fax: 505-247-9101
Human Resources Department:
jobs@itsatrip.org
Web: www.itsatrip.org

Source: http://www.itsatrip.org/about-us/albuquerque-cvb-services/default.aspx

Site Inspections

A site inspection is a physical review of proposed venues, services prior to the actual program. A site inspection may be required at any point in the sales process. A site inspection by the planner may occur prior to the proposal, after the proposal, or after the DMC has been chosen. A site inspection occurring prior to the proposal is a part of the information-gathering visit by the client. Often this is hosted by the destination's CVB or DMO. A site inspection by the planner that occurs after the proposal has been submitted, yet prior to the customer's decision, is used to address questions regarding the execution of the submitted proposal. Finally, a site inspection visit by the planner occurring after the DMC has been chosen is often the first step in the finalization of a program or event. Site inspections can vary in time and detail but always require special attention by busy DMC sales and/or operational executives.

These inspections must be carefully planned and orchestrated to show a customer the venues and services offered as well as to demonstrate the DMC's operational skills, organization, and community contacts and relationships. The site inspection can often be the most critical step in winning a customer's business, as this is when the DMC has an opportunity to develop a relationship with the customer and gain their confidence. Many programs have been won or lost over a seemingly simple lunch conversation during a site inspection.

DMO SERVICES FOR MEETING PROFESSIONALS

The general services that DMOs provide meeting professionals include the following:

- DMOs can offer unbiased information about a wide range of destination services and facilities.
- DMOs serve as a vast information database and provide one-stop shopping, thus saving planners time, energy, and money in the development of a meeting.
- DMOs act as a liaison between the planner and the community. For example, DMOs are aware of community events with which a meeting may beneficially coincide (like festivals or sporting events). They can also work with city government to get special permits and to cut through red tape.
- DMOs can help meeting attendees maximize their free time through the creation of pre- and postconference activities, spouse tours, and special evening events.
- DMOs can provide hotel room counts and meeting space statistics as well as a central database of other meetings to help planners avoid conflicts and/or space shortages.

The specific services that DMOs can provide for meeting professionals are:

- DMOs can help with meeting facility availability—information on the availability of hotels, convention centers, and other meeting facilities.
- DMOs help connect planners to their local transportation network that offers shuttle service, ground transportation, and airline information.
- DMOs provide destination information—information on local events, activities, sights, attractions and restaurants, and assistance with tours and event planning.
- DMOs provide housing services—housing reservations for meeting delegates.
- DMOs are a liaison in destination government and/or community relations—a local resource regarding legislative, regulatory, and municipal issues that may affect a meeting or the meetings industry.

- DMOs can provide access to special venues—as most DMOs have ties to city departments, personnel have the ear of local government officials. Whether an official letter of welcome from the mayor is needed or the blocking of a road for a street party, a DMO can pave the way.
- DMOs can assist in the creation of collateral material.
- DMOs can assist with on-site logistics and registration.
- DMOs can develop pre- and postconference activities, spouse tours, and special events.
- DMOs can assist with site inspections and familiarization tours as well as site selection.
- DMOs can provide speakers and local educational opportunities.
- DMOs can help secure special venues.
- DMOs can provide help in securing auxiliary services: production companies, catering, security, and so on.

The overall job of a DMO is to sell a destination. A DMO wants clients to be happy. It is going to do everything it can to match up clients with the perfect setting and services for their meetings.

What Information Do DMOs Have about Hotels?

DMOs keep track of room counts as well as other meetings coming to the area. In this way, they can help planners avoid conflicts with other events. Moreover, as DMOs have firsthand familiarity with the hotels and with meeting space in the area, they can help planners match properties to specific meeting requirements and budgets.

DMAI'S SERVICES TO MEMBERS AND MEETING PROFESSIONALS

Destination Marketing Association International

As the world's largest resource for official DMOs, **Destination Marketing Association International** is dedicated to improving the effectiveness of nearly 3,000 professionals from 625+ DMOs in more than 25 countries.

DMAI provides members—industry professionals and partners, students and educators—cutting-edge educational resources, networking opportunities, and marketing benefits available worldwide. Founded in 1914, the association's mission is to enhance the professionalism, effectiveness, and image of destination management organizations worldwide. In 2005, the association underwent a brand assessment and changed its name from the International Association of Convention & Visitor Bureaus to the Destination Marketing Association International (DMAI).

As the only association that represents DMOs exclusively, DMAI offers comprehensive year-round education programs, including an annual convention for DMO executives to continue their professional development and network with peers. The association publishes a bimonthly electronic newsletter and an online membership directory, and sponsors DMO-focused research studies through its foundation.

DMAI's DMO members represent significant travel and tourism related businesses at the local and regional level. The association serves as the primary contact point for its destinations for a broad universe of convention, meeting, and tour professionals.

Destination Marketing
Association International (DMAI)
Logo.   *Destination Marketing
Association International (DMAI)*

DMAI actively promotes DMOs worldwide, highlighting the value of using a DMO's services to the media and general public. The DMAI also offers programs and services designed to link DMOs directly with consumers and meeting planners. Meeting planners can access their organization's post-convention history and receive reports via DMAI's **empowerMINT.com** database. The DMAI also sponsors two "Destinations Showcase" trade shows every year, where DMOs exhibit their destinations to meeting professionals. The DMAI offers research, professional development, and a variety of other member services to DMOs.

empowerMINT.com

The premier convention and meetings database, The Meeting Information Network (MINT) houses over 40,000 meetings from 20,000 organizations—including associations, corporations, military reunions, sporting events, and government institutions—in a Web-enabled format accessible from any location at any time. It represents a unique collaboration between 120+ DMOs that voluntarily report detailed meeting history information on the events held in their cities. This online database provides critical marketing and sales direction to thousands of DMOs, hotels, and other convention industry suppliers. Meeting professionals will find that accurate information in empowerMINT.com regarding their meetings will help in the negotiation process. The meeting information is entered into the system by participating DMOs—information they received from firsthand sources, including hotels, convention centers, and meeting professionals. This is one reason why it is important for planners to participate in post-convention meetings.

Meeting Information Network (MINT) logo. *Destination Marketing Association International (DMAI)*

Once meetings are recorded into the database, meeting professionals can encourage suppliers and other interested parties to request a copy of the information in their post-convention reports. This report serves as an organization's meeting "credit report" to the industry. Making sure of the accuracy will reduce the number of unwanted sales calls a meeting planner receives and will make available more qualified information for the next round of negotiations—whether it is with a hotel or a destination management organization.

Destinations Showcase

Destinations Showcase is a fast-paced and productive one-day exhibition and conference owned by the DMAI, where qualified **meeting professionals** attend valuable **education sessions**, **network** with industry leaders and peers, and explore a full range of destinations from throughout the world. *It is where meetings business gets done.*

Destinations Showcase logo. *Destination Marketing Association International (DMAI)*

Exhibitors are exclusively from DMOs and their exhibit facilities. Qualified meeting, convention, exposition, and destination planning professionals have the opportunity to meet face-to-face with professional staff representing destinations from around the world. A low planner-to-exhibitor ratio facilitates a meeting specifically for the purpose of site review and selection. Planners are encouraged to attend "with RFP in hand" and are encouraged to plan ahead with a pre-event exhibitor list.

Shows are held annually in Washington, DC, and Chicago. Full registration is complimentary, and attendance is restricted to qualified meeting professionals only. Meeting planners look for opportunities to earn credit toward the CMP certification at Destinations Showcase. For more information, visit http://www.destinationsshowcase.com.

DMAI Professional Development Offerings

The DMAI provides professional development to DMOs and their employees. It offers the following meeting, convention, training, and certification opportunities to DMO professionals:

- Annual Convention
- Destination Management and Marketing Institute (DMMI)
- CEO Forum
- Leadership Europe COO/CFO Forum
- Sales Academy™ Part I & II and Online
- Shirtsleeve Sessions

Certified Destination Management Executive (CDME)

The DMAI has a certification program that is the equivalent of the CMP designation in the meeting professional community.

Recognized by the DMO industry as its highest educational achievement, the CDME program is delivered under the auspices of Purdue University and the DMAI. The CDME program is an advanced educational program for veteran and career-minded DMO executives who are looking for senior-level professional development courses. The main goal of the CDME program is to prepare senior executives and managers of DMOs for increasing change and competition.

The focus of the program is on vision, leadership, productivity, and implementation of business strategies. Demonstrating the value of a destination team and improving personal performance through effective organizational and industry leadership are the outcomes.

PDM Program

Although PDM is not a designation, like CDME, it is recognized throughout the industry as a highly valuable skills package needed for the destination management career journey. DMO professionals who participate in the PDM Certificate Program acquire knowledge and skills necessary to be more effective and successful destination management professionals.

Accreditation

In fall 2006, DMAI launched the Destination Marketing Accreditation Program (DMAP), starting initially with a beta-test followed by a full program roll-out. Currently utilized by the U.S. Chamber of Commerce, the healthcare industry, and institutions of higher education, accreditation programs are becoming increasingly popular with organizations that wish to define standards of performance for their member constituents and measure their compliance. DMAI research shows that 93% of DMO executives say their organization would seek accreditation if an acceptable program was developed by the association. DMAP aims to provide a good method to assure staff, volunteer leadership, and external stakeholders that their DMO is following proper practices and performing at an acceptable level for the industry. "This new accreditation program will provide a platform for official destination marketing organizations to assure their stakeholders that they have achieved the highest accepted standards," remarked DMAI President and CEO Michael D. Gehrisch.

DMAI Research

DMAI's research arm, the Destination & Travel Foundation, provides destination management professionals with access to insightful, comprehensive, and industry-specific information that

Media Contact: Ryan Smith
(919) 645-2676 office
(919) 270-8346 cell
rsmith@visitraleigh.com

About the Greater Raleigh Convention and Visitors Bureau

Our Mission

- Non-profit organization representing Raleigh and Wake County in the solicitation and servicing of convention business and leisure travelers
- Brings together the interests of city and county government, trade and civic associations, and travel suppliers to build visitor traffic to the area
- Acts as a liaison between potential visitors and the businesses that host them

Formation of the Bureau

- Formed January 1992 by the Wake County Board of Commissioners and the Raleigh City Council, following legislation passed by the 1991 General Assembly
- Formerly the Raleigh Convention and Visitors Bureau, September 1986-January 1992; originally a department of the Greater Raleigh Chamber of Commerce
- Governed by a 12-member Board of Directors
- Funded by a 15 percent share of both the 6 percent Wake County Hotel Occupancy Tax and 1 percent Prepared Food and Beverage Tax
- $3.4 million budget
- 21 full-time and 1 part-time staff member
- Located in One Bank of America Plaza, 421 Fayetteville Street, Suite 1505, Raleigh, NC 27601-1755
- Local: 919.834.5900
  Toll-free: 800.849.8499
  Web site: **www.VisitRaleigh.com**
  E-mail: **visit@visitraleigh.com**

How We're Structured

Sales Department

- Solicit conventions and meetings for the Raleigh area
- Promote Raleigh and Wake County for visitor business to enhance the economic growth and development of the area
- Coordinate sales efforts with hotels and meeting facilities
- Develop and implement marketing plan based on market demands in specific segments
- Conduct sales trips to feeder cities and participate in industry trade shows
- Provide qualified sales leads to hotels
- Conduct site inspections of meeting facilities and attractions
- Aggressively pursue group tour market on a regional and national level
- Respond to visitor information requests from tour companies and travel agencies
- Work with the N.C. Division of Tourism, Film and Sports Development to promote the Raleigh area internationally
- Represent the Raleigh area at trade and travel shows and sales missions

Tourism and Partnership Marketing

- Develop and manage the promotion for Raleigh/Wake County to leisure visitors
- Develop promotional tactics for increasing weekend Occupancy and off-season business at Wake County hotels
- Act as bureau outreach to outlying communities, enhancing strategic alliances and creating programs/promotions to benefit all of Wake County
- Develop potential partnerships with corporations, organizations and associations that will increase awareness and revenues for Wake County
- Develop strategic partnership with industry partners, such as airlines, Amtrak, rental car agencies and private-sector companies on packaging and creating awareness of Greater Raleigh as a leisure market

(Continued)

- Work closely with local, state and regional organizations to develop visitor business to Greater Raleigh
- Coordinate National Tourism Day event

Sports Marketing Department

- Promote Raleigh and Wake County for sports championships, events and sportsrelated activities
- Develop and implement marketing plan
- Provide qualified leads to hotels
- Coordinate sales efforts with hotels and sports facilities
- Work closely with other Raleigh/Wake County and state organizations that pursue sports business
- Represent the Raleigh area at national conferences and trade shows

Convention Services Department

- Encourage repeat business and pre- and post-convention activity
- Provide a housing bureau service free-of-charge for groups using three (3) or more hotels
- Provide registration staff assistance at minimal cost
- Provide complimentary brochures and overall convention consultation
- Provide volunteers to staff information booth for groups of 250 or more people to answer questions about the area
- Assist in planning tours for convention delegates
- Assist in planning special events at unique sites
- Help promote excellent service in the local hospitality industry
- Go-between for the planner and local providers
- Provide pre-convention promotional information to encourage increased convention attendance
- Provide assistance to conventions in obtaining local publicity

Communications Department

- Produce marketing and information materials to promote Greater Raleigh
- Develop public relations and community awareness programs
- Assist local, state and national media
- Manage advertising and creative agencies and coordinate local, state, regional and national ad campaigns
- Work with travel writers to encourage placement of stories about Greater Raleigh in regional and national publications
- Continually maintain, update and promote GRCVB web site
- Manage e-mail mailing list and create and send monthly e-newsletter to list

they can use to enhance the effectiveness of their DMO's day-to-day operations and in their business planning. The DMAI offers a wealth of research and resources that provide statistical data and information essential for calculating economic impact, budgeting and strategic planning, marketing and promotion, and educating stakeholders.

DMAI & DMAI Foundation Research Studies

Futures Study This study is a forward-thinking report that contributed greatly to the ongoing "strategic conversation" in the destination marketing industry and provided a framework for DMOs to plan for the future of their destinations. The research revealed more than 250 specific trends deemed to be relevant to DMOs, which were synthesized into eight globally focused super trends in the key sectors of the business environment. At the highest strategic level, the majority of DMO CEOs identified the following as being significant themes affecting the industry: Relevance, The Value Proposition, and Visibility. The report also reveals a "strategic visitor-centric map" for DMOs, which clarifies the role and contribution of DMOs to the destinations they serve.

DMO Compensation and Benefits Survey This report, conducted biannually, provides a baseline for more than 45 job position compensation levels as well as for benefits packages offered to DMO employees in the United States and Canada.

DMO Organizational and Financial Profile This survey, the most comprehensive of its type for DMOs, provides standards for a variety of operations while also allowing DMOs to compare their operations with their peers. Also conducted every two years, the report includes information on DMO funding sources, available facilities, tax rates, budgets, staff structure, expense categories, and reserves.

MyDMAI This service was launched in 2008 and allows users to augment face-to-face interactions with fellow DMAI members. They can discuss topics of shared interest, provide solutions and best practices, upload documents, submit news, engage with committees, and more.

Destination & Travel Foundation

The DMAI Foundation was created in 1993 to enhance and complement the DMAI and the destination management profession through research, education, visioning, and developing resources and partnerships for those efforts. The DMAI Foundation merged with U.S. Travel Association's Foundation in 2009 to become the Destination & Travel Foundation.

The foundation is classified as a charitable organization under Section 501 (c) (3) of the Internal Revenue Service Code; therefore, donations to the foundation are tax deductible as charitable contributions. A board of trustees, made up of members of the DMAI and representatives from related industry organizations, runs the foundation.

Membership in DMAI

In 2006, DMAI developed three new membership categories separate from DMO members to include students and educators, state and regional DMO associations, and allied members.

Students and educators will find valuable opportunities to learn firsthand how DMOs and tourism boards market their destinations.

FUTURE TRENDS

- The role and function of DMOs will continue to expand. Many are now involved in "managing" the destination. They are helping to guide the community in tourism development, tourism policy, building infrastructure, planning and expanding convention centers, attracting hotel developers, and more.
- Some consider DMO to stand for destination **marketing** organization, while others consider it to stand for destination **management** organization. Furthermore, some experts in the field have suggested that an even better and more descriptive term would be Destination Marketing and Management Organizations.
- The trend of putting destination marketing, tourism services, and convention center operation under one umbrella is likely to continue. This helps to make sales and delivery of the tourism product, especially with large citywide conventions, more efficient and "seamless."
- DMOs will continue to educate the community and stakeholders about the importance and value of face-to-face meetings.
- DMOs will expand their efforts to market their destinations to convention attendees, not only as a place to hold meetings and events but also as a place to live. Thus, the role of DMOs will become, in part, more like that of a Chamber of Commerce.
- DMOs are likely to see continued threats to their budgets. Politicians often try to divert funding away from DMOs and to "more visible" endeavors such as schools. The budget threat is likely to be most severe in the United States where much of the revenue for DMOs come from hotel room taxes.
- The greatest increase in the number and scope of DMOs will likely take place in developing regions such as China and Africa.

HOW TO FIND OUT MORE ABOUT DMOs Visit http://www.destinationmarketing.org, the official Web site of the DMAI. The site contains a listing of DMOs around the world, along with contacts and hyperlinks to more than 600 local DMO Web sites.

Vienna Austria Convention Bureau

Vienna Convention Bureau – About us

The Vienna Convention Bureau is your neutral partner. Our job is to promote Vienna as Central Europe's leading conference city.

We offer our services free of charge to any national or international organizer of meetings, conventions and incentives.

The Vienna Convention Bureau was set up in 1969 as a department of the Vienna Tourist Board with financial support from the Vienna City Council and the Vienna Chamber of Commerce. Additional funding comes from sponsors. In order to hold its corner in today's networked global markets, the Vienna Convention Bureau belongs to a number of international convention and meeting industry associations.

A team of 11 conference specialists, headed up by Christian Mutschlechner, acquire convention, meeting and incentive business from around the globe and play a key role in maintaining Vienna's international reputation as a recognized destination.

Conferences, corporate meetings, and incentives play an important part in Vienna's tourist industry, and account for 12.3% of all overnight stays. Outstanding conference facilities, excellent conference support services and cultural appeal help ensure that Vienna ranks among the leading destinations for international meetings.

Courtesy of Vienna Convention Bureau.

Summary

DMOs are an integral part of the meetings and convention industry. For over 100 years, DMOs have been working diligently to bring meetings and conventions to their destinations and to service these meetings with a variety of free services. Over the years, DMOs have gone from being destination marketers to destination managers, becoming involved in every aspect of their destinations and therefore enriching the experience for meeting attendees and visitors.

The DMAI is the professional association for DMO employees, and it has been providing a wealth of member services to DMOs since 1914.

Key Words and Terms

For definitions, see GLOSSARY, or http://glossary.conventionindustry.org.

Destination Marketing Organization (DMO)
Destinations Showcase
Education session

Destination Marketing Association
International (DMAI)
empowerMINT.com

Meeting professional
Network

Review and Discussion Questions

1. Define the role and function of a destination marketing organization.
2. Name the different ways that DMOs can be funded.
3. Name two things that a DMO does for meeting professionals.
4. Name two things that the DMAI does for meeting professionals.
5. What can the DMAI do for DMOs?

Internet Sites for Reference

1. http://www.destinationmarketing.org
2. www.empowermint.com
3. http://www.destinationsshowcase.com

Contact Information

Destination Marketing Association International (DMAI)
2025 M Street, NW, Suite 500
Washington, DC 20036
Phone: +1-202-296-7888

Fax: +1-202-296-7889
E-mail: info@destinationmarketing.org
Web address: http://www.destinationmarketing.org

Source Note

1. 2009 DMO Organizational and Financial Profile Report 2.

About the Chapter Contributor

DMAI Staff

CONVENTION LEAD SHEET

The convention lead sheet used by DMOs will usually contain the following information:

- Name of the sales representative or account manager.
- The date that the sheet was distributed.
- The file number.
- Name of the primary contact for the group wishing to find space in the city.
  - Their title
- Name of the group or organization.
  - Address
  - City
  - State
  - Zip code
- Telephone number, fax number, and cell phone number of the primary contact.

- The total number of room nights the group anticipates using.
  - Peak room nights and date of peak.
- Dates for the event or meeting.
- Decision date.
- Total anticipated attendance.
- The occupancy pattern.
  - Day
  - Date
  - Rooms
- In sequential order.
- Meeting space requirements
  - Exhibit space
  - Food functions
  - History
  - Competing cities
- Additional information
- Name of person who prepared the sheet and date of preparation.

Adapted from *Professional Meeting Management*, 4th Edition.

CHAPTER 4

Meeting and Convention Venues

An Examination of the Facilities Used by Meeting Planners, Focusing on How Their Financial Structure Dictates Their Relationships with Planner Clients

Cruise ships are sometimes used for meetings and conventions. *Photo by George G. Fenich, Ph.D.*

Chapter Objectives

The chapter provides the reader with an understanding of the following:

- The importance of the physical attributes of the meeting venue to your ability to use it for your event
- How the venue's financial structure impacts your ability to negotiate for your meeting
- The variations in service levels and service availability in different facilities
- Potential hazards often overlooked by novice planners
- What questions need to be asked of a facility in order to ensure the success of your meeting

INTRODUCTION

Meeting planners work in a variety of facilities. These facilities range in size from **hotel** suites that hold a handful of people to major convention centers and outdoor festival sites that accommodate tens of thousands. Any location where two or more people gather is a meeting site. Whether it is a multimillion-square-foot convention center or a street corner under a light pole, people will find a place to gather. The meeting planner's job is to match the meeting and the venue. Thus, the planner must determine two things about the group: Who are they, and why are they here? Most events and meetings are appropriate only for a limited range of facilities. A national political convention would not work on a street corner nor would a board of directors' meeting work in an outdoor **stadium**. For an event to succeed, the characteristics of the event must be properly matched to the facility in which it is held. Whether the

A large tent event.   *Used by permission of Paradise Light & Sound, Orlando, Florida*

venue is the conference room at the end of a suite of offices or the flight deck of an active aircraft carrier, the goal of the meeting must fit with the choice of venue for the meeting to work.

Thus, the planner must be sure to appropriately research the group and the facilities that may fit the group's needs, understand the needs and expectations of the group, communicate the benefits offered by a facility that meet the needs of the group, and verify the arrangements between the group and the venues. Before selecting a meeting venue, the planner must complete a **needs analysis**. A needs analysis is conducted to help guide the planner in formulating meeting objectives and in narrowing down the list of potential venues to those best suited for the event. By performing this important step, the planner can often immediately rule out certain venues, thus streamlining the site selection and planning process. Chapter 9 will discuss the needs analysis procedure in greater detail.

In order to properly exploit the tremendous range of facilities, a meeting planner must be familiar with both the physical characteristics of the venue and its financial structure. The combined impact of these two factors determines a meeting planner's relationship with the facility management and both parties' relative negotiating positions. Many other features of a facility are relevant to the success or failure of any meeting, but an understanding of the significance of the facility's physical form and its financial structure is vital for a meeting planner to effectively use the facility to support the meeting.

The vast majority of meetings take place in conference rooms or offices on the meeting participants' property. Typically, one room in a suite of offices is designated as a conference room, and a handful of colleagues gather to address some current issue. Whether scheduled or impromptu, these meetings rarely involve a meeting planner. However, as these meetings become larger and involve more people, the person who has had the position of scheduling these on-property meetings frequently finds him or herself planning meetings that take place off-property.

HOTELS

The second most common place for a meeting is a hotel. Hotels and their meeting spaces vary widely in size and quality. Virtually all hotels with any meeting space have at least one small **boardroom**. These boardrooms typically seat fewer than a dozen people, and the more elegant examples have permanent large tables and furniture that would be appropriate in the conference rooms of any major corporation. At the other end of the scale, hotel ballrooms tend to top out around 60,000 square feet. **Break-out rooms** vary from a little larger than boardrooms up to about half the size of a main ballroom. The whole facility, including break-out rooms, will likely not exceed 100,000 square feet of total meeting space, although a few are larger. Within the past few years, there has been a surge in the expansion of hotel meeting space. Hotels with over 100,000 square feet of meeting space are no longer rare. Many privately funded hotels such as Gaylord, Sands, or Mandalay Bay are encroaching on the convention venue domains previously dominated by government-funded facilities.

Hotels generally provide a variety of meeting spaces. They typically include a large carpeted ballroom with corresponding themed décor. These ballrooms are generally planned as part of the initial construction of the facility and are often divisible by the use of movable air walls. A common floor plan provides larger divisions flanked by smaller ones accessible from the side corridors. It is not uncommon for the ceiling to be lower in the smaller divisions than in the larger ones. This is not always obvious from printed floor plans. Breakout rooms tend to be decorated and equipped like smaller versions of the ballrooms and serve identical functions for smaller numbers of people.

Some hotels have been so successful at marketing their meeting space that they have found the need to add space. If the construction of additional permanent space is cost-prohibitive or the hotel is concerned that the extra space won't be used on a regular basis, leveling out a parking lot to facilitate tents on an as-needed basis may be a useful alternative. The most common type of event held in a tent is a meal function or themed party. This space allows the hotel to maintain higher room occupancy levels by reducing the gap in the **shoulders** between meetings. Once the tent ceases to be a viable option, due to either weather or zoning issues, many hotels build spaces specifically designed for exhibits. These spaces have a rough, unfinished look to them and tend to be designed more for utility than beauty. These utilitarian facilities are less expensive to maintain and, due to their reduced cost structure, can be more profitable than the glamorous ballrooms.

In contrast to the stark exhibit facilities, many hotels have beautiful outdoor venues to support social and "networking" functions. Pools, patios, atriums, and gardens can all be used as meeting locations. In addition to utilizing outdoor venues, the use of **prefunction space** such as corridors or lobbies adjacent to meeting rooms may provide a location for ancillary event needs. Refreshment breaks, registration desks, and Internet cafes may be situated in these prefunction areas to provide necessary services without compromising valuable meeting rooms. When first inspecting a meeting space, a planner should observe all of the physical attributes of the space. The facility's "hardware" has a significant impact on the delegates' comfort and their involvement in the proceedings.

Hotels tend to be owned by major hotel companies or are franchised by a hotel company to a local owner who manages the facility in accordance with corporate guidelines. Most hotels supporting meeting space are part of a larger corporate entity, which is likely publicly traded or a subsidiary of a publicly traded corporation. The Rosen Hotels in Orlando and the Atlantis in the Bahamas are notable exceptions. Hotels are rarely owned by individuals and almost never owned by local governments. Hotels are intended to be businesses and not charities, thus their mission is to generate profit for the parent company.

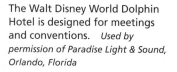

The Walt Disney World Dolphin Hotel is designed for meetings and conventions.   *Used by permission of Paradise Light & Sound, Orlando, Florida*

Meetings are rarely a hotel's primary business. The primary business of almost all hotels is the sale of sleeping room nights. The meeting space in a hotel business is often a **loss leader**, whose primary purpose is to fill what would otherwise be empty sleeping rooms. This single financial fact of life overshadows all other aspects of any negotiation between a meeting planner and a hotel. There are some hotels that derive significant revenue from their extensive meeting spaces, but these revenues are ancillary income and intended to drive their primary business, which remains sleeping room nights. While hotels derive the majority of their revenue from the rooms, many also generate significant income from the restaurants and bars frequented by convention attendees. A smaller percentage of revenue is the result of **concessionaires** at the pools, beach, or spa. This dynamic changes somewhat when the hotel is associated with a theme park or casino. Casinos can be money-making machines and may have a significant impact on a planner's ability to negotiate. Hotels associated with theme parks have a similar effect.

Conventional wisdom states that planners do not pay for meeting space in hotels. However, meeting space costs the hotels money. The interest paid on the investment capital needed to build the hotel, and the staff and materials to clean, maintain, and operate the meeting rooms are some of the most significant costs related to meeting space. These costs must be funded from somewhere. Most often, these costs are covered by requiring a meeting to commit to using a minimum number of sleeping rooms for a minimum number of nights. The hotel's goal is to fill the rooms that would not be filled by its regular customers. The closer the hotel gets to 100% occupancy, the happier the stockholders will be.

By linking sleeping room use with meeting space availability, hoteliers found they could induce meeting planners to use their facilities because the meeting space was free, at least to them. Unfortunately, after the system of financially linking sleeping rooms to meeting space became popular, many hotels discovered that some planners were consistently off in their projections.

Given the popularity of Internet travel booking sites, many planners are realizing that their delegates are finding cheaper rates at the same hotels as the meeting by booking outside the contracted room block. These rooms often wind up not being counted as related to the meeting. The planner can wind up paying **attrition** penalties even if the hotel is sold out due to the number of delegates at that convention. There are clauses that can be added to the contract that address this issue, but they should be discussed with an attorney familiar with these issues. The planner's ultimate goal in this process is to get credit for every room night the hotel sells that it would not have sold if the meeting were held somewhere else. This one issue may be the toughest part of any hotel negotiation.

Another significant source of revenue for most hotels is food and beverage. The hotel's restaurants and bars are generally designed to handle the hotel's "regular" traffic, which is likely a mix of business travelers or tourists. If the hotel has a nightclub, the probability is that its intended clientele is not the meeting delegates, but rather locals or vacationers. The size and staffing levels of these outlets are rarely determined by the needs of the meeting attendees. Banquet catering is intended to fill that need. The scope and quality of hotels' banquet departments vary as much as the quality of the sleeping rooms. In a reaction to the reluctance of some meeting planners to agree to elevated sleeping room rates in order to guarantee meeting space, some hotels have linked banquet revenue with meeting space. Thus, a meeting planner who meets a threshold of spending in the catering department gets a break in the meeting room cost.

Some events do not involve sleeping rooms, and many hotels are reluctant to deal with them. However, the demand for venues to hold the so-called "**local social**" event is great enough that hotels do market to them. In order for the planner of a **local event** to get "free" meeting space, he or she would have to guarantee a minimum amount of catering revenue. Events that do not involve sleeping rooms are generally a hotel's last attempt to derive some revenue out of vacant meeting space. What revenue it derives comes from food service and the commissions paid by other support vendors for the privilege of working in the hotel. These other vendors would include the disc jockey, the florist, limo service, and the decorator among others. If lighting or sound beyond the disc jockey's systems were needed, the in-house audiovisual company would pay a commission back to the hotel. All of these revenue streams are calculated in the decision to accept a piece of social business once all other higher revenue opportunities have been exhausted. Since a planner of a social event is just as likely to fall short of his or her food and beverage projections as a planner of an event involving sleeping rooms, attrition on catering revenue projections is becoming more common.

The décor for a fancy dinner.
Used by permission of Paradise Light
& Sound, Orlando, Florida

Hotels derive revenue from a variety of other non-meeting services as well. Golf courses, spas, equestrian centers, and beaches all provide revenue to the hotel. Hotels often contract with exclusive vendors to provide services within the hotel. Audiovisual companies, **destination management companies (DMCs)**, service contractors, musicians, disc jockeys, florists, and bus companies can all be contracted to the hotel as exclusive vendors of their specialized services. Commissions paid back to the hotel can be as high as 40%. Some hotels charge attrition on those services as well. The hotel's theory is that the hotel and the vendor have made an investment in the facility and equipment for the meeting planner's benefit. Should the planner elect not to use these services, the services should be paid for anyway because they were available. This is particularly common with audiovisual services. Hotels often require planners to use the in-house AV department or an exclusive vendor. If a planner insists on using an outside company, they may have to pay a hefty fee. It is especially important to discuss these expectations early in the negotiating process to avoid confusion later. It is not always safe to assume that the hotel's exclusive vendor has that honor because it is the most qualified. The negotiated size of the projected commission may be the determining factor.

Hotels do pay some commissions, although the discussion to this point has focused on the commissions paid to them. Travel agents and destination management companies as well as site selection companies can be paid a commission for the business they bring to the hotel. One of the questions a planner must ask of every travel professional who recommends a facility is what his or her financial connection is to that facility.

Planners negotiating with hotels need to consider the entire financial package their business will bring to the facility. The more closely aligned the meeting's financial structure is to the needs of the hotel, the better deal the planner can get for his or her meeting. The entire financial package includes not just the revenue from the meeting itself but also the revenue from the sleeping rooms, restaurants, bars, and exclusive vendors. When negotiating with any convention facility, planners are not only negotiating on the basis of what they will use but on the basis of what is available whether they use it or not. The availability of specific **amenities** often drives the delegates' expectations of the facility. It is important that planners match the level of their delegates' expectations with the level of service provided by the hotel at a cost the delegates feel is reasonable.

For instance, hotels attached to theme parks are a special case. It is not uncommon for a theme park-based hotel to include an estimate of how much money the delegates or their families will spend in the attached "entertainment" facilities when they decide whether or not to take a particular piece of business. Clauses relating the number of theme park passes purchased to the availability of meeting room space can appear in some contracts at these hotels. Meetings planned with sufficient free time to allow the delegates to avail themselves to visit the theme parks may have an easier time contracting their desired meeting space.

If the hotel is attached to a casino, it is possible for the hotel to derive more revenue from the casino than it does from the sleeping rooms. The prices charged for the sleeping rooms are fixed in advance of the guests' arrival. The potential revenue derived from the casino is limited only by the availability of credit on the guests' accounts. Meetings then can become a means to bring guests to the casino where they potentially spend more money gambling than they will on other activities. On the other hand, if a group fails to spend enough time and money in the casino during their meeting, the sales department may be told not to contract with the group again in the future.

Seasonality and fluctuating occupancy levels can have a significant impact on the cost of using a facility. A hotel with a severe seasonal variation can have an off-season price that is as little as half of its peak-season price. By paying attention to a facility's seasonal occupancy patterns, meeting planners can find some true bargains. A common misconception among meeting delegates is that the incredibly cheap rate that they pay to use an exclusive resort is due to their planner's negotiating prowess, when it is more likely that the great rate is because of the planner's choice of a venue with extreme seasonal variations.

Aside from the typical considerations when booking meeting space in hotels, such as the size of the space available, attrition penalties for sleeping rooms and/or catering, and seasonality, planners must be aware of move-in/move-out schedules and other groups that are in house. Depending on the size and scope of an event, it may take anywhere from a few hours to a week to set up (or tear down) the physical aspect of an event particularly if there is an exhibition component. This time is essentially a lost opportunity for the hotel because rather than booking another group that could generate money, the space is unavailable. Hotels may charge a rental fee for the space itself to gain back some of that lost revenue, but there is no opportunity to make additional profit through catering or other revenue centers. Planners must keep this in mind and expect to negotiate move-in/move-out dates because hotels prefer to utilize their meeting space as efficiently as possible. In addition, hotels often host meetings for several different groups at any given time. In many cases, this is a non-issue, but when a corporation is promoting a new product launch or discussing proprietary information, they generally prefer their competitors not be in the same facility. Coordinating space is also important when groups may have conflicting behavior. For instance, a significant conflict could arise if a professional organization giving a certification examination was placed in a meeting room adjacent to a daylong band rehearsal. These are considerations planners must be cognizant of during the negotiating and contracting process to ensure that the planning and execution of their event is successful.

Here are the Web sites of some of the hotels mentioned:

http://www.gaylordhotels.com/

www.swandolphin.com

http://marriott.com/property/propertypage/NYCMQ

http://www.mandalaybay.com/

http://www.ihg.com

CONVENTION CENTERS

Conventional wisdom has it that convention centers are huge. Many are, and the biggest are getting even bigger. Convention centers are designed to handle larger events than could be supported in a hotel. Several convention centers feature over a million square feet of meeting and exhibit space. Their very size is both their strength and their weakness. Convention centers are meeting facilities without sleeping rooms and are often little more than large bare buildings with exposed roof beams. Others are mammoth architectural marvels involving magnificent feats of engineering and awe-inspiring vistas.

Compared to hotels, convention centers are more likely to devote the majority of their space to **exhibit halls** and utilitarian spaces than to plush ballrooms. While hotel lobbies are designed to be comfortable and inviting, convention center lobbies are designed to facilitate the uninterrupted flow of several thousand delegates. This difference in design philosophy is evident in every phase of a convention center's operation. Just as hotels have a variety of space sizes, convention centers also have a variety of spaces. In the typical hotel, the ballrooms are the

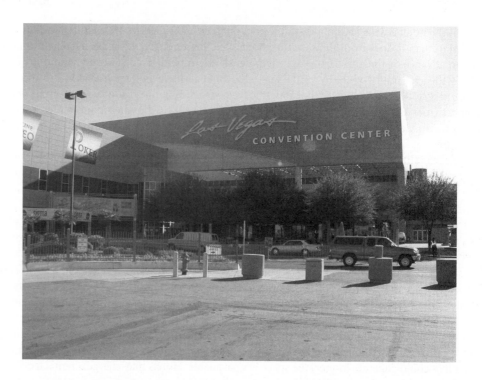

The Las Vegas Convention Center contains over 1 million square feet of space.   *Photo by George G. Fenich, Ph.D.*

largest meeting spaces, followed by the exhibit spaces. In a convention center, the exhibit halls tend to be the largest spaces, followed by the carpeted ballrooms. It would not be unusual for the prefunction spaces in a convention center to be larger than the break-out rooms attached to them, unlike a typical hotel where the prefunction spaces tend to be smaller.

Occasionally convention centers have rooms with built-in stages, a characteristic relatively uncommon in hotels. They are also more likely than hotels to have "congress-style" permanent classrooms, although such rooms would not be as uncommon at conference centers. If we compare the facilities on the basis of the philosophy of their design, it would appear that hotels are designed by psychologists, while convention centers are designed by industrial engineers. Engineering considerations are relevant in both types of facilities, but the difference in scale significantly impacts how hotels and convention centers operate.

Convention centers are often described as utilitarian and occasionally "cold" when compared to hotels. Unlike hotels, convention centers generally do not have spas or swimming pools, exercise rooms, or saunas, restaurants or bars. While a hotel is open around the clock, convention centers can, and do, lock the doors at night and the staff goes home when nothing is scheduled. In a hotel, someone is on duty at all times; whereas if someone is required to be available at odd hours in a convention center, that person must be scheduled in advance. This rigidity of structure and scheduling means that the planner who uses a convention center may need to plan in more detail than the planner who holds the same meeting in a hotel.

Unlike the hotel, which is most likely part of a major corporation, most convention centers are owned by government entities. Professional management is frequently contracted to a private company that specializes in managing such facilities. SMG, Volume Services, and Global Spectrum are three such companies. Many convention centers are actively supported by the local DMO and some DMOs even operate centers. As with everything that concerns government, the managements of these facilities are ultimately responsible to the taxpayers. One controversial issue among convention center managers is whether the public-sector or the private-sector companies can do a better job of managing these facilities. There are strongly held opinions on both sides of the issue. Even with all the discussion, one thing is still true. The quality of a planner's event is as dependent on the planner's relationship with the individuals running the facility as it is with how well the event is planned. Especially in a convention center, the more thorough the planning, the more successful the event.

This management structure creates an environment in which the convention center can take a very long view but at the same time must think short term. Generally, the intent of the government that built the building is that the facility be an economic driver for the whole community.

Therefore, the facility can take events that benefit the community as a whole with less concern for driving the demand for sleeping room nights in the surrounding hotels. This is part of the reason why convention centers, unlike hotels, will take events such as local consumer shows that generate no sleeping room nights. While the convention center may be funded in part by some kind of hotel sleeping room tax, it is not required to maintain a specific ratio between meeting space and sleeping rooms.

How does a convention center make money? After all, the taxpayers will not support a big building forever if it makes no money. Convention centers charge for everything they provide on a pay-per-use basis. Every square foot of the building has a price attached to it. Room rental, by the square foot per day, is the center's biggest single revenue source. Every chair, every table, and every service provided by the convention center has a price. The center makes additional income from catering and the concessions. In a hotel, much of the real cost of holding the meeting is hidden in the sleeping room price; in the convention center, every cost is specifically itemized. This "nickel and dime" approach is the convention center's way of charging for services used and not charging for what is not needed.

One overlooked fact that sets convention centers apart from many other types of facilities concerns the portion of their budget spent on energy. It is not unusual for a convention center to spend more money on utilities than it does on its full-time staff. This is not a reflection of the staffing levels, but rather an indication of how expensive it is to keep a large facility properly climate controlled. Hotels have significant energy bills as well, but unlike a convention center, they are not trying to climate control huge spaces with high ceilings and massive doors that stay open all day.

Similar to a hotel, a convention center has relationships with vendors for services it does not provide internally. Such services might include parking, buses, audiovisual, power, data–telecom, and florists.

In a convention center, catering is more likely to be contracted to an outside vendor than in a hotel. Each of these vendors pays a commission to the center. This commission may not be in cash but may be in the form of equipment owned by the vendor installed in the building. For example, in many buildings, the facility does not own the soft drink vending equipment. The soft drink company with the exclusive rights in the facility owns and services the equipment in return for a specified level of product sales. Another debate in the convention center industry has to do with whether a facility should have "exclusive" or "preferred" vendors. It is no longer safe to assume that any vendor suggested by a facility is either exclusive or preferred unless the vendor is identified as such. Traditionally, catering was the only exclusive service, but in some facilities power, rigging, audiovisual equipment, security, and telecom can be exclusive vendors to the facility. Some of these relationships are the result of governmental regulations, and others are an attempt to avoid liability lawsuits. In contrast, in some convention centers even the catering can

As the old actor said in "The Fantasticks," "See it in lights."
Used by permission of Paradise Light & Sound, Orlando, Florida

be outsourced to vendors other than the ones who have the relationship with the facility. The relationships between the vendors and the facility are fluid and changing. Therefore, no planner should ever assume the nature of the relationships without asking specifically.

It is also not safe to assume that an exclusive vendor is somehow more or less competent than an outside vendor. Many convention industry salespeople have tried to paint their competition into a corner with broad-brush statements that may or may not be true. Determining the competence of the facility's preferred or exclusive vendors is one of the toughest jobs a planner must face; and while there are some guidelines, there are no absolutes. Unfortunately, the success or failure of any given meeting often depends on vendors with whom a planner has no experience.

Given the political climate in which most convention centers operate, combined with the size and scope of the events they support, they tend to be bureaucratic and inflexible. Negotiations can take longer than in a hotel, but a convention center is more likely to publish all its rate information either in print or on a Web site than is any other type of meeting facility. It is possible to go through many convention centers' documentation and know before talking to a salesperson what that event is likely to cost. This is difficult if not impossible to do in many other types of facility. With all this information readily available, it becomes the planner's responsibility to access the information, and not the facility's responsibility to guide a novice planner through the process.

Here are the Web Sites of some of the Convention Centers mentioned:

http://www.mccormickplace.com/

http://www.javitscenter.com/

http://www.moscone.com/site/do/index

http://www.pittsburghcc.com/html/index.htm

Facility Management Company Web Sites:

http://www.smgworld.com/

http://www.global-spectrum.com/

CONFERENCE CENTERS

Many of the most critical meetings determining the future health of an organization involve fewer than twenty-five people. These meetings are often attended by people who understand the importance of the decisions they will make to the careers and livelihoods of the employees of entire corporations. One such meeting involves the review of pharmaceutical research. The people in the meeting will decide whether to continue to fund development of a potential new drug or to abandon it. They will decide which drugs to prepare for regulatory review and which to send back for more tests. The success of these meetings is critical to the survival of the companies that hold them. Hotel boardrooms and conference centers are the ideal venues for such meetings.

For the most part, conference centers are small, well-appointed facilities specifically designed to enhance classroom-style learning. The CIC defines a conference center as a facility that provides a dedicated environment for events, especially small events. The International Association of Conference Centers (IACC) has developed a specific set of guidelines as to what constitutes a "conference center" as opposed to other types of meeting facilities. Adherence to these guidelines essentially guarantees the planner that the facility is well managed and well suited for intense, small group learning situations. Several major corporations run conference centers, including Aramark, Dolce, Sodexho, Marriott, and Hilton. Several smaller companies are also involved, including Conference Center Concepts and the Creative Dining Group.

A planner contemplating using an IACC conference center would be well advised to visit the IACC Web site and ensure that the scope and expectations of the meeting make it appropriate for a conference center in advance of meeting with the facility's salespeople. Conference centers can be either resident or nonresident. The biggest difference between the two is that resident facilities have sleeping rooms and nonresident facilities do not. While it is easy to draw the comparison between hotels and resident conference centers, the comparison would likely be misleading. One of the major differences concerns the conference centers' focus on teaching and learning instead of on elegant parties. This tends to translate into better furniture and a greater tendency toward permanently installed work surfaces as well as permanently installed projection and audio systems.

Many conference centers, whether resident or nonresident, employ a pricing strategy called the **complete meeting package**, which essentially means that whatever the facility owns, the planner may use at no additional charge. This puts the facility's entire inventory of easels, projectors, microphones, and sound systems at the planner's immediate disposal. For the planner, this is a flexible way to work, in that he or she is freed from the task of getting scheduled audiovisual companies to provide their equipment requirements in advance.

Some conference centers are in remote locations. Some of the nonresident centers are part of large corporate office complexes and are offered to the public only when the parent company is not using the facility. The IACC guidelines have a distinctly "corporate" feel to them. The guidelines strictly control the inside of the meeting rooms. The impact in variations of location would be felt less inside the classroom than it would in the supplemental activities the delegates would partake of when not in meetings. Suburban and rural conference centers routinely feature high-quality golf courses, while the more urban centers would link to cultural and sporting activities located in the city centers. Some of the more rural facilities offer horseback riding or outdoor activities like hiking or skiing in season.

When choosing a conference center, a planner should review not only the facilities offered by the center but also the expectations of the delegates attending the event. A nonresident facility might be better if all the delegates are local. A rural facility might be better if the delegates have a tendency to slip away at midday when they should be in classes. A review of the event's history is important in determining if a conference center will work for the event.

Like hotels, corporations generally own conference centers, although some are closely held family businesses. They are not government entities. Therefore, they operate more like hotels than like convention centers except that their meeting spaces are focused almost exclusively on classroom-style education. Conference centers can also have seasonal patterns much like hotels. A conference center located in the midst of several ski slopes will be much less expensive in the summer than it will be in the winter. A conference center located in an urban area may be the same price year round. If the event dates are flexible, moving a week or a month could yield significant savings.

Conference centers using the complete meeting package tend to be entirely self-contained. If outside vendors are used, they will likely be transparent to the planner. By using the complete meeting package concept, the facility ties all its revenue into a single bundle of services. The only variable is the number of delegates who actually show up as opposed to those who register.

Attrition takes on a new meaning in a conference center. It is not unusual for a conference center to charge a planner a fixed price for up to a certain number of delegates. If some of the delegates do not come to the event, the planner is still responsible for the full amount of the contract. This fee is not based on the ability of the facility to resell the rooms. It is based on 100% of the negotiated facility fee regardless how much of the facility is used. Although the planner's tasks on site are less intense than would be the case in a convention center, the planner's ability to predict room night use is very critical. A planner deciding whether to use the complete meeting package or buy their own equipment needs to look beyond the simple cost of the projector or microphone. They need to evaluate the proper use of their time. Is their time well spent hauling a large plastic case through airport security, or is it better spent making sure that the coffee is refreshed and lunch is ready on time? Many planners see their jobs in terms of cost containment. While that is surely part of the job, it would seem that helping guarantee the success of the meeting is the more appropriate goal. Sometimes a penny saved is not a penny earned. Sometimes it is a pound lost in a missed opportunity. The planner's job is to know the difference.

Here are the Web Sites of some of the Conference Center Companies mentioned:

http://www.aramarkharrisonlodging.com/

http://www.hiltondirect.com/

http://www.marriott.com/meeting/default.mi

http://www.dolce.com/

RETREAT FACILITIES

Retreat facilities can be viewed as a special group, much like rural conference centers. They are more likely to be owned by a family or closely held corporation than the other facilities and focus on a smaller portion of the conference center market. Not-for-profit entities, charitable organizations, or religious groups own many of the retreat facilities. Several evangelical organizations run retreat facilities as part of their internal training programs. Other groups can rent these facilities when the parent organization is not using them. In addition to the classroom learning typical of a conference center, retreat facilities often specialize in some unique extracurricular learning opportunities. Some retreat facilities are at dude ranches, others are cabins in the woods where nature is part of the lesson plan, while some are attached to religious organizations where a spiritual message is incorporated into the program. Many planners, out of fear that their delegates may not appreciate the opportunities presented by the unique environment, can unjustly overlook retreat facilities.

These unique meeting environments can be used as a stimulus to energize a moribund group of delegates. The challenge of using these facilities derives from one of their greatest strengths—their relative isolation. Transportation and logistical issues become magnified due to the distance from airports and highways. These impediments can be overcome, and the result can be well worth the effort.

Some examples of retreat Web Sites:

http://www.allaboutretreats.com/

http://www.retreatfinder.com/

CRUISE SHIPS

In a sense, cruise ships are floating hybrids of hotels, conference centers, and full-service resorts. Cruise ships are often underrated as meeting venues; but with proper planning, they can provide a satisfying meeting experience.

The quality of the planning for a cruise event has a greater impact on the success of the meeting than it does with any other type of venue. A ship moves by its own schedule that could have more to do with the tides than it does the ability of a group of guests to be at the dock on time. Failure to properly accommodate the ship's schedule into the transportation plan can have disastrous results. Unlike a building, once the ship leaves port, latecomers are left behind.

Cruise ship meeting rooms are indistinguishable from those found in a hotel.   *Photo by George G. Fenich, Ph.D.*

Cruise ships have long been considered ideal venues for incentive trips. There are few options available to a planner that can provide as romantic an ambiance as a cruise ship. However, romantically inclined couples often have children attached. Many cruise lines have well-developed children's programs that allow the adults to participate in their meetings without being concerned where their children are or what they are doing. In fact, the children's programs on many ships are better developed and provide more opportunities than in many major resorts.

The size and availability of meeting rooms varies widely among different ships. Meeting planners should not only look at the spaces identified as "meeting facilities" but also consider other creative alternatives. Many ships have extensive theaters and lounge facilities that, depending on the size of the group, can be reserved for the group's exclusive use. Theaters that are utilized in the evening for shipboard entertainment are often empty space during the day, thus the rental of these areas by meeting groups generates additional income for the cruise line. These spaces can provide the facilities needed for the business and educational components of the meeting.

In addition to finding creative uses for purpose built facilities on existing ships, new ships are being designed and constructed with the MEEC industry in mind. Royal Caribbean's the Oasis of the Seas boasts a dedicated convention center designed to accommodate up to 300 meeting attendees. Other areas on the ship, such as the ice rink and several nightclubs, were constructed in such a way to allow them to easily transform into meeting venues when needed. The increased popularity of destination weddings has also influenced cruises. Several lines have implemented shipboard wedding packages, thus resulting in the construction of wedding chapels and private reception areas.

Similar to conference centers, many cruise lines offer complete meeting packages. These packages routinely include everything except the bar tab and taxes. By carefully working with the ship's technical staff, it is possible for the entire meeting's technical needs to be accommodated with the on-board equipment. In many ways, this is no different from working with a conference center.

The relative isolation of many conference and retreat centers is one of their greatest strengths as meeting facilities. A ship at sea can be even more isolated. A meeting held while the ship is under way will have a different attendance pattern than the same meeting held when the ship is in port. Schedule planning coordinated with the ship's itinerary can have a significant impact on a meeting's attendance. One issue many planners face is keeping the delegates in the meetings. Hotels adjacent to casinos and theme parks are notorious for having low delegate attendance at sessions. On a ship at sea, out of range of cell phones and pagers, a meeting that requires perfect attendance could have a greater opportunity for success than in many competing facilities. Many planners frequently overlook ships as meeting facilities except for incentive trips, but that shortchanges the potential of these mobile meeting venues.

Some examples of cruise ship Web Sites:

http://www.uniquevenues.com/cruise-ship-meetings.html

http://www.carnival.com/cms/carnivalmeetings/default.aspx

SPECIFIC USE FACILITIES

Theaters, amphitheaters, arenas, stadiums, and sports facilities tend to be underused as meeting facilities, but depending on the needs of the meeting they may support a variety of events. Spectacular and impressive events can be planned for any facility designed for public assembly. Entertainment venues range in size from huge outdoor stadiums to hole-in-the-wall nightclubs. Planners who wish to use these venues can be successful if they are careful to remember that entertainment, not meetings, is the venue's primary business, and services considered standard in a hotel or convention center may not exist in an entertainment venue.

Most of these facilities are focused on events for the general (ticket-buying) public, and a closed event for an invited audience can be a welcome change for their staff. Even though the front-office staff might welcome the meeting planner, the planner needs to carefully determine whether sufficient house and technical staff will be available to support the event. Entertainment events generally occur on evenings and weekends; therefore, staff is frequently composed of part-time employees, or in the case of those who are available during the day, retirees. The availability

An unusual venue for a hospitality event. *Used by permission of Paradise Light & Sound, Orlando, Florida*

and demographics of the staff may or may not be an issue for any given event, but it should be discussed with the facility management prior to signing a contract.

Like convention centers, these facilities are typically owned by government agencies or are public–private partnerships. Specific use facilities are similar to convention centers in the amount of planning required; but unlike convention centers in that while dealing with large numbers of people is their greatest skill, meetings are not their primary business. Depending on the facility's public event schedule, long rehearsal and setup times may not be feasible. If a facility has a resident sports team that might go into postseason play, management might be reluctant to confirm space availability more than a few weeks in advance.

Finances in a special use facility can be a hybrid between the practices of the convention center and those of a conference center. There is generally a fixed fee for the use of the facility and a specific subset of its equipment and services. "Normal" cleanup, comparable to a public event, would likely be included in the facility rental fee. The facility may require a minimum level of staff for which there would be an hourly charge based on a minimum number of hours. All other labor, equipment, and services would be exactly like a convention center on a bill-per-item system.

Among the specific use facilities, theaters can be ideal meeting facilities. They come equipped with comfortable chairs arranged in sweeping curved rows for maximum comfort. They have lighting positions and sound systems built in, and staff members who know how to use them. If delegates are local, they probably know where the theater is and do not need directions. The stages are designed for acoustics and the seats arrayed to enhance visibility. One of the ironies of this industry relates to the amount of time and energy expended converting hotel ballrooms into theaters and how few meetings are actually held in theaters. However, this is beginning to change as theater companies have recognized the cross-promotional opportunities and now advertise their venues as event locations.

On the surface, it would seem that the better technically equipped a theater is, the more likely the meeting's support team would use it rather than bring it in. This, however, is not usually the case. In many theaters, any equipment that is moved must be restored to its original location. The economics of that policy works if the equipment's natural location is in a storeroom somewhere out of the way. Where the policy does not work is when the equipment's location is in an "in-use" position. The cost of putting the equipment back to its in-use location can be greater than merely removing the rental equipment and packing it in a truck for the run back to the warehouse. This is especially true of lighting and projection. If the theater has custom draperies for the stage, those will typically be used because finding replacement drapes in the correct size can be difficult.

Another issue with using the in-house equipment has to do with reliability. Many theaters, particularly educational and community theaters, are not funded to the point where their equipment can be considered properly maintained or reliable. A lighting designer, unsure of the condition of the installed equipment, would likely import his or her own rather than take a risk.

Catering in a specific use facility may require more planning than in some other venues. Given that the venue's primary revenue sources are based on ticketed events, they would probably have a well-developed concessions operation, but may or may not have sufficient catering capabilities. Menu selection may be challenging, depending on the scope of the meeting. Kitchen equipment for a concessions environment may not be capable of supporting the menu needs of a meeting, therefore forcing the planner to contract with an off-site caterer.

COLLEGES AND UNIVERSITIES

It would seem that since colleges and universities devote all their energies to education and research, they should be ideal meeting facilities. Some are, but it is important for a planner to remember that while meetings bring much appreciated supplemental income to an educational institution, few colleges are well-equipped for major meetings, and staff may not be as adept at responding to immediate meeting needs as expected at a full-time meeting facility. The planner using an academic facility needs to investigate and coordinate with multiple members of the institution's organizational structure. It is not sufficient to ask the person in alumni relations who booked the use of the faculty center after hours whether the lawn sprinklers have, in fact, been turned off for the evening. The planner must verify such details directly with the department responsible.

The impact of seasonality on hotels and other meeting facilities is moderate compared to the impact of seasonality on most academic facilities. During summer vacation, many college campuses become ghost towns. A vacant college campus could provide an effective meeting site as a result. The planner who wishes to use a college campus for a large meeting may have to make some extra logistical arrangements. College classrooms are generally open and airy with plenty of light, but they are not known for comfortable furniture. A student chair with a writing arm may be acceptable for a twenty-something, but may not be ideal for a forty-year-old adult. Nevertheless, more and more college campuses are offering conference services to willing clients, particularly those looking for an economical or budget conscious option. Many large universities incorporate their meetings department into the university-wide Hospitality Services umbrella, while smaller colleges often operate a seasonal summer conference division. The increased demand for meetings at institutions of higher learning has prompted these organizations to make an effort to meet that need.

College dorms have beds, and rooms are generally arranged along hallways like hotels, but that is where the similarities end. College dorm rooms have single beds instead of doubles or queens, and most of those are extra long so that standard linen does not fit. It would probably be a good idea to contract with the college's linen service to provide bed linen and towels. While some dorm rooms are singles, the majority are double occupancy. The process of arranging and processing roommate assignments can be a full-time job. If the meeting is large, it might be a good idea to hire an intern for this task. Another issue sometimes overlooked is that dorms generally have bathrooms shared among several rooms. While that might be appropriate for groups of high school and college athletes, it would likely not be comfortable for a meeting of professionals such as doctors or stockbrokers. Newer and some recently renovated dorms have elevators, but many older dorms still do not have ADA-compatible access to upper floors. Considerable savings can be realized using college campuses, particularly if the college's athletic facilities are part of the meeting plan; however, not all meetings work well in this environment.

Many meeting planners have less-than-fond memories of college food. With the advent of professional food service management companies operating many college food service operations, the food quality on many campuses has improved considerably. Planners should be aware, however, that a college dining hall will never be elegant. Equally important is that the quality of the food served is a direct result of the budget available. Any poor quality college food is more likely a function of a small budget than a function of inadequate kitchen capabilities. With an adequate budget, the planner can provide high-quality meals in an academic environment.

College art museums and student centers may provide interesting and exciting locations for meetings. Art museums provide especially interesting opportunities for conversations that can enhance a "networking" event. All the delegates at the event will probably have opinions about the art, motivating strangers to converse. One common mistake planners make when using art centers is the tendency to redecorate them. Without spending a lot of money, it is unlikely that the planner can provide more impressive décor than what the museum's galleries already offer. If the planner feels the need to engage in a massive redecorating project, the art museum may not be the correct venue for the event.

The art centers and theaters at colleges and universities have a unique attribute that many planners and the general public frequently overlook. Unlike the staff in the majority of meeting and special event venues, the venue is not just a job. It is a passion. The people who run these facilities on a daily basis take great pride in and care deeply about the condition of the building and its contents. This is not to say that people in other venues do not care, but usually not with the intensity or even obsession that the academic theater and art directors demonstrate. Any planner who intends to use one of these facilities must understand the sensitivities involved. Equally important, they must convey this message to their own staff. The traveling staff (mere "transients" in the eyes of the permanent employees) must be sensitive to the fact that in spite of the large amount of money they will be spending on this event, they are visitors and not necessarily welcome guests. It is entirely likely that the budget for this one event is greater than the resident staff's monthly or even annual budget, and some jealousies may arise.

Some college conference services Web Sites:

http://www.cce.umn.edu/conferencecenter/

http://www.ces.sdsu.edu/facilities/

UNUSUAL VENUES

Meeting planners continually insist on having meetings in places that were never designed for meetings. Airplane hangars, remote islands, nature preserves, city parks, open meadows, museums, and athletic fields are all unusual venues that are often used for meetings. Perhaps the most common of these unusual venues is a large tent in a parking lot. All of these venues have more in common with each other than they have differences.

None of these venues have support equipment. Virtually everything needed for the event must be brought in. These venues also have little or no staff. In addition to all the normal concerns a planner needs to deal with for an event, the planner using these facilities will need to provide all the support services normally considered the purview of the facility. Such services could include portable restrooms, parking, and trash removal. Weather is an issue in any outdoor venue, but that is no different than would be the case with a pool party at a hotel.

One challenge that frequently catches planners by surprise is obtaining permits. Many local governments require permits to use parks or even private property for special events. Failure to procure the proper permits can lead to an event being shut down at the last moment. Not only must the police and fire department be notified, but in many places the building code office must be notified as well. Tents must usually be inspected by the fire department. In some areas, generators are under the purview of the fire department; in others, there is a special office that deals with electrical issues. This office may be part of the Building and Zoning department or may be part of a designated special events office.

Airport facilities have the additional issue of heightened security. More stringent security measures have been implemented there than ever before. Failure to conform to these security procedures can be detrimental to the event. For those planners who need an aeronautical theme, an airplane museum would likely be a better choice than a working airport. Political rallies are sometimes held at airports just as they used to be held at railroad stations in previous elections. The constant noise of the aircraft in the background does give the impression of excitement, but it can also obscure important parts of a candidate's speech. The quality of the sound system, too often the last item considered, is vitally important to success of the event.

Tents routinely show up as meeting venues. Tents fall into three categories: pole, frame, and clear span. An open-sided pole or **frame tent** set up on the grass is one of the simplest of all meeting venues. It requires little advance planning beyond making sure that the tent rental people can get set up in time. Permits are required in many jurisdictions. Weather is a factor, but adding tent sides and air-conditioning can reduce the impact of weather. The tent may require a floor so that rain drainage flows under the floor and not over the feet of the people in the tent. Lighting or decorating a tent can also be a challenge. To hang lighting in a **pole tent** requires

A fashion show in an airplane hangar. *Used by permission of Paradise Light & Sound, Orlando, Florida*

special brackets to attach the lights to the poles if the poles are sturdy enough to support them; therefore, for a pole tent, supporting the lighting from the floor on boom stands or truss towers may be a better plan.

Clear span tents have a strong roof structure, and it is possible to hang lighting from its beams by using special clamps. Since the purpose of the tent is to create a meeting space where none previously existed, other support services such as power, water, and restrooms may also not exist, and will have to be brought in. If lighting is to be hung in a clear span tent, the lighting should be hung before the floor is put in, since many of the tent floors will not support the scissor lifts used by the lighting and décor people during setup.

All unusual venues share a general lack of support and equipment. All of them have heightened challenges with security and logistics, but some venues have additional, unique challenges.

Access to the meeting site is an issue in some remote locations. One perfectly delightful special event venue in Park City, Utah, is only accessible via horse-drawn sleigh and then only in the winter. Another example is Disney's Discovery Island in Bay Lake. At this location, the only access to the island is via a wooden bridge that is not strong enough to support a vehicle, but its slatted wooden deck makes it impossible to roll catering carts. When the locale was still being used as a special event venue, the only way to bring material to the island was on a float barge. The water was too shallow for anything larger to dock. There are many stories about the "amp rack that almost got away" on the trip to the island. In fact, there are unconfirmed rumors that one amp rack did get away and still rests on the bottom of Bay Lake.

Access can also be an issue even if there are roads directly to the area. Some roads flood in the rainy season, while others are impassable in the winter. Even if the road is substantial enough to support the delivery trucks, it is necessary to determine if there is a dock where supplies can be unloaded or whether a forklift is needed. If a forklift is needed, the planner must determine who supplies the driver as well as any other pertinent logistical questions.

One would think that outdoor sports arenas with their large array of seats or bleachers would be easy venues in which to work, and while they are easier to deal with than many outdoor venues in that they come with restrooms, they also present their own challenges. The irrigation systems for the landscaping at professional or competition fields are fragile enough that driving heavy loads over them can break the piping beneath the surface. Some venues prohibit anything heavier than a golf cart. Forget building a stage on a soccer field unless it is properly padded with plywood sheeting. Pushing that cart of riser tops across the grass is not likely to pass muster with the facility's head of grounds either.

While the technicians have one set of challenges dealing with outdoor sports venues, caterers have another. It is not uncommon for caterers to dump the leftover ice out on the ground, a practice that will kill the patch of grass underneath. Ice should be dumped in a storm drain, on

Osceola Art Festival, 2001. *Used by permission of Paradise Light & Sound, Orlando, Florida*

the pavement, or in a mulched area. Also, portable bars are heavy and can damage the ground underneath. They must be placed on pavement or have a sheet of plywood underneath. That plywood should only be in place a few hours, or the grass underneath will die. There are plastic flooring pieces that will distribute the weight and still allow the grass to breathe. These are preferable to plywood if they are available. Portable bars also leak. If the water was clean, that would not be a problem. However, while most of the runoff from the bars is melted ice, some of it is excess from the soft drink dispensers. This excess contains sugar, which attracts ants. The ants then dig up the grass in search of more sugar, and soon there is an anthill behind third base. The partially melted ice from the shrimp buffet must also be disposed of properly, otherwise the smell from the shrimp will last long after the event is over.

Public parks can be beautiful venues except that they are open to the public. If the event is a public event like an art show, a public park with its regular traffic can be an ideal location. But if the event is more private, especially if it involves alcohol, a public park may not be such a good idea.

When planning an outdoor convention function, an indoor backup plan is vital to the success of the event. For an arts festival like this one, an indoor plan is simply not feasible. However, a professional planner should always recognize the potential for weather to have an impact on the event.

In recent years, unique venues have become more and more utilized for the purposes of holding MEEC gatherings. Companies want their meetings to stand out from competitors; private parties have the desire to host events that are larger than life and feature unusual aspects, and in the wedding business where couples regularly insist on a one-of-a-kind ceremony, unique venues are frequently incorporated to provide the additional "wow" factor. Some venues unaccustomed to this kind of business are now courting groups based upon increased interest and demand. For instance, the Ngala Private Animal Reserve in Naples, Florida, and the Maryland Zoo were both originally intended to house animals and related exhibits. But as a result of interest from group business, both facilities have constructed venues on their properties for the specific meeting and events rentals.

In addition to utilizing unusual venues for meetings and receptions, these locations have become increasingly popular with weddings. Destination weddings occur when a couple chooses to hold their wedding in a location where neither individual resides. For instance, a couple living in Chicago may elect to hold their wedding in Hawaii, as opposed to their hometown. In many cases, these destination weddings take place in an unusual venue. Beaches, botanical gardens, castles, sailboats, or theme parks are some of the many facilities that may be used for a destination wedding. Walt Disney World in Florida plays host to more than 2,500 weddings each year, some of which actually take place in Cinderella's castle in the Magic Kingdom. In short, almost any venue may be used to host an event if the planner is willing to be a little creative.

COMMON ISSUES

Regardless of where an event is held, there are some issues that all events have in common. Many of these issues are logistic, such as transporting delegates from the airport. The following issues are common to most if not all meeting venues, and most if not all meetings.

Obstacles

Perhaps a planner's greatest challenge is to overcome the obstacles in the way of the delegates' ability to be successful as a result of the meeting. The facility can present many obstacles that a planner will need to overcome. An example of such an obstacle would be an understaffed or undersized registration desk. Another would be inadequate parking space for the delegates who drive. Yet another would be a noise ordinance that prohibits loading out between the hours of 10:00 PM and 6:00 AM. Physical obstacles are not limited to disability considerations. There are also questions of how the delegates will get from their rooms to the gala dinner in their formal gowns if it is raining, and whether the busses transporting guests to the off-site venue can get to the actual door of the venue.

Power

Most outdoor special events and many events in smaller indoor venues have power requirements that exceed the power available. A generator usually provides this power, and generators are expensive. Properly anticipating the power needs is even more important in this type of event than one in a traditional meeting venue. With a generator, the planner will pay not only the daily cost to rent the generator, but a fuel charge as well. The fuel consumption is determined by two factors: how long the generator runs, and how much power is actually drawn from it. The fuel cost will be a multiple of the cost per gallon of the fuel, the time the generator runs, and the power consumption. The planner has control over two of the three elements in this equation.

For any meeting or special event using video or name entertainment, more than a few trade show booths or large scenic units will have special power requirements. Power is expensive. The power to run the sound system can be more expensive than the rental of the equipment. Many convention centers offer a discount if the power is requested early. The technical vendors can calculate power requirements fairly easily. If the discount for requesting power early is 30%, which is a fairly common discount, it would make sense to order 10% to 15% more power than estimated. In this way, ample power is available for less than it would have cost to place the power order after all the detailed requirements had been calculated.

Power charges are not based on consumption, but rather on the maximum amount of power deliverable at any one time. To meter the actual power consumption and charge accordingly is illegal in many states. This would make the facility a utility company and subject to rate regulations. It would appear that generator use is charged based on power consumption, but it is actually based on fuel consumption. A generator that is idling uses fuel even if it is supplying no power. Turning a generator off when it is not needed will save money.

Rigging

Plaster ceilings are a production rigger's worst nightmare. Precast concrete roofs with no steel underneath run a close second. Any event involving more than a few hundred people or video image magnification (IMAG) should involve lighting suspended from the ceiling. Unless the facility is unusually well equipped for lighting from ceiling positions, lighting must be accomplished by hanging trusses, and hanging trusses involves rigging. Theaters are generally adequately equipped for lighting without hanging trusses, but not necessarily hotels.

The hotel's contracted rigging company will require access to all floor plans not less than two weeks in advance of the event. While it would seem that two week's lead time on a floor plan should be simple for an event contracted a year in advance, generating an accurate floor plan turns out to be a challenge many planners cannot accommodate. In some jurisdictions, the fire marshal, building code inspector, or safety officer can refuse to allow a show to be hung without a detailed hanging plan. Having to cancel a show at the last minute due to failure to submit paperwork can be a career-ending mistake.

A lighting grip suspended from the ceiling.   *Photo by George G. Fenich, Ph.D.*

Most facilities contract rigging to an outside company for liability protection. This is in addition to the normal reasons one would outsource any task that the facility management may not have enough experience to properly supervise. Given that the rigger's normal job description involves hanging "live loads" over the heads of the general public, they take their work seriously. This sometimes obstructionist attitude is intended to keep people safe and is not meant to impede the event. Adequate advance notification of schedules and requirements can help ensure that the event venue is hung properly and on schedule.

Floors

It is not safe to assume that just because the building has a ground level loading door big enough to drive a tractor-trailer through, that once it fits through the door, the floor will support it. Even though the floor may be made of four inches of steel-reinforced concrete on the ground, the utility boxes in the floor may not be so well designed. One Orlando area facility dug up and repoured the concrete around several floor pockets because the constant forklift traffic drove them into the ground. It is also not safe to assume that a certain size scissor lift can be brought into the ballroom. For events where these issues are relevant, as part of the site inspection, the planner must ask about the floor load because the information is rarely readily available.

Ballrooms are carpeted, and many hotels insist that plastic sheeting be placed over the ballroom carpet during the move-in and move-out process. If the facility has such a requirement, it is important that the Exposition Services Contractor (ESC) and all technical vendors know about it in advance. The requirement to cover the floor with "Polytack" or one of several similar products is becoming more common. Failure to submit a proper floor plan to the people who apply the floor covering or failure to properly schedule the installation can result in expensive delays.

Many academic theaters have polished wood floors on the stages. Nailing or screwing into them is not recommended and is generally a fast way to be refused the use of the venue in the future. These floors are not designed for heavy loads, such as scissor lifts or forklifts. Staffing and equipment requirements may need to be adjusted to compensate.

Access

Not only must the delegates be able to find the venue and its entrance, but the technical support and catering people need to gain access as well. The design of the loading access can have a significant impact on an event's finances. There is a facility in south Florida where the only

A load-out for a large trade show.   *Used by permission of Paradise Light & Sound, Orlando, Florida*

loading access to the ballroom is to back a truck along a sea wall for a hundred yards. A 21-foot truck will not make the corner; a 17-foot truck will. The closest a tractor-trailer can park is a quarter mile away. An event here whose technical support equipment is shipped on a tractor-trailer would need to be unloaded off-site and the equipment trucked in to the loading dock using a smaller truck at considerable additional expense. There is another facility on Florida's west coast where the loading access to the ballrooms is via an open-sided elevator with no top attached at the outside of the building. In this part of Florida, it rains almost every afternoon in the summer. A load scheduled for 4:00 PM in July stands an excellent likelihood of having a problem.

The presence of truck height docks is not enough to guarantee smooth loading. Some facilities, including the WDW Dolphin and the Gaylord Palms, have elevators from the docks to the ballroom. Access to the theater at the Orange County Convention Center involves two elevators and a push down the hall between them. The number and location of the docks is significant. The only Orlando-area major convention hotels with adequate dock space are the Gaylord Palms (in spite of the elevator) and Marriott's Orlando World Center. One would think that the Orange County Convention Center, with half a mile of continuous dock space, would have adequate loading capabilities, but even that fills up on some events, as incredible as it seems. On the other hand, the Morial Convention Center in New Orleans is all on one level, with loading docks lining one entire side of the building.

FUNCTION ROOMS AND SETUPS

Most meetings are held in boardrooms, breakout rooms, or ballrooms. Exhibit halls are considerably larger and most typically are used for large events such as trade shows or concerts, while pre-function spaces are the hallways and foyers outside meeting rooms often used for refreshment breaks or registration areas.

There are a number of factors that must be considered when planners are booking meeting space. Aside from the actual accommodation of meeting attendees and/or exhibitors, it is important to consider other setup aspects such as audiovisual needs, refreshment break areas, and stages and podiums for speakers and panels, among other things. But the most basic layout refers to the type of seating used. The way seating is determined is again directly related to the needs of the group. A meeting where attendees will need to interact with one another during a session will require a different type of setup than one where individuals will be hearing a lecture from a speaker at the head of the room.

In the MEEC industry, there are endless potential types and designs in which rooms may be set up. Since this book is meant to provide an overview of the industry, the three basic room sets are explained here.

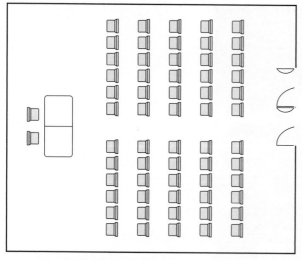

Auditorium or Theater Style Room Set

Classroom Style Room Set

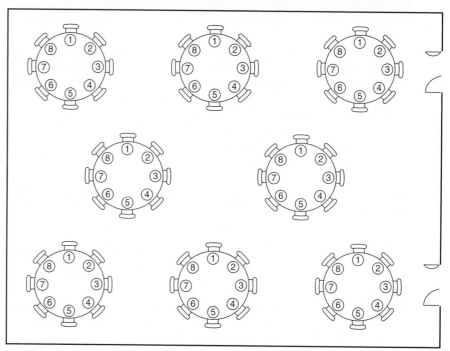

Different meeting rooms set-ups
or layouts

Rounds of Eight

Auditorium and Theater Style

Probably the most common seating arrangement in meetings is an auditorium or theater design.
An **auditorium room setup** is particularly useful when there is no need for attendees to interact
with one another during the course of the session. In this instance, chairs are arranged in rows
facing the same direction. Most commonly those rows will face the head of the room that may be
designated by a stage, head table, lectern, or screen. A speaker or panel will generally run the meeting, often lecturing to attendees who may be taking notes based on the information the speaker is
conveying.

As shown in the image above, all the chairs are arranged in rows while facing the head table
and the two panelists stationed there. Depending on the number of seats required for the meeting, the auditorium style may be altered slightly. For instance, an auditorium room set with 8,000
seats would have several aisles to allow attendees to move freely as needed. The chairs may also be

set up in a V-shape pattern or semicircle to allow those individuals on the far ends of the rows a better line of sight.

Classroom Style

Sometimes meetings may require tables for attendees to use for completing tests, taking notes, or interacting with other attendees to solve presented problems. **Classroom style** is the most common setup used for these types of meetings. In classroom meeting setups, chairs are arranged in a similar manner as in an auditorium, but with tables provided for each row of chairs. These tables are generally six or eight feet long and 18 inches deep. If the design is intended for attendees to be sitting on each side of the table, then 30-inch deep tables (or two 18-inch tables placed back to back) are used to allow sufficient space. In this room setup, the tables are draped, with pads of paper and pencils/pens at each place setting.

Similar to auditorium room sets, classrooms may be modified as needed. Sometimes classrooms are arranged diagonally toward the head table, or even perpendicular to the front of the room. Perpendicular room sets are challenging because it often necessitates a significant number of attendees to have their backs toward the speaker at the front of the room. If the purpose of the session is to work with table partners, this may not be problematic, but a perpendicular classroom setup is seldom wise when attendees need to be focused on the individual on stage.

Rounds

Round tables are sometimes used for meetings, but utilized most often for food functions. In smaller breakout sessions, or those meetings requiring a lot of interaction between attendees, round tables facilitate and encourage communication. All the individuals at the table can easily see their table companions and are seated in close enough proximity to one another to allow collaboration.

Many meeting venues use six-foot rounds (i.e., 72 inches in diameter) or less often five-foot rounds (i.e., 60 inches in diameter). The size of the rounds is important because the diameter dictates how many individuals can comfortably fit. Five foot rounds can accommodate six to eight individuals, while six foot rounds may seat eight to ten.

In the image above, six-foot rounds were used to seat eight guests each. An alternative to full rounds it the crescent rounds. **Crescent rounds** may use full-sized round tables, but will not have seats all the way around the table. For instance, if a head table was placed at the far left side of the room, the planner might choose to eliminate seat numbers 6, 7, and 8 from each of the tables. This would mean that there would be no one seated with his or her back to the head table, and everyone at the table would have a clear view of the speaker.

FUTURE TRENDS

There are a number of trends that will likely become commonplace in the future with regard to meeting and event venues. One of those is the mass utilization of unique venues. Planners are always looking for the newest and freshest ideas to make their events stand out from the competition, and the choice of venue is perhaps the most obvious method for accomplishing that. Attendees also expect to be "wowed" and not see the same cookie-cutter event format year after year. Rather than holding an opening reception for attendees in a convention center hall, the planner can use unexpected venues to keep the attendees guessing and prevent them from getting bored. One year the opening event could be held at Mardi Gras World in New Orleans, the next year at the Cowboys Stadium in Dallas, and the following year at the Seattle Space Needle. In each location, the attendees will have a different experience and leave feeling that their event was one of a kind.

The size and composition of convention centers may also see some significant changes in the next few years. Over the last decade, convention center space in the United States has increased by over 50%, with many second- and third-tier cities building new centers and/or

PCMA Reception at Mardi Gras World, New Orleans.   *Photo courtesy of Jeff Anding, GNOMCVB*

building additions to current facilities. Despite the fact that the MEEC industry is continually growing, the mass construction of convention centers will likely slow down because demand has not caught up to the available supply yet. However, some centers have moved toward adding space that can easily double as business and entertainment venues. This trend may see more growth in lieu of building larger facilities. For instance, the Colorado Convention Center constructed a 5,000-seat theater that can be used for general sessions during the week and concerts on the weekends. Having this space, which includes all the audiovisual needs of a theatrical auditorium, provides a significant cost savings for planners because there are limited production costs.

Summary

RECOMMENDATIONS FOR DEALING WITH ALL VENUES

Obtaining accurate information is essential to planning successful meetings. Detailed and thorough research is the first step in the process. This first step is much easier now than it has been and promises to become even easier, as the Internet and World Wide Web provide planners powerful resources with which to plan their events. Many of the best meeting facilities have extensive Web sites with volumes of available information. Some venues have 360-degree visual imaging that allows a planner to remotely view the facility. This technology is becoming more and more affordable and common. Before calling a sales representative, a planner should visit the facility's Web site and print out everything that might be of interest. Once having studied the material and determined that the facility may be appropriate for the event, then, and only then, should the planner call the facility's salespeople to open the dialogue.

The most important component of dealing with any facility is the development of an open, honest, and trusting relationship with all parties involved. Unfortunately, there are facilities that will take advantage of that relationship, just as there are planners who do not deal honestly with their suppliers. In spite of the risks involved, the attempt must be made, because the success of every event depends on the interaction between the planner and all the other parties. This relationship begins with understanding what each of the participants brings to the relationship and what each needs.

Communication begins with a set of requirements. The more accurate the requirements are, the better. It is important to note, however, that "accurate" and "detailed" are not the same thing. In a contract, the hotel needs to know how many people are coming, but they do not need the names until relatively close to the event. Accurate and timely listings of requirements are the first step in developing a successful relationship. Verification of the documentation returned by the venue is the other half of this communication. Not only should the planner provide requirements, but the venue should also reply and acknowledge that it understands the requirements and how it will fulfill each requirement as appropriate.

The key to working with any venue is fourfold: research, understand, communicate, verify. Research, understand, communicate, verify. Repeat until done! This chapter provides information that can be used by meeting planners in the first two steps of the process. The rest is what separates the best planners from the rest.

Key Words and Terms

For definitions, see GLOSSARY, or http://glossary.conventionindustry.org.

Amenities Amphitheater
Arena
Attrition
Boardroom
Breakout room
Clear span tent

Complete meeting package
Concessionaire
Destination management
    company (DMC)
Exhibit hall
Frame tent

Hotel
Local event
Loss leader
Needs analysis
Pole tent
Prefunction space

Seasonality
Shoulder
Stadium
Theater

Review and Discussion Questions

1. What is the single most important thing a planner can provide a venue to ensure the effective and cost-efficient execution of a meeting?
2. What is attrition, and why should a planner care?
3. What is the most significant single difference between a hotel's meeting space and a convention center's meeting space?
4. What is the most important single activity that facility personnel depend on the meeting planner to provide?

5. How is the financial structure of a hotel different from that of other facilities? What is a hotel's biggest source of revenue? A convention center's?
6. Why is seasonality important to a planner?
7. Why is ceiling height significant?
8. Why should a meeting planner care about copyright laws?
9. What should be a planner's greatest concern on an outdoor event? What should a planner do about it?

About the Chapter Contributor

Kelly Virginia Phelan has over ten years of experience in different sectors of the MEEC industry. As an undergraduate student at Johns Hopkins University in Foreign Policy, she worked as the summer conference manager and organized numerous on-campus recruiting events for the Office of Undergraduate Admissions. Kelly later served as the event coordinator for the 1998 World Lacrosse Championships in Baltimore, Maryland; convention services manager for EPCOT Center in Walt Disney World; event manager for the Iditarod Sled Dog Race in Alaska; and as an event manager for Flamingo, Bally's and Paris Las Vegas Resorts. Presently, Kelly is an assistant professor in the Department of Nutrition, Hospitality, and Retailing at Texas Tech University in Lubbock, Texas.

The Chapter contributor for earlier editions of the text was Bob Cherny, Paradise Light and Sound.

Exhibitions

Chapter Outline

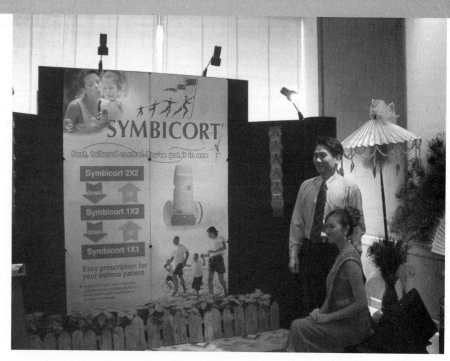

Trade shows are used throughout the world to promote products and companies. This one takes place in Chang Rai, Thailand.   *Photo by George G. Fenich, Ph.D.*

Chapter Objectives

After reading Chapter 5, the reader should be able to:

- Define the different types of exhibitions
- Identify the key players of exhibition management
- Categorize the components of show planning
- Identify the role of the exhibitor and fundamentals of exhibit planning
- Recognize trends in the exposition industry

INTRODUCTION

With more than 14,000 **trade shows** and exhibitions annually in North America alone, the long history of exhibitions has turned into a thriving, ever-changing industry. This chapter provides an overview of the exhibition industry and looks at it from the perspective of the show organizer and the exhibit manager.

HISTORY

Trade fairs began in biblical times and became popular in Medieval Europe and in the Middle East. These fairs served as an opportunity for craftsmen and farmers to bring their products to the center of the town or city to sell their goods as a means of survival.

These were the beginnings of the "public" trade fair and featured handmade crafts, agricultural products, and other specialties. According to the *Art of the Tradeshow*, Germany and France have the first recorded history of organizing the earliest organized fairs. Some examples include the Leipzig Fair in 1165, the 1215 Dublin Fair, Cologne's biannual fair starting in 1259, and Frankfurt's Book Fair in 1445. These types of trade fair, featuring handmade products and produce, continued through the Renaissance period until the beginning of the Industrial Revolution when goods began being mass produced.

The poster announcing the Dublin Fair in the year 1215 AD.
Photo by George G. Fenich, Ph.D.

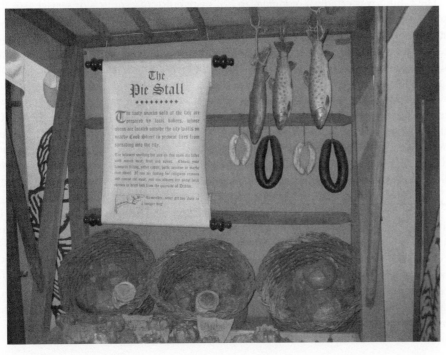

This pie stall from the Dublin Fair of 1215 is not so different than food vendors at festivals today.
Photo by George G. Fenich, Ph.D.

Eventually, the business-to-business industries realized the value of meeting, sharing information, and providing previews of their products to potential customers. This part of the industry blossomed in the late 1800s, with many facilities being built strictly for world-class exhibitions. This buyer–seller format was termed an **exhibition** and typically took place in a large city at a facility built specifically for the exhibition. For example, the Crystal Palace in London was opened for the "Great Industrial Exhibition of All Nations" featuring 13,000 exhibits from all over the world and attracted more than six million attendees. In the United States, facilities were opened in Chicago and Philadelphia to commemorate "world's fairs" that, in reality, were trade shows highlighting the industrial advances of participating countries. In 1895, Detroit started the first joint effort to attract exhibition business, and in 1914 the National Association of Convention Bureaus was formed.

In the early and mid-twentieth century, trade associations grew and saw the potential of trade shows being held in conjunction with their annual meetings as a way to stimulate communication in the industry and expand their revenues gained from the annual meeting. The twentieth century brought exciting and trying times to the exhibition industry, with notable pauses in progress during World War I, World War II, and the Great Depression. Many industry associations formed during this time and recognized the benefits of adding an exhibition to meetings and events. To increase the awareness and value to exhibitions, a group of industry professionals created the National Association of Exposition Managers (which is now named the International Association of Exhibitions and Events) in 1978 and has more than 8,500 members sponsoring, hosting, and organizing exhibits worldwide.

TYPES OF SHOWS

Trade shows

A trade show is typically a business-to-business event. Thus, they are private and not open to the public. The definition of a trade fair has become close enough to that of a trade show that the terms are used interchangeably. The term "trade fair" is more often used outside the United States than "trade show." Trade fairs are discussed in more detail in Chapter 14, "International Perspectives in MEEC." Although the historical definition of exhibition is quite different from today, this term has also evolved to mean a trade show or trade fair. The term "**exposition**" has also evolved to be similar in meaning to trade show. An association meeting may include an exposition, or expo, as the trade show segment of the association's annual gathering. In this chapter, we refer to trade shows, expositions, and exhibitions interchangeably.

The exhibitor is usually a manufacturer or distributor of products or services specific or complementary to those industries represented by the sponsor or organizer. Often, attendance is restricted to buyers from the industry, and business credentials are required for registration. Educational programs may or may not be a part of the trade show program; although in recent years, educational programs have expanded as a method of attracting attendees. Sponsorship or management of the trade show is usually either under the auspices of a trade association or has evolved to come under the sponsorship of a management company. Some trade shows are the result of initiatives by companies and are fully intended to be profit-making ventures. Usually, trade shows are annual events, although some occur more frequently, and others less frequently. Major organizations may also have regional trade shows that are smaller than their standard national or international event. Attendees and exhibitors may come from all over the country or world; therefore, hotel rooms and transportation may be considered in selecting the show's location.

The most common form of marketing to potential exhibitors is advertising in trade publications. Until recently, well-established trade shows and exhibitions had little trouble marketing to potential exhibitors. The exhibit halls were full, and waiting lists of exhibitors were commonplace. However, the past few years have seen many companies downsizing their exhibit space or opting to exhibit at fewer trade shows. Management companies have now placed a renewed focus on marketing to potential exhibitors. Trade shows are now in competition for exhibitors, and exhibition management companies are working hard to retain existing exhibitors and attract new ones.

Examples of U.S.-based trade shows include the following:

- *National Restaurant Show (NRA): The International Foodservice Market* is held annually at McCormick Center in Chicago, Illinois, each May. In 2009, the show attracted more than 37,000 attendees and 15,000 exhibitors.
- *Consumer Electronic Design and Installation Association (CEDIA)* EXPO was held in Atlanta, Georgia, in 2009 with more than 20,000 professionals from the residential electronics systems industry in attendance and over 400 exhibitors displaying the latest home technologies and newest products available in the electronic systems integration.
- *International Builders Show*, the largest building industry trade show in the country, was held in January 2010 in Las Vegas, Nevada.
- *American Society for Cell Biology (ASCB) Annual Meeting and Exposition* was held in San Diego, California, in December 2009. Attendees were scientists and students in academia, industry, government, and higher education; more than 350 commercial and nonprofit exhibits offering new products and services participated in the exhibition.

About The International SPA Association

Since 1991, the International SPA Association has been recognized worldwide as the professional organization and voice of the spa industry, representing more than 3,200 health and wellness facilities and providers in 83 countries. Members encompass the entire arena of the spa experience, from resort/hotel, destination, mineral springs, medical, cruise ship, club, and day spas to service providers such as physicians, wellness instructors, nutritionists, massage therapists, and product suppliers.

ISPA advances the spa industry by providing invaluable educational and networking opportunities, promoting the value of the spa experience and speaking as the authoritative voice to foster professionalism and growth.

Mission of the Association: ISPA advances the spa industry by providing invaluable educational and networking opportunities, promoting the value of the spa experience and speaking as the authoritative voice to foster professionalism and growth.

Vision of ISPA: To be the leader in promoting and enhancing the well-being of the spa industry and the people it serves.

Who Attends?

The ISPA Conference & Expo is the largest ISPA event of the year for spa professionals, and is hosted annually each November. With an 18-year history, ISPA provides spa owners, directors, managers, and suppliers with cutting-edge tips on where the industry is headed and how to ensure that business is sustainable.

In addition, the ISPA Expo brings together the leading suppliers in the industry to network with the decision makers from spas across the globe. Attendees can be the first to see nearly 100 new products before they hit the market, as many companies will be launching new products at the Expo.

Seven Solid Reasons To Exhibit At The 2009 ISPA Conference & Expo

1. Approximately 2,000 spa managers, owners, directors, and other spa professionals attend.
2. 90% of these attendees make the purchasing decisions for their company.
3. Noncompeting hours are scheduled for attendees to explore the Expo floor.
4. 200 exhibitors showcase their newest and most effective products.
5. There are a total of four days of networking with spa professionals from around the world.
6. In a post-Conference survey, exhibitors said they consider the ISPA Conference & Expo to be an important venue for their company to present its products or services to the spa industry.
7. More than 75% of 2008 exhibitors said they planned to exhibit at the 2009 ISPA Conference & Expo.

Benefits Of Exhibiting Include:

- Free listing on www.experienceispa.com with a link to your company's Web site.
- Free listing in the Expo Guide distributed on-site to all Conference attendees. This includes contact information, a 75-word company description, and an indication next to your company name if you are launching new products at the ISPA Conference.
- Free listing in the online Exhibitor Search on ISPA's Web site. This includes contact information, a 75-word company description and 25 words about any new products that you are launching at the ISPA Conference.
- Free pre- and post-Conference attendee list.
- Free webinars to help you and your team make the most out of your Conference experience.
- Free listing in the Auction Catalogue for all exhibitors that donate to the ISPA Foundation Silent & Live Auctions.
- Opportunity to purchase a shelf in the Product Showcases at the Conference.

(Continued)

Trade Show History (2005–2008)

Booth Size	2005 Data	2006 Data	2007 Data	2008 Data
10 x 10 booths	307	291	346	359
10 x 20 booths	18	20	22	24
20 x 20 booths	11	16	17	21
20 x 30 booths	1	2	2	2
Total booths	393	407	470	502
Total number of exhibitors	239	242	280	304

Discussion Questions:

1. How would you describe the trends in terms of the total number of exhibitors and total booths reserved between 2005 and 2008?
2. Research U.S. destinations that could host the ISPA annual convention. The property must have at least 115,000 square feet to exhibit space, 1,000 guest rooms, 150,000 square feet of meeting space, and a large spa for guests.

For additional information on ISPA and the EXPO, visit www.experienceispa.com.

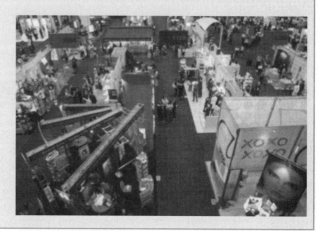

Photo by Mark Ashley. Permission from George Fern Company.

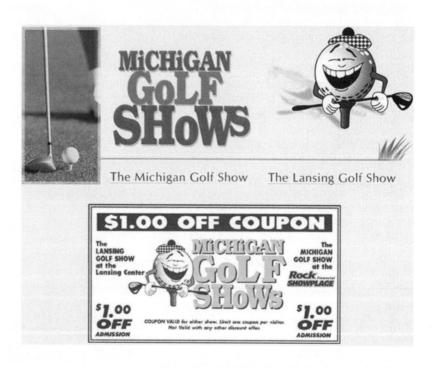

Example of a coupon for a public show.

Consumer or Public Shows

Consumer or **public shows** are expositions that are open to the public and offer a wide variety of products for sale. This type of show is used by a consumer-based industry to bring their goods directly to their market's end user. Show management may or may not charge an admission fee, and shows open to the public are typically held over the weekend. Consumer shows are often

Summary of Characteristics—Public versus private shows

Show Type	Attendee	Registration or Admission	Marketing	Show Days	Location
Trade show	International and national	Preregistration, qualified buyers	Trade publications	Business Week (Monday–Friday)	Large markets with significant meeting space, hotel, and transportation
Consumer Show	Regional or local	Ticket purchase on-site, general public	Newspaper, regional magazines, billboards, radio and TV advertising	Weekends (Friday–Sunday)	Large or secondary markets with large parking areas

regional in nature, with exhibitors traveling from city to city with their displays and products. They also provide excellent opportunities for companies to brand or test market new products.

Public exhibitions also require promotion to be successful. Typically, public shows are marketed through advertisements in trade or local public media. Advertisements may offer discounts for purchasing early tickets or may promote special events or speakers that will attract the largest number of attendees. Promoting public exhibitions is a daunting task because the potential attending audience is so large that it requires a significant expense to reach them through print, radio, and television advertising. Producers must be confident that their investment in promotion will result in reaching the attendance objectives. Producers must also be attentive to other events that may be occurring during the exhibition time period that can affect attendance.

Common types of consumer shows include home and garden, travel-related, and sports-specific shows. Some examples include:

- *Gulf Shore Flower, Garden and Home Show* spotlights sixteen blooming gardens designed and installed by top-rated landscape architects from Southwest Florida in Fort Meyers, Florida, in the spring.
- *The Kansas Sports, Boat & Travel Show* has been one of the most popular shows at the Kansas Coliseum in Wichita. Featuring exhibits in ATV, hunting, fishing, camping, or the freedom of traveling in an RV, tickets for the February event cost $12 for adults.
- *The 2010 Michigan Golf Show in Novi Michigan* will host more than 400 exhibitors with great deals on every aspect of the golf game. This weekend show will cost adult golf lovers $10.

Consolidation Shows (Also Called Combined or Mixed Show)

Consolidation shows are open to both industry buyers and the general public. Exhibitors are manufactures or distributors. Hours may differ based on the type of attendee, allowing the trade professionals to preview the show prior to the consumer buyers. Customer electronics and the automobile industries, which have diverse audience needs, use this format to accommodate the varied industry buyers and retail consumers.

ECONOMIC FORECAST

The trade show and exhibition market is facing a challenging time, but as the economy rebounds from a difficult period, reports are showing initial signs of positive recovery. Attendance, number of exhibits, amount of space, and revenue have seen a decline since 2007; however, exhibitions continue to be a priority in most marketing budgets for corporations and organizations. Now more than ever, the trade show and meeting industry must demonstrate its value, and measuring return on investment is critical to justifying participation and attendance at trade and consumer shows. Industry professionals predict a slow-to-moderate growth between 2010 and 2012 as the trade show industry transforms the face-to-face experience.

According to Center of Exhibition Industry Research (CEIR), performance declined in all four key metrics between 2007 and 2008 based on a survey of more than 300 events. The four metrics include Net Square Feet (NSF), Attendees, Exhibitors, and Revenue.

Prior to 2007, the trade show market consistently showed times of expansion and growth. According the Expoweb.com, spending by exhibitors and attendees resulted in a 5.8% increase in overall spending to $9.15 billion in 2004—a rate not seen since 2000. That follows a 1.5% spending growth rate in 2003, and a decline of 1.2% in 2002. During the first half of 2005, many corporations reported increasing funding for business-related travel, which is expected to drive trade show expenditures up 6.1% to $9.71 billion by the end of the year.

EXHIBITION MANAGEMENT: KEY PLAYERS

Regardless of the show type, there are three key players that ensure that the components of the show come together to accomplish the objectives of each stakeholder—the exhibition organizer, the facility manager, and the general service contractor.

Exhibition Organizer

The exhibition management company (organizer) may be a trade association, a company subcontracted to the trade association, or a separate company organizing the show as a profit-making venture. The show management staff member in charge of the entire exhibit area is called the exhibit manager and is responsible for all aspects of managing the show. Think of show management as the "systems integrator" responsible for implementing the show, marketing it to buyers and sellers, and gathering together all the resources needed for success.

The show management company must also consider the types of programs offered in addition to the event itself. Show programs have evolved to encompass additional programs that serve to boost attendance. Additional programs to consider include:

- Educational programs
- Entertainment programs
- Availability of exhibitor demonstrations and educational/training programs
- Special sections on the trade show floor for emerging companies, new exhibitors, or new technologies
- Celebrity or industry-leader speakers
- Meal programs
- Continuing education units (CEUs) or certifications for educational programs
- Spouse and children programs
- Internet access and e-mail centers

Facility Manager

Facilities are also needed to conduct the trade show. Facilities range from small hotels with limited meeting space to large convention centers. Facilities also include adjacent lodging and entertainment facilities that are used by the exhibitors and visitors. The facility manager, typically known as a convention service manager or event manager, will assist the show manager in arranging the show's logistical details. Show organizers consider a number of variables when selecting facilities,

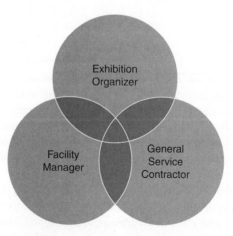

Key Players. *Chart produced by George G. Fenich, Ph.D.*

Reed Exhibitions

Reed Exhibitions is one of the leading organizers of trade and consumer shows in the world. The aim of Reed Exhibitions, with a staff of more than 2,700 employees, is to help associations and corporations produce integrated marketing plans that create unique business and networking opportunities through exhibitions, advertising, and direct marketing initiatives.

Every year this firm manages more than 470 events in 37 countries serving a variety of industries. Reed Travel Exhibitions prides itself on running global travel events, such as Professional Golf Expo, Cannes International Boat & Yacht Show, and the Eastern Sports & Outdoor Show (North America's Largest Outdoor Hunting & Fishing Event). For more information on this show management company, visit their Web site at www.reedexpo.com.

including the size of the facility, services available at the venue (telecommunications, dining, setup and teardown times), cost, availability of service contractors, preferences of exhibitors and attendees, logistical considerations (airline services, local transportation, parking), and lodging and entertainment in the area.

Meeting and convention facilities have kept pace with the growth of the industry. From small, regional facilities to mega convention centers located in major cities, destinations have understood the benefits of attracting trade shows and conventions to their area. Hotels and nontraditional venues are also investing in larger exhibit areas and expanding their meeting space. Many fair grounds, sports centers, and large parking lots or museums, nightclubs, and community centers are being used for expositions. These options must be considered as alternatives to convention centers and large hotels for smaller exhibitions.

The chart that follows shows a range of convention center space available to show organizers.

Convention Center Size

Center	Square Feet Of Exhibit Space	Meeting Rooms
McCormick Place (Chicago)	2.2 Million	114
Orange County Convention Center (Orlando)	2.053 million	94
Las Vegas Convention Center	1.3 million	103
Indiana Convention Center (Indianapolis, IN)	491,045	48
Austin Convention Center (Austin, TX)	246,097	54

Examples of current convention center size.

Source: Meetings & Conventions Facility Annual Directory, 2009.

General Service Contractor

The general service contractor, also known as an official exhibit service contractor or decorator, provides products and services to the **exhibition management company** and the show's exhibitors. Their services are often key to the success of a show. Once selected, the general service contractor will provide the show management and exhibitors with a list of services supplied by the contractor or other subcontractors. Types of services the general service contractors provide include:

- Floor plan development and design
- Aisle carpet and signage
- Custom and modular booths
- Freight handling and shipping
- Storage and warehousing
- Installation, maintenance, and dismantling labor
- Lighting, electronics, and plumbing
- Telecommunication and computer requests
- Sound and audio visual
- Coordination with specialty contractors

Arranging and managing these services for a large show can be quite complex for the exhibition management company and exhibitors. Convention centers, management companies, and even exhibitors have become accustomed to working with various arrangements and companies. Because the service contractors operate in a very competitive environment, they have learned that customer service, fair pricing, and responsiveness to customer needs are important. This enables organizers and exhibitors a level of comfort in relying on service contractors to take care of the problems that arise with organizing a successful trade show.

The general service contractor, in conjunction with the exhibition management company, usually develops an exhibitor service manual that encompasses all details that an exhibitor needs to plan and implement an exhibit program for the show. It also includes the forms needed to order services from the service contractors and the rules and regulations of the exhibition management company, convention center or hotel, and the local government.

Despite the controls and organization put in place by the exhibition management company and service contractors, disputes arise. When this occurs, it is important to get all concerned parties involved in achieving a successful resolution. The show manager is responsible for compliance of exhibitors, attendees, and service contractors to the show rules. See Chapter 6 for more information on service contractors.

CONSIDERATIONS IN PLANNING THE SHOW

Location

Exhibition planners consider a number of variables when deciding on the location of the trade show or public exhibition. It is no secret that the city and venue selected to host the show has a major effect on attendance. Thus, a balance must be attained between location, cost, and the ideal attendance level. Many organizations that conduct annual meetings and trade shows stay in the same city year after year, and thus they can negotiate the best agreements with the local convention center and hotels and still retain the optimum attendance levels. Typically, these are association meetings that have strong educational programs and are held at a desirable site.

However, other organizations or exhibition management companies prefer to move their trade shows from city to city each year. This strategy may help attract additional visitors. Not only is a different local attendance base able to attend inexpensively, but out-of-town visitors may be attracted by local tourist offerings as well.

Organizations and exhibition management companies often survey their membership or potential attendees to assess their preferences on location. The success of convention centers in cities like Las Vegas, Orlando, and San Francisco is indicative of organizations paying attention to the needs and desires of their members and potential audience. Expansion of the convention facilities in each of these cities indicates that these destinations value the revenue generated by large trade and public shows.

Hotel facilities are also a factor to be considered when determining the location of the trade show or exhibition. Are the local facilities adequate for the projected attendance? Are the negotiated room rates within the budget of the typical attendee or exhibitor? What is the proximity to the trade show site, and will local transportation need to be provided? What is the potential for labor problems to arise in the host city or at host hotels? Do the convention center and local hotels comply with ADA requirements?

In addition, the largest trade shows often require dedicated local ground transportation to assist visitors and exhibitors in getting from their hotels to the trade show site. When determining whether dedicated ground transportation is required, consider that safety is often the key decision point. Even if hotels are within walking distance from the convention center, the conditions of the city between the hotels and the center may dictate that it is in your best interests to provide transportation. For example, in New Orleans there are many hotels within walking distance of the convention center, but in the summer when temperature and humidity are both in the 90s, the meeting organizer is better off to provide transportation. When choosing ground transportation providers, be sure to take into account experience, availability, special services, insurance, condition of vehicles, labor contracts, and cost.

Housing and transportation are essential elements to success for any trade show that attracts a national or international audience. A large part of any organizer's time is spent negotiating room

Bus transportation along many routes is necessary for a large convention. *Photo by George G. Fenich, Ph.D.*

blocks in the host city and airline and car rental discounts for attendees and exhibitors. Recently, the trend has moved toward outsourcing housing and transportation arrangements to local convention and visitor bureaus or third-party housing vendors. Regardless of how housing and transportation issues are handled, the expectation is that they will be "transparent" to the attendee or exhibitor.

Another selection factor is weather. Unlike business-to-business trade shows with many people coming from outside the city, public shows rely on the local and regional population for attendance. Locals and regional tourists will not venture out to a public show in the midst of a serious snowstorm or rainstorm. Thus, one episode of bad weather can drastically affect the bottom line of a show producer. The National Western Stock Show, held in Denver each January, is a good example of this. Years with extreme cold and snow greatly reduced the event's attendance. During years of unseasonably mild weather, attendance skyrockets. The solution for the National Western Stock Show has been to extend the show to a sixteen-day period, ensuring that there will be "good days" and "bad days." This has led to a more consistent overall attendance figure from year to year.

Shipping and Storage

Once the location is chosen, the booths and other trade show materials need to be transported to the site. While air freight may sometimes be used, over-the-road freight by truck is the most common method. Charges are typically per hundred pounds and are based on the distance the freight must travel.

Since an exhibitor cannot afford for the freight shipment to arrive late for a trade show, extra time is allowed for transit. Thus, the exhibitor must arrange for temporary storage of the materials at the destination, but prior to the move-in date for the trade show or exhibition. One must also consider storage of the freight containers while the show or exhibition is open. When the show closes, the whole process is reversed. Some Exposition Services Contractors such as GES of Freeman have separate divisions of their company that deal with shipping and storage.

Marketing and Promotion

Without exhibitors, the exhibition will not be successful, and in turn without attendees, exhibitors will not participate or return. Show planners focus their attention to marketing and promotion programs that will fill the exhibition hall with both exhibitors and attendees. Regardless of the type of show, attendance is the key to success. It is primarily the responsibility of the exhibition management company to target and market to the right audience. This is typically done through direct mail, advertising in trade publications, and e-marketing.

Some freight being unloaded in a convention center.   *Used with permission of Paradise Sound & Light, Orlando, Florida*

Exhibition management companies and service companies also offer additional marketing opportunities for exhibitors to consider. Exhibitors want to invest in a show because their potential customers are in attendance. Based on their objectives for the show, exhibitors can choose to invest in a number of programs:

- *General Sponsorships:* These programs usually involve the company's name or logo being included on printed the show's promotional materials or being posted in a prominent place in the exhibit hall.
- *Special Event Sponsorship:* Special events are often conducted during the trade show schedule, such as receptions, press conferences, or entertainment. Companies who sponsor these events have their name or logo mentioned prominently in promotional materials and throughout the event.
- *Advertising in the Show Daily:* Large trade shows usually have a daily newspaper available to all exhibitors and attendees each morning. It reviews the previous day's events and previews what is coming up. Exhibitors have the opportunity to advertise in the show daily.
- *Advertising in the Show Directory:* Almost all trade shows provide attendees with a show directory containing information about the show and exhibitors. Advertising opportunities also exist for this show directory.
- *Promotional Items Sponsorship:* Management companies may offer sponsorship opportunities to companies for badge holders, tote bags, and other promotional items given to registered attendees.

Management companies (for business-to-business trade shows) must provide a convention program that has additional information beyond the exhibit hall to help attract visitors. Often, educational programs are provided as an incentive, or prominent industry leaders are hired to give keynote addresses that attract visitors. Contests, gifts, discount programs, and other tools to attract visitors have been commonplace. Exhibitors are also involved in helping boost attendance at trade shows. Usually, they are given a number of free passes to the show that can be passed on to their best customers. Exhibitors are also encouraged to sponsor or conduct special events and to promote them to their customer base.

Technology

Advances in technology have made trade show and exhibition management, as well as exhibition itself, easier and more productive (for more information, see Chapter 12 on technology).

- The Internet has had a great impact on how exhibitions are marketed to potential visitors. Most shows have sites that allow attendees to register online (private shows) and purchase tickets in advance (public shows). Attendees can view exhibitor lists, review educational programs, and even make their travel arrangements online. They can also view interactive floor plans and select educational programs and/or special events to efficiently plan their time.

- Lead retrieval systems are a great benefit to exhibitors. Systems are in place that enable the exhibit staff to "swipe" an attendee's card or bar-coded badge and capture all of that individual's contact information, saving many hours of entering business card data.
- The use of radio frequency identification (RFID) is now being used by convention and exhibition managers to track attendees' movement and behavior. This advanced technology is beneficial for data acquisition, lead retrieval, and reporting, but raise many issues regarding privacy and use of personal information.
- Technology is also used in promoting a company's products. Many companies now give visitors inexpensive CD-ROMs or flash drives instead of bulky brochures. The electronic format can contain much more information and more elaborate presentations that the potential customer can view at his or her leisure.

Risk and Crisis Management

Organizing and exhibiting at a show can be a risky business. If things are not done correctly, the show can quickly become a colossal failure. Both show organizers and exhibitors need to have a risk management program. A risk management plan does the following:

- Identifies all potential risks for the show management and the exhibitors.
- Quantifies each risk to determine the effect it would have if it occurs.
- Provides an assessment of each risk to determine which risks to ignore, which to avoid, and which to mitigate.
- Provides risk avoidance steps to prevent the risk from occurring.
- Provides risk mitigation steps to minimize potential costs if the risk occurs.

Always keep in mind that an exhibition is a business venture that should be given every chance to succeed. Knowing how to apply risk management principles will help ensure success.

Crisis management has also become critical to trade show organizers. A crisis is different from a risk in that it poses a critical situation that may cause danger to visitors or exhibitors. Examples of recent crises include the 9/11 attacks in New York City, riots during World Trade Organization meetings, and the Hurricane Katrina disaster. Trade shows that were underway on 9/11 were either canceled or curtailed midway through the schedule. Organizing companies suffered deep losses for these events.

Every show organizer should have a crisis management plan that addresses the prevention, control, and reporting of emergency situations. The plan should address the more likely types of emergencies, such as fire, food-borne illness, demonstrations, bomb threats, terrorism, and natural disasters. It should contain all procedures to be followed in the event of an emergency situation.

Consider having a crisis management team who is well versed in assessing the potential for a crisis, taking actions to prevent emergencies, and taking control should a situation occur. The crisis management team should be represented in the site selection process.

EXHIBITORS' PERSPECTIVE

If exhibitors were not successful from a business perspective, exhibitions would not exist. Exhibiting at trade shows or consumer shows is often a key part of a company's integrated marketing strategy. Companies invest a significant portion of their marketing budget into trade show appearances and must see a positive return on their investment. This section of the chapter looks at the issues that face the exhibiting companies.

Why Exhibit?

An exhibition booth is constructed to exhibit products/services and to convey a message. It is important for a company to understand and analyze the benefits of exhibiting at a show prior to beginning the planning. Exhibiting at a trade or public show is the only marketing medium that allows the potential buyer to experience a product or service; and therefore, more money is spent on participating in shows than on traditional advertising or individual sales travel.

The trade show floor at the G2E convention. *Photo by George G. Fenich, Ph.D.*

Additional reasons that companies participate in a trade show or exhibition include the following:

- Branding of their name in the industry
- Annual presentation of products to industry analysts
- New product rollout
- Opportunities to meet with potential and existing customers
- Opportunities to learn about customer needs
- Opportunities to meet with trade media
- Opportunities to learn about changes in industry trends and competitor products

Exhibit Design Principles

Although exhibit design may be limited by the rules established by the exhibit management company, the constraints of the facility, or the business culture of the host country, there are some general principles that can be discussed. These principles include selecting the right layout of the exhibit to meet your purposes, selecting the right size for your company's budget and purposes, and proper use of signage, lighting, and personnel. Exhibits and the space they occupy are a significant corporate investment, and attention must be given to each of these factors.

Exhibit size is a major consideration, if only because of cost. The more space an exhibit occupies, the more it costs in space rental, materials, labor for setup, additional staff, and maintenance. Therefore, be sure to balance the costs with the benefits of having a larger exhibit. A larger exhibit typically means being noticed by visitors, and it creates a better impression if done well. It

Top Reasons Exhibitors Fail

1. Don't understand that every show is different
2. No SMART objectives were set for the show
3. Failure to differentiate your company from your competitors
4. No formal marketing or promotional plan created or shared
5. Logical planning is poor
6. Do not give attendees any reason to visit your booth space
7. Staff is not trained to sell your product or service
8. Exhibiting for all the wrong reasons—did not ensure the "right" buyers would be there
9. Don't know how to measure return on investment
10. Don't do any post show follow-up with leads generated at the show

gives the impression that the company is in a solid financial situation and is a leader in the industry. However, the space must be used well and convey the messages that the company desires to impart to potential customers.

Companies that participate in a large number of shows will have exhibits that range in size from very small (for less important or more specialized trade shows) to very large (for their most important trade shows). For example, Xerox, which exhibits at more than 30 trade shows per year, has very large exhibits for information technology shows but also smaller peninsular or in-line exhibits for specialized trade shows or smaller, regional shows. Some companies even have two or three exhibits at the same trade show: a large one promoting the main theme and message they want to communicate and smaller exhibits in other halls to promote specialized products or services.

Space assignments are often based on a priority points system in which the exhibition management company awards points based on desired space size, total dollars spent in exhibit space, number of years involved, and participation in sponsorship and advertising programs. From the organizer's perspective, this type of arrangement helps retain exhibitors and gives favor to the loyal, highest-paying exhibitors.

When selecting space, the company trade show manager should consider the following:

- Traffic patterns within the exhibit hall
- Location of entrances
- Location of food facilities and restrooms
- Location of industry leaders
- Location of competitors

Exhibit layout is also linked to the objectives a company establishes for the trade show or exhibition. If a company's main objective is to meet as many people as possible and establish its brand in the industry, a large open exhibit is appropriate. This type of layout encourages people to enter the exhibit, and it facilitates a large amount of traffic flow. There will be a few parts of the exhibit that require visitors to stay for a period of time, such as product demonstrations. It is the responsibility of the exhibit manager to notify the show management company if the company is hosting any celebrities, giving a loud presentation from a stage, or is hosting any special events in the booth that would draw an unusually large crowd.

Another type of layout may even purposely discourage people from entering, and parts of the exhibit may be "by invitation only." Why would a company do this? If their purpose at the trade show is to only meet with serious buyers or existing customers, it is important to limit visitors to only those falling in these categories. Therefore, this exhibit layout is set up to minimize traffic through the exhibit.

Most trade show floor plans in the United States are based on a 10-foot by 10-foot grid or an 8-foot by 10-foot grid. This is known as the **standard booth**.

A standard trade show booth.
Photo by George G. Fenich, Ph.D.

Floor plan. *Courtesy of George Fern & Co.*

Lighting can enhance booth
appearance and attractiveness.
Photo by George G. Fenich, Ph.D.

Typically, standard booths are set up side-by-side and back-to-back with an aisle running in front of the booth. Standard booths may also be used to line the inside walls of the exhibit area. Companies may combine standard booths to create an **in-line exhibit** using multiple standard booths to give greater length to the exhibit.

Island booths are created by grouping standard booths together into blocks of four, nine, or larger configurations. Island booths have aisles on four sides and can be an excellent format for medium-sized companies. **Peninsula booths** are made up of four or more standard booths back-to-back with aisles on only three sides.

Multilevel exhibits are often used by large companies to expand their exhibit space without taking up more floor space. The upper floor may be used for special purposes, such as meeting areas, private demonstration areas, or hospitality stations. Exhibitors using multilevel exhibits must be aware of each convention center's unique regulations for this type of exhibit.

As mentioned above, exhibitors must be aware of the location of food facilities, restrooms, entrances, and other special event areas. Each of these factors affects the traffic flow in the aisles and can either hinder or help an exhibit. Although many companies strive to be directly in front of an entrance for exposure, it may create more problems than expected because of the large amount of traffic. The exhibit staff may have difficulty discerning between serious visitors to the exhibit and those just trying to get in or out of the exhibit hall. Food service areas may create unexpected lines at meal times that spill into an exhibit area, essentially making that area useless for that time.

Small exhibitors face a different set of problems. If they have an in-line exhibit, their options are limited in how the exhibit is organized. If they want to maximize interactions with visitors, they may "open" the exhibit by ensuring that there are no tables or other obstructions between the aisle and their staff. If, on the other hand, they want to focus interaction on serious potential customers, their approach may be to block off the inside of the exhibit as much as possible and have meeting areas within the exhibit.

Many people who pass by or through an exhibit only read the signs that the company is displaying. Signage, therefore, is important in planning the exhibit. Signs must communicate the messages that the company wants to convey clearly and quickly to visitors. Detailed itemizations of equipment specifications on signs are almost always ignored. Signs should instead focus on selling points and benefits to the user.

Lighting technology has come a long way in the past twenty years. Today, many companies use pinpoint lighting to focus visitors' attention on their products and signage. Color lighting is often used to accentuate certain parts of an exhibit to communicate a mood for the visitor.

Lighting is also important for areas that will be used for discussions or meetings with potential customers.

Staffing the Exhibit

The most important part of any exhibit is the staff. A company may have an attractive, open, inviting, and informative exhibit space, but if the staff members are untrained, communicate poorly, and do not dress professionally, the exhibit will communicate the wrong message to an attendee about the company and its products or services. Therefore, it is important that, whether for a large or small exhibit, the staff is well prepared and trained to promote the company and represent the product or service professionally.

Staff must be trained to "meet and greet." It is important that visitors are greeted warmly and made to feel welcome to the exhibit. Staff must also "qualify" visitors to determine if they are potential customers or not. By asking the right questions and listening to visitors, they can easily determine whether to spend more time with them, pass them to another staff member, or politely move them through the exhibit. Time is important, especially during the busy times at a trade show. Qualifying visitors is an important step in focusing your staff's time.

Many companies provide product demonstrations or even elaborate productions about their products or services at the booth. This aspect must be well managed and focus the visitors' attention on the main messages the company wants to communicate.

Exhibit staff must also be used wisely. All areas of the exhibit must be covered, and the right people must be in the right places. For large exhibits, greeters should be used to staff the outside of the exhibit. These people will direct visitors to the areas of their interest after initially greeting them. Technical staff may be stationed with the products displayed, being able to provide answers to the more detailed questions that a visitor may present. Corporate executives may roam the exhibit or cluster near meeting areas to enable staff to find them when needed. Often, serious customers want to be introduced to senior executives, and those executives need to be available.

Small exhibits have a special set of staff problems. Usually, the main problem they face is having enough staff to cover the busy times of the trade show, or having too much staff for the exhibit size. Again, it is important that the right people are used to staff the exhibit and that staff assignments are planned according to the show's busiest times.

Free samples are a way for exhibitors to entice attendees to sample their products.   *Photo by George G. Fenich, Ph.D.*

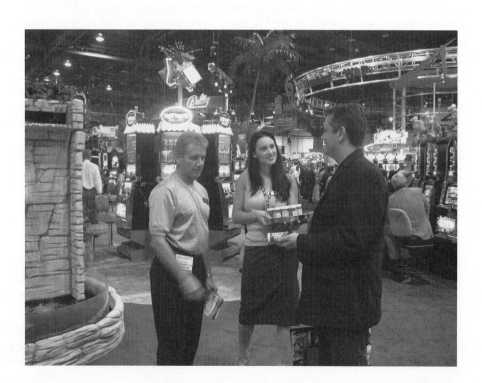

Measuring Return on Investment

In this economic time, companies must select the shows with the right buyers in attendance. Far too often a company analyzes its **return on investment** (ROI) and cannot understand why a particular show was not a success. Perhaps it exhibited at the show for years, and recently their return has dropped. This may possibly be due to not noticing a change in the show's theme and audience; it may no longer be an appropriate venue for the company.

Calculating ROI for each show is more critical than justifying whether or not a company is participating in the right shows and using the right strategy and planning techniques. Often, however, determining ROI is ignored because "we can't tell whether a sale was derived from a trade show lead or not" or "we don't have the data to be accurate." Avoid these excuses by determining actual expenses and revenue generated by the trade show exhibit leads.

When calculating ROI, establish all the expenses that are a part of the show. Typical expenses include:

- Space rental
- Service contractor services (electrical, computer, etc.)
- Personnel travel, including hotel and meals
- Personnel time for non-marketing personnel
- Customer entertainment
- Preshow mailings
- Freight charges
- Photography
- Brochure printing and shipment
- Promotional items
- Training
- Post show mailings

A simple method to determine revenue from the trade show is to set a time limit on business that was the result of leads from the trade show. It is easy to maintain the lead list and determine which resulted in actual business; after a period of time, however, the business may very well be the result of other activities and not participation at the trade show. Thus, one simple formula for measuring show ROI is subtracting expenses (listed above) from revenue generated from the buyers at the show.

Other methods of measuring ROI include evaluating results versus objectives:

- Cost per lead (total investment/total number of leads)
- Percentage of the sales goal achieved (leads gathered/leads identified in objectives)
- Percentage of leads converted to sales (number of sales/leads generated)

Therefore, it is important that an exhibitor continually evaluate its trade show program and ensure that it is exhibiting at the right shows in order to meet its potential customers. Exhibitors can use a variety of tools to measure success. Examples of these include lead retrieval data, in-booth and post event surveys, media clips, and sales tracking.

A company exhibited at a trade show and collected 400 qualified leads and spent a total of $75,000 to exhibit. In the next six months, the company tracked its sales from the show and found it generated 100 new sales totaling $175,000 in new business. Below are the calculations of the return on investment based on the company's objectives for participation in the trade show.

Leads generated = 400 qualified leads

Total cost to exhibit = $75,000

Sales resulting from the show = 100 new sales

Revenue resulting in show sales = $175,000

Target number of leads to gather from show = 700 qualified leads

ROI Calculations

Revenue − Expenses = $175,000 − $75,000 = $100,000

Total cost per lead = $75,000/400 leads = $187.50 per lead

Percentage of goal achieved = 700/400 = 57%

Percentage of leads converted to sales = 100/400 = 25%

FUTURE TRENDS

Exhibitions have been around and will continue to be around for many decades to come. However, as times and economic conditions changes, the trade show industry must adapt in order to both survive and thrive.

- Attendance at future shows may be reduced, but it appears that the buying power of the attendee is greater. Many companies and organizations are not sending multiple representatives to shows and conferences, but are sending the decision makers.
- Technology will continue to push the trade show industry to explore new ways of conducting business. Virtual trade shows will advance and continue to be a supplement to, not a replacement of, the face-to-face event. The human factor is still important in business.
- With information readily available for attendees, exhibitors will have to be creative in their booth design and activities to draw attendees into their space. The use of the booth space, décor, signage, and displays will become even more important as attendees select vendors to engage with at the show site.
- Like associations, organizations and private media firms may be forced to merge shows or events as exhibitors may only be able to participate in a limited number of private or public shows during this tough economic time. This trend allows for creative business agreements, bigger and better shows, and the opportunity to be innovative in event planning.
- Some trade shows are being downsized or even phased out and replaced with **hosted buyer programs**. In these programs, planners are pre-qualified as having the intention to hold a meeting or convention and have the authority to make a decision. These planners have most of their travel expenses covered by the show organizer. The show organizer, in return, schedules meetings between these planners and suppliers such as DMCs or Hotels to discuss planner needs and how the supplier can fulfill those needs. The suppliers pay a fee to participate in these meetings.

Summary

There are three phases of planning to ensure success for the exhibiting company or organization. Prior to the show, the exhibitor must establish measurable and clear objectives the company wants to accomplish by participating. The objectives set the stage for how the exhibit is presented, the messages the signage convey, and the approach that the staff takes with exhibit visitors. Establishing objectives helps the company to give thought as to how the exhibit will operate, and the messages it needs to give to visitors.

A company has to be sure to determine that those attending a particular show are "decision makers" rather than "tire kickers." They want to interface with buyers who will undertake the transaction rather than attendees who have to get approval from a higher authority. A company must consider the demographics and psychographics of people attending a show when deciding where to exhibit and which shows to participate in.

Planning for the exhibit operation is also a key to success. Additionally, significant planning must take place to ensure that everything arrives at the exhibition on time, including the staff, physical booth, brochures, give-aways, and products. The person in charge of the exhibit must coordinate specific requests to the exhibition management company or service companies, synchronize staff schedules, prepare for product demonstrations and a myriad of other details that result in the visitor seeing and experiencing a flawless exhibit. Large companies like Microsoft or IBM will have full-time employees who do nothing but coordinate the company exhibits and the shows in which they participate. Smaller companies will have people who work on trade shows as a part of a larger job, such as marketing manager or director of communications. Whether large or small, trade shows and exhibitions are business ventures that must be thoroughly planned for success.

In order to gauge the success of the show, the exhibition manager and sales team must execute a post show plan. Three components of the post show period must be planned:

- Follow-ups for all qualified leads obtained during the show.
- Monitoring to ensure that all commitments made during the show are fulfilled. Often staff promise visitors that they will send information or have someone call the visitor.
- Evaluation of the results. This includes determining the ROI, giving a budget report, evaluating the response of visitors to the exhibit design, tabulating the survey results, examining the staff feedback, and reflecting upon lessons learned for future performance improvement.

For an exhibiting company, an exhibition is a significant investment from the marketing budget. Therefore, it is critical that planning take place that considers activities before, during, and after the trade show to maximize the ROI. Organizing companies must address the needs of attendees and, just as important, the needs of the exhibitors. Exhibitors are the lifeblood of the trade show, providing the excitement and resources that ensure a show's success.

Key Words and Terms

For definitions, see GLOSSARY, or http://glossary.conventionindustry.org.

Exhibition	Hosted buyer program	Peninsula booth	Trade show
Exhibition management company	In-line exhibit	Public show	Trade fair
	Island booth	Return on Investment	
Exposition	Multilevel exhibit	Standard booth	

Review and Discussion Questions

1. What is the difference between a typical trade show and a public show?
2. Give some examples of services that exhibition service contractors provide to exhibitors.
3. What attributes of an exhibit layout would a company want if its major objective is branding?
4. Describe the layout of a peninsula exhibit.
5. What kinds of additional marketing opportunities do management companies typically offer?
6. Why is risk management important to an exhibition management company? To an exhibitor?
7. What factors are considered by an exhibition management company when determining the location of a trade show or exhibition?
8. What are the three phases of planning that a company trade show manager must address?

References and Internet Sites

TRADE PUBLICATIONS

Convene
 PCMA
 2301 S. Lakeshore Drive, Ste. 1001
 Chicago, IL 60616

Exhibit Builder
 P. O. Box 4144
 Woodland Hills, CA 91365

Exhibitor Magazine
 206 S. Broadway, Ste. 475
 Rochester, MN 55903

EXPO
 11600 College Boulevard
 Overland Park, KS 66210

Facility Manager
 IAAM
 635 Fritz Drive
 Coppell, TX 75019

IdEAs
 5501 Backlick Road, Ste. 105
 Springfield, VA 22151

Meetings and Conventions
 Reed Travel Group
 500 Plaza Drive
 Secaucus, NJ 07094

Tradeshow Week
 12233 W. Olympic Blvd., Ste. 236
 Los Angeles, CA 90064

BOOKS

Chapman, E. (1995). *Exhibit marketing.* New York: McGraw-Hill.

Kent, P. (2006). *The art of the tradeshow.* International Association of Exhibit Management.

Miller, S. (1996). *How to get the most out of trade shows.* Lincolnwood, IL: NTC Business Books.

Robbe, D. (2000). *Expositions and tradeshows.* New York, NY: John Wiley & Sons.

Siskind, B. (1990). *The power of exhibit marketing.* Bellington, WA: Self-Counsel Press.

Weisgal, M. (1997). *Show and sell.* New York: American Management Association.

Internet Sites

Center for Exhibition Industry Research	http://www.ceir.org
EventWeb	http: //www.eventweb.com
ExhibitorNet	http://www.exhibitornet.com
International Association of Exhibitions and Events	http://www.iaem.org
Professional Convention Management Association	http://www.pcma.org
Trade Show Central	http://www.tscentral.com
Trade Show News Network	http://www.tsnn.com

About the Chapter Contributors

Amanda Cecil, Ph.D., CMP, is an assistant professor at Indiana University's Department of Tourism, Conventions and Event Management in Indianapolis, Indiana, and teaches several courses in meeting and exhibition management. Prior to joining the faculty at IUPUI, Dr. Cecil was an exposition manager for Host Communications, Inc., an association and event management association.

Contributor to Previous Editions: **Ben McDonald,** vice president of BenchMark Learning, Inc.

CHAPTER 6

Service Contractors

One of the services provided by Exhibition Service Contractors is Booth Design and Construction. *Photo provided by GES*

Chapter Objectives

This chapter provides the reader with an understanding of the following:

- Service contractors and their role in MEEC
- General services contractors compared with specialty contractors
- Exhibitor-appointed contractors
- Associations in service contracting

INTRODUCTION

An event producer or show manager (or show organizer) may have all the tools at his or her fingertips to promote, sell, and execute a show or conference, but there are many pieces of knowledge, human resources, and equipment that he or she does not have. For example, while you might be a great cook, you do not make the frying pan or the spatula—you turn to experts for that. For exhibitions and events to be produced smoothly and efficiently, the producers and managers must rely on professional service contractors to give the event/show manager and the exhibitors the tools necessary to be successful. These are called **service contractors**. This chapter discusses their various roles in the process, their relationship with the organizer, and their relationship with each other.

DEFINITION OF THE SERVICE CONTRACTOR

Depending on where you are in the world, a person who manages a tradeshow is known as a service contractor, show manager, or an event manager or an event producer. It should also be noted that not all events and conferences have an exhibitor component. If you are going to be doing events/conferences/tradeshows outside of the United States or Canada, be sure to use your network to find the appropriate company that will help you wade through the changes in the meanings of positions, cultural and business changes, language barriers and so much more. Remember, only the United States use feet and inches. In Canada, because much of the business is from the United States, dimensions will be given in feet and inches. Elsewhere in the world, be prepared for dimensions to be metric.

A service contractor is anyone who provides a product or service for the exhibitor or show/event management during the actual show or conference. Service contractors can be the florist, the electrical company, the registration company, staffing agency, and just about every service you can think of. Some service contractors are hired by the show organizers to assist with their needs, and others are hired directly by the exhibitor.

Service Contractor: An outside company used by clients to provide specific products or services (e.g., pipe and drape, exhibitor manuals, floor plans, dance floors or flags). (APEX Glossary http://www.conventionindusry.org/glossary)

MEEC service contractors and their roles have evolved over time. Historically, they were referred to as *decorators*. This is based on their earliest primary function as service contractors, which was to "decorate" the empty space of a convention center or hotel ballroom. This decorating function included pipe and drape, carpets, backdrops, booths, and furnishings.

SERVICE CONTRACTORS RESPONSIBILITIES

Over the years, service contractors have expanded the scope of their activities to match the growing sophistication of MEEC. Today, service contractors can be, and likely are, involved in every aspect of the event from move in, to running the show, to teardown, and move out. As a result, the service contractor provides an important interface between the event organizer and other MEEC suppliers such as hotel convention services, the convention center, exhibitors, local labor, and unions. Many service contractors will work with the organizer to lay out trade show floors, in part because they have spent the time to take careful measurements of every MEEC venue in the host community (Rutherford 1990). Service contractors are also involved before the setup of the show by sending out exhibitor kits and other information.

General Service Contractors

The **general service contractor** (also called the official show contractor or exposition services contractor) is hired by the show manager to handle the general duties necessary to produce the show on-site. (http://www.conventionindustry.org/glossary)

> *General Service Contractor* (GSC) An organization that provides event management and exhibitors with a wide range of services, sometimes including, but not limited to, Installation & Dismantle, creating and hanging signage and banners, laying carpet, drayage, and providing booth/stand furniture. See DECORATOR.

The show may have a contractor appointed by show management whose APEX Glossary definition is

• *Official Contractor* Organization appointed by show management to provide services such as set-up and tear-down of exhibit booths and to oversee labor, drayage, and loading dock procedures. Also known as general service contractor.

General service contractors (GCSs) are responsible for assisting the show organizer with graphic treatments for the entrance and all signage, putting up the pipe and drape or hard wall exhibits, placing aisle carpet, and creating all the official booths, such as association centers, registration, food and beverage areas, lounges, and special areas. More importantly, the GSC offers the show organizer a valuable service by hiring and managing the labor for a particular show. They have standing contracts with unions and tradespeople. They know how to hire enough

Trade show floor layout measured in feet/inches.
Courtesy of Stronco, CA

labor to move a show in and out based on the requirements of the show. It is their responsibility to move the freight in and out of the facility, manage the flow of the trucks coming in and out of the facility, and the storage of the crates and boxes during the show. This is called **material handling** or **drayage**.

It is important to understand the various terms involved in drayage, and this may be a separate services contract, or included with the general services contract for the show/exhibition.

Trade show floor layout, metric measurements. *Courtesy of Stronco, CA*

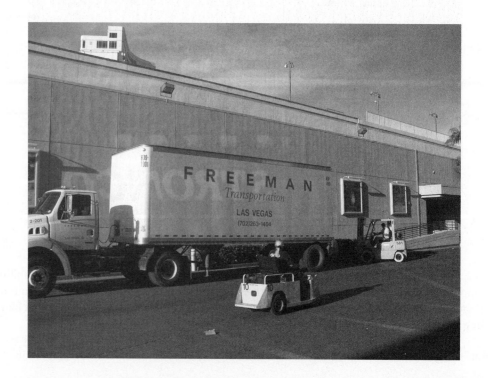

Trucks and equipment from the Freeman companies transport and handle freight. *Photo by George G. Fenich, Ph.D.*

From www.conventionindustry.org/glossary:

Drayage: Delivery of exhibit materials from the dock to an assigned exhibit space, removing empty crates, returning crates at the end of the event for re-crating, and delivering materials back to dock for carrier loading.

Drayage Charge: The cost of moving exhibit materials within the confines of the exhibit hall, based on weight. This charge is calculated in 100-pound units, or hundredweight, abbreviated cwt. (There is usually a minimum charge for all drayage.)

Drayage Contractor: Company responsible for handling exhibit materials.

Drayage Form: Form for exhibitor requesting handling of materials.

Drayage is a somewhat confusing term and may be traced back to medieval times. According to *Webster's New Universal Unabridged Dictionary, S.V.* (1979), "drayage" is the sum charge paid for the use of a dray or drays (a *dray* is a low, strong cart with detachable sides used for drawing heavy loads). Thus, *drayage* is the price paid for having trucks transport products. Today, the transport vehicle can be a truck or a plane, and the fee includes many aspects of the transportation service. Service contractors may charge for services like crating an exhibit in a box, using a forklift to get the box onto a small truck that takes the crate to a local warehouse or storage facility, and then putting it onto an 18-wheeler for over-the-road transport. The reverse happens at the other end and ultimately leads to unloading at the convention center or event site. There, the service contractor will also supervise the unloading of the crate and delivery of it to the proper booth. After the crate is unpacked, the service contractor will arrange for storage of the empty crate until the show is over and the whole process is reversed. The price for drayage is based on the weight, not the size of the materials or crate. The fee is based on each one hundred pounds of weight, and thus is called *hundredweight*. A "bill of lading" is completed by the shipper and delineates what the package contains, who owns it, where it is going, and any special instructions. This is the official shipping document, and authorities at checkpoints like state borders and especially national borders may insist on examining it.

Many GSCs have expanded into specialty areas. Thus, GSCs today may provide audiovisual equipment, security, cleaning, and more. This is done for a number of reasons. One is that the GSCs are building on the relationship they have established with show organizers over years of interaction and rely on the marketing concept of "relationship marketing." Provision of a wide range of services also gives the show organizer the advantage of "one-stop shopping." By using a GSC that provides general and specialty services, the show/event organizer does not have to deal with a multitude of companies to produce the show. Also, providing an array of services allows the GSC to increase revenues and, it is hoped, profitability.

A note of caution if you are the show organizer—you must compare pricing for individual contractors versus putting all your eggs in one basket as described above. What is most cost/time efficient for your event/show?

GSCs not only serve the show organizer, but also are the official service contractor for exhibitors. Exhibitors can rent everything they need for their exhibit from the GSC, from a simple chair to a complete exhibit. Some GSCs will build a booth for exhibitors, store it, and ship it to other shows on behalf of the exhibitor.

The GSC adds value to his or her services by creating the **exhibitor service manual** (exhibitor services kit) along with the show organizer. This manual is a compilation of all the show information, such as dates, times, rules, and regulations for both the show manager and the city. Also included are all the forms necessary for an exhibitor to have a successful show. These forms typically include orders for carpet, furniture, utilities, setup and dismantling, and drayage. Some show organizers also include promotional opportunities to help exhibitors do preshow and on-site promotion. The service manuals can be printed and mailed. Service manuals now exist as CD-ROMs/DVDs/USB drives or on the Web, allowing exhibitors to order services and products from wherever they are.

On-site, the GSC works with both the show organizer and exhibitor to ensure a smooth move in and move out. He or she is often the conduit to a facility to make sure that the rules and regulations are observed. Many times, he or she solves the problems of the exhibitors by finding lost freight, repairing damaged booths or crates, and cleaning the carpets and booths in the evenings.

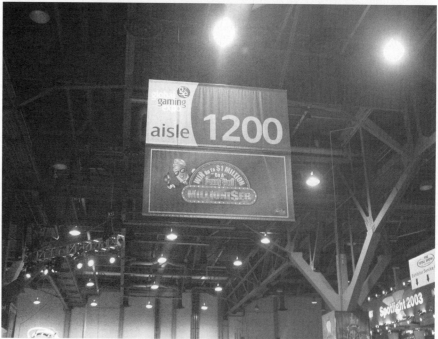

Signage is an important service.
Photo by George G. Fenich, Ph.D.

The services provided can include the following:

To Show/Event Organizers:

- Account Management
- On-site coordination of the event
- Pipe and drape
- Entry areas
- Offices
- Registration areas
- Setup and dismantling of booths
- Planning, layout, and design of exhibit area
- Carpet

This simple example of rigging was used to attract attention to a booth selling chairs. *Photo by George G. Fenich, Ph.D.*

- Furniture
- Signs
- Graphics
- Backdrops
- Interface with labor and unions
- Cleaning
- Transportation services
- Material handling
- Customer Service

To Exhibitors:

- Exhibit design and construction
- Booth setup and dismantling
- Carpet
- Furniture and accessories
- Signs/signage
- Interface with labor and unions
- Rigging
- Material handling
- Exhibitor kit
- Customs brokerage when dealing internationally GF: Good addition

Trade Unions

Exhibition service managers as well as show/event organizers will make use of tradespeople in the community to help set up and tear down the show. Many of these tradespeople will be members of a trade union. Everyone involved in a show should be aware of the local laws and policies in the city, state/province, country that your show/event regarding use of unionized personnel. The primary issue is whether the community is located in a "right to work" state/province. In these states/provinces, an individual working in a specific trade is NOT required to join the trade union representing that skill. Thus, show/event organizers and participants are free to hire whom they please, regardless of whether they are a union member. However, if the community is not in a right-to-work state/province, then people working in the trades such as electricians, plumbers, riggers, and porters must belong to the union. In these communities, there can be significant repercussions if the proper union members are not used. In some locales, an exhibitor cannot

The Case of Exhibiting in a Unionized City

Service contractors can play a pivotal role in dealing with unionized labor. This is especially problematic since (1) the unions and rules vary throughout the United States and other countries, and (2) local labor is essential for putting together an event or trade show. The following portrays one exhibitor's interaction with unionized labor in a city in the northeastern United States. The exhibit, in its crate, was transported to the convention center in a tractor-trailer; and according to local rules, the trailer had to be driven by a member of the Teamsters Union. On arrival at the convention center, the driver opened the back of the trailer but could do no more to facilitate removal of the crate. That required a forklift, and the forklift is considered a piece of heavy equipment, not a truck, and thus had to be operated by a member of the Heavy Equipment Operators Union. So they waited for the forklift operator who then moved the crate to the exhibit booth and placed it on the ground. At that point, the exhibitor was eager to get set up but could do nothing until a member of the Carpenters Union arrived to take the nails out of the crate: Wood and nails are a job for a union carpenter. The crate was opened, but the exhibitor was restricted from doing anything himself that a union member should do. Thus, he waited for a member of the Porters Union to come to take the exhibit contents out of the crate. That was followed by a string of different union members who each did a separate but distinct job and would not infringe on the responsibilities or activities of a different union. So the exhibit frame that was made from pipes had to be assembled by someone from the Plumbers Union: Only plumbers handle pipes. The products and cloth were assembled and laid out by a member of the Stage Hands Union: After all, an exhibit is part of a "show." The sign over the booth required someone from the Heavy Equipment Operators Union to drive a bucket lift, while a member of the Riggers Union occupied the bucket to "rig" the sign. The exhibitor could not even plug his VCR into the electrical outlet provided by show management—that had to be done by a member of the Electricians Union. The telephone had to be plugged into a jack provided by a member of the Communications Workers Union, and the flowers had to be "arranged" by a member of the Agricultural Union. Of course, the cleaning people, security, and other service personnel had to be members of the appropriate union. Furthermore, part of a supervisor's pay in each these unions had to be paid by the exhibitor in proportion to the amount of time that union spent at his booth. Further complicating matters is that, unless special fees are paid, there can be significant time lapses between when one union member finishes one particular job and when the next arrives. And—oh yes—if any union rule is violated or the exhibitor tries to do something himself, all the unions will boycott that booth and refuse to work. Obviously, a service contractor who is knowledgeable about local union rules and has established an ongoing relationship with local labor can be worth his or her weight in gold to an exhibitor or show organizer.

even carry their own materials from their automobile to the trade show booth: They must use a member of the porters union. Prior to signing a contract, you should find out when union contracts are due for negotiations and learn whether past negotiations have been friendly or not. If a strike happened, how long before it was resolved?

However, unions do serve a number of laudable purposes. They represent a class of workers such as electricians when negotiating with management over pay scales and working conditions. Thus, they carry more clout than any single worker could possibly have. Unions also set very specific guidelines regarding termination of an employee and will provide a union member with legal counsel if necessary. In addition, they help to ensure that working conditions are safe and comfortable. Lastly, they work with government agencies to help establish guidelines for the construction trades.

EVOLUTION OF SERVICE CONTRACTORS

Today, general service contractors are evolving and changing to meet the needs of the client and the environment. One of the major changes has been increasing the scope of their work to center on meeting the needs of exhibitors. As is the case with the organizers of events, GSCs have come to the conclusion that it is the exhibitors who are the driving force of the trade show segment of MEEC. Furthermore, they have come to understand that exhibitors have more trade shows and vendors than ever to choose from, along with increased numbers of marketing channels through which to promote and distribute their products. Thus, both GSCs and show/event organizers are directing their attention to the needs of the exhibitor. Exhibitors are reacting to this effort by getting much more specific about their wants and needs, and they are also becoming much more discreet and selective when choosing a service contractor. Exhibitors spend huge amounts of money to participate in a trade show and thus want the best ROI they can get. In today's economic environment, exhibiting companies have to justify the expense of a trade show and are looking to service contractors to help with that justification and to show the value added by participating in the show.

In the long run, service contractors must deliver quality service and products to the user, whether it is the organizer or the exhibitor. Otherwise, both constituents will seek other marketing avenues and strategies, with organizers left out in the cold. The status quo does not hold true any longer, and some companies have decided to forego trade shows in which they have participated for years. The well-known COMDEX Show appears to be facing exactly this type of problem, as is the National Association of Television Production Executives (NATPE). In lieu of exhibiting at an alternative trade show, some companies are developing their own private trade shows targeted to specific target markets or customers.

Still another change for GSCs is that many facilities are now offering to do in-house what used to be the exclusive domain of GSCs. For example, many convention centers are now offering to provide utilities like electricity, water, steam, and gas, and may no longer allow GSCs to do this. Venues are also offering services like cleaning, security, audiovisual, and room setups. This approach is cutting into the business and revenues of service contractors. The venues are creating exclusivity of product versus suggested contractors, leaving the show/event organizer with no choice of service contractor for specific services as listed above.

The advent of **exhibitor-appointed contractors** (EACs, which are discussed later in this chapter) has cannibalized the business of the GSC. This trend began in the mid-1980s, when the courts ruled that service contractors could not have exclusive right to control and negotiate with organized labor (see legal cases "MCM PARTNERS, INCORPORATED, Plaintiff-Appellant, v. ANDREWS-BARTLETT & ASSOCIATES, INCORPORATED, doing business as Andrews-Bartlett Exposition Services, et al., Defendants-Appellees" and "*Reves v. Ernst & Young*, ___ U.S. ___, 113 S.Ct. 1163, 122 L.Ed.2d 525 (1993)").

Thus, an EAC from out of the area had the legal right to compete with GSCs and set up a booth for an exhibitor. EACs are a subset of GSCs that, rather than work from one city or location, work for the exhibiting company and travel throughout the country setting up and dismantling their booths. Their success is based on the long-term relationship they have built with the client company and is known as "relationship marketing." Because the EAC works for the same company over many trade shows and events, the EAC is more knowledgeable about the client company's needs and can provide better service than the broader GSC.

This competition between GSCs and EACs has encouraged the GSCs to provide more specialized, streamlined, and efficient service to exhibiting companies. For example, one GSC now provides exhibiting companies with the same service representative before the trade show opens, during the show, and after the show for reconciliation and billing. This lets the customer deal with one source for ordering of all services and products, a one-stop service desk, and a single master bill representing every product and service used. This is analogous to an individual who gets a different credit card receipt for each transaction but a single, cumulative bill at the end of the month. A service contractor named TEG has a program called the "Gold Advantage" for its best customers that provides a special customer service representative who is available twenty-four hours a day, seven days a week, and a private service center that has a lounge, fax, phone, copy services, and so forth. The large service contractor GES has brought the traditional service desk to the customer by equipping its sales representatives with PDAs so that they can go to a booth and provide on-the-spot service. Freeman Decorating has a program called "ExhibiTouch," where touch screen computer kiosks are located throughout the exhibit floor. A client can go to the kiosk and transact most business requests, ascertain freight status, and print forms like order forms, invoice summaries, and shipping labels.

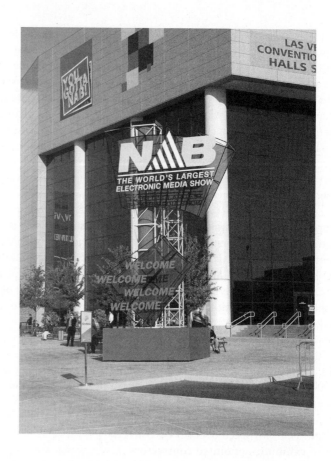

A welcome kiosk outside a convention center, such as this one, is a product supplied by a service contractor. *Photo provided by GES*

General service contractors are also expanding into the area of event marketing. This too is based on the desire by clients to do most of their business with someone or some company they know and trust: relationship marketing. The show/event organizer or association host may sponsor events, but corporations put on most events. As a result, many exhibitors are now responsible for corporate events outside the traditional trade show floor. The GSCs, having developed a long-term relationship with the exhibitor, are now developing corporate events programs, multi-event exhibit programs, private trade shows, new product introductions, hospitality events for clients, multi-city touring exhibitions, and more nontraditional promotional campaigns.

Technology is also changing the way GSCs do business. As with many businesses, the computer is eliminating many activities traditionally done with pen and paper. This includes updating floor plans, tracking freight, and monitoring small package deliveries. For example, as little as ten years ago, floor plans had to be drawn by hand using drafting instruments. A simple booth change, because it affects the entire show layout, could take a week or more to redraft. Now, thanks to computer technology, changes are almost instantaneous. Freeman Decorating, for example, has a program called "Design Vault" on its in-house network. Design Vault includes floor plans and artists' drawings for every major convention facility in the country. Thus, clients can take a "virtual tour" through the venue and make floor plan changes immediately.

General service contractors are also using technology to help them with drayage. Again, pen and paper is being replaced with computer technology that allows tracking of all sizes of shipments to be faster and more accurate. Everything is online so that when a truck enters or leaves a facility, it is in the computer system, and freight managers can go to the central computer to check the status of not only the vehicle but its contents as well. Global Positioning Systems (GPS) on many trucks allow satellite tracking of its location. This technological monitoring happens on the trade show floor, too. An exhibitor can contact the GSC and know which crates are still on the truck and which have been delivered to the booth. Small packages such as brochures can be tracked in the same fashion.

Still another use of technology embraced by GSCs is Web site development. They produce Web sites for show/event organizers that include interactive floor plans, exhibitor show information, booth reservation services, and even personal itineraries for show attendees (Collins 1999).

Floor plan for Vancouver Convention Center is produced by a service contractor.   *Image by Canada-AV, used with permission*

ORGANIZATION OF A SERVICES CONTRACTING COMPANY

Service contractors are businesses, and like most businesses are organized into functional areas. This means that there are different departments grouped by a common activity or function that support the mission of the company. The department that controls and directs the company can be called "administration" and may include the general manager (GM) or CEO, marketing, assistants, receptionists, and the like. Some of the other departments or divisions are as follows:

- **Sales:** Typically divided or broken up into national sales and local sales or special events. Some companies also have a separate "exhibitor sales" department that takes over from national sales in dealing with exhibitors. Exhibitor sales will provide each exhibitor with an inventory of the supplies available and the cost of each item. Exhibitor sales also work to encourage exhibitors to "upgrade" from standard to superior quality products at a higher price. Exhibitor sales typically will have an office and full-time presence at the trade show to facilitate interaction between production and exhibitors, and sell additional products and services on the trade show floor.
- **Logistics:** Handles planning, scheduling, shipping, labor relations, site inspection with show/event organizer, and preparation. This is the department that determines the flow and delivery of booth materials—with booths in the center of the hall being delivered before booths by the doors so that access is not blocked. This department may also work with the exhibit facility and lay out all the different-sized booths, aisles, food service areas, registration, and so on. Today, this is done using computer technology known as CAD/CAM.
- **Drayage and Warehousing:** Transportation of materials, booths, exhibits, etc., along with their temporary storage in the host city. Drayage may include air transport, over-the-road tractor-trailer, and local transportation.
- **Event Technology:** Technology, special effects, reports. This department oversees the planning and subsequent installation of the output of the production department.
- **Event Services:** Exhibitor kits, on-site coordination, registration. The exhibitor kit tells exhibitors everything they need to know about the facility, capacities, rules, regulations, labor, and move-in and move-out times, along with the array of services provided by the service contractor.
- **Production:** Woodworking, props, backdrops, signs, electrical, lighting, metal work, and so on. At Freeman Decorating in New Orleans, clients regularly request backdrops that look like the French Quarter or a swamp. They are produced on large boards like

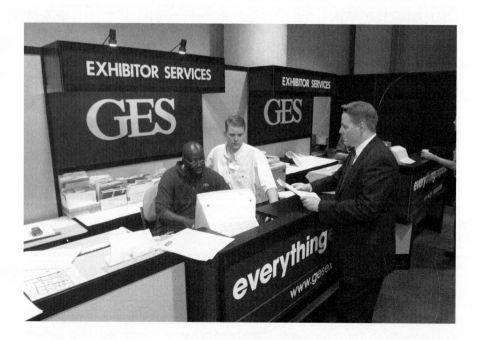

The primary communications link between show organizers and/or exhibitors and the ESC is the service center on the trade show floor.   *Photo provided by GES*

those used in theater productions. However, they are painted by two men who have worked there for years with the backdrop flat on the floor, the men standing up, using paint brushes like those used for oil painting—except that these paint brushes are five-feet long!

- *Accounting and Finance:* Accounts receivable, accounts payable, payroll, and financial analysis.

Two of the largest US GSCs are Freeman Decorating (http://www.freemanco.com) and GES Exposition Services (http://www.gesexpo.com).

The Freeman Companies have three divisions: Expositions, Events and Environments, and Exhibits. Their headquarters is in Dallas, Texas, and they have offices in 23 cities throughout North America. Begun in 1927, they are a full-service contractor for expositions, conventions, special events, and corporate meetings. The company is privately held and owned by the Freeman family and company employees.

GES Exposition Services is headquartered in Las Vegas, but has offices in all the major cities across North America. GES is a wholly owned subsidiary of Phoenix-based Viad Corp; a $1.7 billion publicly held corporation traded on the New York Stock Exchange under the symbol VVI.

In Canada, The Stronco Group of Companies is an all-Canadian privately owned company that was established in 1952. Stronco has been around since the earliest days of trade shows and conventions in Canada. For more than 50 years, it has been through it all, from trade shows and conventions to special performances, sporting events and conferences. Stronco has grown to be the largest privately owned full-service contractor in the trade show and convention services industry in Canada (www.stronco.com).

AV-Canada is a division of Canada, specializing in audiovisual, lighting, and staging (www.av-canada.com). Both bring their expertise across Canada and the United States. They are headquartered in Canada.

Here is a partial listing of full-service show services and general contractors at the time of printing. Included is a list of associations that can help you find a show services company where your event is taking place.

GES	www.ges.com (US & Canada)
Stronco Show Services	www.stronco.com (Canada)
AV-Canada	www.av-canada.com (Canada)
AVW TELAV	www.avtelav.com (US & Canada-member of the Freeman Group)
Freeman Group of Companies	www.freeman.com (US & Canada)
Stagevision	www.stagevision.com (Canada)

SPECIALTY SERVICE CONTRACTORS

To this point in the chapter, discussion has been about GSCs and how they interact with the individual exhibitor and the show/event manager. Now, the focus will broaden to all the potential service contractors that help to create a successful event. **Specialty service contractors** deal with a specific area of show/event production, whereas the GSC tends to be broad and generic. Specialty service contractors can either be official contractors (appointed by show/event management) or EACs (see below). They handle all the services to complete the production, whether a special event/tradeshow/conference or general meeting, including:

- *Audiovisual:* Services and supplies to enhance the exhibit/conference/special event through audiovisual methods.
- *Business Services:* Copying, printing, faxing, and other business services.
- *Catering:* Food and beverage for show/event organizers at the conference/special event and for individual exhibitors who may want to include food and beverage in their booth or at a private client event.
- *Cleaning Services:* Cleaning of public areas of the conference/event, especially carpet along with booths, offices, and nonpublic areas.

- *Communications:* Provides PDAs, cell phones, and wired and wireless services.
- *Computers:* Rental of computers and monitors.
- *Consulting:* This can include pre-event planning, coordination, facilitation, layout and design of the tradeshow/event/conference, and booth design. Often called third-party planners or independent consultants.
- *Décor:* Basic décor company that can enhance staging, general décor theme. Can also provide florals and entertainment.
- *Drayage:* This includes over-the-road transportation of materials for the show, transfers, and delivery of materials from a local warehouse or depot to the show site, airfreight, and returns.
- *Electrical:* Brings electrical power to the exhibits and any other areas that power may be required.
- *Entertainment Agency:* Provides entertainment and acts as liaison between entertainer and show/event organizer.
- *Floral:* Rental of plants, flowers, and props.
- *Freight:* Shipping of exhibit materials from the company to the show and back. There are various kinds of shippers—common carrier, van lines, and airfreight.
- *Furniture:* Rental of furniture for exhibit, often fancier than in your home!
- *Internet Access and Telephones:* Rental of equipment and lines on the show floor or any other area required for the event/conference.
- *Labor Planning and Supervision:* Expertise on local rules and regulations regarding what tradespeople to work with, union requirements, and supervision of workers on site.
- *Lighting:* Design and rental and lighting operators. Could be included with audiovisual supplier.
- *Staffings:* Temporary hiring of exhibit personnel or demonstration personnel, or registration.
- *Utilities:* Plumbing, air, gas, steam, and water for technical exhibits.
- *Photography:* For show/event organizers to provide publicity and to individual exhibitors.
- *Postal and Package Services:* For both organizers and exhibitors.
- *Registration Company:* A company outsourced to manage the entire registration process for an event/conference or tradeshow. They manage all registration processes, including database, payment, badges, and often on-site staffing.
- *Security:* Security to watch the booth during closed hours and to control the entrances when the show is open or general security for an event/conference.
- *Speaker Bureaus:* Work with show/event organizer to find ideal keynote speakers to open/close conference.
- *Translators:* Work with the show/event organizer to do simultaneous translation of speeches and presentations. They also work with exhibitors to provide communication between sales representatives and foreign attendees.

The Translator Who Knew Too Much

A small American company decided that it wanted to exhibit at a trade show in Europe. One of the things it determined was that none of the sales managers who were going to staff their booth spoke any language except English. So it was decided that a translator fluent in Spanish, Italian, and German would be hired. The translator worked so well that she was hired to provide services at another trade show a year later. At this second show, attendees asked many of the same questions asked at the first trade show. Since the questions were repetitive, the translator had learned the answers and would simply answer the attendee without translating and asking the sales managers. Response at this show was low, in spite of high attendance, and reactions to the products being displayed at the booth were poor. When the company manager did a post show assessment, he uncovered the reason. The attendees got the impression that since a mere translator knew about the products, they must be very simplistic and not cutting edge. So at all future trade shows, the translator was told to always translate, ask the sales managers, and never answer on her own!

Besides the standard needs listed earlier, each show has its own needs. A show in the food and beverage industry will have a contractor for ice and cold storage, while a show in the automotive industry might have a contractor who cleans cars.

EXHIBITOR-APPOINTED SERVICE CONTRACTORS

As companies do more and more shows, their exhibits become more involved, and they often want one service supplier working with them throughout the year. Or, they have a favorite vendor who they have worked with in a city where they do many shows. This is particularly true with regard to the installation and dismantling of the exhibit. Most times, show/event organizers will allow this, assuming that a company meets the qualifications for insurance and licensing. This company is called an EAC. As an EAC, they perform the same duties as a specialty contractor but only for that exhibitor, not the show manager. The convention industry council, APEX glossary definition is

Exhibitor Appointed Contractor (EAC) Any company other than the designated "official" contractor providing a service to an exhibitor. Can refer to an Install & Dismantle Company (I&D House), photographer, florist or any other type of contractor.

Some services may be provided only by the official service contractor and are called **exclusive services**. This decision is left up to the show/event manager who makes that decision based on the needs of the show and rules and regulations of the facility or to ensure the smooth move in and teardown of the show. Can you imagine what would happen if every freight company and installation company tried to move its exhibitors' freight in all at once? It would be chaos! So material handling (drayage) is a service that is often handled as an exclusive. Many facilities have very specific guidelines regarding the use of exhibitor appointed contractors. In some cases, the exhibitor must apply to the facility to use one.

RELATIONSHIP BETWEEN CONTRACTORS AND EVENT ORGANIZERS

One of the first actions that show/event organizers take when developing an event is to hire the GSC. This partnership develops as the show develops. GSCs will often recommend cities where a show should be held, the times of the year, and the facilities that fit the event. It is important to hire this company early on.

The process for hiring service contractors is through an **RFP**. The show organizer creates a list of questions and specifications for each show. Other areas of concern include knowledge of the industry, knowledge of the facility, other shows being handled in the same industry, size of the organization, and budget. A sample RFP can be found at http://conventionindustry.org/apex/panels/RFPs.htm.

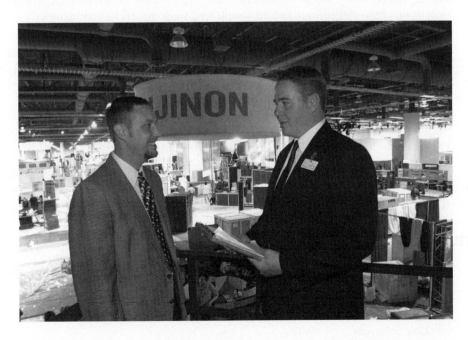

Representatives of the ESC work with show organizers and exhibitors to create a successful event. *Photo provided by GES*

As the show is developed, GSCs watch closely to suggest how marketing themes and association logos can be used in entrance treatments and signage so that when a show comes alive, it looks and feels the way the show organizer wants it. Color schemes, visual treatments, and types of materials all come from the mind of the GSC.

Specialty service contractors work with show organizers to help exhibitors save time and money. Reviewing the past history of a show can tell a service contractor what types of furniture, floral, and electrical needs the exhibitors have used. This permits the specialty contractors to offer money and time-saving tips to the show organizer and pass those savings on to exhibitors. All of this creates a feeling of goodwill among exhibitors who will continue to exhibit at the show.

After a time, the service contractor knows the show as well as the show organizer. This can be added value to the show organizer because as staff changes occur, the service contractor becomes a living historian of the show and its particular nuances.

RESOURCES IN THE SERVICE CONTRACTOR INDUSTRY

There are several associations for individuals and companies in the service contractor industry, including the following:

EIC: Exhibit Industry Council, formed in late 2009 to address the concerns from trade show exhibitors and to promote best practices for serving exhibitors at trade shows, exhibitions, and events. The associations forming the council are: Corporate Event Marketers Association (CEMA), Exhibit Designers & Producers Association (EDPA), Exhibitor Appointed Contractor Association (EACA), Healthcare Convention and Exhibitors Association (HCEA), and Trade Show Exhibitors Association (TSEA).

CEMA: Corporate Events Marketing Association (http://www.cemaonline.com/)

HCEA: Healthcare Convention and Exhibitors Association (http://www.hcea.org/)

Tradeshow Exhibitors Association (http://www.tsea.org/)

ESCA: Exhibition Services and Contractors Association (http://www.ESCA.org). Organization serving general and specialty contractors.

EDPA: Exhibit Designers and Producers Association (http://www.EDPA.com). Organization serving companies engaged in the design, manufacture, transport, installation, and service of displays and exhibits primarily for the trade show industry.

EACA: Exhibitor-Appointed Contractors Association (http://www.EACA.com). Representing EACs and other individual show-floor professionals that provide exhibit services on the trade show floor.

IAEM: International Association for Exhibition Management (http://www.IAEM.org). An association of show organizers and the people who work for service contractors.

CAEM: Canadian Association of Exposition Management (http://www.CAEM.ca). Canadian association of show organizers and the people who work for service contractors.

NACS: National Association of Consumer Shows (http://www.publicshows.com). Association of public (consumer) show organizers and the suppliers who support them.

EEAA: Exhibition and Event Association of Australia (www.eeaa.com.au)

CEIR: Centre for Exhibition Industry Research (www.ceir.org)

TSEA: Trade Show Exhibitors Association (www.tsea.org)

The example of ESCA indicates the professionalism that the various associations strive for. When looking for a show services contractor (or any contractor), be sure to check out the associations they belong to.

FUTURE TRENDS

- Healthy relationships between service contractors and planners will continue to be crucial to mutual success.
- Needs that encourage planners to build lasting relationship with suppliers are
  - competitive pricing
  - flexible contracts

Exhibition Contractors Associations

According to the Exhibition Services & Contractors Association Web site, ESCA is:

- The association for firms engaged in providing services and materials for the hospitality industry:

    Trade shows and exhibitions

    Conventions and meetings

    Sales meetings

- The voice of the exhibition service industry.
- A clearinghouse for the exchange of information between members and all other entities of the vast trade show and convention industry.
- A source for leading general service contractors, specialty contractors, independent contractors, and their suppliers.
- A source for discounts and assistance in the current business climate.

Mission Statement

ESCA is dedicated to the advancement of the exhibition, meeting, and special events industries. Through the education, information exchange, and level of professionalism shared by members and their customers, ESCA promotes cooperation among all areas of the exhibition industry.

Ethics Statement

Members of ESCA recognize the need for standards of professionalism in the relationship between contractor and customer and within the industry as a whole. They recognize that their customers come from every aspect of the exhibition, meeting, and special events industry, ranging from the organizer to the attendee. All ESCA members pledge themselves to conduct their business activities with integrity. ESCA members understand that they are responsible for the professional conduct of persons in their employ. Consequently, they undertake, through exemplary conduct at all times, to secure observance by their employees of this code of ethics.

ESCA members pledge themselves to act in accordance with the following principles of the ESCA code of ethics. Responsibilities of all members include the following:

1. *Accuracy.* ESCA members will provide factual and accurate information about their services and the services of any firm they represent. They will not use deceptive practices.
2. *Disclosure.* ESCA members will provide complete details about terms and conditions of any services, including cancellation and service fee policies, before accepting deposits.
3. *Delivery.* ESCA members will provide all services as stated in their agreement or written confirmation, or provide alternate services of equal or greater value, or appropriate compensation.
4. *Cooperation.* ESCA members will serve in a spirit of partnership with show management, other contractors, facilities management, and exhibitors.
5. *Responsiveness.* ESCA members will offer prompt, reliable, and courteous service at all times.
6. *Compliance.* ESCA members shall abide by all federal, state, and local laws and regulations.
7. *Regulations.* ESCA members will comply with all codes and standards regarding safety, performance, show rules, and regulations.
8. *Confidentiality.* ESCA members will treat every customer transaction confidentially and not disclose any information without permission of the customer, unless required by law.
9. *Conflict of Interest.* ESCA members will not allow any preferred relationships with suppliers and subcontractors to interfere with the interests of their clients.
10. *Disputes.* ESCA members will work with their customers to resolve disputes quickly and fairly, and if necessary, through mediation or then through arbitration.

Contact information for ESCA:
2260 Corporate Circle, Suite 400, Henderson, NV 89074-7701; E-mail: Info@ESCA.org.

- Preferred supplier programs are gaining more and more importance.
- contractors can play a key role in the "greening" of meetings and in sustainability
    - Reducing carbon footprint
    - Embracing use of recyclable materials
    - Using products that are locally produced
- Relationships will continue to be vital
- Service contractors will develop relationships with organizers, planners, and sponsors and help produce meetings and event in multiple locations.

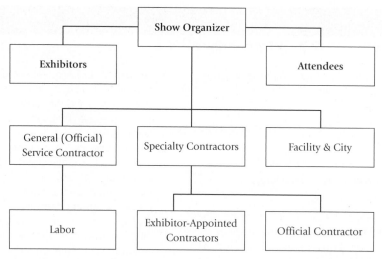

FIGURE 6-1 Relationship between show organizer and service contractors

SO HOW DOES IT ALL WORK?

Take a look at the organizational chart that follows, and you can see how the GSC interacts with the show/event organizer, the facility, the exhibitors, and the other contractors. Remember, exhibitions are like small cities, and the show organizer must provide everything a city does—from safety (security and registration) to a place to work (think of the exhibits as offices), electricity and water, and transportation (shuttle buses). But, it has to be done in a very short period of time, sometimes less than a week. Communication between everyone always must be functioning properly, and often it is the GSC who provides that conduit. The coordination of all the contractors likely is the responsibility of the GSC, who is acting as the right hand of the show organizer.

When you read this Case Study as it relates to September 11, 2001, keep in mind the need to have contingency plans in place. Also, keep in mind the need to ensure that all your contractors become a part of your team and are brought in as early in the process as possible. Each contractor understands its speciality and can add to the success. Each contractor will also have contingency and risk plans in place that the event organizer can add to the overall plans of the particular event/conference.

A Case Study of the Relationship Between Service Contractors and Show Organizers

On September 11, 2001, many exhibitions and events were in progress all over the world. Service contractors worked hand in hand with organizers to get shows moved out, and they held shipments for exhibitors while the airlines were not allowed to fly and trucks were being used to transport emergency equipment.

But, for the trade show industry, the most important factor post-9/11 was how to handle the cancellation of many of the events. Many people were afraid to fly. There were conventions and exhibitions scheduled for the Jacob Javits Convention Center in New York and the Washington area facilities that were being used by emergency crews. These shows were asked to move their dates or cancel. These decisions affected not only the show organizers but also the bottom line for the service contracting industry itself. Many organizations had already spent money on creating show entrances and graphics, and preparing staff to work the shows.

The partnership between show/event organizers and service contractors allowed a compromise. Service contractors billed show/event organizers only for materials purchased to date and then agreed not to receive payment until the show had been rescheduled. Exhibitors were not billed for services they had not used, but were asked to agree to use the same services at a later date. Everyone worked together to provide creative solutions.

Because of the partnership between service contractors and show/event organizers, the effect on trade shows of September 11 was somewhat minimized. Although the combination of the resulting economic slump and fear of travel hurt the technology shows, manufacturing shows showed only a 3% to 10% decline. Many of the shows to have been held immediately after September 11 that were canceled had successful 2002 shows, and there were indications that the future will be strong.

Summary

Service contractors are the backbone of the exhibition/event/conference industry. Their support structure, like the backbone, allows the show/event organizers and exhibitors to create an atmosphere that is smooth and efficient. Understanding the responsibilities of each contractor will allow a show/event organizer to offer the exhibitors the best possible service as well as creating a successful environment for buyers and sellers to do business in the exhibition format.

Key Words and Terms

For definitions, see GLOSSARY, or http://www.conventionindustry.org/glossary

Drayage	Exhibitor service manual	RFP
Exclusive service	General service contractor	Service contractor
Exhibitor-appointed contractor	Material handling	Specialty service contractor

Review and Discussion Questions

1. What types of services do specialty contractors provide?
2. What are some of the questions that should be asked in an RFP?
3. Describe the difference between a general (official service contractor) and an exhibitor-appointed contractor.
4. How can the GSC assist the show/event organizer as it prepares for the exhibition/event/conference?
5. You are the event manager of a large conference that includes a tradeshow component. The trucks are ready to move and the weather sets in. Winter storms are everywhere on the route. Who do you contact? What alternative plans can you make? What if the trucks can't get there in time to set up?

References

Collins, M. 1999. The evolution of the General Services Contractors. *Expo Magazine* (February): 1–5.

Rutherford, D. G. 1990. *Introduction to the Conventions, Expositions, and Meetings Industry.* New York: Van Nostrand Reinhold.

About the Chapter Contributor

Sandy Biback, CMP, CMM, has been involved in the of designing and implementing business events/conferences/tradeshows for over 30 years. Biback currently teaches meetings and conventions at the University of Nevada, Las Vegas, and George Brown College, Toronto, as well as courses in sponsorship design and risk management at Centennial College in Toronto. She is a member of Professional Convention Management Association (PCMA) and Canadian Society of Professional Event Planners (CanSPEP).

Contributor to previous editions: Susan L. Schwartz, CEM,

CHAPTER 7

Destination Management Companies

Chapter Outline

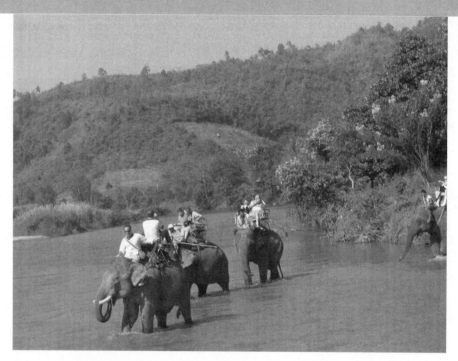

DMCs arrange ground transportation. In Thailand, that includes Elephant Transport.
Photo by George G. Fenich, Ph.D.

Chapter Objectives

After reading this chapter, the reader will be able to:

- Identify the needs that destination management companies meet for their clients.
- Explain how destination management companies interact with meeting planners, local hotels, event participants, and various suppliers within a destination.
- Describe how destination management business is conducted.
- List the competitive factors at work in the business process used by destination management companies.
- Evaluate what projects destination management companies should pursue.
- Detail how destination management companies deliver their contracted services to clients.

INTRODUCTION

One of the many career opportunities that exist within the MEEC industry is providing destination management services. These services include activities such as on-site meeting management, hotel services, convention centers and bureaus, airlines, and catering. Typically, when thinking about careers in the MEEC industry, one may not always consider working in the supplier side of the business. However, services provided at the event destination play a key role in the successful planning and execution of meetings, conventions, and events. This chapter will discuss the business and services provided by destination management companies (DMCs).

DEFINITION OF DESTINATION MANAGEMENT COMPANY

The Convention Industry Council (CIC), an organization of thirty-two affinity organizations that facilitate the exchange of information in the MEEC industry, defines DMCs in their Accepted Practices Exchange (APEX) glossary as:

> ***Destination Management Company*** A professional services company possessing extensive local knowledge, expertise and resources, specializing in the design and implementation of events, activities, tours, transportation and program logistics. Depending on the company and the staff specialists in the company, they offer, but are not limited to, the following: creative proposals for special events within the meeting; guest tours; VIP amenities and transportation; shuttle services; staffing within convention centers and hotels; team-building, golf outings and other activities; entertainment, including sound and lighting; décor and theme development; ancillary meetings and management professionals; and advance meetings and onsite registration services and housing.

Destination management companies may also go by the title of professional congress organizer or ground operator.

Destination management companies (**DMCs**) offer a critical layer of services and are hired by meeting and event planners to provide local knowledge, experience, and resources for corporate and association gatherings. DMCs work cooperatively with airlines, hotels and resorts, convention centers, and other service suppliers in the delivery and implementation of MEEC activities. Successful MEEC events require comprehensive local knowledge of destination infrastructure, local laws and statutes, and regulations. Meeting and event planners must work with local professionals who have qualified information about supplier availability, capabilities, and capacities, gained through actual project work to ensure a successful event.

When discussing DMCs and their services, the industry denotes this as the **client project**, which, be it a meeting, exhibition, event, or convention is typically referred to as a **program**. A program will include all activities and services provided by the DMC to the client while visiting a destination over a specified time.

SERVICES PROVIDED BY DESTINATION MANAGEMENT COMPANIES

Meeting and event planners work closely with DMCs to provide recommendations for destination resources that will best fit and satisfy the goals for a gathering. After these services are determined, a contract is written for the DMC to plan, set up, and deliver those services. Services typically offered by DMCs include:

- Hotel selection
- Event venue selection
- Creative itineraries
- Special event concepts
- Creative theme design
- Event production
- Sightseeing options
- Team-building activities
- Meeting support services
- Transportation planning and delivery
- Dining programs
- Entertainers
- Speakers
- VIP services
- Staffing services
- Budgeting and resource management
- Incentive Travel

DMC services facilitate networking among attendees, celebrating accomplishments, or the introduction of new ideas and/or products. In today's competitive environment, where the impact and return of investment of meetings and events are expected to be measured, planners rely on DMCs to provide unique and creative event concepts that will accomplish the specific goals of the event, be consistent with other activities carried out in the client's program, and stay within the client's budget. Full-service DMCs provide both meeting management support services, such as arrangements for transportation, and all aspects of event production, such as staging, sound, and lights. DMCs often are a reliable resource for entertainment solutions, from a small trio for background music at an intimate cocktail party to the headline entertainment for large **special events**. Familiarity and access to local musicians and entertainers is an important criterion when selecting a DMC. In addition, DMCs often suggest and supply décor such as props, floral designs, and decorations to enhance event spaces and venues.

Transportation logistics are often a key service provided by DMCs. These services include Airport "meet and greet" services, hotel transfers and baggage management, and shuttles. Moving groups of participants—large or small—is an important component of most events that require precise timing and execution, local expertise, and management responsibility. This is best provided by a professional DMC to ensure attendee comfort, convenience, and safety. In addition, many DMCs will provide customized sightseeing tours and recreational activities, such as golf and tennis tournaments.

Because of the creative element associated with meetings and events and the variety of each group's needs and expectations, the list of services that are provided by DMCs is almost limitless. It is important to note that while one client may require a DMC to manage and execute the entire event, another client may contract a DMC to provide only one or two components of the event.

Every element of an event must come together if success is to be achieved. *Used by permission of Paradise Light & Sound, Orlando, Florida*

DESTINATION MANAGEMENT COMPANY VS. DESTINATION MARKETING ORGANIZATION

The DMC business process has been compared to, and often confused with, the services provided by **destination marketing organizations** (**DMO**). Although very different organizations, there are some similarities between their services. DMOs optimize the exposure of a destination, leading it to develop innovative experiences for tourists, enabling the community to develop a sustainable infrastructure to ensure positive returns on investments.

Today's consumers expect a destination to offer customized product and service offerings that match their expectations. The destinations that manage to maximize the satisfaction levels of customers' expectations, and support consumers throughout the buying process, will be the ones to survive and yield maximum benefits. Therefore, DMOs work with the interests of both the community at large and the private companies that provide many of these services.

DMCs will often get leads on new accounts through requests by meeting and event planners that have gone through a DMO. Once the lead has been passed on by the DMO, the DMC will communicate through direct and electronic communications and presentations. These presentations almost always exhibit the DMC's competence using examples of their past successful programs. Once it has been established that the DMC has the expertise to meet the client's needs, it will respond to the client's **request for proposal** (**RFP**).

Typically, potential DMC customers will request that two or more DMCs bid on its program, based on a set of specifications in their RFP. Each DMC will then provide detailed, creative **proposals** for services, which will best satisfy the client's specifications. These proposals are almost always delivered free, intended to win the customer's favor, which is a major issue.

Responding to a client's RFPs is often a considerable cost and requires staff time to formulate a customized proposal; therefore, DMCs must choose wisely when determining what potential business to pursue. Today, the cost for collecting and submitting bids to client's RFPs is controlled by the development of standards for submitting these RFPs electronically. The Convention Industry Council has been a leader in the development of these standards, and templates for the electronic formats can be found and retrieved under the APEX guidelines.

Business Structure of DMCs

Some prerequisites are essential to the destination management process:

- Staff
- Temporary "field staff"
- Office
- Technology
- Licenses and insurance
- Community contacts
- Customer contacts
- History
- Destination resources

A strategically located office is a basic necessity to winning and operating business. Convenient proximity to major hotels, convention facilities, tourist attractions, and event venues is a must. In today's competitive environment, DMCs must have access to the best possible technology. DMC clients are usually associations and major corporations that are used to technology and expect to work with DMCs that are also accustomed to using electronic communications. Communications equipment, office computer capabilities (including database management), imaging software, and high-speed Internet are all expected to be standard tools in today's DMC. The quick processing of information and the ability to make on-the-spot changes and produce professional documents and graphics are becoming an industry standard and a necessity for DMCs.

Given the nature of the services provided by DMCs, they must be legally insured for business liability as well as other standard coverage such as workers' compensation and automobile insurance. Each destination will have unique laws and licensing requirements for the DMC's services. Meeting and event planners must ensure that their chosen business partners are adequately insured and knowledgeable about local ordinances that could affect the successful operation and production of their events.

As with many businesses in the service sector, destination management companies compete in a relationship-driven industry. Customers and planners will literally put their reputations and jobs on the line when selecting a DMC. DMC management and staff should have extensive community contacts among hotels, attractions, convention bureaus, airports, law enforcement, and the supplier community, and must articulate their commitment to building and sustaining positive relationships with their clients. It is through the cooperation from these business partnerships, gained through repeated work experiences, that a DMC can properly service the diverse needs of its clients.

Reputation outside of the destination community, that is, in the client community, is very important to the long-term success of a DMC. The most valuable asset a DMC has is its history of success, which is the best verification a planner can rely on when choosing a DMC partner.

Finally, the destination community must have the necessary resources to support the DMC in the execution of a well-run program or event. It must have a competitive service environment, with many suppliers that have good reputations.

THE DESTINATION MANAGEMENT COMPANY ORGANIZATION

Destination management companies come in a variety of sizes and organizational structures. Given the nature of the services that they provide, it is possible to get started in this business with little start up funding. This section will discuss the range of organizations that operate as DMCs.

Independent Operator

Independent destination management companies are often useful when only a limited or specific service is needed for the success of the event. These operators typically provide a limited array of targeted services such as catering, transportation operator, or tour organizer. The long-term success of independent DMCs is largely predicated on the ability of the owner to develop lasting relationships and goodwill by exceeding clients' expectations. Although it is relatively easy to start this business, the hours and challenges can be long and arduous.

Multi-services Operator

Destination management companies that offer multi-services are typically larger organizations rather than independent operators. Over time, these organizations establish large networks of service offerings. These multi-services suppliers have to be staffed with well-trained professionals who can put together complex, diverse client programs. Often the larger multi-services operator has staff and offices in multiple destinations and can offer its clients a significant advantage in securing high-quality services at a lower cost than can typically be found with an independent operator.

Destination Management Networks

Because local "one-destination DMCs" do not enjoy the same economy of scale that a national DMC such as USA Hosts would, networks of DMCs have been formed. An example of this is "The Network Companies." This group was formed in order to pool resources from individual one-city DMCs for sales and marketing purposes. Other such "DMC groups" exist primarily for the sharing of mutual sales and marketing efforts and expenses.

Destination management networks are a collection of independent destination management companies that pay a fee or commission to be affiliated with a national or regionally based organization. Destination management networks allow meeting and event planners the peace of mind when dealing with DMCs in unfamiliar locations. This arrangement allows for smaller, independent DMCs to remain autonomous while gaining significant advantages typically afforded to the larger multi-services, multi-destination DMCs.

In some cases, particularly with DMC networks, it makes sense to employ professional representation firms to call on particular market segments. Usually, this representation is contracted for a particular geographic location, such as New York, Chicago, or London. These companies typically call on potential and existing customers in the geographic area on behalf of a DMC network. They will seek to familiarize planners about the DMC network while uncovering leads for future business. When appropriate, these representation firms will sometimes also serve as a local liaison between the customer and a DMC partner.

BUSINESS MODEL OF DESTINATION MANAGEMENT COMPANIES

DMC clients are those who plan meetings, exhibitions, events, conventions, and incentive travel programs. When describing the business model of DMCs, the terms *customer*, *client*, and *planner* are used to describe the person, organization, or company for which the DMC is providing services. In some instances, the customer, client, and planner can be three separate entities or the same. The customer is the organization that will be securing and paying for the services provided by the DMC. The client is the representative of the organization who is in a leadership role when making the decision to purchase DMC services. The planner, representing the customer organization, is the person (or persons) whom the DMC works directly with planning and coordinating programs and events.

It is important to note that those who participate in the planning of the services provided by a DMC are almost always staff of the DMC, such as a corporate sales force. It is common for DMCs to service the leisure traveler or tour groups that partner outside of the DMC organization. Increasingly, the value of DMC services is being recognized by large tour operators, and they are often contracted to assist with transportation and/or tours for large groups. A good example of this is cruise ships that employ DMCs to manage land tours, transportation, and excursions.

A DMC may be contracted directly with an organization whose employees or members will be participating in the program, or it may contract with a professional meeting planner who is offering their meeting services to the participating organization (customer) (see flow chart).

Most meeting and event planners consider the DMC as a local extension of their own office while in the destination. They expect the DMC to be their "eyes and ears" in the destination, always acting on their behalf, offering unbiased, experience-based suggestions on logistics, venues, event concepts, and social program content. Planners depend on DMCs to help them design event programs that meet their specific needs, which can vary in size, budget, length, and purpose. For example:

FIGURE 7-1 Sample flow chart

Clients

Destination management companies receive business from several categories of customers. Their contracted programs may come from corporate, association, incentive-based, or special event clients.

CORPORATE ACCOUNTS Given the recent challenges facing the world economy, corporate clients organizing meetings are receiving greater scrutiny. In the past, **corporate meetings** holding a half-day of meetings while spending the remainder of their day on the golf course would not generate much attention. Today, just the location where the corporate meeting is being held can generate negative publicity. Destination management companies must be very sensitive to the constraints and attention that are facing corporate clients when planning and organization meetings.

In addition, corporate clients are reassessing the value of holding face-to-face meetings. It is very important that DMCs focus on working with their clients to ensure that the meetings and events have a higher level of value than could be achieved by not hosting a face-to-face event.

The following is a list of sample event programs that DMCs work on with corporate clients:

- National sales meetings
- Training meetings
- Product introductions
- Dealer and/or customer meetings

ASSOCIATION ACCOUNTS Associations are organizations that are created to support an industry, common interest, or activity. Associations can range from local, state, regional, national, and international groups. Most associations exist to provide networking and educational opportunities to their membership. In carrying out these activities, associations will hold a variety of meetings, conventions, and conferences.

In today's competitive environment, potential conference/convention attendees are being more selective as to which meetings they will attend. Attending a meeting out of town is costly in time and money. The factors involved include the return of investment that the individual believes they will receive by attending the event. DMCs can provide considerable resources and support to help clients create events that will be offered to their membership with the highest impact. The following is a list of sample event programs that DMCs work on with association clients:

- Industry trade shows (food, construction, aircraft, etc.)
- Professional trade shows and conferences (for architects, doctors, teachers, etc.)
- Fraternal organizations (VFW, Lions, etc.)
- Educational conferences (medical symposia, other professional groups)
- Political conventions

INCENTIVE-BASED ORGANIZATIONS Incentive-based meetings and events are organized to recognize and reward employees who have reached or exceeded company targets. This segment of the meetings and event market continues to experience rapid growth. Today's organizations are recognizing the value of providing rewards and recognition for employees' outstanding performance. These events can typically last between three and six days in length and can range from a modest to extravagant getaway for employees and their partners. DMCs can provide the organizing client a range of services that are customized based on the budget of the organization and the desires of the employee. The following is a list of sample event programs that DMCs work on with incentive-based clients:

- Sales incentives
- Dealer incentives
- Service manager incentives

DESTINATION MANAGEMENT COMPANY PROCESS

Unlike hotels, resorts, convention centers, and restaurants, a DMC does not require an extensive capital investment to start up and operate its business. The DMC office is usually located in office space somewhere near the location where most meetings and events take place. Proximity to major airports can be an advantage, since so many program services involve group arrivals and departures.

Primary responsibilities and job titles for a DMC vary from company to company. Many DMCs are small, stand-alone, single-office companies that are locally owned. Other larger companies may have offices in multiple destinations with local staff fulfilling management responsibilities on all levels. (See table and organizational chart that follows.)

Table 7-1 Categories of DMC Job Responsibilities, with Sample Job Titles

Management and Administration
- General Manager
- Office Manager
- Accounting Manager
- Executive Assistant
- Administrative Assistant
- Receptionist
- Research Assistant

Sales and Marketing
- Director of Sales
- Director of Marketing
- Director of Special Events
- Sales Manager
- Sales Coordinator
- Proposal Writer
- Research Analyst

Operations and Production
- Director of Operations
- Director of Special Events
- Operations Manager
- Production Manager
- Transportation Manager
- Staffing Manager

Field Staff
- Meet and Greet Staff
- Tour Guide
- Transportation Manager
- Event Supervisor
- Field Supervisor
- Equipment Manager

To be successful, a DMC's job tasks include finding business leads, proposing appropriate services, contracting services, organizing the group's arrival, delivering the contracted services, and following up with billing and program reconciliation. These task areas are carried out by contracting with supplier companies, hiring **field staff**, and assigning program staff. Field staff, who carry out such functions as tour guides, hospitality desk staff, and airport "meet and greet" staff, are usually temporary casual employees who are hired by a DMC only for the term of the program. It is common for field staff in a destination to work for more than one DMC as the needs arise for their services.

The job titles listed above are examples and will vary from company to company. However, sales and promotion responsibilities, operations and production responsibilities, and management and administrative responsibilities are the basic responsibilities of all DMCs. As in most companies, the levels of authority and reporting lines do vary and are usually based on the size of the company and the qualifications of its staff. For example, a "Director of Special Events" title may appear under both the Sales and Marketing function and the **Operations and Production** function. The position can be either or both, depending on the company and the individual executive's area of expertise.

In many cases, DMCs do not own transportation equipment, props, décor, or other supplies that the DMC packages and sells to its customers. It is common for DMCs to buy or rent from selected suppliers and manage these products and services in the context of the larger event program. As such, the DMC becomes a "contractor" for the services of a myriad of local supplier companies.

FIGURE 7-2 Sample DMC organizational chart

A critical characteristic for the long-term success of DMCs is the ability to objectively recommend and select suppliers for the services contracted. A DMC's value proposition to meeting planners depends on their ability to select the best provider for the services that meet the client's budget and program specifications. Clients must feel confident that the DMC is earning its money for the management services provided and not from some inflated financial "arrangement" made with the supplier companies.

The Sales Process

For DMCs to be successful, new business projects must be continually found and secured for the company. Business opportunities may present themselves in a variety of ways. Not all DMCs service all the clients listed earlier in the chapter. Some DMCs have created successful businesses by specializing in associations' convention business, corporate meetings, or international travel groups. Some DMCs may work with individual travelers, while others focus heavily on the domestic incentive market. However, most DMCs operate in multiple markets, which are usually determined by the nature of their destination.

In other words, the infrastructure and appeal of the destination will often dictate which of the above market segments DMCs will do business with. A destination's infrastructure such as its convention centers, convention hotels, resorts, and airport facilities all play into the equation. Other destination assets such as natural and man-made attractions play heavily into whether or not corporations will plan important meetings and/or incentive travel rewards in a location. Beaches, forests, weather, recreational facilities, fishing, arts, gambling, and theme parks all can enhance a destination's appeal.

Identifying New Business Opportunities

The first stage of the sales process is to discover new business opportunities and pursue those leads. Almost all new business opportunities involve going where the customers are or where the customers do business, such as attending industry trade shows. Some examples of these trade shows are the American Society of Association Executives (ASAE), the Center for Association Leadership, Incentive Travel & Meetings Exposition (IT&ME), and Meetings West. Sales executives representing DMCs must carefully research these trade shows to maximize their sales and marketing resources. Knowing in advance which potential customers will attend and knowing what business opportunities they represent will ensure an increase in the DMC's prospects for creating new client relationships.

Some customers, particularly corporate customers, incentive companies, and meeting management companies, will designate a "preferred" DMC in selected destinations. For DMCs, this is known as a "house account." Whenever house account planners require services, the chosen DMC can help without going through the often-onerous competitive bidding process. These accounts are very important and require careful maintenance. There is considerable competition for them, and competing DMCs are always active in their attempts to take over these accounts. Periodic visits to these customers, and open lines of communication are vital in maintaining these relationships. In addition to continued good service, part of the successful "maintenance" of these relationships may include membership in the same industry organizations as the planners. Attending these organizations' conferences and meetings allows DMC representatives to visit and network among existing and potential planner clients.

Sales efforts at the destination level are considered by most DMCs to be an important part of the sales plan. Creating relationships with local industry representatives who are conducting business with the same customers and planners is an efficient way for DMCs to identify new business opportunities. For example, networking at local hospitality industry functions, such as local Hospitality Sales and Management Association International (HSMAI) monthly meetings or convention bureau "mixers," is a common practice among successful DMCs. In addition, staying abreast of industry news, people who work in the industry, and knowing changes in services and staffing within the local industry make for a well-informed DMC.

Collateral materials are essential to a comprehensive sales and marketing plan. Collateral materials include brochures, letterheads, business cards, proposal shells, and fact sheets for the various activities and services offered by the DMC. In addition to these materials, a DMC will often produce a company newsletter to enhance the company's image and recognition in the industry.

During this phase of the business process, the participants that are actively engaged can fluctuate, requiring the DMC management to constantly monitor costs and other details. With the active involvement by the client, activities and services may be added or removed from the program during this phase. It is important that the DMC representatives are available, responsive, and note these changes. As a contracted member of the customer's team, the DMC is responsible for the destination management portion of the larger, overall customer event—therefore, the DMC must be fully cooperative and flexible. The program's project manager, either an operations or events manager, will assume primary responsibility for the entire program or event. During the setup period, each activity and service for the program is reviewed and confirmed in detail. Full-time and part-time professional program managers, supervisors, tour guides, and escorts are scheduled well in advance.

Program Execution

Destination management companies require the coordination of staff and suppliers into one cohesive program of products and services. After finding the opportunity, creating proposals, earning the planner's confidence, contracting the program, and careful preparations, it is up to the operations and production staff to successfully deliver the program. At this point, everything is "on the line": The image of the customer organization, the reputation of the planner, future prospects for the DMC with the planner, the DMC's reputation in the destination, and the opportunity to profit from the contract are all at risk.

The successful execution of the client's program is very important. If the program is for a large association's convention, the members' perception of the organization is at stake. The American Medical Association, the American Bar Association, and the National Automobile Dealers Association are examples of associations that employ a DMC. Meeting and event planners for these associations are orchestrating major events with thousands of participants on an ongoing basis. The participant's perception of the convention can easily be affected by the quality of the shuttle transportation to and from the convention hall, the quality of the networking events, cocktail parties, meal service, and activities like the annual golf tournament and optional sightseeing tours. All of these services are potentially the DMC's responsibility. The events must live up to the participants' expectations. The activities and tours must be entertaining and well run. The participants are the association planner's customers, and membership renewals and future convention attendance will be affected by the quality of the program delivery.

Similar dynamics are in effect with corporate programs. The annual new model dealer shows for automobile manufacturers have millions of dollars riding on their outcome. Insurance companies reward top sales producers with **incentive programs** that effectively show the best of

DMCs may arrange outdoor performances. *Used by permission of Paradise Light & Sound, Orlando, Florida*

their workforce how the company's top executives value their contributions. Computer companies and software companies produce new product introduction events either as stand-alone events or in conjunction with industry conventions. Often the success of these events has the future of the sponsoring companies at stake.

Through these examples, one can clearly see the tremendous pressure of running a logistically sound and high-quality program. These pressures are riding on the shoulders of the meeting and event planners and the DMCs. The DMC's operations and production staff have one chance to deliver the program. When mistakes or missteps occur, the event cannot be rescheduled for the next day. If the bus and limousine suppliers do not provide equipment as ordered, the departure time cannot be changed. It is the reliability of execution that is the most important issue in the success of a program; price runs a distant second to reliability. However, all DMCs are not equal, and choosing the best fit for a particular program is essential. A close working relationship that fosters confidence, easy communication, and mutual understanding requires that the planner's DMC contact be readily available. Likewise, the planner must be immediately available to the DMC's operation manager throughout the course of the program.

Transportation Services

Transportation management is often a major part of a DMC's business. It encompasses routing, vehicle use, staff requirements, special venue considerations, equipment staging areas, staff scheduling and briefings, maps, and signage. Transportation scenarios and requirements are usually scattered throughout the program itinerary.

Corporate programs usually begin with airport transfers. Airport transportation services customarily include "meet and greet" service and luggage management. Management of the arrival manifest by the airport transportation manager is a key component of the service. The arrival manifest is a detailed list of each guest's name, arrival flight, and time. The manager schedules with the arrival manifest as a guide. People change flights, miss flights, fail to accurately supply flight information, and flights can be delayed or canceled. Because of the inaccuracies common to arrival manifests, the transportation manager must not only expect surprises, but plan for them. Constant communication is necessary between the DMC and the airlines, the transportation equipment suppliers, and the airport meet and greet staff. Equally important is the need to keep open communication with the hotel(s) to which the participants are being transferred and the meeting planner, who may be receiving information about individual participants' changes in travel plans.

Meet and greet services are not limited to the United States. Ugandan dancers and others welcome the Malaysian prime minister.   *Courtesy of Caris Mamu AP Wide World Photos*

When airport transfers are run properly, the participants receive a friendly welcome by someone who knows their name, after which they are directed to the proper baggage belt to identify their luggage. Motorcoaches, minibuses, vans, sedans, and limousines could all be used. A DMC must proactively manage the changes and challenges of airport transportation. The first impression made on a participant is the arrival transfers, and the last impression is the departure transfers.

Transportation requirements of clients often include shuttle services between event venues and the participating hotel(s). Shuttle supervisors, dispatchers, and directional staff, sometimes referred to as "human arrows," manage this personalized service. Whatever the transportation requirement, the DMC is expected to plan, prepare, and deliver the service in a timely and efficient manner.

Production of Events

Event production is also typically a major part of a destination management company's services. Events can be large or small, on a hotel property, or in a remote location. Some examples of events are:

- Cocktail receptions and networking events
- Breakfasts, luncheons, and dinners
- Dining events at unique venues
- Gala dinner events
- Extravagant theme parties
- Outdoor and indoor team-building events

The following are examples of purposes for clients to hold events:

- Events to promote corporate staff and top executives to meet and mingle with their company's middle management
- Events to provide an opportunity for the company's sales people to interact with their largest customers and dealers of the company's products
- Events on the final night of an incentive program with the intent to "knock the socks off" of the attendees and fire them up about the next sales campaign
- Events to provide a casual atmosphere for company employees to network and renew acquaintances since the last meeting

A big challenge for DMCs is large "extravaganza" events. In these events, the production staff must manage the event venue, security, and countless other details. The experience of the DMC management and staff is essential. Holding preliminary meetings that bring together the key suppliers to discuss and provide input on the production schedule is a fundamental step in the planning process. Realistic setup/move-in schedules and cooperative suppliers ensure a smooth-running event.

Operational staff must be familiar with all the necessary municipal regulations regarding insurance, fire safety codes, crowd control, and police requirements. When considering all these issues, there is no substitute for experience, and working with a DMC that has a known track record of success is very important.

Whether planning and operating sightseeing tours, a scavenger hunt, a golf tournament, or running a hospitality desk, strong organizational skills, sound preparation, and a sense of commitment and responsibility are essential traits for a professional DMC operations manager. When everything is riding on the performance of the firms, planners will often bond with the managers and become dependent on them to be their on-site consultants in the community.

Meeting and event planners will often have to deal with on-site questions and requests for VIP arrangements with little advance notice, and the DMC staff will support them in securing appropriate arrangements. Some examples of last minute requests that DMCs are asked to take care of are:

"Where can I send my VP of marketing and her husband for a romantic dinner? She just realized that today's their wedding anniversary!"

"My company president is arriving early in the corporate jet. Can we get a limo to the executive airport in forty-five minutes?"

"The boss just decided he wants a rose for all of the ladies at tonight's party."

"Can we get Aretha Franklin to sing 'Happy Birthday' to one of our dealers during her set at the party tonight?"

A wise person once said, "It is often the little things, the details that separate great events from ordinary ones." Knowing someone's favorite wine, song, or dessert can turn an ordinary event into one that will be remembered forever. These are things that are not included in the contract, but add special touches to an event and are a great opportunities for the production staff to demonstrate their passion of service to the client. A production manager who has developed strong relationships with suppliers can often count on their suppliers to be swept up in the process and suggest ideas for program improvement on their own. Suppliers will do this because they want the event to be the best to establish an ongoing relationship with the DMC for possible future events. Planners are often pleased to be presented with options. For example, being offered confetti cannons for the dance floor area, additional accent lighting, or separate martini bars are all on-site event upgrades.

DMC operations and production managers must be knowledgeable about every facet of the programs and events that they manage. They must be knowledgeable about the customer, the destination, the group's participants, the event venues, the suppliers, the staff, and many other factors. On-site challenges and changes are a fact of doing business for DMC's staff. As a result, operations and production managers must constantly be troubleshooters, looking for what might be an issue later in the program and keeping the planner aware of every important detail that changes or may need to be changed.

Much of an operations or production manager's day is spent confirming and reconfirming services. Constant communication with vendors and suppliers is critical to ensure that final participant counts and timing are accurate. One common task to ensure success of events is the "advancing" of a venue, which is when DMC staff arrives well ahead of a group to make sure that the service staff and the event location are prepared and properly set up. Details such as the number of seats, room temperature, serving instructions, menu inclusions, and beverage service are all examples of items that should be verified when advancing a dinner event.

Operations and production managers are a trusted source of information for the planners, serving as community liaisons for the DMC's customers. DMC representatives are typically asked to recommend restaurants, golf courses, beauty salons, doctors, dance clubs, antique shops, and other service providers. DMC representatives are expected to be experts in all facets of their community for their clients.

Throughout each event, operations and production managers must carefully monitor the original contracted services and all changes that occur after the original itinerary and contracts. Every addition to the program, such as changes in participant counts, times of service, and additional services, must be documented. Accurate, up-to-the-minute data on the actual services delivered must be kept for billing purposes. To avoid billing disputes, it is also important to identify that an authorized representative for the client has accepted the change or addition. Ideally, these authorizations are in writing and approved in advance by the client.

Wrap-Up and Billing

The final invoice for a program should mirror the contract of services agreed upon prior to the execution of the program. Actual services delivered should be outlined along with the number of participants that each charged item is based on. In most cases, items are billed on "lot" costs or on a per-person basis. Lot costs are fixed and independent of the number of participants, such as bus hours, the price of an entertainer, or a décor package for a ballroom. Per-person pricing is based on the actual number of participants, such as food and beverage at a luncheon that is billed at a fixed price per person, plus tax and gratuities.

All additions or deletions to the originally contracted services should appear on the invoice. The "grand total" for the program should be reflected along with all deposits and payments received prior to the final billing. When possible, final billing details should be reviewed and approved by the planner or representative on-site at the completion of the program, while details about the program's operation, additions, and changes are still fresh in everyone's mind. The more time that elapses between the time the program is completed and receipt of the final invoice, the more likely there will be disputes about program details, such as participant counts, times, and items that were approved to be added to the program.

FINDING AND SELECTING A DESTINATION MANAGEMENT COMPANY

When the time comes that meeting and event planners need to find and select a DMC, there are several steps and guidelines that are helpful in ensuring a successful outcome. When searching for DMC candidates, it is best to begin with contacting industry professionals that are managing and executing meetings on a regular basis. One of the best benefits of networking is to have contacts that can be called on to provide advice and guidance when searching for suppliers. If the meeting and event planner is lacking suitable connections, contacting industry groups, such as PCMA, MPI, and ASAE, can be a valuable source. Also, the destination's **CVB** or DMO will have listings of DMCs that operate in and around its destination.

Once a list of potential DMCs has been identified, it is time to identify the best of the group. Factors that may be important before soliciting the RFP selection include:

- How long the company has been in business?
- What are the experience levels of the management and staff?
- What are the perceptions of the planner with the personalities of the management team?
- Is the DMC an affiliated member of any meeting and events professional organizations?
- Is the DMC adequately bonded, relative to the size and complexity of the program?
- What is the quality of the references provided by the DMC both in size of previous programs and ranking of professional providing the references?

The next step in the process is selecting a DMC that best meets the needs and budgetary guidelines. At this point, meeting and event planners should formally notify potential DMCs by a RFP. Once the final selection has been made, it is important to begin working with the selected DMC to ensure that they have historical information related to the organization's participants that may impact the execution of the program.

DESTINATION MANAGEMENT COMPANY RESOURCES

As local experts positioned to assist planners with their programs in a destination, DMCs are expected to provide vital resources for meeting and event planners. The following is a list of examples of what DMCs are called upon to provide recommendations and guidance on.

- *Products:* The products that a DMC offers are presented in a portfolio of services. Besides logistical services, which consist primarily of transportation and related support staffing, these services may also include creative elements that the DMC has designed for the client, such as theme parties, customized tours, and creative team-building activities. The generation of new ideas to meet the changing needs of clients is necessary to remain competitive. The generation of new ideas is a valuable commodity, and DMCs have experienced difficulties with maintaining control of this intellectual property. It is unethical to "borrow" a DMC's creative idea without employing the DMC to execute the idea.
- *Reputation:* A key asset for any DMC is a track record of customer satisfaction. As service is the DMC's primary product, client satisfaction is the best indicator of a DMC's reputation and the ability to meet the needs of its clients. It is often said that a DMC is only as good as the last program or event it has completed. Equally important is the DMC's reputation among the local suppliers. It is critical for the DMC to establish good relationships with key suppliers and for the DMC to have a reputation as a quality, professional company.
- *Experience:* Possibly the most valuable advantage a planner will look for in a DMC is its experience in the industry. Given the almost infinite number of challenges a DMC can face in the course of doing business, experience is often the best teacher. Using a company that has been through the trial and error process is often very important. Considering the relative ease of entry into the DMC business (primarily due to low start-up costs), experience is a critical element that distinguishes newcomers from established professional DMCs.
- *Relationships:* One of the key resources that a DMC is expected to bring to the table is its relationships. In addition to established relationships with quality suppliers, it is also important that it has working relationships with airports, hotels, and other people who can "get things done." The term *destination savvy* is often used to describe DMCs that have the right connections and knows how to use them.

DMCs may make special arrangements for models, this one in costume. *Photo by George G. Fenich, Ph.D.*

- *Suppliers and Vendors:* Other than local knowledge, in many cases everything that a DMC sells to a planner must be purchased from other supplier companies. The DMC is expected by clients to have an inventory of competent, high-quality suppliers who will deliver the services in the final program. A DMC is expected to know the best of the available caterers in the area that have the ability and experience to meet the specific needs and demographics of a group. This knowledge and experience is required for all supplier categories, including transportation equipment, props, lighting, sound equipment, and entertainers. The DMC is expected to know the appropriate combinations of suppliers that make an event a success, and equally important is to know what suppliers not to use. A stable of reliable vendors and suppliers are critical for a successful program.
- *Credit and Buying Power:* The DMC should have ongoing relationships in its community. It should develop good credit ratings through business volume and professional business dealings with hotels, supplier companies, and the independent staff who works for them year round. Unexpected things can, and do happen that require changes and additional services to be added on-site. The DMC must have the "clout" and "buying power" to make things happen quickly and without incident in the eyes of the client or participants.

FUTURE TRENDS

The destination management industry's varied representatives are not immune to the need for change. The following is a list of seven areas that DMC operators should take seriously in order to enhance their leadership and stature in meeting and event management circles and beyond.

1. *Take the Lead in Green Practices.* Be proactive in initiating sustainable practices by implementing leading edge methods for leaving a smaller carbon footprint, educating other parts of the hospitality industry through professional organizational training activities and the development and distribution of training materials. In addition, DMCs should develop new partnerships to share these activities and materials with other businesses in both the private and public sector.
2. *Work Together in Consortiums.* The DMC industry will continue to see a consolidation of service organizations. It will be important for smaller, niche DMCs to bond together in

Brief Case Study: Tourism Crisis and Its Link to Sustainability
By Dr. David Beirman (Senior Lecturer Tourism University of Technology, Sydney Australia)

The Implications of the September 2009 Tsunami in Samoa on Sustainable Coastal Accommodation

On September 28, 2009, an earthquake measuring 8.3 on the Richter scale occurred about 100 kilometers south of the southern coast of the Samoan island of Upolu. The quake generated a massive tsunami, which inundated much of the southern coast of the island of Upolu (Samoa) and large areas of American Samoa. The tsunami caused the deaths of an estimated 144 people (including 10 foreign tourists) in Samoa and a further 65 in America Samoa. Many more people were injured and in Samoa alone over 10,000 people (6% of Samoa's population) were rendered homeless.

The tsunami was especially damaging to the Samoan tourism industry, as many of the Pacific island nation's major coastal resorts were located directly in the path of the tsunami, and all coastal resorts on Samoa's southern and SE coast sustained damage. All the tourists who were killed as a consequence of the tsunami were guests in coastal resorts. The publicity generated by the disaster has proven to be a major challenge to the Samoan tourism industry, and the tourism industry is struggling to restore market confidence in the destination despite the fact that many parts of Samoa including the capital city Apia were untouched by the tsunami.

Since the Indian Ocean tsunami of December 26, 2004, most coastal tourism areas have upgraded tsunami warning systems and procedures; but in this particular case, the time that elapsed from the earthquake to the tsunami actually hitting the southern coast of the Samoan island of Upolu was around ten minutes. Many of the victims were inundated whilst attempting to flee the massive tsunami waves.

As was the case following the 2004 Indian Ocean tsunami and the more recent Samoa event, resort owners and hoteliers are obliged to deal with a challenging question. Should coastal resort owners continue to yield to market demand to place their rooms, bungalows, fales, condos, lanais, or shacks either at the water's edge or as is often the case in upmarket Pacific and Caribbean resorts, over the water? This practice is clearly appealing to guests at resorts, and many resorts respond by placing their most expensive accommodation as close to the ocean as possible. During the Samoan tsunami at two neighboring up market resorts, on the South coast of Upolu, Sinalei Resort, and Coconuts Resort, the most expensive accommodation at each resort suffered the most extensive damage, and not surprisingly in both cases the most expensive accommodation was closest to the sea and most vulnerable to a tsunami wave.

The 2009 Samoan tsunami and the far more extensive damage that was experienced in tourism resorts in Thailand in the 2004 Indian Ocean tsunami oblige coastal resort owners to carefully consider the safety of their guests with at least the same degree of concern about ensuring them a water view. Sustainable planning principles for coastal resorts need to factor in sea surges, tsunamis, hurricanes, and similar storms in planning resort accommodations. This includes planning escape routes, but these recent events also make it necessary to minimize exposure of guests and staff to potential inundation.

Access to the ocean and a sea view is clearly a marketing asset, but hoteliers and resort owners have an ethical and business obligation to minimize the risk of inundation, however slight or infrequent that risk may be. There is also a high level of self-interest involved here. In today's highly litigious society, guests who may be victims of inundation are almost certain to sue the resort, which could incur a far greater cost than the material damage caused by a natural disaster.

Are destination marketing organizations or destination marketing authorities able to impose building or location regulations? In practice, this does not happen. Building and zoning codes normally come under the jurisdiction of either local government authorities or in some cases (especially national parks) state or provincial governments. In very rare cases, mainly for defense establishments, jurisdiction may be exercised by national governments. However, destination authorities and organizations are in a position to exercise influence. Destination authorities and organizations do have a role in licensing, accreditation, and grading of a wide range of tourism and hospitality orientated facilities and enterprises. In this respect, there is the possibility of grading coastal resorts on the basis of risk or lack of risk, placing pressure on resort owners and developers to locate and construct accommodation, which take risk minimization into account.

After the Indian Ocean tsunami, the Thai national government and the provincial authorities of Phuket established upgraded building and location codes for coastal tourism accommodation designed to minimize the risk of guest accommodation being subject to inundation. However, rather than waiting for governments to impose such regulations, the planners and developers of coastal resorts should factor the risk inundation in their planning and construction of coastal tourism resorts. Destination management companies must also take action not to support suppliers who fail to act in the best interests of visitors to their communities.

consortiums to ensure that business remains in the local community and that the overall experience for meeting and event planners is seamless from planning, execution, and payment.

3. *Identify and Develop New Business from Drive-To Markets.* Given the uncertainty of the economy and the unfriendly skies, businesses will begin to look for more local and regional sites for holding their meetings and events. This should lead DMCs to focus on developing new clients from locations that are closer to their destinations.
4. *Develop Crisis Networks.* Issues surrounding the safety and security of meeting attendees will continue to be a concern for corporations and associations. Successful DMCs will develop, implement, and execute crisis plans and business continuity networks in partnerships with other organizations within their communities.

5. *Emphasize Standards of Conduct and Operations.* DMCs will continue to receive scrutiny about the behavior of staff used to provide client services. It will become increasingly important that DMCs implement high standards of conduct for their employees and operations. The standards and operational policies should be defined, recognized, and understood by every employee, client, and the public in general as part of an established image and reputation.

6. *Relationship Management Strategy.* Corporations and associations that conduct business and meeting travel are quickly consolidating their travel, meeting, and event expenses into a more economically efficient model. Local and niche DMCs will need to build strong, lasting relationships with meetings and event planners to ensure that they are on the list of approved vendors.

7. *Attentive to Competitive Forces.* Given the ubiquity of the Internet, and its convenience, successful large DMCs no longer need a continuous presence in a local market. Local, niche DMCs will need to increase the quality of customer contacts and services to meetings and events planners and their attendees, to remain relevant in a competitive marketplace.

Summary

The niche that destination management companies (DMCs) provide in the MEEC industry is important for meeting and event planners. These organizations provide a crucial service because the customer companies and organizations that sponsor meetings and events will always need access to local expertise. The depth of local destination knowledge, the local contacts and connections, the community standing, buying power, and hands-on experience with the implementation of programs and events are not readily available to organizations outside of the destination. DMCs have evolved in some interesting ways. Many of the earlier DMCs evolved from the ranks of wholesale tour operators and ground operators. These early DMCs began by specializing in tours and transportation services for visiting travel groups. In the late 1950s, the specialization in association and higher-end corporate programs demanded a wider range of services, including dining programs, expanded activities, and special events.

Today, the competitive landscape of DMCs is filled multidestination, national DMC companies that operate networks around the world. However, just as individual one-of-a-kind hotels still prosper along with the giant hotel chains, so do unique and specialized one-destination DMCs. The services requested of DMCs by meeting and event planners are still evolving, and destination management services have been secured as a key component for success in meetings and events industry.

Today's network of professionals that work in the destination management segment of the MEEC industry have a wide range of industry associations for support. Founded in 1995, **ADME** is committed to the initiative that professional destination management is a critical and necessary component to every successful meeting or event. As a primary goal, ADME continuously seeks to identify and promote the value of destination management as a necessary resource for planners of meetings, events, and incentive travel programs. ADME's goals also include becoming the definitive source of information, education, and issues-based discussion of destination management for the meetings, events, incentive, and hospitality industries.

Professionals holding positions in the destination marketing field have the ability to gain an important professional designation. The designation of Destination Management Certified Professional (DMCP) was introduced by ADME in January 2000. This professional certification is only available to individuals who have qualified for an extensive examination administered by ADME. Applicants are screened through a detailed questionnaire, which chronicles the applicant's experience and industry education. For more information about ADME, visit their Web site at http://www.adme.org.

The long-term outlook for DMCs is bright. The meeting and event industry that DMCs support is robust, and many existing firms are financially sound and poised to gain market share and increase their brand recognition despite temporary threats and business slowdowns. The industry is full of opportunities for long-term successful career options for new meeting and event professionals.

Key Words and Terms

ADME	DMC	Incentive programs	request for proposal (RFP)
Client project	DMO	Operations and Production	Site inspection
Corporate meetings	Field staff	Program	Special events
CVB	History	Proposal	VIP services

Review and Discussion Questions

1. What is a destination management company?
2. What services are offered by DMCs?
3. Compare and contrast the difference between a DMC and a DMO.
4. Create an organizational chart for a DMC.
5. How do DMCs generate their business leads?
6. What are the resources DMCs provide to a meeting and event planners?
7. Describe the differences between the types of accounts that secure the services of DMCs.
8. What professional organizations support the professionals that work destination management industry?
9. List the services provided by DMAI.
10. Describe key factors that are considered when meeting and event planners are selecting a DMC.

About the Chapter Contributor

Brian Miller is Associate Professor of hospitality operations and technology in the Department of Hotel, Restaurant, and Institutional Management at the University of Delaware. Prior to joining the ranks of academe, Brian spent over 17 years working in hotels, restaurants, and event venues, servicing meetings and events' clients. Brian received the Professional Convention Management Association's (PCMA) award for Educator of the Year in 2005 and continues to work closely with PCMA in the development of faculty and students' programming and initiatives.

Contributor to previous editions: Terry Epton, Executive Vice President, USA Hosts.

Special Events Management

Chapter Outline

Fireworks make an event even more special. This is a special event staged on a battleship in Mobile, Alabama. *Photo by Kenneth E. Manis, Courtesy of Classic Fireworks by Events, Inc., Mandeville, Louisiana*

Chapter Objectives

This chapter provides the reader with an understanding of the following:

- A working definition of a special event
- Understanding the importance of relationships in special event management
- The importance of a workable plan for staging a special event
- The planning tools used in special event management
- The importance of city and community infrastructures when hosting a special event
- The merchandising and promoting of a special event
- Sponsorships for special events
- Target markets for procuring attendance at a special event
- The basic operations for preparing for a special event
- The components of a special event budget
- The breakdown components of a special event
- Future Trends

A WORKING DEFINITION OF A SPECIAL EVENT

The definition of a *special event* is an umbrella term that encompasses all functions that bring people together for a unique purpose. Most events require some sort of planning on the part of the organizer. A special event, such as a city festival or fair, can mean working with **community infrastructure**, merchandising, promoting, and in some cases dealing with the media. The event can be as small as the local community Kiwanis picnic or as large as a global film festival. Special events are imbedded in **meetings, expositions, events and conventions (MEEC)**, and at amusement parks, parades, **fairs, festivals, and public events**.

The CIC glossary includes the following definition related to special events:

Special Event One time event staged for the purpose of celebration; unique activity.

Special Events Company This type of company may contract to put on an entire event or only parts of one. A Special Events *Production* Company may present special effects and theatrical acts. They sometimes hire speakers as part of their contract. Source: http://www.conventionindustry.org/glossary

A special event can bring organizations together for the purpose of fund-raising, establishing a city or community as a local, regional, or national destination, and to stimulate the local economy. The event can also be an opportunity for an association or a corporation to favorably position itself with a community or with the mass consumer. Sponsoring a specific type of event can provide a marketing edge and another avenue for reaching customers. For example, Buick Automobiles sponsors numerous PGA golf tournaments, in part because the demographics of the audience match its target clientele. Volvo does the same thing with the U.S. Open tennis tournament. Busch Beer sponsors NASCAR races, Nokia sponsors the Sugar Bowl football game, and Macy's sponsors the Thanksgiving Day parade: The list goes on and on.

Orchestrating a special event takes more than an idea. It takes planning, understanding your target market, having basic operational knowledge, using effective communications, working with volunteers or volunteer organizations, working within a budget, promoting the event, and even creating the logistics for breaking down an event. Simply stated, the event planner needs to understand: the "who, what, where, and why" of the special event.

It All Begins with a Relationship

What do these special events have in common: a wedding reception, a 5K charity run, the Macy's Thanksgiving Day parade, and a company picnic? All are very special events, though very different. And, all are planned by someone who must understand the goals, the needs, and the desires of the client they are serving. The planner has a responsibility to the client to do everything in his/her power to reach the goals of the client, while working within the parameters of the given location, city, or facility.

How does the planner begin to truly understand the vision of his/her client? And how does the client begin to trust the efforts of the planner? Special events management begins and evolves by developing a very important relationship between the client and the planner. The planner must listen to the clients, hear their words, and see their vision. The planner should have the capability to put that vision into a reality for the clients, given the expertise and the professionalism of the planner.

A planner and a client must have clear lines of communication between them. And as they talk and listen to each other, a viable plan can unfold. The planner must always understand that the success of any event must begin with a relationship. Listen to the client, do what you say you will do, tend to the little things, and communicate without fail.

No matter what the profile of the event, each and every special event is, indeed, very special to someone, or to many. It becomes a great challenge to meet (and exceed) the expectations of your client.

Another smaller, but very successful event that draws more than 125,000 visitors to Central Pennsylvania is the summer Central Pennsylvania Arts Festival. This festival brings people to downtown State College and the University Park campus of Penn State to celebrate the arts with its nationally recognized Sidewalk Sale and Exhibition, a gallery exhibition, and music,

The Presidential Inauguration Day Parade

While the tradition of the Inaugural parade dates back to the Inauguration of George Washington, the first organized parade unfolded at the Inauguration of James Madison in 1809. Here, Madison was escorted to the Capitol by a troop of cavalry. After taking his oath of office, Madison then watched the parade of militia. In William Henry Harrison's time, in 1841, floats were introduced to the parade. In addition, military bands, political groups and college groups became parade participants.

As history progressed, African Americans joined Abraham Lincoln's Inaugural parade for the first time, increasing even further the number of participating groups in the parade. In 1873, President Grant reordered the events of the Inaugural Day to make the parade *after* the Inaugural Ceremony, rather than *before*. This tradition continues today.

Reviewing stands were built in 1881 for the Inauguration of President James Garfield. To combat the cold and sometimes harsh weather conditions, the grandstands became enclosed. Reviewing stands were also built for visitors.

Women became participants of the parade in 1917, and then, in 1921, President Warren Harding became the first president to ride in an automobile. This set a precedent until 1977, when President Jimmy Carter chose to walk in the parade with his wife and daughter, from the Capitol to the White House. The first televised Inaugural Parade was held in 1949 for President Harry S. Truman.

The largest parade occurred in 1953 at the Inaugural Parade of President Dwight D. Eisenhower. The parade included seventy-three bands, fifty-nine floats, horse, elephants, military troops, and civilian and military vehicles. The parade lasted for over four-and-a-half hours.

The size and sophistication of the parade has developed tremendously over the last 200 years, and the Inaugural Parade has evolved into a nationally lauded special event. At the 2009 Inauguration Parade, President Barack Obama hosted 15,000 participants, including 2000 military personnel. Forty-six bands were chosen to participate of the 1,000 that applied. Today, millions of Americans can view the parade, whether via television viewing, Internet access, or in person. This parade has truly become a tradition of celebration for all Americans.

Today, the Armed Forces Inaugural Committee is responsible for the organization of the parade, and the Presidential Inaugural Committee is responsible for selecting all participants of the parade. (http://inaugural.senate.gov/history/"daysevents/inauguralparade.cfm)

2009 Inauguration Day Parade.   *Courtesy of Totalphoto, Dreamstime LLC—Royalty Free.*

dance, and theatrical performances in a variety of traditional and nontraditional venues (http://www.arts-festival.com/).

A film festival can be a dream come true for moviegoers as they seek out famous actors who might be walking right next to them, as on the streets of Park City, Utah, during the Sundance Film Festival. Founded in 1981, the festival has grown to international recognition, attracting tens of thousands of visitors each year to this quaint little town to view over 3,000 film submissions.

These special events came from an historical tradition that ultimately grew to attract thousands of visitors to some very remote areas. Continuing to attract visitors requires planning and planning tools, such as an understanding of the community infrastructure, merchandising and promoting the event, developing sponsorships, and working with the media. This is the art and science of special events management.

Using Festivals in the Off-Season: "Rockin' Mountains"

The typical image of the Rocky Mountains and Colorado is one of snow-covered peaks in winter dotted with skiers. But what happens when summer rolls around and people cannot ski? What do the ski resorts do, shut down? The answer is a resounding "No!" They put on music festivals using the same facilities occupied by skiers in the winter. The setting is idyllic, with music carrying through the clean air with the awesome backdrop of mountain peaks.

This use of Colorado mountain ski facilities to host off-season musical events started in 1949, when concerts were held in the town of Aspen. At the time, it was called the Goethe Bicentennial celebration. Some of the events included the Minneapolis Symphony Orchestra playing in a tent that held 2,000 people. This special event has continued and grown into the Aspen Music Festival and School. During the summer of 2006, the event included more than 800 international musicians. During these periods, students, faculty, and visiting musicians perform almost 250 classical pieces, ranging from symphonies to children's programs. There are three major **venues**. The largest one is a tent that holds more than 2,000 people and is made from the same fabric as the Denver airport terminal.

Another ski resort that has turned to musical events to attract visitors in the off-season is Telluride, Colorado. Nearly every summer weekend, the town hosts a musical event. The biggest special event is the Telluride Bluegrass Festival, which has been held for over thirty years. It runs for four days in June and attracts 10,000 people per day. Telluride also hosts a Jazz Festival, a Chamber Music Festival, and a Blues and Brews Festival.

In Winter Park just west of Denver, three weekends are occupied with music festivals. Concertgoers sit on the slopes and watch bands perform against the backdrop of the Continental Divide. A Rockfest features an eclectic line-up of Post-Pop artists ranging from the latest breakout bands to "old-school" favorites. In July, Winter Park holds the "Hawgfest," a Harley-Davidson inspired blowout targeted to baby boomers. They also hold a Jazzfest with music that runs the gamut from the best in Smooth to Progressive Jazz.

The towns of Aspen, Breckenridge, and Telluride have banded together to form the Colorado Music Alliance. This organization has hosted and marketed events in these three locations, plus a number of small, somewhat isolated communities, including Silverthorne, Crested Butte, Estes Park, Durango, Steamboat Springs, and Nederland. This proves that festivals are a good way of drawing tourists who would not otherwise travel to an area during the off-season. They bring economic activity when there would be none, and the attendees may like the location enough to come back during the busy season.

HISTORY AND BACKGROUND

Festivals and special events have been part of human history since time immemorial. Humankind has celebrated births, weddings, and deaths throughout history and held special gatherings like the Olympics and gladiatorial combat. However, most historians credit the use of the term "special event" in modern history to a Disney imagineer named Robert Janni. The problem Disney faced was that the families who frequented the theme park were worn out after a day of adventure and most left by 5 PM each day, even though the park stayed open hours longer. In order to keep attendees at the park, he proposed producing a nightly parade called the "Main Street Electric Parade" with numerous floats decked out with lights. It was a success in keeping people in the park in the evening. When asked by a reporter what he called this parade, he replied "A Special Event." The use of special events to attract or maintain crowds is still used to this day.

A special event is a celebration of something—that is what makes it special. Goldblatt (2005:6) defines a special event "as a unique moment in time celebrated with ceremony and ritual to satisfy specific needs."

Special Events can include:

- Civic Events
  - Centennials
  - Founders' Day

- Mega-Events
  - Olympics
  - America's Cup
  - Hands Across America
  - World's Fairs
- Festivals and Fairs
  - Marketplace of ancient days
  - Community Event
  - Fair = not for profit
  - Festival = for profit
- Expositions
  - Where suppliers meet buyers
  - Education
  - Entertainment
- Sporting Events
  - Superbowl
  - World Series
  - Masters Golf Tournament
  - Belmont Stakes
- Social life-cycle events
  - Wedding
  - Anniversary
  - Birthday
  - Reunion
  - Bar Mitzvah (Bat Mitzvah)
- Meetings & Conventions
  - Political National Convention
  - National Restaurant Association convention in Chicago
  - PCMA annual conference
- Retail Events
  - Long-range promotional event
  - Store opening
  - New product rollout
    - X-box
    - i-Tunes
- Religious Events
  - Papal Inauguration
  - The Hajj (Mecca)
  - Easter
  - Quanza
- Corporate Events
  - Holiday parties
  - Annual dinner
  - Company picnics
  - Conferences/meetings

Source: Adapted from Goldblatt, Joe. (2005). Special Events: event leadership for a new world (4th ed.). Hoboken, New Jersey: John Wiley and Sons.

PLANNING TOOLS FOR A SPECIAL EVENT

Special events management, like any other form of managing, requires planning tools. The first of these tools is a vision statement of your event. This vision statement should clearly identify the "who, what, when, where, and why" of the event. As the event begins to unfold, it is important to keep those involved focused on the vision. This can be accomplished by continually monitoring, evaluating, and, where possible, measuring the progress toward the outlined goals of the event (see chapter on "Planning and Producing MEEC Events").

Jane Byrne at the Chicago St. Patrick's Day parade.   *Courtesy of Mayor's Press Office, City of Chicago*

The "who" of planning an event are those people or organizations that would like to host and organize it. In the case of the St. Patrick's Day Parade in Chicago, Illinois, it is the city that hosts and coordinates the marchers, the floats, and the bands. The "what" was a parade demonstrating Irish pride and local tradition. The "where" of the Parade is downtown Chicago, with the floats and bands marching down Michigan Avenue. The big question of "why" is one of tradition, pride, fun, and tourism. This, in turn, promotes the city and brings revenues to the local businesses. When the city decided to serve as the host of this event, it needed to incorporate the tools of special event management.

Some of the management tools that are used in staging events are as follows:

a. Flow charts and graphs for scheduling. Look at any program for a meeting; there are start and end times, times for coffee breaks, a time for lunch, and a time that the meeting resumes and ends. The flow chart can be as "romantic" as a wedding ceremony **agenda**. The chart can be the order or sequence of floats for a parade, the program for a talent show, or the agenda for a weeklong international conference. A flowchart scheduling an event's activities helps guide attendees and guests and makes the execution of the event flow smoothly.

b. Clearly defined setup and breakdown **schedules**. These provide the event manager with an opportunity to determine tasks that may have been overlooked in the initial planning process.

c. Policy statements developed to guide in the decision-making process. Policy statements provide a clear understanding of commitments and what is expected to fulfill them. Some of the commitments to be considered are human resources, sponsors, security, ticketing, volunteers, and paid personnel.

Understanding Community Infrastructure

Another key ingredient for planning a successful event is an understanding of the infrastructure in the community where the event is to take place. This infrastructure might include the CEO of the company, politicians, prominent business leaders of the community, civic and community groups, the media, and other community leaders. Without a "buy-in" from the city leadership, a community is less inclined to be supportive. The role of business leaders in the infrastructure could be to provide sponsorships, donations, staff, or a possible workplace for the coordination of the event. Many times, community groups serve as volunteer workers for the event and are also an extension of the advertising for it.

Early on it must be recognized whether or not a community or a company is truly committed to hosting any type of special event that will call on its support not only with the financial

FIGURE 8-1 Elements of the promotional mix for successful special event management

commitment but also in the physical and emotional commitment it will take to manage an event from start to finish. For a promoter or special events management company to maintain a positive reputation, there needs to be a solid infrastructure in place.

Merchandising and Promoting the Special Event

Merchandising and promoting a special event is another planning tool for attracting attendance and increasing the overall profitability for the event. Just because a community decides to host a craft fair or street festival does not mean that there will be the attendance necessary to meet vendors' and visitors' needs. Profit for the vendor and a memorable experience for the attendee are two main objectives for a special event. The special event requires all the promotional venues that an event management company or civic group is able to afford.

Understanding and utilizing the **promotional mix model** (see figure above) is pivotal in order to meet the goals of the event marketing plan. The role of promotion in special events management is the coordination of all the seller's efforts to set up channels of information and persuasion to sell or promote the event. Traditionally, the promotional mix has included four elements: advertising, sales promotion, publicity and/or public relations, and personal selling. However, this author views direct marketing and interactive media as additional elements of the promotional mix. Modern-day event marketers use many means to communicate with their target markets. Each element of the promotional mix is viewed as an integrated marketing communications tool. Each of these elements of the model has a distinctive role in attracting an attendee to the special event. Each takes on a variety of forms, and each has certain advantages.

Distinctive Roles of the Promotional Mix Model

Advertising is defined as any paid form of nonpersonal communication about the event. The nonpersonal component means advertising that involves mass media (e.g., TV, radio, magazines, and newspapers). Advertising is the best known and most widely discussed form of promotion because it is the most persuasive, especially if the event (e.g., a home and garden show) is targeted toward mass consumers. It can be used to create brand images or symbolic appeals for the brand, and generate immediate responses from prospective attendees.

Direct marketing is a form of advertising that communicates directly with the target customer with the intent of generating a response. It is much more than direct mail or catalogs. It involves a variety of activities, including database management, direct selling, telemarketing, and di-rect-response ads, the Internet, and various broadcast and print media. An example of direct mar-keting is a company like Mary Kay Cosmetics or Tupperware. Rather than distribution channels, they rely on independent contractors to sell their products directly to consumers. These contractors directly communicate with the customer, maintain their own database, bring the product directly to the customer through "parties," receive direct response, and finally after the sale is made they deliver the product directly. The Internet has also fueled the growth of direct marketing. Interactive or Internet marketing allows for a back-and-forth flow of information; users can participate in and modify the form and content of the information they receive in real time. Unlike traditional forms of marketing, such as advertising, which are one-way forms of communication, this type of media allows users to perform a variety of functions. It enables users to receive and alter information and images, make inquiries, respond to questions, and make purchases. Many event attendees will go to a Web site to garner information about a special event such as a concert and purchase their tickets directly online. For a special event such as the Aspen Music Festival, attendees can go to the festival's official Web site, view the schedule, learn about the event and the surrounding area, purchase tick-ets, and request additional information—all forms of direct marketing. In addition to the Internet, other forms of interactive media include CD-ROMs, kiosks, and interactive television.

Sales promotion is generally defined as those marketing activities that provide extra value or incentives to the sales force, distributors, or the ultimate consumer with the intention of stimulating the sale. A popular form of sales promotion is the coupon. Many events will use a two-for-one attendance coupon to stimulate attendance on slower days.

Publicity and public relations is divided into two components. Publicity is the component that is not directly paid for, nor has an identified sponsor. When an event planner gets the media to cover or run a favorable story on a special event, it affects an attendee's awareness, knowledge, and opinions. Publicity is considered a credible form of promotion, but it is not always under the control of the organization or host of the event. In the case of Punxsutawney Phil, the groundhog used in the city's quest to determine if spring is six weeks away, all of the national broadcasting television stations send a camera crew and reporter to publicize this unique event. If those reporting the event have a positive experience, it will favorably affect the public's perception of the event. Unfortunately, the reverse is also true; the planners have little control.

Social Media has exploded as a preferred strategy for promotional initiatives. Social Media reaches the masses with minimal expense and relative ease of effort. This is also known as viral marketing. While there are many vehicles of social media, some of the more commonly used mediums include Facebook, Blogging, LinkedIn, Ning (a forum medium for subgroups), and Twitter. Each of these mediums allows a message to be sent simultaneously to many people, projecting a controlled and positive message to the reader. In addition, the message that is sent is delivered immediately to the reader. For more information, see Chapter 12, Technology.

There are a variety of special events that take place to promote a destination or an occasion. One example is Groundhog Day celebrated in Punxsutawney, Pennsylvania. Once a small town event, millions of television viewers now awake to the early morning cheers and chants for Punxsutawney Phil, the beloved groundhog who will let us know if we are in for another six weeks of winter should he see his shadow.

Groundhog Day History

European Roots

(Adapted from "Groundhog Day: 1886 to 1992" by Bill Anderson)

Groundhog Day, February 2nd, is a popular tradition in the United States. It is also a legend that traverses centuries—its origins clouded in the mists of time with ethnic cultures and animals awakening on specific dates. Myths such as this tie our present to the distant past when nature did, indeed, influence our lives. It is the day that the Groundhog comes out of his hole after a long winter sleep to look for his shadow.

- If he sees it, he regards it as an omen of six more weeks of bad weather and returns to his hole.
- If the day is cloudy and, hence, shadows less, he takes it as a sign of spring and stays above ground.

The groundhog tradition stems from similar beliefs associated with Candlemas Day and the days of early Christians in Europe, and for centuries the custom was to have the clergy bless candles and distribute them to the people. Even then, it marked a milestone in the winter and the weather that day was important.

The Roman legions, during the conquest of the northern country, supposedly brought this tradition to the Teutons, or Germans, who picked it up and concluded that if the sun made an appearance on Candlemas Day, an animal, the hedgehog, would cast a shadow, thus predicting six more weeks of bad weather, which they interpolated as the length of the "Second Winter."

Pennsylvania's earliest settlers were Germans, and they found groundhogs in profusion in many parts of the state. They determined that the groundhog, resembling the European hedgehog, was a most intelligent and sensible animal and therefore decided that if the sun did appear on February 2nd, so wise an animal as the groundhog would see its shadow and hurry back into its underground home for another six weeks of winter.

The Germans recited:

For as the sun shines on Candlemas Day,

So far will the snow swirl until the May.

This passage may be the one most closely represented by the first Punxsutawney Groundhog Day observances because there were references to the length of shadows in early Groundhog Day predictions.

Another February 2nd belief, used by American 19th century farmers, was:

Groundhog Day—Half your hay.

New England farmers knew that they were not close to the end of winter, no matter how cloudy February 2nd was. Indeed, February 2nd is often the heart of winter. If the farmer didn't have half his hay remaining, there may have been lean times for the cows before spring and fresh grass arrived.

The ancient Candlemas legend and similar beliefs continue to be recognized annually on February 2nd due to the efforts of the Punxsutawney Groundhog Club.

Source: http://www.groundhog.org/faq/history.shtml

PUBLIC RELATIONS   The purpose of public relations is to systematically plan and distribute information to attempt to control or manage the image and/or publicity of an event. It has a broader objective than publicity because its purpose is to establish a positive image of the special event. Public relations can be the reason for hosting the special event altogether. Tobacco companies have used special events like a NASCAR race (Winston Cup) or tennis tournament to create a more positive image with consumers.

Personal selling is the final element of the promotional mix model, and it is a form of person-to-person communication in which a seller attempts to assist and or persuade prospective event attendees. Typically, group tour sales are the best prospects for personal selling of a special event. There are several touring companies that purchase large groups of tickets for special events. Unlike advertising, personal selling involves direct contact between the buyer and seller of the event, usually through face-to-face sales. Therefore, personal selling is more appropriate and feasible by meeting face-to-face with a group representative, while meeting face-to-face with each individual prospective attendee is not. Some examples of events that group tours attend may include: the Indianapolis 500, the Kentucky Derby, or the Jazz Fest in New Orleans. Group tour organizers will meet face-to-face with event planners or talk via the telephone to purchase tickets for an event.

Sponsorships for Special Events

Sponsorships help to ensure profitable success for an event. They are an innovative way for event organizers to help underwrite and defray costs. Sponsorships should be considered more than just a charitable endeavor for a company—they can be a strong marketing tool.

Event sponsors provide funds or "in-kind" contributions and receive consideration in the form of logo usage and identity with the event. Recent trends of sponsorships show rapid growth. Sponsorship can take many forms. A large corporation, for instance, may have the means to provide financial sponsorship for an event. The mid-size and smaller organizations, however, may need to be more creative in their sponsorship methods. A smaller organization may, for example, provide product, rather than the financial contribution. Therefore, you may not see their banner hanging at the event, but you will have their product in your hand.

Many types of special events require sponsorship to be successful. **Sporting events** have long been the leader in securing sponsorships for teams and athletes. However, their market share

---

The Great Garlic Cook-Off
Gilroy, California

The Annual Garlic Festival is held in the "Garlic Capital of the World," Gilroy, California, at Christmas Hill Park during the last full weekend of July.

This festival's origin lies in the pride of one man, Rudy Melone. Melone felt that Gilroy should celebrate its superior production of the "stinking rose," otherwise known as garlic. He then began what is referred to as "the preeminent food festival in America."

In December of each year, the Gilroy Garlic Festival begins its request for original garlic recipes. Citizens of Canada and the United States are asked to participate. Recipes are then submitted by amateur chefs, and eight are chosen to participate in the festival cook-off. Winners are awarded monetary prizes for their work well done.

Another tradition practiced by the Garlic Festival is the nomination of a "Queen of Garlic." To date, only twenty-four women can claim this title. Contestants are judged on a personal inter-view, talent, a garlic speech, and evening gown competition. The queen represents Gilroy at various festivities before and during the festival.

Over the last twenty-eight years, the Garlic Festival has attracted over three million attendees and raised money for local nonprofit organizations. Over 4,000 volunteers are recruited to work the event and participate in activities like picking up trash, parking cars, and serving lemonade. The Gilroy Garlic Festival is not only known for its garlic pride and knowledge but for its ability to bring the community of Gilroy together. Its Web site states "Where else can one feast on food laced with over two tons of fresh garlic, enjoy three stages of musical entertainment, shop in arts and crafts, view the great garlic cook-off and other celebrity cooking demonstrations, spend time in the children's area, visit interactive displays set up by many of our sponsors, soak up some glorious sunshine, and mingle with a fun bunch of garlic-loving people?" (http://www.gilroygarlicfestival.com/)

has dropped as companies begin to distribute sponsorship dollars to other events, such as city festivals and the arts. This shift in sponsorships from sports events to that of festivals and the arts over the past decade has emerged because companies are cognizant of the effective tool that a sponsorship can be for overall company marketing plans.

There are five compelling reasons why company sponsorships are an important option to consider

1. Economic changes (both upturns and downturns)
2. Ability to target market segments
3. Ability to measure results
4. Fragmentation of the media
5. Growth of diverse population segments

Changes in the economic climate of the country will affect the goals, spending, and expectations of the sponsoring organization. In times of economic health, companies (both large and small) may be willing and able to more freely spend their promotional dollars on sponsorship. In economic downturns, however, organizations are likely to feel the necessity to account for the return they are receiving on their promotional spending. In other words, the sponsorship is seen as an investment, and the organization would like to know if, in fact, they are receiving a return on their investment. In either economic climate, sponsorships promote the intangible benefits of company visibility and overall goodwill.

When looking for sponsorships for a special event, organizers must determine if the event fits the company. Planners must always examine the company's goal, and be sure to research the competition. Special event organizers should aid the sponsors with promotional ideas that will help them meet their goals. Promoters of an event need to ensure that sponsors get their money's worth. Remember that sponsors have internal and external audiences to whom they are appealing.

"Cross-promotional opportunities" allow the sponsor to achieve the greatest visibility possible by capitalizing on more than one promotional opportunity within one event. For example, if PepsiCo sponsored an event, then that company would likely gain notable visibility through banners, logos, etc. However, to further capitalize on this sponsorship, PepsiCo might further request that only Pepsi products be sold at the event. Therefore, they are gaining notoriety through banners, advertising logos, etc. They are gaining visibility through the product that is being served at the event, and they may likely be earning revenue on the product that they are serving. This sponsorship would, therefore, serve as a triple benefit to the corporation. The internal audience of a corporation is its employees, and they must also be sold on the sponsorship of the event. A company needs to provide opportunities for employee involvement. If the special event is a charitable marathon, employees may be asked to actually participate in the marathon or raise funds for the charitable cause. Those employees who participate may be featured in promotional material or press releases.

New York City Marathon

Sponsorship

The New York City Marathon boasts 30,000 runners with more than 2 million spectators—the largest live sporting event in the world, broadcast to over 330 million viewers in more than 154 territories. Television coverage includes a live five-hour telecast on WNBC in New York, a one-hour national telecast on NBC, and various live and highlight shows internationally.

New York Road Runners and the New York City Marathon are fortunate to have the support and commitment of our fine sponsors and strategic partners. Their continued support makes the New York City Marathon a world-class event year after year.

Sponsors

Adecco	Dole	Nextel
Aestiva	Gatorade	Poland Spring
Aleve	Georgia Pacific	Pontiac
Amtrak	ILX Systems	PowerBar
Andersen	Lamisil AT	Ronzoni
Best Buy	Mirror Image	Saranac
Breathe	Moishe's	Tiffany & Co.
Right	Motorola	Time Warner
Chock Full	New York	Cable
O' Nuts	Apple	UPS
Dannon	Association	Walrus Internet

Source: http://www.nyrrc.org/nyrrc/mar01/about/sponsors.html

Selling to the external audience of the corporation (the consumer) is done in a variety of ways. First, the company might feature its logo on the event's products. The company can promote its affiliation with the special event by providing its logo for outdoor banners and specialty advertising items, such as T-shirts, caps, or sunglasses. The types of specialty products are limitless and excellent venues for advertising. The sponsoring company may wish to appoint an employee spokesperson to handle radio or television interviews.

Working with the Media for an Event

Generating media coverage for a special event is one of the most effective methods for attracting attendance. Ideally, an event organizer wants to garner free television, radio, and print coverage. In order to attract the media, a promoter must understand what makes for good TV, radio, or print coverage and what does not.

When a camera crew is sent to film an event by assignment editors at a TV station, they will look for a story that can be easily illustrated with visuals captured by a camera. They also look for a vignette that can entertain viewers in thirty seconds or less. If an event organizer wants television or radio stations to cover the event, he or she needs to call it to their attention with a press release or press conference. There are no guarantees that the station or the newspaper will air the footage or print the story; however, the chances are better if a camera crew shoots footage or a reporter does an interview. Thus, the event has free advertising. Remember, special events provide ideal fodder for the evening news. This can be an interview with a celebrity who will be attending the event or an advance look at an art exhibit.

Within the promotional mix model, the biggest way to attract attention to the event is with television, radio, and print media through publicity. This "free" type of promotion offers something that advertising cannot match—credibility. These media sources are an excellent way to reach the mass consumer.

Event organizers try to present the unusual to the press. At the opening of a steak restaurant in a hotel in Tulsa, Oklahoma, a special event was staged where the management hosted a "Moo-Off." Community leaders were invited to a dinner featuring the restaurant's signature food and beverage items. They were then asked to "Moo" in the voice of their favorite celebrity. The audience bellowed their Mae West Moos, Jack Nicholson Moos—even an Elvis Presley Moo. Moo-ers were gonged by specially selected judges (city leaders). The winner of the event donated the cash prize to a community charity. The event caught the attention of the media and was featured on the evening news. The event organizers used well-timed radio segments to enhance the credibility of the Moo-Off. The restaurant manager was featured on local radio stations during morning and afternoon drive times, which peaked TV interest on the day of the event. Although it initially appears that the promoters of the Moo-off did not have to work too hard to obtain media coverage, their professional expertise in advance promotion of this event is what guaranteed its success. Once the media found out about the Moo-off, the event sold itself; the organizers' main work was to ensure that the media found out about it.

Promoters of special events have long recognized what TV and radio coverage can do for an event. Here are some helpful hints for attracting television and radio coverage:

1. Early in the day is considered the best time to attract cameras and reporters. Remember, a crew must come out, film, get back to the studio, edit the film, and have the segment ready for the 5:00 or 6:00 PM newscast that night.
2. The best day of the week to attract news crews is Friday. That is because it is usually a quiet news day. Saturday and Sunday have even fewer distractions, but most stations do not have enough news crews working the weekend who can cover an event.
3. Giving advance notice for a special event is very helpful to assignment editors. Usually about three days' notice, with an explanation of the event via a press release and telephone follow-up, is very helpful in securing media coverage. If an interview is involved, a seven-day notice is a good time allotment for coverage.

UNDERSTANDING THE TARGET MARKET FOR YOUR SPECIAL EVENT

Bringing special events to a community has not changed much over the years; however, consumers have changed. They are much more selective and sophisticated about the events they will attend. Since the cost of attending events has risen, consumers are much more discerning

A Very Special Wedding

A couple from Texas wanted to be sure that their wedding was special, so they decided to have it in New Orleans. They were enamored with the charm of the city: moss-draped oak trees, antebellum homes, and horse-drawn carriages. They decided to invite 100 people and contacted a local DMC to make the arrangements. Their specification was that the DMC arrange a rehearsal dinner for 12 people and a reception for 100. Such costs as transportation to New Orleans, hotel accommodations, and the church were not part of the bid. Their stated budget for this wedding reception and dinner was $250,000. That's right—a quarter of a million dollars or $2,500 per guest! When the planner heard this, her reaction was twofold: (1) how could she possibly put together this event and spend that much money, and (2) if that was their proposed budget, she would try to up-sell them.

The rehearsal dinner was held in a private dining room at the famous Arnaud's restaurant in the French Quarter. The real money was spent on the reception. They rented the art deco Saenger Theater for the evening, but there was a problem. Like most theaters, the floor sloped toward the stage. So, they removed all the seats and built a new floor that was level, not sloped. The interior of the theater was so beautiful that it needed little decoration. The New Orleans Police Department was contracted to close the street between the church and theater to cars so that the period ambiance would not be disturbed for the couple and their guests while being transported in their horse-drawn carriages. When the couple and their guests entered for the evening, they were greeted by models in period costume and served mint juleps while a gospel group sang. A blues band followed, and the night was topped off by not one but two sets by Gladys Knight and the Pips. The affair was catered by Emeril Lagasse and only included heavy hors d'oeuvres, not even a sit-down dinner. The ultimate cost for this event was almost $300,000, and the couple was delighted.

The planner was Nanci Easterling of Food Art, Inc.

about how they spend their entertainment dollars. This creates a demand for quality for any special event.

Understanding your target market is one of the most important components in the overall success of the event. It is critical for the event marketer and planner to know the participant audience. Age, gender, religion, ethnicity—all must be understood. Depending on the type of event, the planner must have an understanding of participant restrictions (i.e., religious, dietary) and participant needs. The event must be based on the overall needs and desires of the target market.

The most valuable outcome a special event can generate for a community is positive word of mouth. In order to create this positive awareness, an organizer recognizes that the event cannot appeal to all markets. A promoter will determine the target market for the community's event.

Target marketing is defined as clearly identifying who wants to attend a certain type of event. For example, a Miley Cyrus concert has been determined to appeal to a young female audience between the ages of six and fourteen. To stage a profitable concert, promoters will direct their advertising dollars to that particular targeted audience. Subsequently, all promotional items will also be geared toward that age group.

Most communities know that a special event will have a positive economic impact on the community and the region. This has created competition to attract events. A city will commonly use inducements to lure the special event to the community. These inducements may include free entertainment space, security, parking, and even the "key to the city" to the celebrity providing the entertainment. A "city wide" is a commonly used term for those large events or conventions that impact the entire city. City wides are key to urban economics. When a large event or convention is hosted in a particular city, the economic effects are positive. Hotel rooms may completely sell out across the city, eateries are busy, and retail and cultural attractions may flourish due to the "city wide."

A successful event has two vital components. One is that the community is supportive of bringing the event to the city, and second is that the event meets the consumers' need. For example, every year on Labor Day weekend, New Orleans is host to a special event called "Southern Decadence." This three-day event is targeted to gay and lesbian people, and they "strut" around

Miley Cyrus in Concert.   *Courtesy of Chrishg, Dreamstime LLC—Royalty Free.*

the city freely. New Orleans is probably one of the few communities in the United States that would be supportive of bringing such an event to its city

PREPARING FOR THE SPECIAL EVENT

Basic operations for staging an event need to be established and include the following:

1. Secure a venue.
2. Obtain **permits**.
   a. Parade permits
   b. Liquor permits
   c. Sanitation permits
   d. Sales permits or licenses
   e. Fire safety permits
3. Involve **government agencies** where necessary (i.e., if using city recreation facilities, work with the department of parks and recreation).
4. Involve the health department if there will be food and beverage at the event.
5. Meet all relevant parties in person so that any misconceptions are cleared up early.
6. Secure all vendors and suppliers for the event.
7. Recognize the complexities of dealing with the public sector. Sometimes public agencies have a difficult time making decisions.
8. Recognize the logistics that a community must contend with for certain types of special events, such as street closures for a marathon.
9. Set up a security plan, which may include the security supplied by the venue and professional law enforcement. (Pay attention as to which security organization takes precedence.)
10. Secure liability insurance (the most vulnerable area are those liabilities attached to liquor and liquor laws).
11. Determine ticket prices if the special event involves ticketing.
12. Determine ticket sale distribution if the special event involves ticketing.

In a Land Far, Far Away

Gansbaai, South Africa-based Grootbos Private Nature Reserve overlooks Walker Bay and provides guests a unique opportunity to view flora, fauna, and marine life. Its lodges are a two-hour drive from Cape Town, accessed by tar road or helicopter, and it's the destination of choice for people planning weddings, incentives, birthday parties, and product launches. Popular event spots at Grootbos include the wine cellar, main lodges, and the pool area. For a taste of local events, marketing and reservations manager Florentina Heger says nothing beats a "South African braai at our boma nestled in the Milkwood Forest"—or, in other words, a South African barbecue in an open outdoor event space. Picnics in the Milkwood Forest are also popular, with lunch accompanied by violinists, cello players, or published authors reading their works. Dinner could consist of a six-course gala event or dishes served in small portions to encourage guests to circulate and mingle as they eat. Weddings here are typically beach affairs with whales in the distance and sushi, Champagne, and salmon- and trout-wrapped mussels served after the ceremony. http://specialevents.com/venues/events_destination_known_20011110/

13. Other basic business support functions include:
    a. Accounting systems (general ledger, financial reporting, accounts payable, accounts receivable, and payroll)
    b. Human resource systems (recruiting, personnel records, and job classifications and descriptions)
    c. Accommodations (talent, media, officials, support staff, and spectators)
    d. Registration
    e. Marketing and advertising the event
    f. Ticketing (mail order, seat inventories, seat assignments, and gate sales)
    g. Scoring and results (scoreboards and displays)
    h. Develop timelines, checklists, and schedules for setup, execution of event, and wrap-up of event

The type of special event being held will determine the degree of preparedness needed. The larger the event, the more involved the checklist. Preparedness should produce a profitable and well-managed event.

THE SPECIAL EVENT BUDGET

For any event to be considered a success, it must also be considered profitable. Profitability requires understanding the six key elements involved in the cost of an event. The basic items that make up the costs for a special event include the categories that follow.

Rental Costs

Depending on the type of event, renting a facility such as a convention center or ground space to put up a tent requires payment of a daily rental charge. Convention centers usually sell the space based on a certain dollar amount per square footage used. Most facilities charge for space even on the move-in and move-out days. Multiday events can usually negotiate a discount.

There are, of course, variations to the rental cost of event space. If, for example, an association is holding a conference in a hotel, the event space may be free of charge or offered at a reduced rate if a certain number of hotel rooms are booked by the participating group. Furthermore, if the group requires food and beverage, then often the rental space if provided at a reduced rate.

Security Costs

Most convention centers, rental halls, and hotels provide limited security. This could mean that a guard is stationed at the front and rear entrances of the venue. Depending on the type of event, such as a rock concert performed by a band that has raucous fans, more security may be required.

It is hard to believe that this is the inside of a tent used for a special event. *Used by permission of Paradise Light & Sound, Orlando, Florida*

European Soccer (Football) matches require even more security. Actual costs will depend on the city and the amount of security needed.

Production Costs

These are the costs associated with staging an event. The costs vary depending on the type of special event. For example, if the special event is a large home and garden show, there are costs associated with the setup of the trade show booths. As with many home and garden shows, exhibitors bring in elaborate garden landscapes that are very time consuming and labor intensive to set up and break down. Labor costs for decorators need to be calculated to estimate the production costs based on the type and size of trade show booth. There are also electrical and water fees needed for a home and garden show, and these costs must be included in the production costs. Other production costs include signage or banners for each booth and pipe and drape fees.

Labor Costs

The city where the special event is being held will affect the labor costs involved in the setup and breakdown of the event. Some cities are unionized, and this can add higher costs to an event because of the higher wages. Holding an event in very strict union cities means that the organizer of the event must leave more of the handling to the union crew. In some cities, the union allows the exhibitor to wheel his or her own cart with brochures and merchandise. In other cities, exhibitors cannot carry anything other than their own briefcases.

When selecting a city for an event, the role of unions has been an important influence. Most special event organizers will pass the higher costs on to the exhibitor or will increase ticket prices.

Marketing Costs

The costs associated with attracting attendees can make up a large portion of the budget (see the Statement of Revenues and Expenses below). Here, the event organizer examines the best means of reaching the target market. Trying to reach a mass audience may mean running a series of television commercials, which can be very expensive. Most event organizers use a combination of promotions to attract the attendee. There will be elements of advertising, direct marketing, publicity and public relations, sales promotion, interactive or Internet marketing, and personal selling. All of these need to be budgeted.

Talent Costs

Virtually all special events use some type of talent or performers. They may include keynote speaker, band or orchestra, sports teams, vocalists, animals, etc. While the organizer may have grandiose thoughts about the quality of the talent used, price has to be considered and matched to the special event budget. The high school class reunion probably cannot afford to have Jennifer Lopez or Taylor Swift perform.

Before an event, it is essential that a planner do a projection of all costs and revenue. These projections are essential to whether a community will host another event. Repeat events are much easier to promote, especially when the organizers have made a profit. Before and during the event, it is critical that billing updates are completed and presented to the client on a regular (sometimes daily) basis. Any discrepancies or new costs should be handled at the point they occur. There should be no cost surprises at the end of an event.

BREAKDOWN OF THE SPECIAL EVENT

Special events have one thing in common: They all come to an end! Breaking down the event usually involves a number of steps. Once the attendees have gone, there are a variety of closing tasks that an organizer must complete.

First, the parking staff should expedite the flow of traffic away from the event. In some cases, community police are able to assist in traffic control.

A debriefing of staff should take place to determine what did or did not happen at the event. There may be issues pending that will need documentation. It is always best to have written reports to refer to for next year's event. Consider having the following sources add information to the report:

1. *Participants:* Interview some of the participants from the event. A customer's perception and expectation is an invaluable insight.
2. *Media and the Press:* Ask why it was or was not a press-worthy gathering.
3. *Staff and Management:* Get a variety of staff and other management involved in the event to give feedback.
4. *Vendors:* They also have a very unique perspective on how the event could be improved. Exhibitors and vendors MUST complete a survey. Because of their great perspective, exhibitors can provide some outstanding and constructive feedback for planning the next event.

The following should also be included in a final report on the event:

1. Finalize the income and expense statement. Did the event break even, make a profit, or experience a loss?
2. Finalize all contracts from the event. Fortunately, most of everything involved with putting together the event will have written documentation. Compare final billing with actual agreements.
3. Send the media a final press release on the overall success of the event. Interviews with the press could be arranged. This could be especially newsworthy if the event generated significant revenues for the community.
4. Provide a written thank you for those volunteers who were involved with the event in any way. A celebration of some sort with the volunteers may be in order, especially if the event was financially and socially successful.

Once the elements of breakdown have taken place, the organizers can examine the important lessons of staging the event. What would they do or not do next year?

FUTURE TRENDS

The twenty-first century brings some evolving ideas into special events. The following are some noteworthy thoughts from special event planners, designers, and coordinators:

- Less is the new more. Clients are seeking the simple with a "flare."
  - Clients want to appear to be responsible in their spending. Excessive overspending is no longer the desirable trend.

Weddings are a very special event and can be big business. This is especially true for Disney where thousands of couples are married each year.   *Courtesy of Ting-Li Wang, The New York Times*

- "Stylish minimalism" refers to the idea that clients still want style, flare, and innovation in the overall event, but choose to uphold a conservative budgetary perception.
- Quality is paramount, at a cost that the client sees as a "value."
- Frivolous events are seen as wasteful; events should have a purpose.
- Many events are now targeted toward service or charitable causes. This provides purpose to an event. Events may be targeted toward medical concerns (i.e., cancer research, heart disease, autism awareness, etc.) or toward relief on a national or international level (Haiti Relief, Hurricane Katrina Relief, etc.).
- Clients are looking for an entire "package"—an experience. The event planner is truly planning an experience—often referred to as "experience management." Some event planners believe that a good event should captivate the audience, and offer "change" every half hour.
- Going green—environmentally, event planners are urged to consider green solutions. Earthy, environmentally friendly efforts are becoming the expectation. Interestingly, because of the perceived lack of sophistication, "eco-friendly" efforts are more likely to be incorporated into an event, rather than a primary means of service. For example, recycled coffee cups may be offered at a coffee station, along with china cups and saucers.
- Technology is key in promotional efforts. More Internet promotions are desired, as event managers are able to quantify the number of "hits" that they receive on their promotional initiative. This serves to quantifiably validate the expense and time of promotion.
- Every client has his/her own unique set of needs and wants. Every client wants the undivided attention of the planner; his/her needs must be recognized throughout the entire planning and execution of the event.
- Quality, cost, and relationship are three components that must be in balance for every special event.

Summary

Creating a memorable event requires that an organizer meet and exceed an attendee's expectations. Recognizing that the special event could be for a meeting or convention, a parade, a festival, a fair, or an exhibit requires understanding the objectives of the event. Having the planning tools in place is the keystone for success in managing the gathering. Special events management works with and understands the community infrastructures to help support the event.

It can be costly if in advance a planner does not decide which part of the promotional mix model of the event is used. The promotional mix model includes advertising, direct marketing, interactive or Internet marketing, sales promotion, publicity and public relations, and personal selling. Helping to defray costs by seeking sponsorships for a special event is another way to successfully market an event, and it is also an important marketing tool for the corporation sponsor. Generating and working with the local and or national media is the most effective way for attracting attendance. An organizer also needs to understand what makes for good media coverage, and whether it is for print or broadcast. The target market for the special event must always be considered in the objectives, the promotions, and the continuation of the event.

The basic operations and/or logistics for the event follow the planning and promoting. A checklist of the items that need to be handled or looked into is a must for any planner. Planners should also create checklists that will help develop the overall special event budget. This budget requires regular reviews of the statement of revenues and expenditures. The breakdown is the final step and includes another checklist for the closure of the event. Always remember your volunteers—without them, the event would not take place!

ISES: International Special Events Society

About ISES

The International Special Events Society (ISES) is composed of more than 4,000 professionals and 41 Chapters all over the world representing special event producers (from festivals to trade shows), caterers, decorators, florists, destination management companies, rental companies, special effects experts, tent suppliers, audiovisual technicians, party and convention coordinators, balloon artists, educators, journalists, hotel sales managers, specialty entertainers, convention center managers, and many more.

ISES was founded in 1987 to foster professionalism through education while promoting ethical conduct. ISES works to bring professionals together to focus on the "event as a whole" rather than its individual parts. Membership brings together professionals from a variety of special event disciplines, including caterers, meeting planners, decorators, event planners, audiovisual technicians, party and convention coordinators, educators, journalists, hotel sales managers, and many more

professional disciplines. The solid peer network ISES provides helps special event professionals produce outstanding results for clients while establishing positive working relationships with colleagues.

ISES Mission

The mission of ISES is to educate, advance, and promote the special events industry, its network of professionals, and its related industries. To that end, it strives to:

Uphold the integrity of the special events profession to the general public through its "Principles of Professional Conduct and Ethics"

Acquire and disseminate useful business information

Foster a spirit of cooperation among its members and other special events professionals, and

Cultivate high standards of business practices.

The preceding information is from the ISES Web site. If you would like additional information about ISES, please contact ISES Headquarters, 401 N. Michigan Ave., Chicago, IL 60611-4267, USA; phone: 800-688-ISES (4737) or 312-321-6853; or e-mail: info@ises.com.

NACE: The National Association of Catering Executives

About NACE

The National Association of Catering Executives, the oldest and largest catering association in the world, encompasses all aspects of the catering industry. Dedicated to promoting career success for its members and the professionalism of the industry, NACE offers educational programs, professional certification, chapter initiatives, networking opportunities, recognition and awards programs, a job bank, community service projects, and the industry's

most prestigious annual conference. In helping its members enhance their business and careers, NACE helps the industry reach its highest potential.

Mission of NACE

The mission of NACE is "to provide catering and event professionals superior education, networking and resources to enhance career success and deliver excellence to clients."

For more information on this association, go to the Web site: www.nace.net

PCMA: Professional Convention Management Association

About PCMA

The PCMA has approximately 6,100 members from the United States and Canada, including planner professionals, suppliers, faculty, and students. PCMA began in 1956 in Philadelphia, PA, and was incorporated as an organization in 1957. The signature event for PCMA since 1956 has been the Annual Meeting, held every January in cities across the country and in Canada. The attendance at the annual meeting has grown from its original single digits to more than 3,000 participants each year. PCMA also developed its Education Foundation in 1985. The role of the Foundation is to support educational programming to improve professionalism in the meetings industry. Since 1986, PCMA has published *Convene* magazine as a resource to meetings industry professionals.

Mission Statement of PCMA

The mission of the PCMA is to deliver superior and innovative education and promote the value of professional convention management.

For more information on this association, go to the Web site: www.pcma.org

MPI: Meeting Professionals International

About MPI

MPI is the meeting and event industry's most vibrant global community. MPI membership comprised more than 24,000 members belonging to 71 chapters and clubs worldwide.

Mission Statement of MPI

To make our members successful by building human connections through:

- Knowledge/Ideas
- Relationships
- Marketplaces

For more information on this association, go to the Web site: www.mpi.org

HSMAI: Hospitality Sales and Marketing Association International

About HSMAI

The HSMAI is a global organization for sales and marketing professionals in all segments of the hospitality industry. The HSMAI was founded in 1927, and is composed of 7,000 members from 35 countries and chapters worldwide. HSMAI has a strong focus on education, and promotes networking and customer/client connections.

Mission Statement of HSMAI

To be the leading source for sales and marketing information, knowledge, business development, and networking for professionals in tourism, travel, and hospitality.

For more information on this association, go to the Web site: www.hsmai.org

There are many resources, including magazines, journals, and Web sites, that serve as excellent reservoirs of information for the special events professional. Magazine resources include, but are not limited to *Special Events, CaterSource, Biz Bash,* *Event Solutions, and Events Design.* Additionally, each professional association typically has a resource publication dedicated specifically to the market it serves within the organization (http://specialevents.com/).

Key Words and Terms

For definitions, see GLOSSARY, or http://glossary.conventionindustry.org.

Agenda	Government agencies	Permit	Schedule
Community infrastructure	Meetings and conventions	Promotional mix model	Venue
Fairs, festivals, and public events			

Review and Discussion Questions

1. Discuss the types of events that a city might host.
2. What does the vision statement of an event provide for an organizer?
3. Discuss the importance of the planner/client relationship in event planning.
4. Discuss the types of planning tools that aid in successful event management.
5. What are the distinctive roles of the promotional mix model?
6. What are the benefits for sponsorships at a special event?
7. What are some tips for working with broadcast media?
8. What are some basic operations for staging an event?
9. Discuss costs associated with the event budget.
10. Outline the elements of breakdown for a special event.
11. Consider special event opportunities for your community. How would you offer advice as an event planner to encourage attendance?

About the Chapter Contributor

Joy Dickerson received her Ed.D. in innovation and leadership; she also holds her master of science degree in human resource management and bachelor of science degree in hotel, restaurant, and institutional management. She is an Associate Professor at Widener University in Chester, Pennsylvania, and the Director of Cooperative Education for Hospitality Management students. She serves as the co-advisor to the school's student chapter of PCMA and the advisor to the student chapter of NACE.

Dr. Dickerson was supported, in part, in production of this chapter by:

Scott Barnes, Stephen Starr Events, Philadelphia, PA www.starr-restaurant.com/events/

King Dahl, MGM Mirage Events, Las Vegas www.mgmmirageevents.com

David Halsey, The Meetinghouse Companies, Elmhurst, IL www.meetinghouse.com

Tom Kehoe, Kehoe Designs, Chic www.kehoedesigns.com

David Merrill, AOO Events, Los Angeles www.aooevents.com

Contributor to previous editions: Cynthia Vannucci, Metropolitan State College in Denver.

The ABC Special Event

Statement of Revenues and Expenses

Revenues	Budget	Actual
Admission	$ 5,000	$ 6,000
Exhibit booth sales	$ 10,000	$11,000
Food and beverage sales	$ 2,000	$ 4,000
Total	**$ 17,000**	**$21,000**
Expenditures		
Rental	$ 1,000	$ 1,000
Labor (security)	$ 500	$ 500
Production	$ 2,000	$ 3,000
Marketing costs	$ 3,000	$ 4,000
Talent	$ 0	$ 500
Total	**$ 6,500**	**$ 9,000**
Surplus	**$ 10,500**	**$12,000**

CHAPTER 9

Planning and Producing MEEC Gatherings

Chapter Outline

Planning and organizing of National Political Conventions are functions of the MEEC Industry. *Courtesy of James K. Clark, Pearson Education/PH College*

Chapter Objectives

This chapter provides the reader with an understanding of the following:

- The differences in association and corporate meeting planning
- The motivations that influence meeting objectives
- Writing clear and concise meeting objectives using the *SMART* technique
- The purpose of a needs analysis
- The process of site selection
- The information needed on an RPP
- Establishing budgetary goals
- The importance of evaluation
- The process of registration for a meeting or event
- The process of arranging housing for a meeting or event
- The elements of a meeting and event specification guide
- The importance of a pre- and post-convention meeting

INTRODUCTION

A meeting planner or organizer may be familiar with all of the elements of the MEEC industry. However, it takes good planning, organizing, directing, and control to put these diverse elements together and "make it work." In order to accomplish this, the organizer needs to understand the group, its wants, and its needs: Who are they? Why are they here? Then objectives can be set that will guide the program delivery to meet these wants and needs while staying within budget constraints. It should be noted that this chapter on planning and producing MEEC gatherings only touches upon the major issues involved. There are many textbooks, reference manuals, trade press, and Web-based content available that go into more detail. This chapter will focus on the planning of meetings: The reader is reminded that the "process" and steps of planning are the same for any event, whether business or leisure oriented.

SETTING OBJECTIVES

Creating Meeting and Event Objectives

The first thing a planner needs to determine is (1) Who is the group? and (2) Why are they here? This is followed by asking, "What is the objective of this event?" This simple question is the basis of much of the planning process. Webster's dictionary defines an *objective* as "something aimed at or strived for" along with "being the aim or goal" (*Webster's Unabridged Dictionary,* 2nd ed., S. V. "objective"). All meetings and events should begin with clear, concise, and measurable objectives. Meeting objectives are the basis for virtually all components of the planning process, whether it is for corporate meetings, association meetings, special events, trade shows, or virtual meetings held via the Internet. The objective of the meeting will impact site selection, food and beverage requirements, transportation issues, and especially program content.

Most people attend meetings for three reasons: education, networking, and to conduct business. Some people participate in association **annual meetings** for the networking and educational offerings. Others may attend primarily to develop business relationships and to make sales. If the planner does not design the program content and scheduling to accommodate these objectives, then the attendees may become dissatisfied.

Another key point is that program planning, especially for association meetings, begins months or years before the actual event. The average meeting attendee does not understand how much effort goes into planning even simple events, let alone something as complex as an association's annual meeting and trade show. As with much of the hospitality industry, the real work goes on behind the scenes, and unless something goes wrong, the attendees are blissfully unaware of the planning process and the coordination and cooperation necessary to produce an event. The meeting planner and the support staff should be invisible to the attendee.

Good meeting objectives should focus on the attendees. What will make the attendees want to attend the meeting? What will be their **return on investment** (ROI)? What makes your event more desirable than your competitor's event? Following are some of the key meeting planning components that are directly affected by the meeting objectives.

IMPORTANCE OF EDUCATION

A key component of MEEC is to provide an environment conducive to education. Sponsors of meetings are increasingly cost-conscious with the planning and implementation of their events and have high expectations for the ROI achieved by employees or association members. Poor planning in logistics or in program content can spell disaster for the meeting planner. Gone are the days when conventions were viewed as primarily recreational events and expense accounts were plentiful. If the actual benefits of attending the meeting cannot be justified, then funding to attend or membership fees for an association may be withheld. In cases where the attendee is paying out of his or her own pocket to attend, good program content becomes a much more critical issue. People are usually much more careful with their own money than with someone else's. It is a fact that attendee expectations are seldom lowered. If you provide child care and all meals one year, then the same (or better) services will be expected the subsequent year. It is a constant challenge for the meeting planner to continuously improve the content and execution of meetings and conventions while keeping the price of attendance affordable.

Professional Certifications

Increasingly, people within a particular industry seek to differentiate themselves by becoming "certified" or "licensed" in a specific skill or to recognize that they have achieved a certain level of

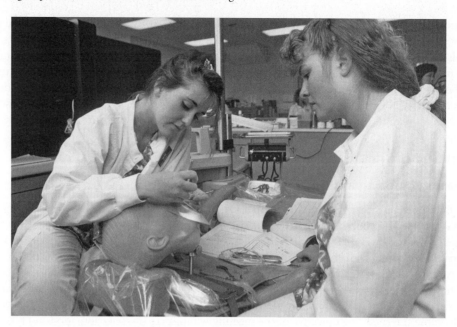

Medical education is an important part of MEEC.
Courtesy of Robert Harbison

competence in a career field. Most people cannot afford the luxury of quitting their job to go back to school for academic instruction. Instead, they rely on their professional associations to provide current information and continuing education in their particular field. Programs may be offered at the annual convention, at regional seminars, or through distance education over the Internet. Individuals receive **continuing education units (CEUs)** for each workshop they attend, and these CEUs will be a part of the qualifications to become certified or licensed. Physicians are a good example. To retain their medical license, doctors are required to take a certain amount of **continuing medical education (CME)** courses to keep current with innovations in health care. The MEEC industry also has numerous professional certifications (see chapter 1).

NEEDS ANALYSIS

As part of setting objectives for a meeting, a **needs analysis** must be undertaken. A **needs analysis** is a method of determining the expectations for a particular meeting. A needs analysis can be as simple as asking senior management what they want to accomplish at a meeting and then designing the event around those expectations. It should be remembered that the needs of corporate and association meeting attendees are very different (see chapter 2). The first step is to know your attendees by asking the question "Who are they?" A planner must collect demographic information of both past and prospective attendees. This is much easier for an annual event, such as an association meeting or corporate management meeting. The planner keeps a detailed **group history** of who attended the meeting, their likes and dislikes, and all pertinent information that can be used to improve future meetings. Questions to consider include the following:

- What is the age and gender of past attendees?
- What is their level of expertise—beginner, intermediate, advanced?
- What is their position within the organization's hierarchy—new employee, junior management, or senior management?
- What hotel amenities are preferred—indoor pools, spas, tennis courts, exercise rooms, wireless Internet access?
- Are there specific dietary restrictions for attendees (i.e., Kosher, Muslim, vegetarian, diabetic, etc. or other medical dietary needs)?
- Who is paying the expenses? Most people are more cost-conscious if they are paying out of their own pocket rather than a company expense account.
- Will meeting attendees bring guests or children to the event?
- Are networking opportunities important?
- How far are attendees willing to travel to attend the meeting?

- Will international guests who require interpreters attend?
- Are special accommodations needed for people with disabilities?
- What are the educational outcomes expected at the meeting?

Some of this information can be answered by questions on the meeting registration form. Other information can be obtained through association membership or company records. Most planners do some type of evaluation after an event to provide feedback that can be used to improve the next meeting. This is covered later in the chapter.

DEVELOPING *SMART* OBJECTIVES

Once the planner has determined the needs of the attendees and sponsoring organization, objectives must be written in a clear and concise format so that all parties involved in the planning process understand and are focused on common goals. A common method of writing effective meeting objectives is to use the **SMART** approach. Each letter of the SMART approach reminds the planner of critical components of a well-written objective.

Specific: Only one major concept is covered per objective.

Measurable: Must be able to quantify or measure that you have, or have not, achieved the objective.

Achievable: Is it possible to accomplish the objective?

Relevant: Is the objective important to the overall goals of the organization?

Time: The objective should include when the objective must be completed.

It is also good to begin meeting objectives with an action verb (e.g., *achieve, promote, understand, design*) and include cost factors if applicable. You should list by name the person or department responsible for achieving the objectives.

Examples of Meeting Objectives

- The Meetings Department of the International Association of Real Estate Agents will "generate attendance of 7,500 people at the 2012 annual meeting to be held in Orlando, FL."
- The Education Committee of the National Association for Catering Executives (NACE) will "create a NACE professional certification program by the 2013 annual meeting."
- The Brettco Pharmaceutical Corporation will "hold a two-day conference, October 2 and 3 in Chicago, IL, for the 12 regional sales managers to launch 5 new product introductions for 2013. Total meeting costs are not to exceed $15,000."
- Jill Miller will "complete the graphic design for the convention program by May 3, 2012."

Designing well-written meeting objectives can be a very positive activity for the meeting planner. Objectives serve as signals to keep the planning process focused and on track. At the end of the meeting, the planner can communicate to management what goals were achieved or exceeded, or what was not achieved and why. If objectives are met, it helps demonstrate the ROI that the meeting planner provides to the organization. If objectives are not met, then management can focus resources on finding out the causes of failure and correcting them for the next meeting.

SITE SELECTION

The site selection process can begin after meeting objectives are developed. The objectives will guide the planner in deciding the physical location for the event, type of facility to use, transportation options, and many other meeting components. Depending on the type of meeting, site selection may take place days, weeks, months, or years before the actual event. For major conventions, a city is usually selected three to five years in advance. Some large associations, such as the American Library Association, have determined meeting sites (cities) decades into the future. However, small corporate meetings usually have a much shorter lead time of a few weeks or months.

Contrary to popular belief, the association meeting planner is usually not the final decision maker when it comes to which city will be selected to host a convention. Typically, determining the actual site selection is a group decision made by a volunteer committee, with much input from the board of directors and the association staff. The meeting planner will review numerous reference materials, talk with other planners, and may make recommendations but usually does not personally make the final decision. The corporate planner may have more influence over site selection, especially for smaller meetings. But for larger corporate meetings, the CEO or chairman of the board may make the decision. Sometimes locations are chosen because of the availability of recreational activities like golf, not because the meeting facilities are outstanding. It differs with each organization.

Meeting planners are regularly bombarded with site selection information. There are several trade publications like *Successful Meetings*, *Meetings and Conventions*, *Convene*, and *Corporate Meetings and Incentive Travel* that meeting planners may subscribe to for low or no cost. Most are available online in addition to traditional print versions. These magazines are either independently owned or are affiliated with one of the major meetings-related professional associations, such as the PCMA and MPI. The magazines are funded through advertising sales from hotel chains, transportation companies, convention facilities, and many other service providers to the meetings industry. Other key advertisers are the actual locations competing for the convention dollar. There are common special advertising inserts or destination guides that promote regions ("Meetings on the Gulf Coast"), individual cities ("San Antonio Meeting Planners Guide"), states ("Conventions in California"), and countries ("The Korean Connection: Asia's Convention Destination"). These special advertising segments can showcase local culture, attractions, and facilities; provide testimonials of past events; and serve to entice the planner to consider their location. Other special supplements are designed to showcase other characteristics, such as "Second-Tier Cities," "Unique Venues," "Meetings on College Campuses," "Cruise Ship Conventions," "Affordable Meetings," or "Golf Destinations."

Other factors to consider in site selection are the rotation of locations and the location of the majority of the attendees. In the United States, the planner may want to hold a major convention in the East (Boston) one year, the South (New Orleans) the next, the Midwest (Chicago) the third year, and the West (San Francisco) the fourth year. This allows attendees to enjoy a wide variety of meeting locations, and attendees who live on one side of the country are not always traveling many hours and through several time zones to attend the meeting. But if most of the attendees live on the East Coast, it may be preferable to hold the meeting in a city conveniently located there. However, some conventions, such as the National Association of Broadcasters, MAGIC Marketplace, International Builder's Show, or the Consumer Electronics Show, are so large that they are extremely limited to their choice of cities due to the amount of sleeping rooms, meeting, and exhibition space required. IMEX has been held in Frankfurt Germany for years and is now expanding into the United States using only Las Vegas.

The Links at Spanish Bay, part of the famous Pebble Beach Golf Resort, is often chosen as a site for small meetings and incentive trips. *Photo by George G. Fenich, Ph.D.*

Cost is another consideration. In addition to the costs incurred by the meeting planner for meeting space and other essentials, the cost to the attendee should be considered. Some cities, mostly first-tier cities, are notoriously expensive for people to visit. It all depends on what is important to your attendees—cost or location. Another option is to hold a meeting in a first-tier city at a first-class property in the off-season or during slow periods, such as around major holidays. Most hotels discount prices when business is slow. As witnessed by the global economic downturn beginning in 2008, most hotels had to reduce their rates to attract a shrinking volume of MEEC gatherings.

The mode of travel is another factor in site selection. How will the attendees get to the location? Air? Road? Rail? In recent years, most major airline carriers have been struggling to survive. Many people are still cautious about flying due to terrorism threats, the ordeal of getting through security at airports, packed airplanes, additional baggage fees, and a host of other challenges that make air travel distasteful. The availability of flights (**air lift**) can also be an important consideration in site selection. Those cities with the greatest number of flights include Chicago, Atlanta, Dallas, and Washington, DC. There are some cities that are convention destinations (have a convention center) and have no air lift, including Anchorage (AL), Huntington (WV), Davenport (IA), and Wheeling (WV).

The type of hotel or meeting facility is another major consideration. There are a variety of choices, including metropolitan hotels, suburban hotels, airport hotels, resort hotels, and casino hotels. In addition, there are facilities especially designed to hold meetings called "conference centers." The **International Association of Conference Centers** (IACC) is an association in which the member facilities must meet a list of over thirty criteria to be considered an approved conference center. Visit http://www.iacconline.com/ for more information. Other options are full-service convention centers, cruise ships, and university campuses. These facilities are discussed at length in the chapter, "Meeting and Convention Venues."

Meeting space requirements are also critical in the site selection process. How many meeting or banquet rooms will be needed? How much space will staff offices, registration, and pre-function areas require? Floor plans with room dimensions are readily available in the facilities' sales brochures or on their Web sites. Good diagrams will also provide ceiling heights, seating capacities, entrances and exits, and location of columns and other obstructions. Most major hotel chain Web sites (http://www.hyatt.com, http://www.marriott.com, http:www.hilton.com) will provide direct links to their hotels and their specification information.

REQUEST FOR PROPOSAL

Once the meeting objectives are clearly defined and the basic location and logistics are drafted, the meeting manager creates an RFP. The RFP is a written description of all the major needs for the meeting. The **Convention Industry Council** (CIC), a federation of over thirty MEEC industry associations, has created a standardized format that may be used. It is copyright free and may be downloaded at http://www.conventionindustry.org.

Once the RFP is completed, it is disseminated to hotel properties and convention facilities that may be interested in submitting a bid for that meeting. Typically, the meeting planner can submit the RFP via the Internet directly to preferred hotels and the **Convention and Visitor Bureaus** (CVBs) of desirable cities for distribution to all properties, or can submit it to the DMAI Web site at http://www.destinationmarketing.org. Some hotel chains, such as Hyatt, guarantee a response to an RFP within twenty-four hours of receipt. The RFP also serves to allow hotels to examine the potential economic impact of the meeting and decide whether or not to create a bid for it. If the group has limited resources and can only afford an $89 room rate, then major luxury hotels may not be interested in the business. However, smaller properties or hotels in second-tier cities may be very interested in hosting the event. If a meeting facility decides to submit a proposal, then the sales department will review the meeting specifications and create a response.

Fam trips (familiarization) are another method of promoting a destination or particular facility to a meeting planner. Fam trips are a no- or low-cost trip for the planner to personally review sites for their suitability for a meeting. These trips may be arranged by the local CVB or by the hotel directly. During the fam trip, the hotel or convention facility tries to impress the planner by showcasing its property, amenities, services, and overall quality. Throughout the visit, the planner should visit all food and beverage outlets, visit recreational areas, see a variety of sleeping rooms, check all meeting space, monitor the efficiency of the front desk and other personnel, note the cleanliness and overall appearance of the facility, and if possible meet with key hotel personnel. A seasoned meeting planner always has a long list of questions to ask. A lot depends on the selection of hotel. Make a mistake, and the whole meeting could be in jeopardy.

Once the planner has reviewed the RFPs and conducted any necessary site visits, then the negotiations between the planner and the sales department at a facility can begin. This process can be quite complex, and careful records of all communications, concessions, and financial expectations should be well documented.

BUDGETARY CONCERNS

Following the objectives, budgetary issues are usually the next major consideration in planning a meeting or event. How much will it cost to produce the event? Who will pay? How much will attendees be charged for registration, if anything? What types of food and beverage events are planned, and what will be served? Will meals be provided free or at an additional cost to the attendee? What additional revenue streams are available to produce and promote the meeting? If the event is being held for the first time, the planner will have to do a lot of estimation of expenses and potential revenues. An event that is repeated benefits by having some historical data to compare and project costs. The basis for a meeting budget can be developed by establishing financial goals, identifying expenses, and identifying revenue sources.

Step 1: Establish Financial Goals

Financial goals are important and should incorporate SMART. They may be set by the meeting planner, association management, or by corporate mandate. Basically, what are the financial expectations of the event? Not every meeting or event is planned for profit. For example, an awards ceremony held by a company to honor top achievers represents a cost to the company. No profit is expected. Similarly, a corporate sales meeting may not have a profit motive. The ultimate goal of the meeting may be to determine how to increase business and thus "profit," but the meeting itself is not a profit generator; it is an expense for the company. Most association meetings, on the other hand, rely heavily on conventions to produce operating revenue for the association. For most associations, the annual meeting (and often accompanying trade show) is the second highest revenue producer after membership dues. The financial goal for an annual meeting may be based on increases or decreases in membership, general economic trends, political climate, competing events, location of the event, and many other influences. For any event, there are three possible financial goals:

- Break even: revenue collected from all activities cover the expenses. No profit is expected.
- Make profit: revenues collected exceed expenses.
- Deficit: expenses exceed revenues.

Step 2: Identify Expenses

The CIC manual (2000) suggests categorizing expenses by their different functions:

- **Indirect costs** are listed as overhead or administrative line items in a program budget. These are organizational expenses not directly related to the meeting, such as staff salaries, overhead, or equipment repair.
- **Fixed costs** are those expenses incurred regardless of the number of attendees, such as meeting room rental or audiovisual equipment. You could even set a specific dollar amount for profit as a fixed cost.
- **Variable costs** are those expenses that can vary based on the number of attendees (e.g., food and beverage).

Expenses will vary according to the overall objectives of the meeting and will be impacted by location, season, type of facility, services selected, and other factors. For example, a gallon of Starbucks coffee in San Francisco at a luxury hotel may cost you $80 or more. A gallon of coffee at a moderate-priced hotel in Oklahoma City may only cost $25 or less.

Step 3: Identify Revenue Sources

There are many ways to fund meetings and events. Corporations include meeting costs in their operating budgets. The corporate planner must work within the constraints of what is budgeted. Associations usually have to be a bit more creative in finding capital to plan and implement an event. Associations have to justify the cost of the meeting with the expected ROI of the attendee. It can be quite expensive to attend some association meetings. Consider a hypothetical example of one person attending an association annual meeting: transportation ($300), accommodations for three nights ($450), food and beverage ($200), registration fee ($500), and miscellaneous ($100), for a total of $1,550. Depending on the city and association, this amount could easily double. It is a complex process to create an exceptional and affordable event. If the registration fee is too high, people will not attend. If it is too low, the organization may not achieve revenue expectations. But there are more possible sources of funding available other than registration fees. These include the following:

- Corporate or association funding
- Private funding from individuals
- Exhibitor fees (if trade show)
- Sponsorships
- Selling logo merchandise
- Advertising fees, such as banners or ads in the convention program
- Local, state, or national government assistance
- Selling banner ads or links on the official Web site
- Renting membership address lists for marketing purposes
- Establishing "official partnerships" with other companies to promote their products for a fee or percentage of their revenues
- Contributions in cash or in-kind (services or products)

Estimating expenses and revenues can be accomplished by first calculating a break-even analysis—in other words, how much revenue must be collected to cover expenses.

COST CONTROL

To stay within budget and reach the financial objectives, it is important to exercise cost control measures. Cost control measures are tools for monitoring the budget. A large event for thousands of people may be managed by only a few meeting planning staff. The opportunities for costly mistakes are rampant. The most important factor is to make sure that the facility understands which person from the sponsoring organization has the authority to make additions or changes to what has been ordered. Typically, the CEO and the meeting planning staff are the only ones who have this "**signing authority**." For example, an association board member may have an expensive dinner in the hotel restaurant and say "put it on the association's bill." The restaurant cannot do so without the approval of a person who has signing authority. This helps keep unexpected expenses to a minimum.

Another cost control measure is to accurately estimate the number of meals that will be served. The **guarantee** is the amount of food that the planner has instructed the facility to prepare and will be paid for. If the planner estimates 500 people will attend a dinner and only 300 show up, the planner is responsible for the 200 uneaten dinners—an expensive waste of money. This is covered in depth in the chapter on "Food and Beverage."

CONTROL IN MEEC

Creating and implementing most meetings is a team effort. Many meeting planners will conduct an evaluation after each meeting to obtain feedback from the attendees, exhibitors, facility staff, outsourced contractors, and anyone else involved in the event. Individual sessions may be evaluated to determine whether speakers did a good job and whether the education was appropriate. Overall, evaluations may collect data on such things as the comfort of the hotel, ease of transportation to the location, desirability of location, quality of food and beverage, special events and networking opportunities, and number and quality of exhibitors at a trade show convention. This information may be collected by a written questionnaire after the event as well as by telephone, fax, or Web-based collection methods. One of the fastest and least expensive is to broadcast an e-mail with a link to the questionnaire. Many software packages are available that will design, distribute, collect data, and tabulate results for you. No special knowledge of statistics is required. Programs range from no cost (http://www.freeonlinesurveys.com, http://www.surveymonkey.com, and http://www.zoomerang.com) to several hundred dollars (http://www.surveypro.com). The data concerning speakers and logistics will assist the meeting planner and program planning committee to improve the programming for subsequent years.

Just as in setting good objectives, the meeting planner must first determine what is to be evaluated. For example: What information is needed, who will utilize it, and how will the results be communicated to those who participate in the evaluation? Evaluations can be time-consuming and expensive to design and implement. It may cost thousands of dollars to print, disseminate, collect, and analyze evaluations. Unfortunately, some of the data collected by planners are often filed away and not used appropriately—especially if the results are negative toward the event. No board of directors or CEO wants to hear that the site they selected to hold a meeting did not meet attendees' expectations. However, negative comments may ultimately turn into a favorable marketing tool. If the attendees indicate they did not like the location of the meeting (Chicago in February), then by selecting a warmer climate (Palm Springs) for the next meeting, the planner can promote how much the attendees' opinions matter and that the organization will follow the directives of the attendees.

Designing the Evaluation

A good evaluation form is simple, concise, and can be completed in a minimal amount of time. An evaluation for a meeting can be a single sentence: "Was this meeting a good use of your time?" Response options can be "Yes" or "No." This would be good for short departmental meetings or training sessions. For larger events with multiple sessions and activities, a more in-depth evaluation is called for. A good source for questions can be to review your event goals and objectives. If the meeting is an annual event, it is important to ask similar questions each year so that data may be collected and analyzed over time.

Timing is also an issue with administering evaluations. If you collect data on-site immediately after an event, you may increase your response rate. You can remind attendees to complete and return evaluations before moving on to the next session. Other planners prefer to wait a few days to ask for feedback. This gives the attendee time to digest what actually occurred at the meeting and form an objective opinion when not clouded by the excitement of the event.

The process of evaluating a meeting should begin in the early stages of meeting planning and tie-in with the meeting objectives. Costs for development, printing, postage, analysis, and reporting should be included in the meeting budget. The evaluation serves as a valuable component of a meeting's history by recording what worked or did not work for a particular event. It is a cyclical process whereby the evaluation results feed directly into next year's meeting objectives. Committees plan most large meetings. Evaluation results are the means by which information is passed from one committee to the next.

PROGRAM IMPLEMENTATION

Once the basic objectives of the meeting have been identified, the site selected, and the budget set, the meeting program can be developed in detail. Some major concerns involved in this process are: Is the programming to be designed in a way that facilitates communication between departments within a corporation? Is the programming geared toward training new employees in the use of a particular computer system? Is the programming geared to educate the members of a professional association and lead toward a certification? To address these concerns, the planner must consider several factors, including:

- Program type
- Content, including track and level
- Session scheduling
- Speaker arrangements
- Refreshment breaks and meal functions
- Ancillary events
- Evaluation procedures

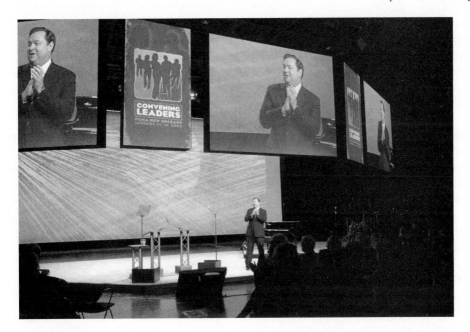

General session at the PCMA
Annual Convention in New
Orleans.   *Photo by Jeff Anding,
GNOMCB*

Program Types

Each type of program or session is designed for a specific purpose, which may range from providing information to all attendees, discussion of current events in small groups, hands-on training, and panel discussions. The following are typical descriptions of the major program types and formats.

GENERAL OR PLENARY SESSION   A general or plenary session is primarily used as a venue to communicate with all conference attendees at one time in one location. Typically, the general session is what kicks off the meeting and includes welcoming remarks from management or association leadership; outlines the purpose or objectives of the meeting; introduces prominent officials; and recognizes major sponsors or others who helped plan the event, ceremonial duties, and other important matters of general interest. General sessions last between 1 and 1.5 hours. Often, an important industry leader or a recognizable personality will give a **keynote address** that will help set the tone for the rest of the meeting. For a corporate meeting, this may be the CEO or the chairman of the board. An association may elect to hire a professional speaker in a particular subject area, such as business forecasting, political analysis, leadership and change, technology, or a topic that would be motivational to the audience. Many planners use highly recognizable political, sports, and entertainment personalities. These individuals are hired not because of their personal knowledge of the association and the various professions it represents but as a "hook" to attract people to come to the meeting. As a note, it is not uncommon to spend $75,000 to $100,000 or more (plus travel expenses) to hire a well-known sports or entertainment figure to speak at a general session. General sessions may also be held at the end of a convention to provide closure and summarize what was accomplished during the meeting or as a venue for presenting awards and recognizing sponsors. Attendance at closing general sessions is typically smaller than with opening sessions as people make travel plans to return home early.

CONCURRENT SESSION   A concurrent session is a professional development or career enhancement session presented by a credentialed speaker who provides education on a specific topic in a conference-style format. Alternately, several speakers may form a panel to provide viewpoints on the topic at hand. Group discussions at individual tables may also be incorporated. Concurrent sessions typically serve groups of 150+ attendees, and several sessions may be offered simultaneously at a specific time. They typically last between 1 and 1.5 hours.

WORKSHOP OR BREAKOUT SESSIONS   Workshops or breakouts are more intimate sessions that offer a more interactive learning experience in smaller groups. Participants may learn about the latest trends, challenges, and technologies of a specific field. These sessions are often presented by experienced members or peers of the association and may involve lectures, role-playing, simulation, problem solving, or group work. Workshop sessions usually serve groups of 150 or fewer attendees. These are the mainstay of any convention, and dozens or even hundreds of workshops may be offered throughout the course of the event, depending on the size of the meeting. A large association, such as the American Library Association, has more than 1,000 workshop sessions at its annual convention. Workshops typically last between fifty minutes to an hour.

ROUNDTABLE DISCUSSION GROUPS   Roundtables are small, interactive sessions designed to cover specific topics of interest. Basically, eight to twelve attendees convene around a large round table, and a facilitator guides discussion about the topic at hand. Typically, several round-table discussions will take place in one location, such as a large meeting room or ballroom. Attendees are free to join or leave a particular discussion group as desired. Roundtables can also be useful for continued and more intimate conversation with workshop speakers. The role of the facilitator is to keep the discussion on track and not allow any one attendee to monopolize the conversation.

POSTER SESSIONS   **Poster sessions** are another more intimate presentation method often used with academic or medical conferences. Rather than utilizing a variety of meeting rooms to accommodate speakers, panels or display boards are provided for presenters to display charts, photographs, a synopsis of their research, etc. for viewing. The presenter is scheduled to be at his or her display board at an appointed time so that interested attendees may visit informally and discuss the presentation.

Program Content

The average attendee will only be able to sit through three to six sessions on any given day. It is critical that the attendee be as well informed as possible about what each session will offer and the appropriateness of the session to his or her objectives for attending the meeting. For association meetings, programming objectives are developed months in advance and used extensively in marketing the convention to potential attendees. Program content is not a "one-size-fits-all" proposition. The content must be specifically designed to match the needs of the audience. A presentation on Basic Accounting 101 might be good for a junior manager but totally inappropriate for the chief financial officer. A good way to communicate to attendees how to select which programs to attend is to create tracks and levels. **Track** refers to separating programming into specific genres, such as computer skills, professional development, marketing, personal growth, legal issues, certification courses, or financial issues. A variety of workshops can be developed that concentrate on these specific areas. **Levels** refer to the skill level the program is designed for, whether it is beginning, intermediate, or advanced. Thus, the speaker who is assigned a session can develop content specifically tailored for a particular audience. Attendees can also determine if a session meets their level of expertise.

Session Description

Workshop 14: Effective E-Mail Marketing:
Corbin Ball, CMP, Corbin Ball & Associates
3:30 PM to 4:45 PM (1530–1645)
Room 314

Over 35 billion e-mail messages are sent daily. This is more than the combined total number of phone calls, faxes, and paper mail messages sent. This is expected to grow to 50 billion messages in 2010. How can your company develop email effectively as a primary marketing vehicle? What are the most effective options to do so?

Attend this session to:

- Discover the top ten steps in developing effective e-mail marketing campaign.
- See recent e-mail surveys about customer expectations.
- Understand delivery options for bulk e-mailing.
- Enhance your own e-mail effectiveness.

Track: Marketing

Level: Intermediate

Adapted from the IAEM annual meeting program 2002.

SESSION SCHEDULING

Timing is critical in program development. The planner has to orchestrate every minute of every day to ensure that the meeting runs smoothly and punctually. Each day's agenda should be an exciting variety of activities that will stimulate attendees and make them want to attend the next meeting. One of the biggest mistakes planners make is double-booking events over the same time period. If a planner schedules workshops from 8:00 AM to 1:00 PM and the tee time for the celebrity golf match is at 12:30 PM, then he or she stands to lose any of the attendees who want to attend the golfing event. Trade shows are another challenge. If workshops are scheduled at the same time that the trade show floor is open, attendees must choose between the two options. If attendees choose to attend the education sessions, the exhibitors will not get the traffic they expect. Conversely, if attendees go to the trade show rather than attend sessions, there may be empty meeting rooms and frustrated speakers.

Another major issue is allowing enough time for people to do what comes naturally. Do not expect to move 5,000 people from a general session into breakout sessions on the other side of the

---

Typical Association Meeting Schedule

While no two conventions are the same, the following time line provides a good idea of a typical meetings flow.

Day One

8:00 AM. Staff office and pressroom area setup
Exhibition setup begins
Preconvention meeting with facility staff
Registration set up

Day Two

8:00 AM. Association board meeting
Registration opens
Staff office opens
Exhibition setup continues
Set up for preconvention workshops
1:00–4:00 PM. Preconvention workshops (with break)
Various committee meetings
Program planning committee finalizes duties for meeting
5:00 PM. Private reception for board members and VIPs
7:00–9:30 PM. Opening reception

Day Three

6:30 AM. Staff meeting
8:00 AM. Registration opens
Coffee service begins
9:00 AM. General session
10:30 AM. Break
10: 45 AM. Concurrent workshops

12:00–1:30 PM. Lunch
1:30–5:00 PM. Exhibition open
5:00 PM. Registration closes

Day Four

6:30 AM. Staff meeting
8:00 AM. Registration opens
Coffee service begins
9:00 AM–4:00 PM. Exhibition open
12:00–1:30 PM. Lunch provided on show floor
1:30–2:30 PM. Workshops
2:45–3:45 PM. Workshops
4:00–5:00 PM. Workshops
Teardown of trade show begins
5:00 PM. Registration closes
7:00 PM. Cocktail reception
8:00–10:00 PM. Banquet and awards ceremony

Day Five

7:00 AM. Staff meeting
8:00 AM. Registration opens
Trade show teardown continues
9:00–10:30 AM. Closing session
Pack up staff office
Pressroom closed
10:45 AM–12:00 PM. Program planning committee meets
12:00 PM. Registration closed
3:00 PM. Postconvention held with facility staff

convention center in ten minutes. Plan thoughtfully. Allow sufficient time for people to use the restroom, check their e-mail or voicemail, say "hello" to an old friend, and comfortably walk to their next workshop. If these delays are not planned for in advance, then there may be attendees disrupting workshop sessions by coming in late—or worse, by skipping sessions.

REFRESHMENT BREAKS AND MEAL FUNCTIONS

As with scheduling workshops, it is important to provide time for attendees to eat and refresh themselves throughout the day. Food and beverage functions can be quite expensive. But, depending on the objectives of the event, it may be more productive to feed attendees than have them wandering around a convention center or leaving the property to find a bite to eat. Refreshment breaks provide the opportunity to catch up with old friends, make business contacts, network, and grab a quick bite or reenergize with a cup of coffee. Breaks and meals are excellent opportunities for sponsorship. Companies gain attendee recognition by providing food and beverages. Attendees get fed, and the planner does not have to pay for it. Everybody wins!

Cocktail receptions and dinners provide their own set of challenges. Overindulgence in alcohol can not only be detrimental to the health of attendees but also has the potential to cause liability issues for the meeting planner. If alcoholic beverages are provided, staff should be trained as to when to stop serving individuals who have consumed too much. Provide lots of healthy snacks, and limit salty foods. There are a variety of ways the planner can limit alcohol consumption. Drink tickets or a cash bar will greatly reduce consumption. Remember, hung-over attendees are not very focused!

SPEAKER ARRANGEMENTS

For large conventions, it is almost impossible for the meeting planner to independently arrange for all the different sessions and speakers. The meeting department often works together with the education department to develop the educational content of the meeting. In addition, a program committee comprised of industry leaders and those with special interests in education will volunteer to assist the meeting planner. These volunteers will work diligently to arrange what topics are appropriate for sessions and who the likely speakers might be. It is the job of the committee to be the gatekeeper of educational content. Subcommittees may be created to focus on finding a general session speaker, workshops, concurrent sessions, student member events, and so on.

VOLUNTEER SPEAKERS   Most associations cannot afford to pay all of the speakers at a large convention. A moderate-sized convention of 2,500 people may have 100 or more sessions offered at a three-day event. Remuneration for speakers may range from providing no assistance at all to paying a speaker fee and all expenses, such as the case with a paid general session speaker.

Benefits of Using Volunteer Speakers
- Reduces expenses (the person may already have budgeted to attend the meeting, so no housing or transportation costs are required)
- They are knowledgeable about what industry topics are important
- Popular industry leaders may increase attendance at sessions
- Builds relationships between speaker and event sponsor

Challenges of Using Volunteer Speakers
- May not adequately prepare for presentation
- May not be a good presenter, even if knowledgeable about topic
- May have a personal agenda; uses session to promote self or company

PAID SPEAKERS   A more expensive but often more reliable source of speakers is to contact one of the many speaker bureaus who represent thousands of potential speakers for your event. A **speaker bureau** is a professional talent broker who can help find the perfect speaker to match your event objectives and your budget. Typically, a speaker bureau has a stable of qualified professionals who can talk on whatever topic you desire. Fees and other amenities range from the affordable to the outrageous. If you are a small Midwestern association of county clerks, you are not going to be able to afford Michael Jordan as your keynote speaker at your annual meeting.

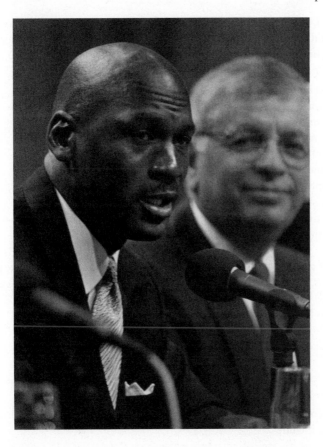

Michael Jordan not only plays basketball but is a speaker as well.   *Courtesy of Morry Gash, AP Wide World Photos*

However, you might be able to afford a gold medal Olympian from the 1990s who can talk about teamwork and determination for a bargain price of $4,000.

Providing high-priced, popular, paid speakers will most likely increase attendance at your meeting. The smart way to provide such talent is to have the costs of the speaker sponsored by a key exhibitor or leader in the industry. The general session is a high-profile event, and it may be cost-effective for a company to fund the keynote speaker to promote itself to a maximum number of attendees. For example, a $30,000 speaker for a group of 5,000 attendees is only $6 per attendee. That may be less expensive than designing and distributing a traditional mailing!

Another source for speakers is local dignitaries, industry leaders, and university professors. As they are local, you will not incur transportation and lodging costs. In addition, their services are often free or very affordable. The local convention and visitors bureau or university can assist you in finding people who are willing to assist you. A small gift or honorarium is customary to thank these individuals for their time and effort.

Online Speaker Bureaus

Sources for well-known or affordable speakers can be found at a variety of Web sites. Speakers are separated into several categories based on subject matter and price. Streaming video is often available for you to view actual presentations online. Otherwise, the speaker bureau should be able to supply you with a videotape or DVD of any person it represents. The best way to determine if a speaker is right for your audience is to attend an actual session and decide for yourself if he or she is worth the expense. Web sites to visit include:

- http://www.nsaspeaker.org (National Speakers Association)
- http://www.Speakers.com
- http://www.LeadingAuthorities.com
- http://www.Premierespeakers.com
- http://www.nsb.com

SPEAKER GUIDELINES Speaker guidelines or speaker kits should be developed to inform the speakers (paid and nonpaid) of the logistics required to speak at an event as well as to clearly define the expectations of the organization. Speaker guidelines vary from one group to the next, but most should include the following:

- Background information about the association
- Date and location of meeting
- Special events or activities the speaker may attend
- Date, time, and location of speaker's room for presentation
- Presentation topic and duration
- Demographics and estimated number of attendees for the session
- Room set and audiovisual equipment requests and availability
- Request for short biography
- Names of other speakers, if applicable
- Remuneration policy
- Dress code
- Location of **speaker ready room**, where he or she can practice or relax prior to speaking
- Instructions for preparing abstracts or submitting final papers (typically for academic conferences)
- Instructions for having handouts prepared
- Transportation and lodging information
- Maps and diagrams of hotel or facility
- Deadlines for all materials that must be returned
- Guidelines for speaking to the group (i.e., attendees are very informal; attendees like time for questions and answers at the end of session)

It is not uncommon to include a variety of contractual agreements that must be signed by the speaker. These include:

Presenter Contract. This is a written agreement between the presenter and the sponsor to provide a presentation on a specific topic at a specific time. A contract should be used regardless of whether the speaker will be paid or not. The contract will verify in writing expenses that will be covered, the relationship between the two parties, promotional material needed to advertise the session, deadlines for audiovisual and handout materials, disclosure statements pertaining to any potential conflict of interest, selling or promoting products or services, penalties for failure to perform the presentation, and allowable conditions for termination of the contract.

Tape, CD-ROM, and Internet Authorization and Waiver. If the session will be recorded in any way, or if content will be made available on a CD-ROM or on a Web site via print or streaming video, the speaker must be informed and must agree. Some speakers do not want their presentation materials to be accessed on the Internet, where they may be easily copied and used by others. Selling digital recordings of programs is an additional revenue stream for associations. Since attendees are limited in the number of sessions they can attend each day, by purchasing recordings of missed sessions, they can have the information from the sessions they missed.

AUDIOVISUAL EQUIPMENT

Most hotels and meeting facilities do not allow meeting planners to provide their own audiovisual equipment, such as LCD projectors, televisions, and VCR/DVD players. The rental and servicing of this equipment is a huge revenue stream for facilities. Audiovisual equipment is extremely expensive to rent. In many instances, it costs as much to buy the equipment as it does to rent it. A 27-inch television, which may be purchased at a discount store for $250, may cost the planner that amount in rental fees *each day!*

Thus, controlling audiovisual costs is very important. You may wish to inform speakers that only an LCD projector and laptop computer are available. Thus, the speaker can craft his or her presentation to the media available. Another good idea is to provide speakers with a template to use in preparing overheads and handouts. You can request that all slides and handouts be developed with a certain font, such as Arial or Times New Roman, and dictate the text and background colors that should be used. Also provide a crisp logo for the organization or event. This will provide some uniformity in the "look" of your meeting.

Attendees often expect traditional paper handouts at educational sessions. In an effort to reduce expenses and conserve resources, some groups have opted to put all handouts on a CD-ROM and make it available free or for a nominal charge. Likewise, some groups will post all the handouts on their company Web site rather than distribute it at the meeting. If handouts will be used, remember to request a master copy well in advance of the meeting. You can e-mail the masters to a convenient copy shop at your destination and have everything printed and delivered to your meeting facility. Unfortunately, the fate of most handouts is to be thrown away at the hotel (too heavy to pack) or never referred to again.

MANAGING SPEAKERS ON SITE

For a large meeting with multiple speakers, keeping track of who is where and what is going on is a monumental task. Recruiting volunteers or hiring temporary staff to assist you will make a big difference. The worst thing that can happen is to have a speaker not show up for your meeting and you do not realize it. Likewise, most speakers expect some sort of recognition for their time and effort. They want to feel "special." This checklist will help.

A new trend is to develop "preconvention" session activities so that attendees come better prepared to the education session. Social media such as Facebook, MySpace, Twitter, and Blogs can be created months in advance for people to begin discussions on a topic. The speaker may facilitate discussion and will design the actual presentation based on what has transpired online. Similarly, some speakers will preassess the attendees to determine the level of knowledge of the group. After the session, attendees can be reassessed, and the amount of learning that occurred may be measured.

Ancillary Activities

There are a variety of activities that may be incorporated before, during, and after the actual scheduled program. In today's hectic business environment, many people try to squeeze a short vacation into their meeting schedule. More and more we are seeing husbands, wives, significant others, and children attending meetings as guests. Some meeting attendees tack on a few extra days at the beginning or end of the scheduled meeting to spend some quality time with their family and friends. Likewise, while the meeting attendee is attending workshops and trade shows, the guests want something to keep them occupied. Tours, shopping excursions, cultural events, sport events, dinners, museums, festivals, and theatrical shows are all popular diversions. Every city, no

Keynote speakers do not always stand at a podium: here the format is a discussion.   *Photo by George G. Fenich, Ph.D.*

matter how small, has something of interest to explore. The key is not to let these ancillary activities interfere with your overall program objectives. **Ancillary activities** should not be more attractive than the program. Ancillary activities must be provided, and it is important that they are appropriate to the age, gender, and interests of the guests.

If possible, limit participation in planning ancillary activities for two reasons: additional effort and liability issues. As a planner, you need to concentrate on what is going on in the meeting facility. You do not want to worry about whether the bus to the mall is on time. If possible, outsource the management of ancillary activities to a local **DMC**. A DMC is a company that specializes in arranging activities and is an expert on the local area (see Chapter 7 on DMCs, for more information). Likewise, if something should happen and people are injured at an event that you arranged, you do not want to worry about liability issues. A prime example is if child care is offered by the sponsoring organization, additional insurance may be needed to protect the organization from any liability issues. Child care is definitely a service that must be outsourced to a professional child care service. Special licensing is needed to ensure the safety and security of children.

Accent on Arrangements is a company that specializes in children's programs at meetings and conventions. The following is from their Web site.

What makes ACCENT on Children's Arrangements different from other providers?

Age-Appropriate Adaptation – From infants to teens, ACCENT on Children's Arrangement's professional programming is geared toward the needs of each age group and offers children the opportunity to meet new friends, learn new skills and play fun games.

Customized Service and Planning – ACCENT on Children's Arrangements creates customized programs to meet each client's needs and budget. The same thing doesn't work for every group, environment, time of year or setting and ACCENT on Children's Arrangements takes all of this into consideration when planning a program.

Edu-tainment–ACCENT on Children's Arrangements combines education with entertainment to produce a unique concoction of Edu-tainment.

High Level of Supervision – Without dampening the fun or hampering the activities, all children are carefully supervised by responsible, CPR-trained adults that have been specially trained to meet ACCENT on Children's Arrangements high standards. All care givers have to meet ACCENT's stringent screening, selection and training process as well as necessary legalities. ACCENT thoroughly performs criminal checks and background references on all care givers.

Safety and Security – ACCENT on Children's Arrangements photo security procedure, "SecurChild(r)", is a positive identification system for check-in and out (ACCENT photographs and documents the parent or guardian who drops off the child and ensures that only that person picks up the child). Camera-monitored children's centers are optional. Additionally, ACCENT prepares in-depth Fire and Emergency safety plans specific to each meeting location.

Staff and Management Team

ACCENT's Management Team has years of experience in the education and hospitality field and understands the special requirements of children's programs. Key members of the management team are ACCENT's Program Managers who work with a group

from the beginning and are responsible or developing a curriculum that fits the group, the meeting location and the needs of the children. ACCENT's Program Managers are on-site for the entire program and are responsible for the successful implementation.

Flexibility – ACCENT on Children's Arrangements works its magic in any major destination site from early morning, to late in the evening. Headquartered in New Orleans, Louisiana, the company is set up to take all children's programs on the road and travel with clients, offering consistency and reliability no matter where the client event is planned.

Registration – Starting with group publicity and inclusion in all meeting communication, ACCENT is a partner in the registration process providing customized pre-event registration online, by phone, mail or fax. In addition, ACCENT creates parental consent and waiver forms and sets up on-site registration for larger programs.

Experience – ACCENT's founder, Diane B. Lyons, is a recognized leader in the meeting industry, she has a master's degree in education and professional experience as a teacher. She created ACCENT on Children's Arrangements to meet the emerging needs of professional parents and for more than 14 years, ACCENT on Children's Arrangements has been the leading provider of children's programs throughout the country, cultivating and constantly revising programs to ensure they meet the needs of meeting planners, parents and children nationwide.

A Promise - Diane B. Lyons founded ACCENT on Children's Arrangements in 1991 with one employee, one office and one promise:

To provide children's services at corporate, society, association, and other group meetings and events that exceed the most stringent safety and security needs while captivating the attention of children and easing the concerns of parents.

For more than 14 years, ACCENT has been exceeding that promise and has grown into a 12-person headquarters office with 10 part-time staff throughout the U.S. and more than 200 contract employees due to the company's dedication to its clients and its commitment to exceeding client expectations.

ACCENT on Arrangements, Inc., Headquarters
615 Baronne Street, Suite 303 New Orleans, LA 70113
phone: 504-524-1227 fax: 504-524-1229
email: info@accentoca.com

The safest route is to provide a list of local activities and the Web site address of the convention and visitors bureau. Let the attendees plan their own activities. Be warned: When holding meetings in popular resort locations like Orlando, Florida, or Las Vegas, Nevada, the "attractions" available can quickly become "distractions" for your attendees. It is not uncommon to lose a few attendees in Las Vegas when the call of the slot machines is louder than an hour-long workshop on a dry topic.

REGISTRATION

Registration

To attend most conventions or trade shows, some type of registration is typically required. Registration is the process of gathering all pertinent information and fees necessary for an individual to attend the meeting. It is much more than merely collecting money. Registration data are a valuable asset to any association or organization that is sponsoring an event. Registration begins several weeks prior to the event and usually lasts right up to the final day. Discounts are often provided to attendees who register in advance. They are offered an **early bird special** incentive to send their money in, for example, six weeks early. The association can then use that money to pay deposits or bills coming due. By registering early, the planner can determine if registration numbers are at anticipated levels. If not, it can increase marketing or negotiate with the hotel or meeting facilities about lowering expectations and financial commitments that may have been promised.

Data collected on the registration form may include name, title, occupation, address, e-mail, phone, fax, membership category, desired workshop sessions, social functions, optional events, method of payment, special medical or dietary needs, and a liability waiver. A recent addition has been to ask attendees where they are staying and their length of stay so that the impact of the meeting can be determined. Some organizations inquire about the size of the company, number of employees, or financial responsibility of the attendee (such as does he or she make or recommend purchase decisions). This registration data can be used before, during, and after the meeting.

Prior to the meeting, the data can be given or sold to exhibitors or advertisers so that they can promote their company, products, and services before the actual meeting. It may also be used to market to potential attendees who have not committed to attending. Advertising "we have 7,500 qualified buyers attending this year's convention" may entice more companies to register or exhibit. Preregistration data can also help the planner monitor interest in special events or particular workshops that may be popular. If a particular workshop is getting a lot of interest, then the planner can move it to a larger room or increase seating.

During the meeting, registration data can be used as a promotional tool for the press to gain media attention for the organization, sponsors, and exhibitors. It can also help the local DMO in justifying the costs of marketing and soliciting groups to come to their city. Hard facts, such as using 3,000 rooms and 200,000 square feet of meeting space, are music to the ears of hospitality companies. For the attendees, technology now allows us to automatically access, via computer, who is at a particular meeting and beam the entire attendee list onto a PDA for future use.

After the meeting, registration data can be used to update association membership records, solicit new members, or sold to interested parties. Most important, it can be used to help the planner with logistics and to promote the next meeting. By examining registration data over time, it gives the organization a better view of who is attending its meeting and if there are any trends apparent, such as changes in gender, age, education, or title of attendees.

Registration Fees

There may be several different pricing structures for a single meeting. For association meetings, members typically receive a discount on the cost of registration. This helps encourage people to become members of the association. But not all members will pay the same price. For example, in 2010 PCMA charged professional members (meeting planners), $625; suppliers (hotel sales people, CVBs), $725; university faculty, $415; and student members, $205. These are the early bird preregistration prices available until about six weeks prior to the convention. After the **cutoff date** for preregistration, all prices increased by $50 to $100. All attendees, regardless of how much they pay, receive the same opportunities for education and networking, and are invited to the scheduled meals, breaks, and receptions. However, additional activities, such as golf, tours, or special entertainment functions, may incur a separate cost.

For some events like the Exhibitor Show, an annual trade show for people in the exhibition industry, registration fees are priced based on what the attendee wants to attend. Entrance to the trade show is free, but education sessions may cost up to $150 per workshop. Additional events, such as dinners and receptions, may be purchased separately. All-inclusive registrations are also an option with full registration and attendance to all education programs costing well over $1,000.

Associations usually offer substantial registration discounts to their members. The "non-member" rate to attend may well exceed the difference between the cost of membership and the member rate, making it desirable to join the association. This is a clever way for associations to increase their membership base and provides an opportunity to promote other products and services to the new members. Registration fees are often waived for VIPs, members of the press, speakers, and local dignitaries. Complimentary registrations must be monitored closely because there may be costs involved if the meeting has food and beverage or if other events are available.

Preregistration

Preregistration is the process of registering attendees weeks or months in advance of an event. This benefits the planner in several ways. It provides information about who will be attending a meeting or event. It can help the meeting planner determine room capacities for educational sessions and can help the session speaker to estimate the number of people who may attend a session. Typically, advanced payment is also required to preregister. By receiving payment weeks or months ahead of the event, the planner can use that money to pay bills or make necessary deposits for services. The early bird discount is a major incentive to preregister. Logistically, as people are arriving for the event, preregistration can reduce congestion in the registration area as well as reduce long lines and waiting time. A quick check-in to collect a name badge and other meeting materials and to confirm the person's arrival is all that is necessary.

Whether it is paper-based or electronic, the prospective attendee must complete a registration form, the more simple and easy to complete, the better. A one-sided registration form is easier to fax than a form with printing on both sides.

ON-SITE REGISTRATION Like the front desk of a hotel, the registration area is the first experience an attendee has with a meeting, convention, or trade show. A slow or inefficient registration process can set the tone for the entire meeting. The registration area should be heavily staffed the first day and should remain open throughout the event. If international guests are expected, registration materials may need to be translated, and interpreters may be necessary to facilitate a smooth check-in. If a trade show is involved, having a separate area for exhibitor registration is a good idea.

Registration desk at a conference. *Photo by George G. Fenich, Ph.D.*

Registration is one of the areas often outsourced by the meeting planner, especially for large events. It is a complex process that requires much training on the part of the registration attendants. Some hotels or convention centers have arrangements with temporary agencies that provide staff that do registration on a regular basis. Some registration management companies handle housing as well.

HOUSING

Not all meetings require housing arrangements. But if housing is needed, there are basically four methods of handling housing for attendees:

1. Attendees arrange for their own room. Lists of hotels may be provided, but the meeting sponsor makes no prior arrangements regarding price negotiations or availability.
2. A group rate is negotiated by the planner at one or more properties, and attendees respond directly to the reservations department of their choice.
3. The meeting sponsor handles all housing, and attendees book rooms through them. Then the sponsor provides the hotel with a rooming list of confirmed guests.
4. A third-party **housing bureau** (outsourced company) handles all arrangements either for a fee or paid by the CVB.

Having attendees make their own hotel reservations is the easiest method. It totally removes that responsibility from the planner. But remember, the facility is going to base its pricing to host the event on the total revenues it anticipates from the group. Sleeping rooms represent the largest amount of potential revenue for the hotel. If you do not block rooms, you will most assuredly pay a premium for renting meeting space and other services. The room block is a key negotiation tool for the planner.

The last three options require that the meeting planner establish a rate for the attendees. The room rate will reflect prior negotiations with the sales department in which the total value of the meeting to the facility is considered. A certain number of rooms will be reserved, called a "block," and rooms are subtracted from this inventory as attendees request them. This can be a gamble for the meeting planner. As with food and beverage events, the planner must estimate how many people will be attending. If the planner blocks 100 rooms and only 75 attendees show up, he or she may be held responsible for part, or all, of the cost of those rooms. The difference between rooms blocked and rooms "picked up" (actually used) is called **attrition** (for more information on attrition see chapter on legal issues). A serious challenge to planners these days is attendees booking rooms outside the block. That is, they bypass the hotels for which the planner negotiated special pricing and find other accommodations. If the host hotel charges $199 per day and a smaller and less luxurious hotel down the street is charging $99, a certain percentage of the attendees will opt for the lower price. Sometimes, by calling the hotel directly or by using a discount hotel broker on the Internet, attendees can get better prices in the same hotel for less than what the planner negotiated. If large numbers of attendees do this, then the meeting planner is going to get stuck paying for a lot of unused rooms. One method of reducing this potentially expensive problem is to establish review dates in the hotel contract, whereby the planner can reduce (or increase) the **room block** by a certain percentage at a certain time. The closer to the actual meeting dates, the less likely the hotel will allow a reduction in room block. The hotel must have time to try and sell any unused rooms and recoup any losses. A hotel room is a perishable commodity if it is not sold each day; the potential revenue is lost forever.

Having attendees call or reserve rooms online directly with the hotel is a good option. The attendees should benefit by the negotiated room rate, and the hotel handles the reservation processing directly. The meeting planner will need minimal involvement. For larger meetings where multiple properties are used, it is advisable to provide a range of hotel prices to accommodate the budgets of all the attendees.

Handling attendee reservations in-house is possible but is easiest with small groups. If the event is a small, high-profile event, the planner can have attendees reserve rooms with the organization, and a **rooming list** will be created to give to the hotel. The rooming list should include type of room, ADA requests, smoking or nonsmoking, arrival and departure dates, names of additional guests in the room, and special requests. Handling reservations in-house can be quite time-consuming and may require additional staffing. Alternatively, a housing bureau can be of great assistance.

Registration and Housing Companies

Several companies have developed over the last few years that specialize in handling both conference registration and housing. Visit their Web sites at the following addresses:

ConferenceDirect	http://www.conferencedirect.com
Experient	http://experient-inc.com
International Conference Management	http://conference.com
Passkey	http://Passkey.com
StarCite	http://StarCite.com

Outsourcing the housing process to a third-party vendor or DMO is most prevalent with medium and large meetings. Some groups, such as the National Association of Broadcasters or Consumer Electronics show, are so large that they require most of the hotel rooms in the host city. Housing for a so-called **citywide** meeting is best left to professionals who have the most current technology and are well equipped to handle thousands of housing requests. Making reservations through a housing service can be done by mail, phone, fax, and Internet. The housing bureau may charge a fee per transaction. This cost may be paid by the sponsoring organization, or in some cases the local CVB will absorb some or all of the cost. Indeed, many CVBs and even hotels operate their own housing bureaus as a service to meeting planners.

MEETING AND EVENT SPECIFICATION GUIDE

One of the challenges in the meeting and events profession is that there are few standardized policies, procedures, and terminology. To begin a codification of definitions and standardized practices, an industry-wide task force called the **APEX Initiative** was created. As mentioned in Chapter 1, *APEX* stands for Accepted Practices Exchange, and one of its first accomplishments was the development of accepted practices regarding terminology. Another APEX initiative was the standardization of resumes and work orders, which are the primary record of communication and logistics between the meeting planner and the facility. The APEX Resumes & Work Orders Panel was established in January 2002 to review common practices and to develop standards. The committee found that many terms were used interchangeably to describe the document used by a planner to communicate specific requirements for a function. Some of these terms included *catering event order, meeting resume, event specifications guide, staging guide operations manual, production schedule, room specs, schedule of services, working agenda, specifications sheet,* and *group resume* (Green and Witham 2002). After a considerable amount of effort and input from all types of meeting planners, hotel convention service managers, DMCs, exhibit managers, and CVBs, the panel created a format that, if adopted, will greatly facilitate the communication between planners and the entities that service their meetings.

The panel proposed that the term **Specification Guide** be adopted industry-wide to describe this document. It is defined as:

> **Specifications Guides (Spec Guide).** The industry preferred term for a comprehensive document that outlines the complete requirements and instructions for an event. This document is typically authored by the event planner, and is shared with all appropriate vendors as a vehicle to communicate the expectations of services for a project. The industry accepted practice is to use the APEX Specifications Guide, which can be found at the Convention Industry Council Web site (www.conventionindustry.org).

> The Specification Guide is a three-part document that includes the following:

> 1. *The Narrative:* general overview of the meeting or event
> 2. *Function Schedules:* timetable outlining all functions that compose the overall meeting or event
> 3. *Function Set Up Orders:* specifications for each separate function that is part of the overall meeting or event. This is used by the facility to inform setup crews, technicians, catering and banquet staff, and all other staff regarding what is required for each event.

The APEX panel also recommended a standardized timetable for communication between the planner and the facility and service providers. Recognizing that these guidelines may differ

Size of Event	Submit ESG in Advance	Receive Return From Facility and Vendors
1–500	4 weeks	2 weeks
501–1000	6 weeks	4 weeks
1000+	8 weeks	6 weeks

depending on the size, timing, and complexity of the individual event, they do provide a useful general format.

The Specification Guide contains quite a bit of detailed information. Both the meeting planner along with catering and convention services staff will need access to a copy. If any changes are made, they should be recorded in all copies. Fortunately, as software is created and disseminated into the industry, this document will be easier to maintain and update. Some planners and CSMs now download this information onto their PDA, so a five-pound, three-ring binder is reduced to a few portable ounces. Changes to the Spec Guide can be made easily and beamed to the appropriate people.

PRE- AND POST-CON MEETINGS

What is certain for all meetings is that changes to the Spec Guide are unavoidable. In fact, one of the chief responsibilities of a good meeting planner is to react and manage change—often unexpected change.

Pre-convention Meetings

A day or two prior to the actual beginning of a meeting, the planner should partake in a **pre-convention** (pre-con) meeting. This is a gathering of all critical people representing all departments within the facility who will impact the group. In addition to the CSM, who is the primary contact for the planner, the following representatives may be requested to attend the meeting: catering or banquet manager or food and beverage director; audiovisual representative; sales manager; accounting manager; front desk manager; bell staff or concierge; housekeeping manager; security manager; engineering manager; switchboard manager; recreation manager; and all outside service providers, such as transportation, special events, and decorators. Often the general manager of the facility will stop by, be introduced, and welcome the planner. The pre-con meeting allows the planner to meet and visually connect with all the various people servicing the event. In most cases, this will be the first time the planner meets many of these people. Each representative is introduced, and any changes or additions of duties in their respective departments are reviewed. After the individual departments have been discussed, the planner should release the person to return to his or her duties. The Specification Guide is reviewed page by page with the CSM. All changes are made, guarantees are confirmed, and last minute instructions are conveyed. The pre-con is basically the last time the planner has the opportunity to make any major changes without disrupting the facility. Once an event is in progress, it is very difficult and potentially costly to make major changes. If the planner decides one hour before a session that the room should be set with only chairs rather than with tables and chairs as listed on the Function Set Up Order, it can cause havoc. Additional staff may be needed to remove the tables, and the planner may be charged for the labor. Sometimes the last-minute request of a planner cannot be fulfilled. If fifty tables are requested just prior to an event, the hotel may not have them available or may not have scheduled staff for set up.

Post-convention Review

At the conclusion of a major meeting, the meeting planner will create a written document to record all key events of the meeting. This is used for planning the next meeting. It also serves as a "report card" for the facility and the meeting manager. It will include what went right as well as what went wrong. Then, a post-convention (post-con) meeting is held. It is smaller than the pre-con and may include the planning staff, the CSM, the food and beverage director, the audiovisual manager, and a representative from the accounting department. This is the time to address any discrepancies in billing, service failures, and problems, or to praise facility staff for a job well done. Most major meetings will have a post-con; smaller meetings may not. In some cases, the planner is just too mentally and physically exhausted to conduct a post-con meeting immediately following the event. A good night's rest and peace and quiet may be needed first.

FUTURE TRENDS

• The focus on meeting and event Return on Investment (ROI) will only become more intense.

ROI Measurement Practices, Planners						
	Overall		**Association**		**Corporate**	
	2010	**2009**	**2010**	**2009**	**2010**	**2009**
Do not measure	7%	7%	7%	5%	7%	7%
Use subjective estimates only	20%	20%	22%	18%	19%	21%
Use both subjective and objective means	51%	47%	54%	51%	48%	45%
Use objective measures only	23%	27%	18%	27%	26%	27%

Source: FutureWatch 2010, used with permission of Meeting Professionals International.

• Planners will need to keep the "WOW" factor in mind. Attendees are looking for new and innovative programming, facilities, and food—what was done in the past is no longer acceptable.

The WOW factor was certainly evident at this reception that took place in the New Orleans Superdome. The DMC that produced it won an award.
Photo by Jeff Anding, GNOMCVB

• Technology will play an increasingly significant role in planning and producing MEEC events.
• Lead time for planning MEEC events continue to bifurcate. Small event lead times will get shorter while large events will get longer.
• Corporations and associations will continue to downsize their in-house meeting and event staff—outsourcing to third party and/or independent meeting planners will increase.

Business Travel Outlook 2010 and Beyond—On the Road Again, Slowly

- **What's hot?** Same-day business trips, coach-class air, upscale lodging at mid-scale prices, free breakfast, and free high-speed Internet access.
- **What's not?** First/business class air, hotel suites, limo transfers, 3-star Michelin dining, and awakening to read about your company's profligate ways in the Wall Street Journal.

Reasons Not Traveling on Business* Oct 2009

- Company travel restrictions 34%
- Current economic conditions 32%

- Reduction in people attending meetings 13%
- Using technology alternatives 8%

*next six months |
Source: Ypartnership/U.S. Travel Association, October 2009 travelhorizons (TM)
http://www.hospitalitynet.org/news/154000320/4044819.search?query=smith+travel+research+2010+forecast

Summary

Planning a meeting or event is a long process that often requires input from a lot of people or committees. Setting clearly defined objectives is the first essential step in creating effective program content and managing logistics. The planner must begin with a clear understanding of the purpose and expectations of the meeting. The objectives will impact site or city selection, type of facility used, and the services required. The planner must also understand the motivations of the attendees: Why should they attend? Is attendance voluntary or mandated by management? Planning a corporate event compared to an association event can be very different processes. Education has replaced recreation as the driving force for most meetings. However, people like to be entertained as well as educated, so the planner must attend to all the needs of the attendees and provide both. The format of the education sessions as well as the setup of the meeting space should be appropriate to the objectives of the meeting.

Once the objectives are clear, a needs analysis should be conducted to further guide the planner in selecting appropriate meeting space, speakers, and amenities that are expected from the attendees. The demographics of attendees must also be considered. Meetings and conventions represent enormous economic potential for cities. In the site selection process, the RFP is the announcement of what is required by the planner. CVBs and individual hotels must evaluate the potential of the meeting and respond accordingly. Interested properties may invite the planner for a fam trip to visit the property.

Evaluations of individual sessions, the overall conference, exhibitors, and other key items should be conducted to provide information for subsequent events. Creating a user-friendly format will ensure a good response.

Education has replaced recreation as the driving force for most meetings. However, people like to be entertained as well as educated, so the planner must attend to all the needs of the attendees and provide both. The format of the education sessions as well as the setup of the meeting space should be appropriate to the objectives of the meeting. Program content should be designed with both a track and level that will target the majority of the attendees. Housing and registration are important components in implementing the plan for a meeting or event. Both paid and voluntary speakers can be utilized—each has positives and negatives. Care must be taken to ensure that speakers are adequately prepared to address the group and are contractually obligated to perform. Finally, ancillary activities like shopping trips, tours, child care, and other services that enhance an attendees' meeting experience should be planned thoughtfully so as not to interfere with the scheduled programming.

Because of the complexity of the meeting planning process, this chapter can only highlight some of the planning and producing activities involved. There are many additional resources available including: The MPI Planning Guide, Events Design and Experience by Graham Berridge, Art of the Event: Complete Guide to Designing and Decorating Special Events (The Wiley Event Management Series) by James C. Monroe and Robert A. Kates, Special Event Production: the Process by Doug Matthews, Event Entertainment and Production (The Wiley Event Management Series) by Mark Sonder, and Professional Meeting Management, 5th edition, In addition, most MEEC-related professional associations have a wealth of information available on their Web sites and in their publication archives.

Key Words and Terms

For definitions, see GLOSSARY or http://glossary.conventionindustry.org

Annual meeting	Concurrent Session	Convention Industry Council	Convention and Visitor Bureaus
APEX initiative	Continuing Education Unit	(CIC)	(CVBs)
Attrition	(CEU)	Continuing Medical Education	Cutoff date
Citywide		(CME)	

Destination Management
    Company (DMC)
Early bird rate
Fam trip
Housing Bureau

International Association of
    Conference Centers
Keynote address
Level
Needs analysis

Poster session
Return on Investment (ROI)
Room block
Rooming list
Signing authority

SMART
Speaker Bureau
Speaker guidelines
Specifications Guide
Track

Review and Discussion Questions

1. Why would a planner hire a high-paid nationally known speaker for the keynote address?
2. What is the purpose of using program formats, levels, and tracks in designing effective meeting programming?
3. What is the purpose of using speaker contracts?
4. What are the benefits and challenges of using volunteer speakers compared to paid speakers?
5. Why are speaker guidelines used, and what should be included?
6. What are the benefits and challenges of providing ancillary activities?
7. What are the benefits and limitations of outsourcing components of a meeting, such as housing or registration?
8. How can planners use registration data before, during, and after a convention?
9. How does preregistration assist the planner in planning a meeting?
10. Describe the four different methods of housing.

11. What is the purpose of an ESG? What information should it contain?
12. Explain the benefit of having a pre-con and post-con meeting.
13. Why would a planner hire a high-paid nationally known speaker for the keynote address?
14. What is the purpose of using program formats, levels, and tracks in designing effective meeting programming?
15. What are the benefits and challenges of using volunteer speakers compared to paid speakers?
16. What are the benefits and challenges of providing ancillary activities?
17. What are the benefits and limitations of outsourcing components of a meeting, such as housing or registration?
18. Describe the four different methods of housing.
19. Explain the benefit of having a pre-con and post-con meeting.

References

Ramsborg, G. C., Miller, B., Breiter, D., Reed, B. J., and Rushing, A. (2006). *Professional meeting management*, 5th ed. Chicago: Professional Convention Management.

Convention Industry Council. (2000). *The convention industry council manual*, 7th ed. McLean, VA: Convention Industry Council.

Green, R., and J. Withiam. (2003). Preliminary report of the APEX Resumes & Work Orders Panel. Conference presentation, International Association for Exhibition Management Annual Convention, Orlando, FL, December 11.

Las Vegas Convention and Visitors Authority. (2006). Las Vegas visitor statistics. http://www.Ivca.com/press/statistics-facts/index.jsp. Accessed October 27, 2006.

MacLaurin, D., and T. Wykes. 1997. *Meetings and conventions: A planning guide.* Toronto, Ontario: Meetings Professional International Canadian Council.

State of the industry report. (2003). *Successful meetings.* p. s7, January.

About the Chapter Contributor

Curtis Love, Ph.D., is an associate professor in the Tourism and Convention Administration Department and associate director of Graduate Studies for the William F. Harrah College of Hotel Administration at the University of Nevada–Las Vegas (UNLV). His teaching and research concentrations are in the area of meetings, conventions, and exhibitions. Prior to joining UNLV, he was the vice president of education for the Professional Convention Management Association.

CHAPTER 10

Food and Beverage

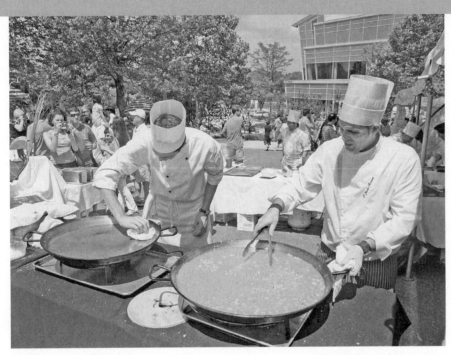

Meals are not always prepared in a kitchen. *Courtesy of Schootalot, Dreamstime LLC—Royalty Free*

Chapter Objectives

This chapter provides the reader with an understanding of the following:

- Types of catering operations and types of caterers
- Relationships between the catering department and other hotel departments
- Purpose of the meal function
- Types of meal functions, menu planning, menu design, and pricing
- Types of beverage functions, beverage menu planning, and pricing
- Liquor laws and third-party liability
- Space requirements and room setup

INTRODUCTION

Food and beverage is an area that many meeting planners shy away from by outsourcing its planning and negotiation to third-party planners. It is often a mystery to many planners as to what is negotiable, how caterers price their services, and where caterers will make concessions.

The CIC Glossary provides the following definition:

Caterer (1) a food service vendor, often used to describe a vendor who specializes in banquets and theme parties. (2) An exclusive food & beverage contractor within a facility.

The quality of the food and beverage functions can impact the overall impressions of a meeting. While many simply see food as fuel, for others it is an important component of the overall experience. From planning menus to negotiating prices, catering is one area not to leave to chance. It is one of the major expenses of a meeting and an area where Murphy's Law prevails. Furthermore, the importance of cuisine must be emphasized. The choices and preparation of food have changed dramatically over the past few years—whether to go organic, ethnic, or vegetarian for example. It is posited that food revenue is increasing steadily due to the increased choices of cuisine. However, beverage revenue may be in decline because sponsors of events do not want to assume liability for alcohol consumption.

Here are some questions to ask when planning for food and beverage:

1. Who will I work with planning the event?
2. Who will be on-site during the event?
3. When can I expect your written proposal?
4. What is your policy regarding deposits and cancellations?
5. When is the final payment due?
6. Are there other charges for setup, delivery, overtime, etc.?
7. Do you take credit cards? Do you take personal checks?
8. When must I give you my final guarantee?
9. What percentage is overset above the guarantee?
10. What is the sales tax, and what are your gratuity and/or service charge policies?
11. What are the chef's best menu items?
12. What are your portion sizes?
13. Will wine be poured by the staff or placed on the tables?
14. How many staff will be working the event?
15. What are your substitution policies for vegetarian plates and special meals?
16. Could you pass wine or champagne as guests arrive?
17. How many bartenders will be used during the cocktail hour?
18. Do you provide table numbers?
19. What size tables do you have?
20. What are the options for linen, chair covers, china, stemware, flatware, and charger plates?
21. What decorations do you provide for tables, buffets, and food stations?
22. Are you ADA compliant?
23. Can you provide a podium, mike, and overhead projector?

CATERED EVENTS

Catered events generally have one host and one bill, and most attendees eat the same meal. (Exceptions would be if an attendee arranged vegetarian, low-fat, or other special meals.) A mandatory gratuity is added to the check that can range from 18% to 24% of the total bill, and taxes can add another 5% to 9%. The distribution of this gratuity varies widely among hotel companies. In some companies, the gratuity goes exclusively to the servers and bartenders. In other hotels, a portion goes to management, such as the catering manager or the CSM. A gratuity differs from a tip, as a tip is voluntary and is given at the discretion of the client for service over and above expectations. Service charges are a murky area, but they generally do not go to the service personnel. The lesson here is: when in doubt, ask.

Catered events can be held in just about any location. **Off-premise catering** transports food—either prepared or to be prepared onsite—to a location such as a tented area, museum, park, or attraction. Sometimes food is prepared in a kitchen and is transported fully cooked to the event site. At other times food is partially prepared in a kitchen and is finished at the site, or everything can be prepared from scratch at the site. Mobile kitchens can be set up just about anywhere, using generators and/or propane and butane as fuel to heat cooking equipment. Caterers also generally must rent equipment, including tables, chairs, chafing dishes, plates, flatware, and glassware.

On-premise catering is defined as being held in a facility that has its own permanent kitchens and function rooms, such as a hotel, restaurant, or convention center. This allows the facility to keep permanent furniture, such as banquet tables and solid banquet chairs in their inventory. Meeting

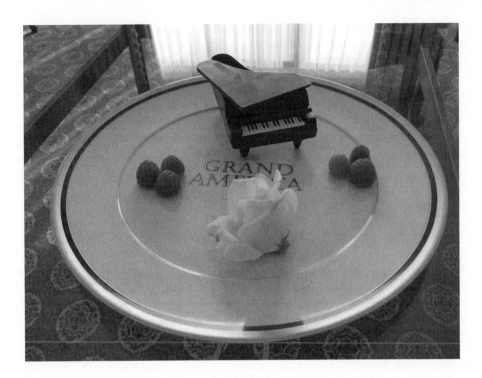

This 'wow' plate presentation was produced on-premise by the Grand America Hotel in Salt Lake City, UT.   *Photo by George G. Fenich, Ph.D.*

planners are usually locked into using the catering department of the hotel at the site of the meeting. In a citywide convention, one hotel is usually named the host hotel and holds most of the food functions, although some events often move attendees to a variety of venues. However, many meetings have at least one off-premise event, often the opening reception or closing gala or a themed event. Attendees want to experience some of the flavor of the destination, and they often get "cabin fever" if they never leave the hotel. Events can be held at an aquarium, a museum, a winery, or an historic mansion. For example, in Dallas, many events are held at Southfork Ranch, site of the television show *Dallas*.

Off-premise Catering

In Orlando, it is much easier logistically to transport a 20-person board of directors dinner to a local restaurant than to transport 1000+ attendees to Disney World. As a meeting planner, you may be responsible for simultaneously coordinating both off-premise catering events. In this case, a shuttle bus system must be set up to transport attendees back and forth, which can be expensive.

Many notable and excellent restaurants have banquet rooms, and bigger restaurants have banquet sales coordinators. Arnaud's in New Orleans has a six-person sales staff, so banquets are big business. In Las Vegas, a trend in recent years has celebrity chefs create their own signature restaurants within the hotel, separate from the hotel's own food service operations. These restaurants, such as Spago in the Forum Shops at Caesars Palace or Delmonico's at the Venetian, also have their own banquet sales staff. The Web has made it easy to research what local restaurants have to offer. The MIM List, a free e-mail listserver for meeting planners sponsored by *Meeting News* magazine, is a great place to ask for suggestions and advice: http://www.mim.com.

For an off-premise event, the first step for a meeting planner would be to create an RFP and send it to event managers or caterers in the area. The RFP would include basic information, such as the objective of the event, information on the company, workable dates, number of attendees, and approximate budget, as well as any special requests, such as the need for a parade area. Many catering companies have online RFPs. Once the planner has had the opportunity to review the proposals, an interview and, if possible, a site inspection would follow. During the site inspection, look at the ambiance of the space, the level of cleanliness and maintenance, and other amenities that may be required, such as parking and restrooms.

In many cases, off-premise events will be outsourced with a DMC. DMCs are familiar with the location and have relationships established with unique venues in the area. For example, in Las Vegas the Liberace Mansion is available for parties. In New Orleans, Mardi Gras World, where the parade floats are made, is an outstanding setting for a party. Just about every destination has some distinctive spaces for parties: Southfork in Dallas, the Rock and Roll Hall of Fame in Cleveland, the Getty Museum in Los Angeles, and so on.

Destination management companies also know the best caterers, decorators, shuttle companies, entertainment, and any other supplier of products or services you may require. While DMCs charge for their services, they often can get quantity discounts because of the volume they purchase throughout the year. And if there is a problem with the product or service, the DMC can usually resolve it faster because of the amount of future business that would be jeopardized.

Two of the challenges with off-premise events are transportation and weather. Shuttle buses are an additional expense for the meeting. Weather can spoil the best-laid plans, so contingency measures must be arranged. Back-up shelter should be available, whether it is a tent or an inside function room. For example, outdoor luaus in Hawaii are frequently moved inside at the last minute because of the frequent tropical storms that pop up there.

During the initial site inspection, obtain a copy of the facility's banquet menus and policies. Do they offer the type of menu items that would be appropriate for your group? Ask if they are prepared to handle custom menus if you decide not to use their printed offerings. When planning custom menus, always check the skill level of the culinary team in the kitchen and the availability of special products that may be required.

Other important considerations include the demographics of the group. Menu choices would be different for the American Truck Drivers Association and the International Association of Retired Persons. The typical truck driver would probably prefer a big steak, while a retired person would likely prefer a smaller portion of chicken without heavy spices. You need to consider gender, age, ethnic background, profession, and so on.

On-premise Catering

Most meals are catered on-premise during a meeting. Serving attendees all at once prevents strain on the restaurant outlets, keeps attendees from leaving the property, and assures that everyone will be back on time for the following sessions.

Conference centers offer a complete meeting package, which includes meals. Breakfast, lunch, and dinner are generally available in a cafeteria-type setup at any time the group decides to break. This keeps the group from having to break just because it is noon if they are in the middle of a productive session. If more than one group is in the facility, they will each be assigned different areas of the dining room. Refreshments are usually available at any time as well, allowing breaks at appropriate times. Conference centers can also provide banquets and receptions on request.

Convention centers and stadiums usually have concession stands open. More and more, trade shows are holding their own opening reception or providing lunch on the show floor to attract attendees into the exhibits. Most convention centers are public entities, and the food service is contracted out to companies like ARAMARK or Sodexho. These contract food service companies often have exclusive contracts, and other vendors or caterers are not allowed to work in the facility.

The above venues generally also have full-service restaurants on the property. If the group will use the restaurant, check the capacity and hours relative to the needs of the group. For example, CHRIE held its annual convention at a major hotel in Palm Springs, California, during late July. They attracted about 700 attendees and were virtually the only people in the 1,500-room hotel. CHRIE felt that the five free standing restaurants would be more than adequate to meet the dining needs of the group (dining off-site was not a practical option). This would normally be true. However, since it was low season for the hotel, they closed all but two of the restaurants, with the result that CHRIE convention attendees were faced with waits of over two hours to be seated for dinner.

Meeting planners also need to stay abreast of current food trends. They do so by reading trade journals, such as *Meeting News, Successful Meetings, Convene,* or *Meetings & Conventions.*

Table 10-1 Types of Functions

Continental breakfast	This is typically a bread or pastry, juice and coffee, although it can be upgraded with the addition of sliced fruit, yogurt, and/or cold cereals. Most are self-service with limited seating, unless an additional fee for "seated continental service" is assessed.
Full, served breakfast	This would be plated in the kitchen and would normally include some type of egg like Eggs Benedict, a meat like bacon or sausage, a potato item like hash browns, fruit, and coffee.
Breakfast buffet	An assortment of foods with a variety of fruits and fruit juices, egg dishes, meats, potatoes, and breads.
Refreshment breaks	These are often beverages only but may include snacks, such as cookies, bagels, or fruit.
Brunch	This is for a late-morning meal and includes both breakfast and lunch items. A brunch can be a buffet or a plated, served meal.
Buffet lunch	This can be a cold or hot buffet, with a variety of salads, vegetables, meats, etc. A deli buffet can include a make-your-own sandwich area.
Box lunch	These are for carrying away from the hotel for a meal in a remote location. They can be eaten on a bus if there is a long ride to a destination (such as a ride from San Francisco to the Napa Valley for a day's activities) or eaten at the destination (such as a picnic area to hear the Boston Pops Orchestra). Box lunches can also be provided to attendees at a trade show.
Full, served lunch	This is a plated lunch, usually a three-course hot meal, and often includes a salad, a main course, and a dessert. A one-course cold meal is sometimes provided, such as a Grilled Chicken Caesar Salad.
Receptions	These are networking events with limited seating, which allow for conversation and interaction during the event. Food is usually placed on stations around the room on tables and may be served butler style. Beverage service is always offered at these events. Light receptions may only include dry snacks and beverages and often precede a dinner. Heavy receptions would include hot and cold appetizers, perhaps an action station, and are often planned instead of a dinner.
Dinner buffet	This would include a variety of salads, vegetables, entrees, desserts, and beverages. Often meats are carved and served by attendants.
Full, served dinner	This could be a three- to five-course meal, including an appetizer, soup, salad, main course, and a dessert. Food is preplated in the kitchen and served to each guest seated at round tables in the dining room. This style of service is often referred to as American Style Service.
Off-site event	This is any event held away from the host hotel. It could be a reception at a famous landmark, such as the Queen Mary in Long Beach, or a picnic at a local beach or park.
Theme party	This is a gala event with flair. It can be a reception, buffet, or served meal. Themes can run the gamut. An example would be an international theme, where different stations are set up with food from Italy, China, Japan, Mexico, Germany, etc.

Many of the event and food trade publications, such as *Event Solutions*, *Special Events*, *Hotel F&B Director*, and *Catering* are wonderful resources. Online versions are linked on this Web page: http://tca.unlv.edu/pub. BizBash is also a great place to see creative things that others are doing: http://www.bizbash.com.

STYLE OF SERVICE

There are many ways to serve a meal, from self-service to VIP white-glove service. While there is some disagreement on a few of the following definitions, the following are based on the CIC glossary. The White House protocol is also being followed in this book. The White House

Dessert Buffet Table.   *Photo by George G. Fenich, Ph.D.*

publishes the *Green Book*, which explains how everything is to be done for presidential proto-col. However, because of confusion in the area, it is important to be sure that the planner and the catering representative agree on what the service styles mean for the event. (Unfortunately, the *Green Book* is not available to the public, as it also includes information on presidential security, etc.)

- *Buffet:* Food is attractively arranged on tables. Guests serve themselves and then take their plates to a table to sit and eat. Beverages are usually served at the tables. Buffets are generally more expensive than plated served meals because there is no portion control, and surpluses must be built in to assure adequate supplies of each food item. Be sure to allow adequate space around the table for lines to form. Consider the flow, and do not make guests backtrack to get an item. For example, place the salad dressings after the salad so that guests do not have to step back on the next guest to dress their salad. Provide one buffet line per 100 guests, with 120 being the break point.
- *Attended Buffet/Cafeteria:* Guests are served by chefs or attendants. This is more elegant and provides better portion control.
- *Combination Buffet:* Inexpensive items, such as salads, are presented buffet style, where guests help themselves. Expensive items, such as meats, are served by an attendant for por-tion control.
- *Action Stations:* Sometimes referred to as *performance stations* or *exhibition cooking*, **Action stations** are similar to an attended buffet, except food is freshly prepared as guests wait and watch. Some common action stations include pastas, grilled meats or shrimp, omelets, crepes, sushi, flaming desserts, Caesar salad, Belgian waffles, and carved meats.
- *Reception:* Light foods are served buffet style or are passed on trays by servers (**butler service**). Guests usually stand and serve themselves and do not usually sit down to eat. Receptions are often referred to as "Walk and Talks." Plates can add as much as one-third to food cost because people often select more items or larger portions, but plates should al-ways be included with reception food service. Control can be managed by selecting appro-priately sized plates. Some receptions serve only finger food (food eaten with the fingers), while others offer fork food (food that requires a fork to eat).
- *Family Style/English Service:* Guests are seated, and large serving platters and bowls of food are placed on the dining table by the servers. Guests pass the food around the table. A host often will carve the meat. This is an expensive style of service. Surpluses must be built in.

- *Plated/American Style Service:* Guests are seated and served food that has been preportioned and plated in the kitchen. *Food is served from the left of the guest.* The meat or entree is placed directly in front of the guest at the six o'clock position. *Beverages are served from the right of the guest. When the guest has finished, both plates and glassware are removed from the right.* **American Service** is the most functional, most common, most economical, most controllable, and most efficient type of service. This type of service usually has a server/guest ratio of 1:20 or 1:30, depending on the level of the hotel.

- *Preset:* Some foods are already on the table when guests arrive. The most common items to preset are water, butter, bread, and appetizer and/or salad. At luncheons, where time is of the essence, the dessert is often preset as well. These are all cold items that hold up well.

- *Butler Service:* At receptions, *butler service* refers to having hors d'oeuvres passed on trays, where the guests help themselves.

- *Russian Service:* (1) Banquet Russian: The food is fully prepared in the kitchen. All courses are served either from platters or an Escoffier dish. Tureens are used for soup and special bowls for salad. The server places the proper plate in front of the guest, who is seated. After the plates are placed, the server returns with a tray of food and, moving counterclockwise around the table, serves the food from the guest's left with the right hand. With this style of service, the server controls the amount served to each guest. (2) Restaurant Russian: Guests are seated. Foods are cooked tableside on a *rechaud* (portable cooking stove) that is on a *gueridon* (tableside cart with wheels). Servers place the food on platters (usually silver), and then guests serve themselves. Service is *from the left.*

- *Banquet French:* Guests are seated. Platters of food are assembled in the kitchen. Servers take the platters to the tables and serve from the left, placing the food on the guest's plate using two large silver forks or one fork and one spoon. Servers must be highly trained for this type of service. The use of the forks and spoons together in one hand is a skill that must be practiced. Many hotels are now permitting the use of silver salad tongs.

- *Cart French:* Less commonly used for banquets, except for small VIP functions, this style is used in fine restaurants. Guests are seated, and foods are prepared tableside using a rechaud on a gueridon. Cold foods, such as salads, are prepared on the gueridon, sans rechaud. Servers plate the finished foods directly on the guest plate, which is then placed in front of the guest *from the right.* Bread, butter, and salad are served from the left, while beverages are served from the right. All are removed from the right.

- *Hand Service:* Guests are seated. There is one server for every two guests. Servers wear white gloves. Foods are pre-plated. Each server carries two plates from the kitchen and

White Glove Service.   *Courtesy of Howard Sokol, Getty Images Inc.— Stone Allstock.*

stands behind the two guests assigned to him or her. At a signal from the room captain, all servings are set in front of all guests at the same time, synchronized. This procedure can be used for all courses, just the main course, or just the dessert. This is a very elegant and impressive style of service used mainly for VIP events because the added labor is expensive.

- *A La Carte:* Guests are given a choice of 2–3 entrees, with a minimum of 2 predetermined courses served before the entrée choice.
- *Waiter Parade:* An elegant touch where white-gloved servers march into the room and parade around the perimeter carrying food on trays, often to attention-getting music and dramatic lighting. This is especially effective with a Flaming Baked Alaska Dessert Parade. The room lighting is dimmed, and a row of flaming trays carried by the waiters slowly encircles the room. When the entire room is encircled, the music stops and service starts. Guests are usually applauding at this point. (Flaming dishes should never be brought close to a guest. In this case, after the parade, the dessert would be brought to a side area, where it would be sliced and served.)
- *Mixing Service Styles:* You can change service styles within the meal. The whole meal does not have to conform to one type of service. For example, you can have your appetizer pre-set, have the salads "Frenched" (dressing added after salads are placed on table), the main course served American, with a dessert buffet.

MENUS

In times past, menus rarely changed. Today, change is necessary to keep pace with the changing tastes of the public. Most food trades journals run features on "What's Hot and What's Not." Here are some items that are generally always "hot."

Table 10-2 Hot Menu Items

Seasonal food	Locally grown produce, in season, was first popularized some years ago by Chef Alice Waters. These items include food at its peak flavor.
Ethnic foods	With the influx of peoples from other cultures into the United States has come the unique cuisine of many areas of the world. The American palate has grown beyond the ethnic foods of the past, such as Italian, Chinese, and Mexican, to include the foods of many Asian countries, the Middle East, and South America.
High-quality ingredients	People may pinch pennies at the grocery store, but when they eat out at a banquet, they want the best. No longer satisfied with frozen, sweetened strawberries, they want fresh Driscoll strawberries on their shortcake. They want giant Idaho baked potatoes and Angus beef.
Fresh ingredients	Frozen, canned, and dried foods, once seen as the newest, greatest technology, have worn out their novelty. The loss of these food's flavors during preservation has made fresh food highly prized.
New and unusual ingredients	With improvements in production, technology and transportation, new foodstuffs have appeared in marketplaces that were previously unknown to most Americans. These include artisanal breads and cheeses, heirloom tomatoes, lemon grass, Yukon Gold potatoes, purple potatoes and blood oranges.
Safe foods	Organic foods and foods free from pollution and pesticides.
Highly creative presentations	Plate presentations are increasingly important. We eat with our eyes before anything hits our taste buds. Contemporary presentations should focus on the primary menu components, and garnishes should be minimal (based on the time food might be on display or stored in a hot box).
Excellent service	Food served promptly (while still hot) and friendly, courteous service are important considerations in the enjoyment of a meal.

Table 10-3 Food Consumption Guidelines		
Type of Reception	**Type of Eaters**	**No. Hors D'Oeuvresper Person**
2 hours or less (dinner following)	Light	3–4 pieces
	Moderate	5–7 pieces
	Heavy	8+ pieces
2 hours or less (no dinner)	Light	6–8 pieces
	Moderate	10–12 pieces
	Heavy	12+ pieces
2–3 hours (no dinner)	Light	8–10 pieces
	Moderate	10–12 pieces
	Heavy	16+ pieces

FOOD CONSUMPTION PATTERNS

The most important information in deciding how much food to order is the history of the group: Who are they? Why are they here? A pretty good determination can be made based on previous years. If this is a new group, or the history is not available, then consider the demographics of the attendees.

Some General Guidelines

Guests will eat an average of seven hors d'oeuvres during the first hour. They will generally eat more during the first hour of a reception. These general guidelines will vary based on the demographics of the group.

The amount of food consumed may also depend on how many square feet of space is available for guests to move around in (smaller equals less consumption).

MENU RESTRICTIONS

Banquet servers should know the ingredients and preparation method of every item on the menu. Many attendees have allergies or are restricted from eating certain items like sugar or salt due to health concerns. Others do not eat certain foods due to their religious restrictions, and others are vegetarians who do not eat meat. There are three basic types of vegetarians:

- Type one: vegetarians who will not eat red meat, but will eat chicken and fish.
- Type two: "lacto-ovo" vegetarians who will not eat anything that has to be killed, but will eat animal by-products (cheese, eggs, milk, etc.).
- Type three: "vegans" who will not eat anything from any animal source, including animal by-products such as honey, butter, and dairy.

A recent article in Meetings and Conventions (January 2010) states that venues are creating more interesting vegetarian entrees that even appeal to "carnivores." When in doubt, assume attendees who identify themselves as vegetarian are vegans. To serve a vegan a plate of vegetables with butter and/or cheese would not be appropriate.

Other dietary restrictions include people who are lactose intolerant, which means they have difficulty digesting anything containing milk or milk products. Today, people have imposed dietary restrictions upon themselves in an effort to eat in a more healthy fashion, including those on low carbohydrate diets, high fiber diets, etc. Religious restrictions may also impact food and diet. For example, people who maintain a Kosher diet will not eat anything that is not blessed by a Rabbi, not mix dairy products with meat products, and will keep separate kitchens for dairy and for meat.

It is a good idea to have attendees fill out a form indicating if they have any menu restrictions. This information can then be communicated to the catering manager, who will ensure that the proper number and type of alternative menu items are available. At meetings of the National Association of Catering Executives, attendees are provided with complete menus of every event, along with a form where they can indicate which meals they need to have changed.

There Are New Ways to Save Money on Food and Beverage

- Make receptions shorter: reducing the before dinner reception from two hours to one can produce significant savings.
- Delay Dessert: instead of having dessert as the third course for lunch, eliminate it and serve more creative items at the afternoon break, thus saving money.

- Can the Bottles: eliminate the bottled water and replace with a re-usable container that is given to each attendee at registration. This not only saves money but is "green" and present "sponsorship opportunities" as well.

Source: *Meetings & Conventions*, January 2010.

FOOD AND BEVERAGE ATTRITION

Most planners do not like **attrition** clauses, although they benefit both planner and hotel because they set down legal obligations for both sides and establish liability limits. When a contract is signed, both parties want the food and beverage guarantee to be met. But caterers want to be certain and up-front, while planners want to wait until the last minute to give the final guarantee. If the guarantee is too high, the planner might have to pay for it in the form of attrition.

Attrition hits the planner in the pocketbook if the **guarantee** is not met. The planner agrees in the contract to buy a specific number of meals or to spend a specific amount of money on group food and beverage; the caterer's obligation is to provide the service and the food. If the guarantee is not met, the planner must pay the difference between the guarantee and the actual amount or an agreed-on percentage of the actual amount (see Chapter 11 on "Legal Issues," for more information on attrition).

The planner may also lose concessions that he or she has negotiated. Function space often is provided free of charge because of the revenue the group brings into the hotel through sleeping rooms and catered events. If the revenue does not come in, the hotel can charge for services that normally would have been complimentary, such as labor. The hotel could also reassign or reduce space being held for the planner if minimums are not met.

Catering sales managers must strive to maximize revenue per available room. They need a way to guarantee that money when booking a group. Meeting planners should know how much revenue their meeting produces before negotiating an attrition clause. Caterers should pin down how much money the group will be spending on catering instead of getting a head count, since food prices fluctuate.

When using a dollar amount guarantee, provide some flexibility as to how the money may be spent. The contract can indicate that food and beverage fees could be reduced if the catered event is replaced with other business.

AMENITIES OR GIFTS

Many hotel CSMs, the DMC, and so on like to say "thank you for your business" with a token of appreciation that may be an in-room amenity. The meeting planner may also be offered the opportunity to send in-room amenities to meeting VIPs. When sending an in-room gift during the meeting, do not just send the customary fruit and wine basket. Give some thought to the person and what he or she might like. Sending a bottle of wine to the room of a recovering alcoholic or a big box of chocolate truffles to a diabetic would be a bad move. However, something that shows the planner gave some thought to the gift will impress VIPs. For example, if a VIP likes a particular wine, be sure that same wine is placed in the room.

Cut fruit and cheese do not last, so only send whole fruit and small packaged cheeses. In areas of high humidity, open crackers stale quickly, so only include small packages. Bottled water is always appreciated. If the sender knows nothing about the client's tastes, a gift certificate for room service would give the client choices and may be a luxury not normally indulged in. Or, you may give the client a certificate for a massage or to the gift shop for something he or she can take back home. Flowers are pretty, but attendees do not enjoy them because they spend little time in their rooms, and flowers do not fare well on an airplane.

BEVERAGE EVENTS

Reasons for a Beverage Event

Beverage events are popular and include refreshment breaks and receptions. Beverage breaks not only provide liquid repasts and possibly a snack but also allow the attendee to get up, stretch, visit the restroom, call the office, and possibly move into another room for the next breakout session.

Receptions are slightly different because most include alcohol and probably more variety and quantity of food options. Reasons for receptions include:

Socializing: To loosen guests up—it is easier to sell to a relaxed potential client.

Networking: To look for a job or business leads.

Categories of Liquor

The three categories of liquor are beer, wine, and spirits. Beer and wine are considered soft liquor, and spirits are considered hard liquor. There are three categories of spirits: **Well**, **Call**, and **Premium** brands.

Well Brands: These are sometimes called "house liquors." It is less expensive liquor, such as Kentucky Gentleman Bourbon. Well brands are served when someone does not "call" a specific brand.

Call Brands: These are priced in the midrange and are generally asked for by name, such as Jim Beam Bourbon or Beefeater's Gin.

Premium Brands: These are high-quality, expensive liquors, such as Crown Royal, Chivas Regal, or Tanqueray Gin.

How Beverages Are Sold

BY THE BOTTLE   *Common for open bars and poured wine at meal functions.*

The planner pays for all of the liquor bottles that are opened. A physical inventory is taken at the beginning and end of the function to determine liquor usage. Most hotels charge for each opened bottle, even if only one drink was poured from it. This method saves money but is inconvenient to monitor and calculate. The planner will not know the final cost until the event is over. Usually, the group history will give some indication of how much consumption to expect. Open bottles may not be removed from the property. Unopened bottles may not be removed unless the

Service of alcoholic beverages is a part of many functions.   *Photo by George G. Fenich, Ph.D.*

hotel has an off-sale liquor license. You can, however, have them delivered to a hospitality suite or to the room of a VIP to use during the meeting.

BY THE DRINK *Also called "Consumption Bar".*

The host is charged for each individual beverage consumed during the event. Normally, the price per drink is high enough to cover all relevant expenses (limes, stirrers, napkins, etc.). Individual drink prices are set to yield a standard beverage cost percentage set by the hotel. This is the amount of profit the hotel expects to make from the sale of the liquor. Cost percentages range from 12% to 18% for spirits and usually around 25% for wine. The planner will not know the final cost until the event is over.

PER PERSON This method is more expensive for the planner but involves less work and hassle. The planner chooses a plan, such as premium liquors for one hour, and then tells the caterer how many people are coming ($25 per person × 500 guests = $12,500). Costs are known ahead of time—no surprises. Tickets are collected from attendees at the door, and the guarantee is monitored.

CHARGE PER HOUR *This is similar to per person.*

This method often includes a sliding scale, with a higher cost for the first hour. This is because guests usually eat and drink more during the first hour, then level off. You must provide a firm guarantee before negotiating a per-hour charge. Or, you can combine *per person, per hour:* $25 per person for the first hour, and $20 per person for the second hour, so hosting 100 guests for a two-hour reception would cost $4,500 [$25 × 100 = $2,500 (+) $20 × 100 = $2,000 (=) $4,500]. No consideration is given for those who arrive late or leave early; the fee is $45 per person, regardless.

FLAT-RATE CHARGE The host pays a flat rate for the function based on the assumption that each guest will drink about two drinks per hour for the first hour and one drink per hour thereafter. (Check history and demographics of your group.) Costs will vary based on the number of attendees; whether well, call, or premium brands are poured; and the type of food served.

OPEN BAR *Also called "Host Bar."*

Guests do not pay for their drinks; a host or sponsor pays for them. Guests usually drink as much as they want of what they want. Liquor consumption is higher because someone else is paying. The sponsor can be the meeting itself, an exhibitor, a similar organization, and so on. For example, at the Super Show, which features sporting goods, Nike may sponsor a bar.

CASH BAR *Also called "No-Host Bar."*

Guests buy their own drinks, usually purchasing tickets from a cashier to exchange with a bartender for a drink. At small functions, the bartender may collect and serve, eliminating the cost of a cashier. Cashiers are usually charged as extra labor. Cashiers provide better control and speed up service. Bartenders do not have to handle dirty money and then handle glassware.

Calculate Total Cost to Determine the Best Option

If the hotel charges $80 for a bottle of bourbon that yields twenty-seven 1¼ ounce drinks, each drink costs the client $2.96. If guests are expected to drink two drinks per hour, for a one-hour reception for 1,000 people, purchasing by the bottle would cost $6,000.

If purchased by the drink, at $4.00 per drink, the same group would cost $8,000.

If purchased at $10 per person, it would cost $10,000.

So, you can see, the hotel makes more money selling per person.

Table 10-4 Number of Drinks per Bottle

		1 Ounce	1¼ Ounce	1½ Ounce
Liter	33.8 ounces	33	27	22
5th—750 ml	25.3 ounces	25	20	16

COMBINATION BAR A host purchases tickets and gives each attendee a certain number (usually two). If the guest wants a third drink, he or she must purchase it himself or herself. Or, the host can pay for the first hour, and the bar reverts to a cash bar for the second hour. This method provides free drinks to guests but retains control over costs and potential liability for providing unlimited drinks.

LIMITED CONSUMPTION BAR Pricing by the drink. Cash register used. The host establishes a dollar amount. When the cash register reaches that amount, the bar is closed. The host may decide to reopen as a cash bar.

Labor Charges

Extra charges are usually levied for bartenders and/or barbacks, cocktail servers, cashiers, security, and **corkage**. These items are negotiable, depending on the value of the business. For example, if a bar sells over $500 in liquor, the bartender charge may be waived.

A "barback" is the bartender's helper—restocking liquor, keeping fresh ice, clean glasses, and so on—at the bar so that the bartender will not have to do it himself during service.

"Corkage" is the fee added to liquor brought into the hotel but not purchased from the hotel. The hotel charges this fee to cover the cost of labor, use of the glasses (which must be delivered to the room, washed, and placed back in storage), mixers, olives, lemon peels, and so forth.

One bar or bartender per every 100 guests is standard. If all guests are arriving at once, or if there is concern about guests standing in long lines, one bar or bartender for every 50 or 75 guests can be used. Unless yours is a very lucrative group, the hotel passes on the labor charges to you.

Spirits

All premium brands are available in 750 ml and 1 liter bottles. One 750 ml bottle equals 20 (1¼ ounce) servings. A one-liter bottle equals 27 (1¼ ounce) servings. Consumption will average three drinks per person during a normal reception period.

Wine

All premium brands are available in 750 ml bottles and/or 1.5 liters (magnums):

> One 750 ml bottle = five 5-ounce servings
>
> One 1.5 liter bottle = ten 5-ounce servings

Consumption will average three glasses per person during a normal reception period, assuming that 50% of the people will order wine; you should order thirty 750 ml bottles for every 100 guests.

Champagne should be served in a flute glass instead of the classic "coupe" because there is less surface exposed to the air, so the bubbles do not escape as fast, causing the champagne to go flat (see figure that follows).

HOSPITALITY SUITES

Hospitality suites are places for attendees to gather outside of the meeting events. They are normally open late in the evening, after 10:00 PM, but occasionally around the clock. Three types of hospitality suites are:

> *Morning:* Continental breakfast
>
> *Afternoon:* Snacks and sodas
>
> *Evening:* Liquor and snacks

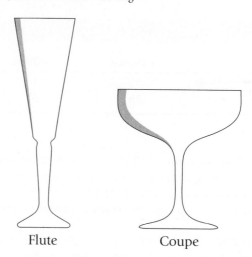

Flute   Coupe

FIGURE 10-1 Flute and Coupe

Some suites offer a full bar, and some beer and wine only. Some have lots of food, others have only dry snacks. Some offer desserts and specialty coffees. Consider ordering more food if the attendees have had an open evening.

Hospitality suites are usually held in a client's suite on a sleeping room floor, usually handled by room service, and usually sold by catering. Sometimes they are held in a public function room and are both sold and serviced by catering.

Hospitality suites can be hosted by the sponsoring organization, a chapter of the organization, an exhibitor, a nonexhibiting corporation, an allied association, or a person running for an office in the organization.

Watch for "underground hospitality suites" where unofficial parties pop up. In these types of hospitality suites, you only gain liability and lose revenue. The court case resulting from the Tailhook Scandal, in which a female was groped in a hallway at a military meeting at the Las Vegas Hilton, set a precedent that a hotel can no longer claim that it does not know what is going on within the property.

Another factor to keep in mind is that liquor laws vary from state to state and county to county. You should always check the laws in your specific location.

Examples

In Las Vegas and New Orleans, liquor can be sold 24/7.

In California, liquor cannot be sold between 2 AM and 6 AM.

In Atlanta, liquor may not be served until noon on Sundays.

In some states, liquor may not be sold at all on Sundays.

There are generally four types of illegal liquor sales, wherever you are located:

- Sales to minors
- Sales to intoxicated persons
- Sales outside legal hours
- Sales with an improper liquor license

There are on-sale licenses, off-sale licenses, and beer and wine licenses. Licenses also stay with the property. For example, if your hotel has a liquor license, it is not valid in the public park across the street. The caterer would need to obtain a special temporary permit.

Planners who wish to bring their own liquor into an establishment must check local laws and be prepared to pay the establishment a per-bottle corkage fee.

ROOMS

Room Setups

The way the room is set up is a critically important area to be familiar with. How the room is set up can affect the flow of service, the amount of food and beverage consumed, and even the mood

Grand Hall

FIGURE 10-2 Sample room layout

of the guests. The ambiance can make or break a meal function—be it a continental breakfast or a formal dinner. (See figure that follows.)

Room setup includes tables, chairs, decor, and other equipment, such as portable bars, stages, and audiovisual equipment. It is essential that you communicate *exactly* how you want the room to be set to the banquet setup manager. This is accomplished on the Banquet Event Order (BEO) form and by using room layout software. These types of programs allow you to place tables, chairs, and other equipment into a meeting room plan. Free room layout software demos can be downloaded from the following sites:

- *Meeting Matrix:* http://www.meetingmatrix.com
- *Optimum Settings:* http://www.ceosoft.com
- *Room Viewer:* http://www.timesaversoftware.com

Room Rental Charges

Can they be waived? It varies depending on the venue. If the event is part of a meeting with room nights, it is easier to negotiate away the room charge from the hotel. When undertaking catering events at hotels that are handled by the catering department rather than the sales department because there are no room nights involved, a planner rarely encounters a rental fee for the space. Rather, there will be a minimum sales amount on the room. The group may have to spend $50,000 to secure a ballroom for an event, which frequently means that guests eat *very* well. However, in event venues, otherwise known as off-premise venues, it depends on how the venue has set up its charge/profit schedule. Most off-site venues charge a rental fee. Some charge a rental fee, some an admission fee per guest, and a few charge both and then add on catering, rentals, and service costs. Which type of charge is used almost always depends on how big or profitable the event is. Everything is negotiable. At several venues, it may be possible to negotiate removing the rental charge when bringing a large or highly profitable event to the property; it varies depending on the venue. If the event is part of a meeting with room nights, there sometimes is no charge from the hotel.

AISLE SPACE Aisles allow people to move easily around the room without squeezing through chairs and disturbing seated guests. They also provide a buffer between the seating areas and the food and beverage areas. Aisles between tables and around food and beverage stations should be a bare minimum of 36-inch wide (3 feet), but it would be preferable to have 48 inches. Also, leave a three-foot minimum aisle around the perimeter of the room. Cross aisles should be 6-foot wide. Check with the local fire marshal for local rules and regulations. Because of the major hotel

Banquet room set with tables for a function.   *Used by permission of Paradise Light & Sound, Orlando, Florida*

fires in Las Vegas in the early 1980s, the local fire marshal must check and approve any layout for 200 or more people.

TABLES   Allow 10 square feet per person at rectangular banquet tables. Allow 12.5 square feet per person at rounds. This assumes the facility is using standard 20- by 20-inch chairs.

Remember to deduct space taken up for furniture before calculating the number of people. Include large sofas found in many hospitality suites, buffet tables, portable bars, plants, decor and props, check-in tables, and so forth. Also, allow three square feet per person for dance floors. And always remember to check local fire codes.

Service

REQUIREMENTS   One bartender per every 100 guests is standard. If guests will arrive all at once, or you do not want long lines, you could have one bartender for every 50 or 75 guests, but there may be an additional labor charge.

Table 10-5 Space Requirements			
Space Requirements for Tables			
Rounds	60-inch round =	5-foot diameter =	Round of 8
	72-inch round =	6-foot diameter =	Round of 10
	66-inch round =	Compromise size	Seats 8–10
Rectangle	6-foot long	30-inch wide	Banquet 6
	8-foot long	30-inch wide	Banquet 8
Schoolroom or classroom	6- or 8-foot long	18- or 24-inch wide	
Half-moon table	Half of a round Table		
Serpentine	¼ hollowed-out round table		
Space Requirements for Receptions			
Minimum (tight)	5½ to 6 square feet per person		
Comfortably crowded	7½ square feet per person		
Ample room	10+ square feet per person		

Service is critical. Many excellent meals are ruined by poor service. Meal service levels can run from one server per eight guests to one server per forty guests. Most hotel staffing guides allow for a ratio of 1/32, but most meeting planners want 1/20 or 1/16 with either poured wine or French Service.

Savvy meeting planners negotiate for the following:

General

Rounds of 10:1 server for every two tables

Rounds of 8:1 server for every five tables

With poured wine or French Service

Round of 10:2 servers for every three tables

Round of 8:1 server for every two tables

Buffets 1/30–40

One server per thirty to forty guests

1 runner per 100 to 125 guests

French or Russian Service

Rounds of eight or ten

One server per table

One busser per three tables

Supervision. One room captain. One section captain for every 250 guests (25 rounds of 10).

Set Over Guarantee. This is negotiable. It is the percentage of guests that the hotel will prepare for beyond the guarantee, in case additional, unexpected people show up.

Average overset is 5%, but you must look at the numbers, not just the percentages.

100 guests = 10% overset

100–1,000 guests = 5% overset

Over 1,000 guests = 3% overset

COCKTAIL SERVERS Cocktail servers can only carry from twelve to sixteen drinks per trip. Counting the time to take the order, the time to wait for the drinks at the service bar, and the time it takes to find the guest and deliver the drink, it takes at least fifteen minutes per trip to the bar. This only makes it possible to serve from forty-eight to sixty-four drinks per hour. Cocktail servers are usually only used at small or VIP functions.

SERVICE TIMING Fifteen minutes before you want to start serving, dim the lights, ring chimes, start music, open doors, and so on to get the guests to start moving to their tables.

The salad course should take from twenty to thirty minutes, depending on dressing or style of service. The main course should take from thirty to fifty minutes from serving to plate removal. Dessert should take from twenty to thirty minutes.

A typical luncheon: One hour and fifteen minutes

A typical dinner: Two hours

Tablescapes

The tabletop is the stage—it sets expectations and should reflect the theme of the event. Once seated, the focus is mainly on the table, so it is imperative that it not be overlooked.

The centerpiece should not block sight lines for people sitting across the table from each other. Centerpieces should be low or high with a Lucite or slender pole in the middle portion.

A garland of flowers set off this coffee station.   *Courtesy of Dorling Kindersley Media Library*

The *cover* is the place setting and includes placement of flatware, china, and glassware.

Napery is the term to include all table linens, including tablecloths, overlays, napkins, and table skirting.

Other décor may include ribbons, greenery, or other items relating to the theme of the meal.

Examples

Trailing flower garlands or ribbons between place settings

Different colored napkins at each cover

Different napkin folds at each cover

Creative centerpieces

Edible centerpieces, such as a basket of bread

Major props for tablescapes can be rented from prop houses, service contractors, party stores, or be provided by the hotel or club. Other props are small, decorative pieces that can be found in many places, such as:

Auto supply stores

Toy or crafts stores

Garden centers

Ethnic food stores or import shops

Travel agencies (destination posters)

Sports clubs or stores

Medical supply stores

Military surplus stores

FUTURE TRENDS

- There will likely be gradual and sustained efforts to embrace and integrate "green" products and practices.
- There will be a focus on big/bold flavor profiles.
- There is a trend toward fresh, local/specialty foods.
- The trend is toward clean/slick/simple presentations and efficient service.

The following is from the article entitled "The Simple Palate"

Food trends

- *Classic Dishes Are New Again:* fads are on hold. People are looking for sophisticated interpretations of familiar food.
- *Chicken Is Back in Style:* there is a movement toward "anti-luxury," so chicken is preferred over beef for a closing dinner.
- *Small Surprises:* even if budgets for meals are reduced, a "wow" item can be included to build some "buzz."
- *Breakfast Can Be Tweaked:* some venues are allowing multiple groups to share the same breakfast buffet, thus saving cost. Another trend is to consolidate breakfast and lunch into brunch, thereby making it one meal instead of two, which results in cost savings.
- *Easier Prep:* planners will choose foods that don't require extra labor such as making special sauces or preparing individual servings.
- *Meal Mingling:* more meals are focusing on networking opportunities in lieu of a large, long, sit-down meal. Lunches are going to a more "grab and go" style or on small, tapas style items. Dinners are now receptions.
- *Organic Décor:* using cotton tablecloths instead of linen, low-cost candle scapes instead of laurels. "Compostable" plates and utensils are now more common.
- *Locally Grown:* the green movement has created more interest in products that are locally grown. The "story" of where food came from is being included on printed menus.
- *Waste Reduction:* there is continued focus on reducing the "waste" produced by meetings, conventions, and events.

Source: *Meetings and Conventions*, January 2010.

This 'wow' dessert included a chocolate hand.   *Photo by George G. Fenich, Ph.D.*

Summary

Food and beverage is an integral part of most meetings. Astute planning can save a tremendous amount of money. Knowing what is negotiable and how to negotiate is critical. Food and beverage events create memories and provide a necessary service beyond being a refueling stop. While most attendees do not specify food and beverage events as a reason for attending a meeting, when asked later about a meeting, they will often rave (or complain) about these events. Catered events can set the tone of the meeting and create great memories that can result in future business, not only from the planner but also from every guest in attendance.

Key Words and Terms

For definitions, see GLOSSARY, or http://glossary.conventionindustry.org.

Action station	Buffet	Corkage	Off-premise catering
American Service	Butler service	Guarantee	Room setup
Attrition	Catered event	On-premise catering	

Review and Discussion Questions

1. What is the first step for a meeting planner when planning for an off-premise event? List five types of functions and give a brief description of each.
2. Describe how Family Style/English Service and Plated/American Style service differ.
3. What is the most important information to consider when deciding how much food to order for a group?
4. What is the average number of hors d'oeuvres a guest will eat during the first hour of an event?
5. What are the three categories of liquor?
6. What is the function of a hospitality suite, and what are the three types?
7. What are the important aspects of an event that are affected by how the room is set up?
8. When catering an event at a hotel, and no room nights are involved, which department handles the booking of the event?
9. Why is it imperative that the tabletop not be overlooked?

About the Chapter Contributors

Perry Lynch joined the faculty of the Rosen College of Hospitality Management at the University of Central Florida in 2006, after a 23-year career in catering and convention service with Marriott Hotels.

Contributor to earlier editions: Patti J. Shock is a professor and chair of the Tourism and Convention Administration Department in the Harrah College of Hotel Administration at the University of Nevada–Las Vegas.

CHAPTER 11

Legal Issues in the MEEC Industry

Knowledge of legal issues will help to keep MEEC organizers out of court.   *Courtesy of Dreamstime LLC—Royality Free.*

Chapter Objectives

This chapter provides the reader with an understanding of the following:

- The fine points of negotiation between the organizer and suppliers
- The concept of risk management and ways to deal with risk
- Taxation
- Employment laws
- The concept of intellectual property and how it relates to MEEC
- Ethics and unique applications in MEEC

INTRODUCTION

Whether we like it or not, we live in a very litigious society. Thus, legal issues are becoming increasingly important, especially in the MEEC industry. There are legal aspects or issues in almost everything we do as meeting planners and organizers. Contracts are a part of virtually every event and have become increasingly complex: Mere humans have difficulty reading them! We enter into negotiations regardless of whether we are the buyer (meeting organizers) or suppliers (hotels, DMCs, caterers, and so forth). We have to be concerned about risks such as "acts of

God," people getting injured, and failures to perform. We also have to be concerned with national, state, and local laws that impact how we put on an event, who we employ, and the entertainment we use. In this chapter, we delve into many of these issues and provide some insight into this important area. Remember that this chapter does not take the place of consulting with an attorney who is knowledgeable about MEEC and licensed to practice in your jurisdiction.

NEGOTIATION

Negotiation is the process by which a meeting planner and a hotel representative (or other supplier) reach an agreement on the terms and conditions that will govern their relationship before, during, and after a meeting, convention, exposition, or event.

While many believe that the goal of a negotiation is to create a "win–win" situation, one in which both parties feel satisfied about the outcome, in fact the real "winner" may be the party who is better prepared entering the negotiation and has a good idea of what he or she wants. In this regard, hotel representatives generally have an advantage over planners, since the hotels usually know more about the planner's organization than the planner knows about the lodging industry or the specific hotel under consideration. There are almost as many approaches to negotiating strategy as there are negotiators. One negotiator has offered these tips:

- *Do your homework.* Develop a "game plan" of the outcomes sought, and prioritize your needs and wants. Learn as much about the other side's position as you can.
- *Keep your eyes on the prize.* Do not forget the outcome sought.
- *Leave something on the table.* It may provide an opportunity to come back later and renew the negotiations.
- *Do not be the first one to make an offer.* Letting the other person make the first move sets the outside parameters for the negotiation.
- *Bluff, but do not lie.*
- *When There is a roadblock, find a more creative path.* Thinking "outside the box" often leads to a solution.
- *Timing is everything.* Remember that time always works against the person who does not have it and that 90% of negotiation usually occurs in the last 10% of the time allocated.
- *Listen, listen, listen . . . and do not get emotional.* Letting emotions rule a negotiation will cause one to lose sight of what result is important.

When negotiating meeting contracts—or any agreements—it is wise to keep some general rules in mind. While a good contract negotiation is a "win–win" situation, providing something for each party, the real "winner" in a negotiation is usually the one who is best prepared and/or the one who has the best bargaining leverage. The following general rules will help with the negotiation of a meeting contract:

- *Go into the negotiations with a plan.* A skilled negotiator knows his or her "bottom line," that is, what is really wanted and what proposals can be given up to reach a compromise result.
- *Always go into a contract negotiation with an alternative location or service provider in mind.* Bargaining leverage is better if the other party knows you can go somewhere else with your business.
- *Be thorough.* Put everything negotiated in the contract, and do not be afraid to utilize an addendum, provided that it is referred to in the body of the contract. Develop your own contract if necessary.
- *Do not assume anything.* Meeting industry personnel change frequently, and oral agreements or assumptions can be easily forgotten or misunderstood.
- *Be specific.* For example, do not state "food and beverage prices will be guaranteed *12 to 18* months out." Instead, specify that "food and beverage prices will be guaranteed (or negotiated) 12 months prior to the meeting."

- ***Beware of language that sounds acceptable but is not specific.*** For example, what does a "tentative first option" mean? Words like "reasonable," "anticipated," and "projected" should be avoided, since their meaning is different to different people.
- ***Do not accept something just because it is preprinted on the contract or the proposal is given to you by the other party.*** Everything is negotiable.
- ***Read the small print.*** For example, the "boilerplate" language about indemnification of parties in the event of negligence can make a major difference in the resolution of liability after an accident or injury.
- ***Look for mutuality in the contract's provisions.*** For example, do not sign a contract in which the "hold harmless" clause only protects one of the parties. Such provisions should be applicable to both parties. And never give one party the unilateral right to do anything, such as change the location of meeting rooms without consent of the meeting organizer.

In addition to the general "rules" applicable to all contract negotiations, there are some special rules about hotel contracts that should also be kept in mind:

- Remember that a meeting contract provides a "package" of funds to a hotel. Think in terms of overall financial benefit to the hotel (i.e., its total income from room rates, food and beverage, and so on), and allocate this to the organization's benefit.
- Never sign a contract in which major items like room rates are left to future negotiation. Future rates can always be set as a percentage of then-current "rack" rates or as a predetermined increase over existing rates (such as the Bureau of Labor Statistics' Consumer Price Index, officially called the "Consumer Price Index for All Urban Consumers" or CPI-U). And, although it may be unlikely, you may provide for a decrease in rates if the market falls. Also indicate the specific date when final rates are to be determined. For example, a contract could indicate that the room rate, if not guaranteed, is to include the increase over the CPI-U, "x" percent off the then-current rack rate, or 5% per year over the current group rate, whichever rate is less.
- Specify special room rates—such as for staff and speakers—and indicate any upgrades for them. Indicate whether these are included in the complimentary room formula, and specify what that formula is.
- While it is preferable to have specific meeting and function rooms designated in the contract, they should be assigned at least six to nine months prior to the meeting, depending on the time of the first promotional mailing. Do not permit a change in assigned meeting rooms without approval of the meeting organizer.
- Do not agree to any changes that are not spelled out either in the contract or in a later addendum. If an addendum is used, make sure that it references the underlying agreement; and if it is signed at the time of the agreement, make sure that the agreement references the addendum. Be sure that all documents are signed by individuals who are authorized to bind the parties.

One of the most frequently overlooked yet most important parts of a hotel contract includes the names of the contracting parties. While the meeting's organizer is listed (an independent planner should always sign as an agent for the organizer or have an authorized representative of the organizer sign), the name of the hotel is, in almost all cases, simply listed as the name on the hotel marquee, like "Sheraton Boston."

But the hotel's name is merely a trade name—that is, the name under which the property's owner or management company does business. In today's hotel environment, it may actually be a franchise of a national "chain" operated by a company that the planner has never heard of. For example, one of the country's largest hotel management companies is Interstate Hotels & Resorts, Inc. Included in the more than 300 hotels that it manages are properties operating under the following "chain" names: Marriott, Holiday Inn, Hilton, Sheraton, and Radisson. Thus, if a contract with one of Interstate's properties simply states that it is with the "Gaithersburg (MD) Marriott," the planner might never know that the actual contracting party is Interstate Hotels & Resorts.

Negotiating is a difficult and oftentimes frustrating experience. *Courtesy of Redbaron, Dreamstime LLC—Royalty Free.*

Every meeting contract should contain the following provision, usually as the introductory paragraph:

"This Agreement dated _____ is between (official legal name of entity), a (name of state) (corporation) (partnership) doing business as (name of hotel) and having its principal place of business at (address of contracting party, not hotel) and (name of meeting organizer), a (name of state) (corporation) (partnership) having its principal place of business at (address of meeting organizer)."

Sleeping rooms generates the major share of hotel revenue, so this is often the biggest concern to hotels.

Catered food and beverage is also important but only if it is the "right" kind of food and beverage function, since not all functions are equal in value. For example, a seated dinner for 100 people is worth more to a hotel—in revenue and profit—than a coffee break or continental breakfast for the same number of people.

The type of entity organizing the meeting. Hotels know from experience that certain types of meeting attendees are likely to spend more at hotel food outlets (restaurants, room service, etc.) than other types of attendees who may venture outside the property for meals at more expensive restaurants. From experience, a hotel is also able to estimate the number of attendees who will not show up or who will check out early. Early departures and no-shows deprive the hotel of expected revenue.

If a meeting planner is going to successfully negotiate with a hotel, the planner should:

• Understand the relative strengths and weaknesses of the meeting as a "piece of business" that the hotel may be interested in: "how much is the piece of business worth?"

• Understand how a hotel evaluates business.

• Understand the competitive marketplace in which the hotel operates—for instance, its strengths, weaknesses, and occupancy patterns.

• Position the meeting in its best light, using detailed information and history of prior meetings to support this approach. The hotel may base its evaluation of a meeting, especially one it has never hosted before, on its perception of the industry or profession represented by the meeting organizer. Thus, the meeting organizer can counter any negative impressions, or buttress positive ones by providing the hotel with as much information as possible on the organizer's meeting history. Especially helpful is information pertaining to previous meeting room blocks and subsequent room utilization, total spending on sleeping rooms, food and beverage, equipment rental, and ancillary services like recreational activities or in-room movies.

• Many hoteliers, particularly those who have been in the industry for many years, sum up meeting negotiations with this simple maxim: "**Dates, Rates** *and Space—You Can Only Have Two.*" By this maxim, for example, the planner can get the dates and meeting space he or she wants for a meeting, but may have to give a little on the rate. In reality, much more than space, room rates, and meeting dates are negotiable. Consider contract issues such as complimentary room ratios, cutoff dates, rates after cutoff, attrition and cancellation clauses, meeting or exhibit space rental, comp suites, staff rates, limo service, audiovisual rates, VIP amenities, parking fees, and food and beverage provisions. In short, *everything* about a hotel (supplier) contract is negotiable. Likewise, in any other vendor or supplier contract, there are many negotiable items.

• Determine where the meeting organizer can be flexible. A negotiation often requires both parties to make concessions in order to reach an equitable, acceptable agreement. For example, if a planner understands that the meeting's space-to-rooms ratio is greater than customary, the planner can help his or her position by altering program format, eliminating 24-hour "holds" on meeting or function space that allows the hotel to sell the space in unused hours. The planner who refuses to be flexible is not likely to get the best deal. Changing arrival and departure dates to more closely fit the hotel's occupancy pattern can also lead to a successful negotiation. Moving the meeting forward or backward one or more weeks can also result in savings, especially if the preferred time coincides with a period of high sleeping room demand.

To understand how a hotel approaches a meeting negotiation, the planner must first know about the hotel. Some of the necessary information is obvious:

• The hotel's location—is it near an airport, downtown, or close to a convention center?
• The hotel's type—is it a resort with a golf course, tennis court, and other amenities; a "convention" hotel with a great deal of meeting space; or a small venue with limited meeting facilities?

However, some of the information that is important to know is not so obvious, and may in fact change depending on the time of the year. For example, it is important to know the mix between the hotel's transient business (that derived from individual business guests or tourists) and groups; within the group sector, it is valuable to know how much business is derived from corporate, government, and association sources. It is also important to know what the hotel regards as "high" season, when room demand is highest, and "low" season, when demand is at its annual low. This information is important because it helps the planner understand the hotel's position in the negotiation process, and it may provide some helpful hints in structuring a planner's proposal to meet the hotel's needs.

Seasonal fluctuations may be driven by outside factors, such as events in the city where the hotel is located. For example, an informed planner will know that it is difficult to book rooms in

Jazz Fest draws upwards of 100,000 attendees per day to New Orleans in late April.   *Photo by George G. Fenich, Ph.D.*

New Orleans during Mardi Gras or during that city's annual Jazz Fest (in late April and early May) because hotels can sell their rooms to individual tourists at higher rates than to groups. Many hotels in Palm Springs, California, are heavily booked during spring break; therefore, favorable meeting rates may be difficult to obtain then.

The arrival and departure patterns of the majority of a hotel's guests are also important for a planner to know. For example, a hotel in Las Vegas is generally difficult to book for weekend meetings, since that city attracts large numbers of individual visitors who come to spend the weekend. A hotel that caters to many individual business guests may have greater availability on Friday and Saturday nights, when business travelers are not there. A national survey indicates that, for typical hotels, occupancy is lowest on Sunday evenings and highest on Wednesdays.

While hotels generate revenue from a variety of sources—and recently have become more sophisticated in analyzing these "profit centers"—the primary source of hotel income is sleeping room revenue; one industry research report estimates that, on the whole, more than 67% of all hotel revenue is generated from sleeping rooms.

Sleeping room revenue is also profitable, with more than 73% of the income going to the "bottom line" as gross profit. This profit figure does not take into account expenses for marketing, engineering, general and administrative overhead, or any items related to debt service, such as mortgage payments and insurance. While food and beverage operations is the second largest source of revenue, this source is far less profitable, with about 25% being recorded as "profit."

Hotels set their sleeping room rates—at least the published or so-called **rack rates**—in a number of ways. First, the hotel wants to achieve a total return on its investment. However, since nearly 50% of all rooms in all hotels are sold at less than rack rate, hotels vary their actual rates depending on a number of supply and demand factors, including time of year (which is a function of demand).

Most hotels have adopted the concept of **yield management**, also called revenue management, pioneered by the airline industry. In this approach, hotels are able to vary their rates almost daily, depending on the actual and anticipated demand for rooms at a particular time. The "yield management" concept may have some negative impact on meeting planners. For example, a planner who books a meeting fifteen to eighteen months in advance may find that, as the meeting nears, total hotel room utilization is lower than the hotel anticipated, so the hotel, hoping to generate additional revenue, will promote special pricing that may turn out to be less than what was offered to the meeting organizer. A contractual provision prohibiting this practice—which many hotels will not agree to—or at least giving the meeting organizer credit toward its room block for rooms booked at these lower prices can help take the sting out of yield management practices.

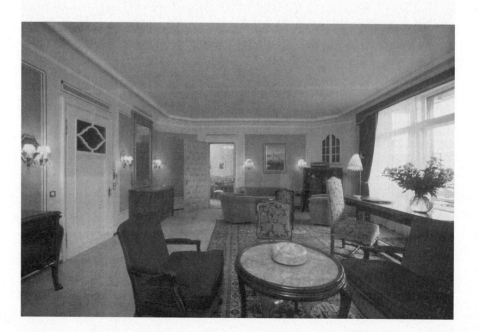

Suites like this one are sometimes rented by exhibitors and vendors to host parties for clients.
Courtesy of Robin Smith, PhotoLibrary.com

CONTRACTS

In far too many instances, **contracts** for meetings, conventions, and trade shows, and the ancillary services provided in connection with these events, contain self-serving statements, lack specificity, and fail to reflect the total negotiation between the parties. This is understandable since neither meeting planners nor hotel sales representatives generally receive training in the law governing these agreements.

By definition, a contract is:

"[a]n agreement between two or more persons which creates an obligation to do . . . a particular thing." (*Black's Law Dictionary* (6th ed.), 1990, p. 322).

A contract need not be called a contract but can be referred to as an *agreement*, a *letter of agreement*, a *memorandum of understanding*, and sometimes a *letter of intent* or *proposal*. The title of the document or understanding is not important—its contents are. For example, if a document called a "proposal" sets forth details of a meeting and contains the legal elements of a contract, it becomes a binding contract when signed by both parties. So technically, you could call it a duck . . . and it might still be a contract!

The essential elements of a contract are:

- An offer by one party.
- Acceptance of the offer as presented. This is typically done by signing the contract.
- Consideration (i.e., the price negotiated and paid for the agreement). Although consideration is usually expressed in monetary terms, it need not be—for example, mutual promises are often treated as consideration in a valid contract.

Offers can be terminated prior to acceptance in one of several ways:

- At the expiration of a specified time (e.g., "This offer is only good for 24 hours." After twenty-four hours, the other party cannot accept it because it expired.).
- At the expiration of a reasonable time period.
- On specific revocation by the offeror. In this case, however, the revocation must be communicated to the offeree to be effective.

A rejection of the offer by the offeree or the proposal of a counteroffer terminates the original offer, but a request for additional information about the offer is not construed as a rejection of the offer. For example, if an individual responds to an offer by saying, "I accept, with the following addition," that is not really an acceptance but the proposal of a counteroffer, which the original offeror must then consider and either accept or reject.

Often, a meeting contract proposal from a hotel will contain a specified termination period for the offer. These "offers" are usually couched in the phrase "tentative first option" or in a similar wording. Because the meeting organizer pays or promises nothing for this "option," it is, in reality, nothing more than a contract offer, which must be specifically accepted by the meeting planner. There is no legal obligation on the part of the hotel to keep the option or offer open for the time period stated.

In a meeting context, the hotel, venue, or vendor is usually the offeror—that is, the written agreement is generally proposed, after some preliminary negotiation, by them to the planner. The meeting organizer becomes the offeree, but a counteroffer is often made.

In order for an offer to be accepted, the acceptance must be unequivocal and in the same terms as the offer. Any deviation from the offer's terms is not acceptance; it is a counteroffer, which must then be accepted by the original offeror in order for a valid contract to exist.

Acceptance must be communicated to the offeror using the same means as the offeror used. In other words, if the offer is made in writing, the acceptance must be in writing. Mere silence on the part of the offeree is never construed as acceptance, and an offeror cannot impose an agreement on the other party by stating that the contract will be assumed if no response is given by a specified date.

As indicated, consideration is the price negotiated and paid for the agreement. While consideration generally involves money paid for the other party's promise to perform certain functions—for example, money paid to a hotel for the provision of sleeping rooms, meeting space, and food and beverage functions—it could also be an exchange of mutual promises, as in a barter situation.

Consideration must be what the law regards as "sufficient," not from a monetary standpoint, but from the standpoint of whether the act or return promises results in either a benefit to the promisor or a detriment to the promisee. The fairness of the agreed exchange is legally irrelevant; thus, the law is not concerned about whether one party "overpaid" for what he or she received. One need not make an affirmative promise or payment of money; for instance, forbearance, not doing something that someone is legally entitled to do, can also be a consideration in a contract.

It is important that both promises must be legally enforceable to constitute valid *consideration*. For example, a promise to commit an illegal act is not *consideration* because the law will not require one to commit that act.

Although a contract does not have to be in writing to be enforceable, every law student learns that it is better to have a written document since there can be less chance for a misunderstanding about the terms of the agreement. However, under what is called the "Statute of Frauds," some contracts must be in writing to be enforceable. This statute was first passed in England in 1677, and in one form or another has become a part of the law of virtually every state in the United States. The exception is Louisiana, where law is based on French Napoleonic code.

Among the agreements that must be in writing are contracts for the sale or lease of real estate and contracts that are not to be performed within one year of agreement. The latter includes contracts for meetings and other events that are to be held more than one year in the future. The former could also include a meeting contract, since the agreement might be construed as an organizer's "lease" of hotel space. The law requires these contracts to be in writing because they are viewed as more important documents than "ordinary" agreements. However, as indicated, planners are strongly encouraged to put all contracts in writing to avoid the possibility of misunderstandings.

A valid written contract must contain the identity of the parties, an identification or recitation of the subject matter and terms of agreement, and a statement of consideration. Often, where the consideration may not be obvious, a contract will state that it is entered into for "good and valuable consideration, the receipt and sufficiency of which are acknowledged by the parties."

When a contract is in writing, it is generally subject to the so-called "parol" evidence or "four-corners" rule of interpretation. Thus, where the written contract is intended to be the complete and final expression of the rights and duties of the parties, evidence of prior oral or written negotiations or agreements or contemporaneous oral agreements cannot be considered by a court charged with interpreting the contract. Many contracts contain what is often called an "entire agreement" clause, which specifies that the written document contains the entire agreement between the parties and supersedes all previous oral or written negotiations or agreements.

Parol Evidence

Parol evidence (or evidence of oral agreement) can be used in limited instances, especially where the plain meaning of words in the written document may be in doubt. A court will generally construe a contract most strongly against the party that prepared the written document; and if there is a conflict between printed and handwritten words or phrases, the latter will prevail.

Many contracts, especially meeting contracts, contain addenda prepared at the same time or sometimes subsequent to the signing of the contract. In cases where the terms of an addendum differ from those of the contract, the addendum generally prevails, although it is a good idea when using an addendum to specifically provide that in the event of differences, the addendum will prevail.

Planning and executing a meeting may involve the negotiation of several contracts. Obviously, the major—and perhaps most important—agreement is the one with the hotel and/or trade show facility. However, there can also be agreements covering a myriad of ancillary services, such as temporary employees, security, audiovisual equipment, destination management (e.g., tours and local transportation), entertainment, outside food and beverage, exhibitor services or decorating, and housing bureaus. Moreover, agreements may be negotiated with "official" transportation providers like travel agencies, airlines, and rental car companies.

Attrition, cancellation, and termination provisions in a hotel are frequently confusing. If not carefully drafted, they can lead to many problems (and much expense) if a meeting organizer does not fill the room block or wishes to change his or her mind for some reason.

Attrition

Attrition clauses (sometimes also referred to as *performance* or *slippage clauses*) provide for the payment of damages to the hotel when a meeting organizer fails to fully utilize the room block specified in the contract. Most hotels regard the contracted room block as a commitment by the meeting organizer to fill the number of room nights specified. However, in at least one case, a court determined that the room block did not represent a commitment by the meeting organizer; that decision was predicated, in part, on contract language that indicated that room reservations would be made by individuals and not by the meeting organizer.

A well-written attrition provision should provide the organizing entity with the ability to reduce the room block by a specified amount (e.g., 10%–20%) up to a specified time prior to the meeting (e.g., six to twelve months) without incurring damages. Thereafter, damages should only accrue if the organizer fails to occupy a specified percentage (e.g., 85%–90%) of its adjusted (not the original) room block. Occupancy should be measured on a cumulative room night basis, not on a night-by-night basis.

Because hotels sometimes offer rates to the general public as part of special promotional packages that are lower than those available to the meeting attendees, it is important that the meeting room pickup be measured by all attendance, regardless of the rate paid. This may involve some extra work on the part of the hotel and the meeting organizer, but the result could save the organization money, especially if the meeting attendance is not as expected. For example, the meeting contract could include language similar to the following:

> Group shall receive credit for all rooms used by attendees, regardless of the rate paid or the method of booking. Hotel shall cooperate with Group in identifying these attendees and shall charge no fee for assisting Group.

Using this language, an organization would submit its meeting registration list to the hotel and ask that the hotel match the list against those guests who are in-house at the time. An alternate approach, which many hotels reject, is to have the hotel give the group its in-house guest list and have the group do the matching.

Damages triggered by the failure to meet a room block commitment should be specified in dollars, not measured by a percentage of some vague figure such as "anticipated room revenue." The latter may provide the hotel with an opportunity to include estimated spending on such things as telephone calls, in-room movies, and the like. The specified damages should be based on the hotel's lost profit, not its lost revenue. With sleeping rooms, for example, the average industry profit margin is 75% to 80%, so the per-room attrition fee should not exceed 80% of the group's single room rate. The industry standard for food and beverage profit is 25% to 30%. In any event, damages for failure to meet a room block commitment should never be payable if the hotel is able to resell the rooms; the contract should impose a specific requirement on the hotel to try and resell the rooms and, if possible, require the hotel to resell the rooms in the organization's room block first.

Attrition clauses often appear in the portion of a contract that discusses meeting room rental fees, with the contract providing that meeting room rental fees will be imposed, typically on a sliding scale basis, if the room block is not filled. If the clause appears in conjunction with meeting room rental, it should not also appear somewhere else, resulting in a double charge, and language should be inserted making it clear that the meeting room rental fee is the only charge to be imposed in the event that the room block is not completely utilized.

Some meeting organizers have attempted to insert a provision that is, in essence, the reciprocal of an attrition clause. Such a provision would state that if the group exceeds its room block by a specified percentage (usually the same as the attrition percentage), the hotel would provide a monetary payment of a specified amount to the organizer's master account, recognizing the additional revenue generated by the larger-than-anticipated attendance. Hotels, however, have been generally reluctant to agree to such a provision, even though it can be argued that it is merely the reciprocal for damages for failure to fill a room block.

Cancellation

This is the provision that provides for damages should the meeting be canceled for reasons other than those specified, either in the same clause or in the termination provision. More often than not, this provision in a hotel-provided agreement is one-sided. It provides damages to the hotel in the event the meeting organizer cancels. A properly drafted agreement should provide for damages in the event either party (including the hotel) cancels without a valid reason. However, as indicated previously, some contract drafters believe that damages should not be specified in the event of a hotel cancellation because it only provides the hotel with an amount that it can use to buy out of an agreement.

If a cancellation clause will trigger a monetary payment to the hotel, the payment should be specified in dollars (not percentages of something) and should be based on the hotel's lost profit rather than lost revenue. When lost room revenue is involved, make sure to measure lost sales against the normal occupancy for the particular time of the year, not against the hotel's capacity. Damages should not be payable if the hotel resells the space. While many contract drafters strive for mutuality in provisions, there is a difference of opinion regarding specified damages in a contract for cancellation by the hotel. Some believe that this is important; others point out that it only provides the hotel with a predetermined figure that it can use to "buy out" of a deal and that may not actually reflect the true damages to the meeting organizer of hotel cancellation.

The meeting organizer should not have the right to cancel solely to book the meeting in another hotel or another city, or for the hotel to book another, more lucrative meeting in place of the one contracted for. However, a meeting organizer should be able to cancel, without payment of damages, if the hotel ownership, management, or brand affiliation changes, if the meeting size outgrows the hotel, if the hotel's quality rating (as measured by the American Automobile Association or Mobil Travel Guide) changes, or for reasons that make it inappropriate or impractical to hold the meeting there. The latter language should be broad enough to cover so-called boycott situations, where a group decides not to hold a meeting in a particular location because of action taken by the state legislature. As an example, the organizer of a major shooting sports trade show (SHOT) canceled the event after the sponsoring city sued gun manufacturers who were the show's major exhibitors.

In some cases, cancellation is provided without damages as long as it is done within a specified time (e.g., two to three years) prior to the meeting. This gives the hotel ample opportunity to resell the space.

The damages triggered by a cancellation are sometimes stated on a sliding scale basis, with greater damages being paid the closer to the meeting date the cancellation occurs. Damages should be expressed as "liquidated damages" or cancellation fee, not as a penalty, since the law generally does not recognize penalty provisions. As with damages in an attrition clause, damages should be expressed in dollar amounts, not room revenue (so that sales tax can be avoided) and should only be payable if the hotel cannot resell the space.

Termination

Sometimes called a **force majeure** or **Act of God** clause, this provision permits either party to terminate the contract without damages if fulfillment of the obligations imposed in the agreement is rendered impossible by occurrences outside of the control of either party. This usually includes such things as labor strikes, severe weather, and transportation difficulties. This provision sometimes contains the "inappropriate or impractical" situation referred to in the discussion of cancellation provisions. However, many hotels seek to limit termination to situations where performance becomes illegal or impossible, so some negotiation is usually required.

Example Terminology

Provide the ability to cancel a meeting without penalty or damages if:

a. Hotel ownership, management or brand affiliation (often called the "flag") is changed.
b. The meeting outgrows hotel space or substantially shrinks in size.
c. The hotel does not perform satisfactorily at an earlier meeting (e.g., in the event of a multiyear contract with the same company).
d. An adverse change in the hotel's quality rating, as measured by the American Automobile Association or the Mobil Travel Guide.

Contracts provided to planners by hotels generally vary significantly from property to property, even within the same chain. Some of the variance can be attributed to the fact that some "chain" properties are managed by outside parties, making standardization difficult. Often, however, it has been the result of a lack of attention to the meeting contracting process by the chains themselves. Some hotels have resisted development of "standard" contracts, saying that all meetings are different and thus one contract cannot "fit all." More recently, though, most major hotel chains have adopted or are considering "standard" agreements, even though some of the provisions contain multiple options for use by sales representatives.

Because of the differences in contracts supplied by hotels, and because it is often so easy for planners, even experienced ones, to overlook key elements of a contract, many meeting organizers are developing their own "standard" contract. While many meeting organizers may be unsure of the costs involved in having a competent attorney prepare this type of document, such costs are minimal when compared with the time (and therefore expense) involved in reviewing each and every contract proposed by a hotel, whether the review is conducted by counsel or by a meeting planner or other staff member.

An organizer's development of its own contract will ensure that its particular needs are met and will minimize the chances of subsequent legal problems caused by a misunderstanding of the terms of the agreement.

Dispute Resolution

No matter how carefully a contract is written, disputes may occur either because the parties might disagree as to their individual rights and obligations or because one of the parties may perform less than had been promised. These controversies seldom involve precedent-setting legal issues; rather, they concern an evaluation of facts and interpretation of contract terms. When these differences arise, parties often prefer to settle them privately and informally in the kind of businesslike way that encourages continued business relationships.

Sometimes, however, such resolution is not possible. This leaves the "aggrieved" party with three options: forget the possibility of reaching a solution and walk away from the problem, go to court and sue, or resolve the dispute through other means.

Going to court can be an expensive and time-consuming proposition, with crowded court dockets delaying a decision for several months, or in some cases several years. Counsel fees can mount up quickly, especially if extensive pretrial proceedings are involved. Depending on the court's location, one of the parties may have to expend additional fees for travel expenses. Since court cases are matters of public record, potentially adverse publicity may result.

For this reason, arbitration is gaining favor as a means of settling disputes. *Arbitration* is defined as "settlement of a dispute by a person or persons chosen to hear both sides and come to a decision" (*Webster's New Universal Unabridged Dictionary*, S.V. "arbitration"). Under rules administered by the American Arbitration Association, arbitration is designed for quick, practical, and inexpensive settlements. It is, at the same time, an orderly proceeding, governed by rules of procedure and standards of conduct prescribed by law. Either party can utilize lawyers, but there is a minimum of pretrial procedures. If arbitration is chosen as the dispute-mechanism procedure in the contract, the parties also generally agree that the results are binding; that is, they cannot be appealed to a court of law. The contract should also specify the location of the arbitration. Arbitration is not generally a matter of public record, so all of the proceedings can remain private.

While the filing fee required to commence an arbitration proceeding is generally higher—often considerably so—than that required to begin litigation in the courts, the overall cost of arbitration is frequently significantly lower. This is because of the absence of extensive pretrial maneuvering and because attorneys are often discouraged or even prohibited from participating as representatives of the parties. The "downside" to arbitration is that some believe arbitrators may often "split the difference" in a dispute, seeking an equitable solution rather than following the letter of the law.

If the parties choose arbitration as a means of settling disputes, the choice should be made before disagreements arise, and language governing the arbitration option should be included in the meeting contract. The contract should include the location of the arbitration proceeding. If arbitration is not selected, the contract should spell out which state's law (e.g., where the meeting took place or where the meeting organizer is located) will be utilized to resolve a court dispute.

Under the American system of justice, each party to a court suit or arbitration proceeding is required to bear the costs of its own attorneys unless the agreement provides that the winning party is entitled to have the loser pay its attorneys' fees and costs.

Finally, a well-drafted contract should specify the damages to be awarded in the event of a breach by either party. Such an approach takes the decision out of the hands of a judge or an arbitrator and leaves the dispute resolver only to determine whether a breach of the agreement occurred. Damages are typically stated as "liquidated damages"; that is, damages that the parties agree in advance will be the result of a breach. Courts will generally not honor a contract provision that imposes a "penalty" on the one breaching the agreement, so that term should be avoided. As an example, a conference was held in a Las Vegas hotel, but the meeting organizer failed to pay the $57,000 master bill presented by the hotel for the meeting expenses. After multiple unsuccessful efforts to get the meeting organizer to pay the bill, the hotel decided to bill the individual attendees for a pro rata share of the master bill. After many upset attendees and much negative media, the hotel reversed its position and went back to pursuing the meeting organizer for the payment.

RISK MANAGEMENT

What Is Risk? What Is Risk Management?

All meetings involve an element of **risk**. *Risk* is the possibility of suffering loss or harm. *Risk management* is the process of assessing, analyzing, mitigating, and controlling risk. *Risk* is the "what" and *risk management* is the "how." Risk is used here as an umbrella term to include loss or harm caused by everyday occurrences as well as emergencies, disasters, crises, and catastrophes, all of which are defined differently based on the scope and impact.

Imagine that an exhibition is to be held outdoors and during setup, torrential rains come, making it impossible to complete setup or to hold the exhibition. This is an example of a risk. Now imagine that the wise exhibition planner has rented tents under which the exhibits can be placed so that the show can go on. That's risk management.

How do you plan for natural risks like earthquakes, tornadoes, etc. *Courtesy of Akiyosiaki, Dreamstime LLC—Royalty Free.*

The stages of risk management are:

1. Preparedness (assessment and analysis)
2. Mitigation
3. Response
4. Recovery

The outdoor exhibition example above can be used to simply and quickly walk through the steps of risk management.

1. *Preparedness:* The exhibition organizer would have *assessed and analyzed* the possible risks during the planning stage. Risks identified during the assessment might have included not only rain (and other inclement weather) but accidental injuries, violence, airline stoppages (preventing exhibitors or attendees from getting to the destination), etc. In analyzing these risks, the exhibition planner looks at the *probability* that each risk would occur and the *consequences* if it did. The planner probably decided that an airline stoppage was less likely to occur than rain, and so might focus more on planning for rain.

2. *Mitigation:* In the *mitigation* stage, the planner would try to determine what he or she could do to decrease the probability that rain would occur (and quickly realize it's hard to control the weather!), and to decrease the consequences if it did rain. Realizing that the latter was more manageable, the planner would have had a tent rental company on standby (or rented them just in case if the budget allowed), contracted with a backup indoor venue, purchased event cancellation insurance in case the exhibition was rained out, and carefully monitored the weather reports on the days leading up to the exhibition.

3. *Response:* The tricky thing about risk response is figuring out both *when* to respond and *how.* If two days prior to the event dates, the weather forecast is calling for 60% chance of rain on the exhibition date, should the planner implement the rain plan? Does that mean getting the tents or just alerting exhibitors to the possible change in plans? If the planner waits until the morning of the exhibition, does that give him or her enough time to implement the rain plan? The answers to these questions really depend on the size and scope of the event as well as the nature of the plan.

4. *Recovery:* A risk that results in loss or harm can cause damage to property, people, or to more intangible aspects—like the organizer or planner's reputation. In the case of the outdoor exhibition, recovery might just include refunding exhibitor's or attendee's fees who didn't attend, or filing a claim with the insurance company. In the case of a full-blown disaster or crisis, however, the recovery stage can be much more serious and take a much longer time.

Despite recognizing the importance of risk management, research suggests that less of half of all MEEC planners have a risk management plan in place. (*Source:* Kline, S. & Smith, S. (2006). *Crisis planning for the meeting and convention industry.* Chicago, IL: PCMA.) Some of the reasons cited for not having a plan include: lack of time or staff, it is not required by their organization, lack of budget, and lack of knowledge about how to create a risk plan (*Source:* Hilliard, T.W. (2009). Crisis Prepared Meetings: Crisis Preparedness Program Components and Factors Influencing Their Adoption by Meeting Planners.)

How Risk Management Affects Your Meeting or Event

Risk management isn't just another thing that planners have to do; it is just part of the meeting planning process. It should inform decisions on a myriad of meeting and event logistics. For example, the meeting organizer may decide not to choose a coastal destination for an event during hurricane season. The planner may decide to choose one facility over another because security is better, and so on.

PREPAREDNESS AND MITIGATION   Conducting a risk assessment and analysis will also help the planner determine which mitigation measures should be implemented. Examples of some common mitigation measures include:

- Contracts—signed prior to the meeting or event, contracts mitigate risk by narrowing or shifting liability to the responsible party or they specify exactly what the monetary damage fees (e.g., attrition or cancellation) might be for underperformance of the contract.

- Insurance—the mitigation effect of insurance is that it shifts some of the liability for financial loss to the insurance company. In exchange for paying a premium, the meeting organizer knows that the insurance company will pay a claim for loss or damage if it falls within the boundaries of the insurance policy.
- Security—hiring security guards to provide physical security and/or monitor property is a way of mitigating the risk of injury or loss.

RESPONSE   Meeting and event planners focus primarily on the preparedness and mitigation stages of risk management. That is, planners are responsible for determining what the risks might be, how they might affect the meeting or event, and implementing measures to reduce the likelihood that the risk will occur and the impact if it does occur. However, not everything is within the control of the planner.

Should a realized risk adversely affect a meeting or event in spite of the best planning, the planner needs to have a risk team ready to respond. Depending on the nature of the realized risk, the response may be as simple as sending an announcement to participants about a change in the program. Or, it may be as complex as having to help coordinate an emergency evacuation and provide first-aid to the injured. A simple response will be up to the planner's risk team. A complex response will likely require emergency professionals: firefighters to put out a fire, police to regain control of a crowd, and emergency medical professionals to administer first aid. The response must fit the realized risk.

RECOVERY.   Recovery also depends on the nature of the realized risk. If the rain in our ongoing example is so bad that the outdoor exhibition has to be cancelled, recovery would include insurance paying claims for the losses suffered by the exhibition organizer as well as the actions by the organizer to overcome any bad press, upset members or exhibitors so that the organization can survive both from a financial and a public relations standpoint.

• *Workers' compensation* insurance is mandatory in all states. It provides coverage for employees who are injured on the job. While most states permit employers to either self-insure or purchase coverage from private companies, a few states (such as Nevada) require employers to purchase this insurance only through a state fund. This could cause a problem if an organization holds a meeting in Nevada and hires temporary employees to perform services at the meeting. To avoid this problem, organizations should utilize only independent contractors for temporary staffing or hire individuals provided by a temporary agency.

• *Comprehensive general liability* (CGL) policies are the commercial equivalent of a homeowner's policy. They protect the organization against personal injury claims and loss (including theft) or damage to the insured's property as well as the property of others. Although these policies are designed to cover "all risks," they frequently have exclusions, and it is important to carefully review what is not covered as well as what is included within the policy's scope.

It is not clear from many of these policies whether they insure against events that occur outside of the organization's premises, such as at meetings, conventions, and trade shows. If they do not cover these types of events, they should be amended to cover them or additional insurance should be secured. Furthermore, many general liability policies may not cover liability resulting from alcoholic beverage service without a specific amendment. Athletic events, such as "fun runs," may also be excluded from coverage without a specific endorsement. In addition, it is important to be sure that the policy specifically refers to and covers contractual liabilities, like those that would be incurred under a meeting contract.

Another coverage that should be checked as part of any CGL policy is alcohol server liability. Serving alcoholic beverages at an event, especially if the guests are going to drive home afterward, can subject the organizing entity to the risk of litigation if an attendee becomes intoxicated at the event and then is involved in an automobile accident. Such an occurrence led to a lawsuit in Washington, DC, against a company holding a holiday party for its employees at an off-site location.

Planners should review the definition of who is the "insured" under the policy, since it may be important to extend coverage to the organization's employees and volunteers as well as the organization itself. Frequently, a hotel or convention center will require that it be designated as an "additional named insured"; this is easily done through the insurance broker who procured the policy.

How much insurance to carry is also a concern for planners. While multimillion dollar awards are all too common in liability cases, the typical general liability policy has coverage limits of 1 to 2 million dollars. If additional coverage is desired, it is relatively easy to obtain an "umbrella" policy that provides coverage in the 2 to 10 million dollar range.

• *Association professional liability* (**APL**) policies protect the organization and its officers, directors, staff, and volunteers against personal liability arising from their official actions. This type of policy is broader than a traditional directors and officers (D&O) liability policy in that it covers the organization as an entity as well as individuals.

Unlike many other forms of insurance, APL policies issued by different companies vary greatly, and organizations may find that certain coverages, such as antitrust or libel protection, may not be available from a particular company. Therefore, it is important to obtain several sample policies and premium quotations in order to properly evaluate options. The lowest-cost policy may not always be the best.

The APL policy generally does not protect the organization against the kind of liability that is covered by the CGL policy. APL premiums are generally considerably higher than those for general business liability, although some carriers are attempting to cut premiums by writing APL policies in conjunction with comprehensive general liability coverage.

• *Event cancellation* policies are a specialized form of protection, insuring against unforeseen circumstances, such as labor disputes, inclement weather, or damage to the convention or meeting facility. The failure of a featured speaker or entertainer to appear may or may not be included in the coverage. These policies often cover the organization's personal property (such as computers and other equipment) utilized at the convention or meeting and the loss or theft of on-site convention receipts. However, this coverage is generally in excess of any other existing personal property or loss of money coverage that an organization may carry. It is not intended to be used as "first dollar" coverage against loss to personal property and/or money and receipts.

Planners should seek to include coverage for reduced attendance as well as total cancellation at an event, although most policies will not protect against the lack of attendance for reasons other than unforeseen circumstances. Many policies will include so-called remedial action taken by a meeting organizer, such as purchasing fans to deal with a failed air-conditioning system. In addition, some policies will provide automatic coverage for smaller meetings (e.g., under $50,000 budgeted gross revenue) when an organization's major meetings are covered. This coverage only applies to the period of time the coverage is in force for major meetings. These policies also do not protect against liability to third parties.

• *Exhibitors liability* policies provide protection to the organization for damage caused by exhibitors. In addition, these policies generally protect the organization for loss or damage that it causes as part of its convention or meeting management. Many policies also provide host liquor liability coverage. One company quotes a premium on the basis of $50 per exhibitor, with a $500 minimum. This type of coverage may not be necessary if all exhibitors are major companies and the exhibitor contract includes a provision requiring indemnification of the organization for damage caused by the exhibitor's negligence.

AMERICANS WITH DISABILITIES ACT

Federal legislation makes it illegal to discriminate against or fail to provide a "reasonable accommodation" for people with disabilities. The legislation resulted in passage of the Americans with Disabilities Act (ADA) of 1990, which places responsibility on the owners and operators of public facilities to make reasonable accommodations for people with many types of disabilities. A **disability** is "a physical or mental impairment that substantially limits a major life activity of an individual." This may include people in wheelchairs, those with visual impairments, hearing impairments, and food intake restrictions as well as "invisible disabilities" like those who having cancer, epilepsy, or other conditions that may not be immediately visible. The ADA Amendment Act of 2008 became effective January 1, 2009; so criteria for identifying a person with a disability and the appropriate "reasonable accommodation" have been more broadly construed in recent years.

Anne Jakob, CMP, and her husband, Bob, both require special accommodations because they use motorized wheelchairs.
Photo by George G. Fenich, Ph.D.

The following is the stated purpose of ADA:

1. to provide a clear and comprehensive national mandate for the elimination of discrimination against individuals with disabilities;
2. to provide clear, strong, consistent, enforceable standards addressing discrimination against individuals with disabilities;
3. to ensure that the federal government plays a central role in enforcing the standards on behalf of individuals with disabilities; and
4. to invoke the sweep of congressional authority, including the power to enforce the Fourteenth Amendment and to regulate commerce, in order to address the major areas of discrimination faced day-to-day by people with disabilities.

Source: The Americans with Disabilities Act of 1990, Titles I and V, The U.S. Equal Employment Opportunity Commission; ADA Amendments Act of 2008 (P.L. 110-325).

This act applies to meeting planners and organizers. They must (1) determine the extent to which attendees have disabilities and (2) make reasonable efforts to accommodate the special needs of those attendees at no cost to the attendee. As a result, we now see sections on registration forms asking if the attendee has any special needs. One of the most common relates to dietary needs, such as the individual who is lactose intolerant (cannot drink milk or consume milk products). The planner would not have to provide milk substitutes for that attendee because the situation does not impair a major life function. Another example is the attendee who is hearing impaired. The planner would have to provide a "sign language" interpreter. Readers may have seen these interpreters in class or during important speeches. For those with vision impairment, the planner may have to provide documents with extra large type or produced in Braille. Failure to accommodate attendees with disabilities can result in legal action and fines. Furthermore, the accommodations requirement is not limited to attendees. It applies to employees as well.

The planner must be aware of the ramifications of the ADA and be sure that all facilities used meet the standards. The planner must also be sure that their activities and programs meet the guidelines set forth in the act. Be aware, however, that this act only applies to events and meetings in the United States. Canada does not have the equivalent of the ADA, and many of its facilities do not meet the standards put forth in the Act. Accessibility and accommodation of those with disabilities varies significantly from county to county.

Guidelines for Addressing ADA

- General Areas
  - Staff training
    - Etiquette
    - Language
    - Role play
  - Providing opportunities for persons with disabilities to identify themselves and request accommodation
    - Membership applications
    - Meeting registrations
    - Certification process applications
  - Providing accommodations for blind and visually impaired
    - Technology orientation
    - Mobility specialists
    - Tactile maps
    - Scribes or readers
  - Providing accommodations for individuals who are deaf or hard of hearing
    - Technology
    - Relay service
    - TDD/TTY
    - E-mail
    - Captioning
      —Real time
      —Open or closed
    - Interpreters
      —American Sign Language (ASL)
      —Pidgim Sign English (PSE) and Signing Exact English (SEE)
      —Oral interpretation
    - Boards and committees
  - Providing minutes and documents in alternative media
    - Braille
    - Text files
  - E-mail
  - Voting
    - Visual signals
    - Auditory signals
  - Providing chat rooms or video for conference calls
  - Providing access at social functions

Some of the other tasks a meeting planner should consider:

- At least one staff member should be designated as the contact person for disability accommodations. That person should coordinate with the housing venues regarding those with disabilities who might identify themselves on one form but not the other.
- Put together a list of vendors who could provide support for people with disabilities at the conference site.
- Registration forms for the meeting or event should include places for people with disabilities to identify themselves and request accommodations.
- Registration forms for housing should also include a place for those with disabilities to identify themselves and request accommodations.
- Be sure that disability accommodations are included in your meeting budget. At least 7% to 10% of the budget should be allocated for accommodating people with disabilities.

(Source: P. Critta, and D. Hulse, 2003, "Becoming an Advocate for all attendees," *Convene*, February, pp. 48–49.)

INTELLECTUAL PROPERTY

The right of the authors of "original works of authorship" includes literary, dramatic, musical, artistic, and certain other intellectual works (*Source: U.S. Copyright Office – Copyright Basics*).

Many meetings and trade shows feature events at which music is played, either by live musicians or through the use of prerecorded CDs. Music may be provided as a background (such as at a cocktail reception) or as a primary focus of attention (such as at a dinner dance or concert). At trade shows, individual exhibitors as well as the organizing entity can provide music.

Regardless of how music is provided, it is important to remember that under the federal **copyright** act, the music is being "performed," and according to many court decisions, the entity organizing the event is considered to be controlling the "performance," even if that "control" means only hiring an orchestra without telling them what to play. The only recognized exemption to the "performance" rule is for music played over a single receiver (radio or TV) of a type usually found in the home.

The American Society of Composers, Authors and Publishers (**ASCAP**) and Broadcast Music, Inc. (**BMI**) are membership organizations that represent individuals who hold the copyright to approximately 95% of the music written in the United States. ASCAP and BMI exist to obtain license fees from those who "perform" copyrighted music, including radio stations, retail

Disk Jockey.   *Courtesy of 36clicks,*
Dreamstime LLC—Royalty Free.

stores, hotels, and organizations that organize meetings, conventions, and trade shows. A 1979 decision of the U.S. Supreme Court conferred on ASCAP and BMI a special, limited exemption from normal antitrust law principles. This decision has enabled them to develop "blanket" licensing agreements for the various industries that utilize live or recorded music.

Following negotiations with major meeting industry organizations (such as the International Association of Exhibition Managers and the American Society of Association Executives) in the late 1980s, both ASCAP and BMI developed special licensing agreements and fee structures for meetings, conventions, trade shows, and expositions. These special agreements were designed to replace earlier agreements under which hotels paid licensing fees for meetings held by others on the property. Although the negotiated agreements technically expired at the end of 1994, ASCAP and BMI have extended them on a year-to-year basis, with slight increases in licensing fees. (Copies of the current ASCAP and BMI music licensing agreements may be obtained from ASCAP at http://www.ascap.com or BMI at http://www.bmi.com.) Under court decrees, ASCAP and BMI are forbidden to grant special "deals" to individual meetings, so the agreements, which must be signed, are the same for all meetings and cannot be altered to meet the needs of a particular meeting. Failure to sign these agreements—and agreements with *both* organizations must be signed—could subject a meeting or trade show organizer to costly and embarrassing litigation for copyright infringement.

Under copyright law, an organization cannot meet its obligation by requiring the musicians performing the music or the booking agency or hotel that provided the musicians to

Jibbitz, Inc., the official maker of snap-on accessories for Crocs (shoes), attended the WSA trade show as an exhibitor. At the trade show, the Jibbitz exhibit staff noticed another exhibitor promoting the sale of snap-on accessories for Crocs. Because Jibbitz, Inc. (as a wholly-owned subsidiary of Crocs, Inc.) was the only official maker of these accessories, it filed a trademark infringement lawsuit against the other exhibitor. Jibbitz, Inc. was awarded $56 million in damages.

Copyright Symbol. *Courtesy of Fabinus08, Dreamstime LLC—Royalty Free.*

obtain ASCAP and BMI licenses. The entity organizing the event must obtain the requisite licenses.

Recording or Videotaping Speakers

An organization organizing a meeting will often want to make audio or video recordings of certain speakers or programs, either for the purpose of selling copies to meeting attendees to those who could not attend, or for archival purposes.

Speakers or program participants have a common law copyright interest in their presentations, and the law prohibits the organizing organization from selling audio or video copies of the presentation without obtaining the written permission of the presenter. Many professional speakers who also market books or recordings of their presentations frequently refuse to provide consent to be recorded by the meeting organizer.

Permission can be obtained by having each speaker whose session is to be recorded sign a copyright waiver, a simple document acknowledging that the speaker's session is going to be recorded and giving the organizing entity permission to sell the recordings made of the speaker's presentation. If the recording is to be done by a commercial audiovisual company, a sample waiver form can usually be obtained from that company, or the sample form following this summary can be used.

LABOR ISSUES

Preparation for on-site work at meetings and trade shows often involves long hours and the use of individuals on a temporary or part-time basis to provide administrative or other support. It is therefore important for organizations to understand how federal employment law requirements impact these situations.

The Federal Fair Labor Standards Act (FLSA), adopted in 1938, is more commonly known as the law that prescribes a minimum wage for a large segment of the working population. Another major provision of the FLSA, and one frequently misunderstood, requires that all workers subject to the law's minimum wage coverage *must* receive overtime pay at the rate of $1^1/_2$ times their "regular" rate of pay *unless* they are specifically exempted by the statute.

There are many common misconceptions that employers have about the FLSA's overtime provisions, including the following, all of which are not true:

- Only hourly employees (and not those paid on a regular salary basis) are eligible for overtime.
- Overtime pay can be avoided by giving employees compensatory time off instead.
- Overtime need only be paid to those who receive advance approval to work more than forty hours in a week.

Over the years, the Department of Labor regulations and court decisions have made it clear that overtime pay cannot be avoided by a promise to provide compensatory time off in another workweek, even if the employee agrees to the procedure. According to the U.S. Department of Labor, the only way so-called "comp time" is legal is if it is given in the same week that the extra hours are worked or in another week of the same pay period and if the extra time off is sufficient to offset the amount of overtime worked (i.e., at the time-and-one-half rate).

The use of comp time is probably the most common violation of FLSA overtime pay requirements, and it occurs frequently. This is because many employees, particularly those who are paid by salary, would rather have an extra day off from work at a convenient time to deal with medical appointments, holiday shopping, or simply "attitude adjustment." Compensatory time is also frequently—but not legally—provided when a nonexempt employee works long hours in connection with a meeting or convention, then is given extra time off in some later pay period to make up for the extra work.

Overtime cannot be limited to situations where extra work is approved in advance. The law is also clear that premium pay must be paid whenever the employee works in excess of forty hours per week—or is on call for extra work—even when the extra effort has not specifically been approved in advance. Thus, if a nonexempt employee works a few extra hours in the days prior to a meeting to complete all assignments for that meeting, the employee must be paid overtime.

Overtime pay is not limited to lower salaried employees or those paid on an hourly basis. The FLSA requires *all* employees to receive overtime unless they fall under one of the law's specific exemptions. The most generally available exemptions are the so-called white-collar exemptions for professional, executive, and administrative employees.

In order to determine whether an employee falls within one of these exemptions, one should review the FLSA and applicable regulations and interpretations carefully. What is explained here is simply a summary. It is also most important to remember that the exemptions only apply to those whose actual work activity falls within the definitions; job titles are meaningless in determining whether an employee is exempt.

- The professional exemption is available only to those whose job requires that they possess a skill obtainable only through an advanced degree. This is generally limited to lawyers, physicians, architects, and some engineers. An employee whose employer prefers, or even requires, an advanced degree cannot be exempt from overtime unless the actual job being performed—such as general counsel—requires such an education.
- The executive exemption is available only to those whose primary duty is management and who regularly supervise the work of two or more full-time employees (or their part-time equivalents). Thus, someone who has the title "Director" but who only supervises an administrative assistant or secretary is not exempt from overtime under this category.
- The administrative exemption is probably the most difficult to understand, although it may be available to those employees who cannot qualify under either of the other two white-collar exemptions. According to the Labor Department regulations, an administrative employee is one whose primary duty is the performance of nonmanual (i.e., office) work directly related to management policies and who, in the course of that work, generally exercises discretion and independent judgment. The regulations make clear that an administrative assistant is not exempt from overtime merely because he or she exercises discretion over such things as what office supplies to order or how to process meeting or convention registrations. These decisions are viewed as merely carrying out established management policy.

It is important for all employers to know which of their employees are exempt from overtime pay requirements and which are not. This is especially significant when employees are asked to work long hours at meetings or conventions, particularly those held out of town, or to "pitch in" and help complete a large mailing or project. When in doubt about overtime, an organization should review job descriptions with a competent human resources professional or experienced counsel.

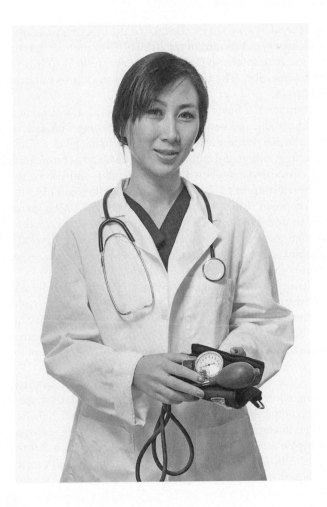

Doctors are exempted from FSLA overtime regulations. *Courtesy of Geotrac, Dreamstime LLC—Royalty Free.*

ETHICS IN MEEC

The preceding part of this chapter deals with legal issues, and the planner can look to legislation or legal advisors for assistance in dealing with them. There are many other issues, actions, or activities in MEEC that may be legal but may raise questions of ethics. *Webster's New Universal Unabridged Dictionary* (1972, S.V. "ethics") defines *ethics* as "(1) the study of standards of conduct and moral judgment; moral philosophy, (2) the system or code of morals of a particular philosopher, religion, group, profession, etc." Ethics guide our personal and professional lives. Furthermore, the issue of ethics has come to center stage with the unethical practices of Enron, Imclone, Martha Stewart, and others. Ethics is addressed on the evening news and on the front page of newspapers today. The MEEC industry, by it very nature, offers a multitude of opportunities for unethical behavior or practices.

William Brown said in a series of articles in *Convene* (June 1998, July 1998, September 1998) that there is "no right way to do the wrong thing" as it relates to ethics. He goes on to stress the importance of harmonizing ethics at three levels—personally, interpersonally, and professionally. How someone responds to an issue regarding ethics is personally and culturally based. What is ethical behavior in one community or society may be considered unethical in another. Loyalty to personal friends versus an employer is another ethical consideration faced in the MEEC industry. Ethical issues and personal conduct are an important aspect of any industry, including MEEC. The topic cannot possibly be covered in a few paragraphs. Thus, readers are encouraged to seek additional sources of information on this topic.

SUPPLIER RELATIONS

Many planners feel suppliers are out to make a buck and will do anything they can to get the contract for an event. Some believe that suppliers and vendors will promise anything but may not deliver on their promises. While promising more than can be delivered, or embellishing their abilities may be legal, it may not be ethical. On the other hand, many suppliers and vendors feel meeting planners tend toward overstatement, for example, in estimating the number of rooms they will use in a hotel and the amount their group spends on food and beverage. This too is an ethical question. The solution to these issues is to put everything in writing, preferably in the contract.

Even with a contract, the buyer (planner or organizer) and the seller (vendor, supplier) should be as open, forthright, and honest as possible in dealing with each other. A relationship not built on trust is a fragile relationship, at best. Furthermore, given the increasing importance of relationship marketing, honest and ethical behavior can lead to future business.

Still another ethical issue deals with the ownership and use of intellectual material. Destination management companies (DMCs) in particular often complain that meeting planners submit requests for proposals (RFPs) to many suppliers and the DMCs spend quite a bit of time, energy, and money to develop creative ideas and programs to secure the planners business. However, there are many cases in which a planner will take the ideas developed by one DMC and have another implement them, or the planner may then do this on his or her own. Is this legal? Yes. Is it ethical? No.

Still another issue for suppliers concerns the offering of gifts. Should a DMC employee or sales representative accept gifts and privileges from a supplier or vendor? If amenities are accepted, is there some obligation on the part of the salesperson to repay the supplier by steering business in the vendor's direction? When does one cross the line from ethical to unethical behavior? Is it proper to accept a Christmas gift, but not proper to accept football tickets when offered?

Another ethical question regards so-called familiarization or "fam" trips. Fam trips bring potential clients on an all-expenses-paid trip to a destination with the hope that they will bring their business to the community. But what if a planner or organizer is invited on a fam trip to a destination but has no intention of ever holding a MEEC gathering in that location? Should the planner accept the trip? If accepted, is there some implicit expectation that the planner *will* bring business to the locale? Although it is perfectly legal to accept a trip with no intention of bringing business to the locale, is it ethical?

The planner or organizer of a large MEEC gathering has significant clout and power based on the economic and social impact of the gathering. He or she may ask for special consideration or favors based on this power. It may be ethical to exert this influence on behalf of the group such as when negotiating room rates, catering rates, and comp services. However, is it ethical for the planner or organizer to request personal favors that only benefit himself or herself? Is it ethical for the planner to accept personal favors from a supplier or community?

Examples of ethical issues and questions abound in the MEEC industry. An individual must adhere to a personal code of ethics, and many industry associations have developed their own code of ethics to which members must adhere. Colleges and universities have recognized the need to address ethics by implementing courses on the subject. The discussion of ethics in this chapter is meant to make readers aware that ethics is an important aspect of the study of the MEEC industry, but it is not meant as a comprehensive treatise.

FUTURE TRENDS

- Legal issues and precedents continue to vary by geographic region—even within the same country.
- As developing countries mature, the complexity of legal issues will increase.
- Who has the upper hand in negotiation—the organizer or the vendor—will depend upon the economy. In a good economy where demand is strong, the supplier has the upper hand; in a weak economy, it is the organizer or buyer.
- Attrition penalties will also vacillate with the economy: more attrition penalties in a strong economy, fewer in a weak economy.
- With the work of APEX, contracts will become more standardized in MEEC, which follows the pattern of other industries.
- The need for competent legal advice will remain: for organizers and vendors alike.

Summary

Legal issues are an increasingly important factor in the MEEC industry. This chapter is meant to provide insights into some of these issues, such as negotiation, contracts, labor, and intellec- tual property. There are other issues that were not discussed, and entire books are devoted to them. Readers are reminded to seek legal counsel whenever appropriate.

Key Words and Terms

For definitions, see GLOSSARY, or http://glossary.conventionindustry.org.

ADA	BMI	Dates, Rates, Space	Rack rates
APL	CGL	Force majeure, Act of God	Yield management
ASCAP	Contract	Negotiation	
Attrition	Copyright	Parol evidence	

Review and Discussion Questions

1. Discuss the negotiation process. What are the important points for each party to be aware of?
2. Define a contract.
3. What laws are important to know with regard to contracts?
4. Discuss negotiating contracts.
5. Discuss attrition.
6. What is the difference between cancellation and termination with regard to events?
7. Discuss the different types of risks a planner may face and how to deal with them.
8. What is the ADA, and how does it impact events and gatherings?
9. What is intellectual property, and why should a planner or organizer be aware of it?
10. What are some of the labor issues unique to MEEC?

About the Chapter Contributors

Tyra Hilliard is Associate Professor of hospitality management at the University of Alabama in the Restaurant, Hotel, and Meetings Management program. She is also an attorney and consultant in the areas of legal issues and risk management for meetings and events.

Very active in meetings industry organizations, Tyra served as the Chair of the Convention Industry Council's APEX Contracts Panel and has also served as a member of many meetings industry committees. She was recognized as the 2009 Educator Honoree at the PCMA Education Foundation Professional Achievement Dinner. In addition to speaking frequently at U.S. conferences, Tyra has presented educational and training programs to international audiences in Canada, Mexico, Denmark, Germany, Spain, Turkey, Qatar, China, Taiwan, and Singapore. Her eclectic tourism and hospitality career includes working as an association meeting planner, a catering manager, and a convention and visitors bureau sales manager. Her industry experience gives her a unique perspective on the legal and business aspects of meeting and event management.

Contact information:

Tyra W. Hilliard, Ph.D., JD, CMP, Associate Professor
University of Alabama
College of Human Environmental Sciences
Department of Hospitality Management
Box 870158
Tuscaloosa, AL 35487-0158
Phone: (205)348-6157
Fax: (205)348-3789
Tyra.Hilliard@gmail.com
www.ua.edu

Contributor to previous editions: James M. Goldberg is a principal in the Washington, DC, law firm of Goldberg & Associates, PLLC.

Technology and the Meeting Professional

Satellite technology is used to beam MEEC programming to remote locations.   *Courtesy of Nn555, Dreamstime LLC—Royalty Free*

Chapter Objectives

After reading this chapter, the learner will be able to:

- Recognize how technology currently impacts meeting professional
- Identify new technologies that support meeting marketing and communications
- Understand the critical technology terms that apply to the hospitality industry
- Recognize the best Web portals for researching industry information
- Understand how social media is impacting the meetings industry

INTRODUCTION

In the past four years, the technology game has shifted from a top-down approach to one that is bottom-up. The drivers of information are not only the creators (in the Meetings, Expositions, Events and Conventions [MEEC] industry, they would be the event organizers), but now are the attendees themselves. Blogs, **Twitter**, conference wikis, and Facebook, among other tools, have created a seismic shift in how information is distributed.

The fear of many planners is that the virtual tools now available will eradicate the need for live meetings. Most experts agree that this will not happen, as we are still a species that needs face to face communication. An event in **Second Life** will not (at least today) replace the need for a national convention. What it will do is transform and extend the meeting beyond the four walls of a conference room or exhibit floor, and provide more opportunities for connections to occur.

What does this mean for today's planner? It's pretty straightforward, actually. Planners who don't embrace the new tools, especially while they try to engage their younger constituents, will struggle to succeed. A basic understanding of technology is as important a skill set for today's planners as their knowledge of site selection, food and beverage, and room setups.

While all of those tools are in use in our industry, there is still a larger amount of more mature technology applications that still are incredibly useful for today's meeting planner. More than ever, today's planner needs to understand all of the technological tools available, if for no other reason than to be able to correctly decide which one(s) is the best for their group. Remember the questions about what you need to know about a group: Who are they? Why are they here?

From mature to breaking technologies, this chapter will provide the information required to be knowledgeable about what technology is impacting our industry . . . and how it will help ensure success.

BEFORE THE EVENT OR CONFERENCE

Technology-savvy meeting professionals have more tools than ever before to help research, promote, and organize their event. Once the primary use of technology in our industry, it still can be said that technology applications are of great support to the conference planner in this phase of the event's lifecycle. From desktop uses to virtual site selection support, not to mention the ubiquitous Web-based marketing tools, the planners certainly have plenty of choices in making the process work for them.

Virtual Site Selection and Research

ONLINE RFPs As the World Wide Web developed in the mid-late 1990s, one of the first tools available, both through Convention & Visitors Bureau Web sites and hotel and third-party planning sites, was the one that allowed the planner to create an efficient online **RFP** (Request for Proposal—the tool many planners use to distribute information to hotels about potential meetings). While the model has adapted from a fee-based RFP to a free approach, the idea remains the same: allow the planners to input their specs easily, and allow the Web to be the conduit for distributing the information to potential cities and hotels.

Without standardization, each RFP has its own nuances, which could cost the planner time in completing each one required. Planners still need to determine which vehicle (CVB-based, hotel-based or third party-based) is best to distribute their meeting specs.

Some planners eschew the RFP forms, and just use e-mail and the Internet to save time in their process by allowing an Office-based spec sheet to be distributed via e-mail. No matter how one looks at it, the technology is saving significant time in helping planners distribute their meeting requirements.

VIRTUAL TOURS Industry stats have estimated that over one-half of all meetings are booked without a formal site inspection, a number that continues to grow. While there is no substitution for visiting a hotel, the Web's visual capabilities have allowed planners to at least get a sense of a facility if time or budgetary restrictions prevent their inspection.

The concept of a virtual site inspection has morphed over the years, from its meager beginnings in using only pictures of meeting rooms. Videos and 360° panoramic tours of meeting spaces and sleeping rooms moved that forward a number of years ago. The current and future use of this concept is in hotel directed site visits and virtual properties.

The next wave in the **virtual tour** is being showcased by Virtual Visit (http://www.virtualvisit. ca). The hotel directed site visit is a tool that allows the hotel to literally walk the planner through the space, focusing on areas of interest to both parties. This tool is ideal for remote site inspections, but can also be used in tandem with a traditional site visit (perhaps used with a tablet PC), where the planner can call up alternate room setups and capacity information at a single click.

What's next for virtual site selection? How about a hotel in Second Life, with its meeting space identical to how it looks in person? A place where planners can do a complete tour of the hotel anytime they wanted. If you think that's a crazy idea, think again. A few years ago, Starwood Hotels designed their new Aloft brand entirely in Second Life before ever breaking ground in "first life." Using Second Life, as well as blogs and wikis to enhance communications, they engaged the virtual community to help them improve upon their design ideas of the product.

In 2009, a company named Layar (www.layar.com) created the first reality browser, allowing users to use their mobile devices (supported with built-in GPS and camera) to display real-time information on top of live images. Just think about how that blend of virtual and real life might ultimately enhance the planners' information during their site visit. It is still in beta, and clearly not ready for use, but as a mashup (see mashup section later for more on this) idea in our industry, it could revolutionize the planner's task.

Meeting Industry Information Portals

While less elegant, but still enormously useful, industry information **portals** continue to thrive. While search engines are incredibly useful for general research, our industry has a great deal of information at the fingertips of the savvy Web users who can find resources and tools at their disposal in a few clicks. There are many sites that have great information, but their discussion is focused only on where registration (or paid subscription) is not a requirement of entry.

Any discussion of information portals for the hospitality industry begins with the Web site of Corbin Ball (http://www.corbinball.com). From his home page, linking onto his favorites page presents the viewer with nearly 3,000 industry-related Web sites, organized categorically. Ball keeps the site updated frequently, and has plenty of additional information of value for the meeting professional.

Convention and Visitors Bureau (CVB) pages are rich with information for the planners to orchestrate their meeting. The information available through drop down menus on their sites replaces the more archaic printed city guides.

The only difficulty with the CVB sites is finding their Web addresses (URL). Sometimes they are obvious, but not always. When you don't know them, it is good to know the site of the Destination Marketing Association International (http://www.destinationmarketing.org). Formerly the IACVB (International Association of Convention & Visitors Bureaus), this site's resources include a listing of CVBs from the United States and over 20 countries worldwide.

While its Web location has shifted a few times, an essential resource for planners is a searchable database with information on tens of thousands of hotels. The Meetings Industry Megasite (www.mimegasite.com) is jointly managed by two of the most popular industry publications, *Meeting News* and *Successful Meetings*. Under the site's "Tools and Resources" navigation bar is the Hotel/Facility Search, which is sponsored by Cvent (www.cvent.com), an industry **online** registration mainstay. The searchable database is an essential tool for planners in their site selection quest.

MARKETING AND COMMUNICATIONS

Another revolution in the past few years has once again shifted the nature of this aspect of the planner's job. Looking at this in 2005, we were thrilled to have Web sites replacing the old school (and very expensive) direct mailings. While Web sites still have great value, the past years have seen the rise of social network sites as a critical tool as to how we market and communicate with our clients, customers, and constituents. Real-time communication is now the expected norm, and organizations that are not offering this are becoming less relevant, especially to a younger audience who grew up using technology and sees its inherent value.

Web sites and Strategic Communications

It used to be all about one-way communication: information sent from the event organizers to the (potential) attendees. In the past few years, as social network sites have become synonymous with real-time communication, the model of event communication has clearly become a two way model.

Web sites are still an important part of the communication conversation. Not only do they need to integrate a two-way communication model, but they still must serve the purpose of efficiently providing critical information to the conference goers. The best online event models have both successful social media strategies, and are easy to find, navigate, and make purchases from the event Web site.

Event Web sites

Overshadowed in the social media revolution is that one-way tools still have importance. The event Web site is to today what the conference marketing brochure was a generation ago: a place to provide information, create interest, and hopefully, get people to register for the conference.

The best Web sites integrate a two-way strategy (blogs/comments, or a Twitter fountain being two examples), but having that site that can allow people to find out everything they need to know about the event is of critical importance. The core rules of a successful conference Web site include:

The need for a clear, easy way to find information.

Focus on the 5 W's about the conference (who, what, where, when, and why)

The ability to make the sale (in the MEEC industry, the payment process on the registration form).

A frequent issue with event organizers is not getting information on the Web site early enough. While there is no definitive time frame, it is clear that if you're running an annual event, information about next year's meeting should be ready to go live the day that this year's meeting concludes. It's just common sense. If people are pleased with the conference, why shouldn't you allow them to register for next year when their memories are still vivid from the past event?

Web 2.0 and Social Media

The Web site is one facet of the e-marketing strategy of the technology-savvy meeting professional. Social networks are the hottest, but not the only tools available to the planners to enhance their event marketing and communications.

The term Web 2.0 refers to all of the online tools where the operative word is interactivity. Any Web site that allows two-way communication, as well as all **social media** (which inherently do this), is considered to be Web 2.0. For many people, the terms Web 2.0 and social networks are interchangeable.

Social Networking. *Courtesy of Icefields, Dreamstime LLC—Royalty Free.*

SOCIAL NETWORKS   The past decade has seen the ascension and dominance of these services. Social networks have always been at the root of the MEEC industry's success. A conference gathering about a specific topic (such as the Annual Widget Convention) is nothing more than a large social network of Widget professionals gathering to learn and share from one another.

For the past few years, organizations such as Meeting Professionals International (MPI) have used customized social networks to create an incredibly useful tool for attendees, both prior to attending the event and on-site and post event networking. They also are using all of the social media to orchestrate their communication strategy. Indeed, that is a very smart approach, as you don't know which of the services each member of your audience is using. This holistic approach is the best one to ensure that your message reaches everyone.

The only difference is now the social network is online, as well as face to face. The applications created over the past decade have enabled real-time communication in this area. Facebook, LinkedIn, and Twitter would be considered the big three, but by no means the only players.

Facebook's event pages, viral marketing, and social interaction make it a great platform for communication (and marketing) to occur about the meeting. A good Facebook event page helps create buzz to an event, especially when supported by an active community (as always, the planner needs to understand his or her own group to see what works best). The most visual of the big three, and the one with the largest community, it is becoming an essential part of the marketing strategy for all groups.

Twitter is the fastest growing social network. Twitter is considered a microblog, whose limitation is only 140 characters in an update. Even with that limitation, Twitter has features that can greatly enhance an event. Use of the hashtag (#) in Twitter offers a threaded conversation about a topic (or an event), allowing a group sharing of information to occur. Event visualization for Twitter (such as www.twitterfountain.com or www.visibletweets.com) is being used more to share tweets at the event with the entire group, by projecting them on a screen in a common area (such as registration).

LinkedIn is considered more of a business network than a social network. However, it is also more of an individual networking tool. While LinkedIn has groups (which are a great tool), there is no place to promote an event directly. The Senior Planners Industry Network (SPIN) is one of many vibrant meeting communities on LinkedIn.

By no means, these three services are the only social networks available for the planner. Customizable networks (some free, some premium) are in favor with many groups. The benefits of a customized network are just what it seems to be—to be able to design the layout and content to meet the specific event needs.

Pathable (www.pathable.com) and IntroNetworks (www.intronetworks.com) are two platforms (premium) that event planners have used to tailor the social network for their event. While they each have a different interface and strengths, both serve as an excellent vehicle to blend the actual event with the virtual access that the Web (and mobile Web) provides.

Ning (www.ning.com) is a free service that allows anyone to easily and quickly create a social network. Not only is this tool good for specific events, but a number of meeting industry professionals have used Ning to create online communities for our industry. Some examples include EventPeeps (www.eventpeeps.com) and Meetings Diva (www.meetingsdiva.com).

The Meetings Community (MeCo) has been a Google Groups-based network since 2006. With over 3,000 members, MeCo (www.groups.google.com/group/meco) is an online industry community, with no marketing allowed. MeCo also has a presence in Second Life (the MeCo Mansion).

RSS   Possibly the most important approach to the Web today is in the use of **RSS** (Really Simple Syndication). This is a tool where a Web site creates or gathers a feed of information about a specific topic, and publishes it as an RSS feed. This information is updated continuously, so it has the effect of always updated content. If you look at any Twitter page, as an example, a link to the page's RSS feed is on the right column. This means that you can read anyone's tweets via RSS. This feed could be the cornerstone of a well-designed topical Web site, or it could be gathered and read by the recipient in his or her own RSS reader.

Similar to the social network, RSS feeds on an event Web site help to create a "stickiness" to the site (a site that is sticky is one where people like to stay, or return to). The Web site that provides topical RSS feeds is one that is constantly providing the reader with pertinent information. Imagine if Jane Planner runs the conferences for a National Widget Association. Why would the association's members want to go to her Web site? Primarily, if the information on the site is useful. Once they've been there, the only reason to return is if the information is updated. And that's what a successful RSS feed can do to enhance a Web site. It can provide a steady stream of continuously updated content, making the Web site the place to return for information that would help them at their job.

Hundreds of meeting professionals have blogs, podcasts, and other RSS feeds to which one can subscribe. The Meetings Industry Megasite (www.mimegasite.com) offers free streams of content and articles on various topics and destination guides. Also, blogs and podcasts wouldn't be the force they are without RSS providing the distribution.

In addition to streaming RSS onto your Web site, many knowledgeable users maintain their own ability to read RSS feeds. Both Google and Yahoo have personal services (free of charge) to gather and customize their own home page to provide news of importance to the reader. Plus, there are dozens of free RSS reader products on the market that provide the same service.

If you believe the adage that on a Web site, content is king, how much better does it get than to be able to provide a stream of current information (at little to no expense), all of which gets the potential attendee to always want to return. And, what do you know, when they do, they may just see the link to the conference, and choose to learn more about other ways your organization can help them.

BLOGGING   The blog, or Web log, is an online diary that is posted to the Web. Part of the social networking fabric that is the new Web, **blogging** allows everyone to become part of the Web, by posting anything that is on his or her mind. In 2009, Technorati (www.technorati.com), as site that follows all things blog, indicated that they were following over 110 million blogs. Blogging inherently is a two-way medium, as most blogs allow for people to respond and further the discussion on the posted blog.

The use of the blog in the marketing of a conference is simple. Create a dialogue between the organizers and their audience. Since blogs have a built-in comment functionality, it is a two-way communications tool that can greatly help organizers get a pulse of what is on the minds of their attendees.

While blogs are a very easy point of entry into social media, and a great way to enhance your Web presence, it is surprising how few planners and suppliers maintain and update blogs on a regular basis. To some extent, the explosion of Facebook and Twitter is at part to blame. Still, planners would be wise to create and update a blog to help enhance their event communications.

PODCASTING   Quick quiz. The mp3 player is:

A way cool music player

A 1000+gb backup hard drive for your files

The future of distance learning

The answer, of course, is all of the above. For now, let's focus on the distance learning aspect. Wikipedia (http://www.wikipedia.org) defines podcasting as "the method of distributing multimedia files, such as audio or video programs . . . for playback on mobile devices and personal computers."

Consider Jane Planner's boss' blog. Well written and informative, it provides a great tool to communicate with your colleagues . . . as long as they are at their computer. But how about for that long morning and evening commute? Many organizations have taken blogs and other information, and by creating podcasting content, enable the user to listen to the information on their mp3 player.

The event podcast is essentially an extension of what planners have been doing for many years. A generation ago, planners would audio tape sessions, and then distribute (sell) the tapes to those who couldn't attend. Podcasts can do that by digitizing the recording. However, as our attention spans have gotten shorter (and with the proliferation of free available podcasts online), the event podcast may find itself to be more of a marketing tool than revenue stream. Still, it provides a great way to extend the event to those who couldn't attend.

VIRAL VIDEO Do you have a YouTube channel for your event? If you don't, you should consider it. The success of YouTube has shown how powerful a tool video can be through its viral marketing abilities. Organizations such as MPI and PCMA have hundreds of videos on YouTube, helping to share content and enhance their event marketing. The creation of easy-to-use video cameras, including those built into mobile phones, as well as the Flip Camera (www.theflip.com), has placed video marketing into everyone's hands.

EVENT WIKIS A wiki is a collaborative Web site that can be edited by anyone. The pillar of wikis is, of course, Wikipedia (www.wikipedia.org), which is an encyclopedia created and maintained by us all. So why not extend this concept into your event? Some groups have already done so, using free wiki creation tools (such as www.wetpaint.com) to create a community wiki for their event. The American Library Association, for a number of years, has created wikis for each of its events, with a great deal of success.

Since a wiki is a shared, collaborative Web site, you could consider the customized social networks discussed earlier a wiki as well as a social network. In fact, you could consider the shared documents in Google Docs that we discussed as nothing more than a wiki. And, you'd be 100% correct.

E-BLASTS Twenty years ago, Jane Planner could (and would) send out as many direct mail pieces as she could. She would do so as frequently as her budget would allow, since she knew that the more information that landed on the desk of the buyer, the greater the likelihood that they might attend the function.

Five to ten years ago, Jane would have taken advantage of e-mail as her primary marketing tool. And, if she uses it correctly today, she still can reap great benefits from a well-orchestrated e-blast strategy.

However, as we stated earlier, the rules have changed. We are so inundated with spam e-mail (some experts have estimated the percentage of spam we receive as high as 85% of our daily e-mail), that multiple, unsolicited e-mails are having the inverse effect. People are tuning out all communications with that particular sender.

Instead of just blasting the audience with e-mail after e-mail, Jane Planner may be wise to heed a different set of marketing rules to best promote her conference to her audience.

Opt-in Just because you have obtained an e-mail address, it is not an open invitation to commence spamming. In fact, the technology-savvy approach would be to establish a dialogue, and confirm that the recipient wants to be included in future mailings. This way, not only will those e-mails get to the people who may actually wish to attend, but they won't have the potential affect of designating the sender as a spammer (which could put all of her e-mailing at risk).

Don't Overdo It Once you've received the OK to e-mail, don't begin a barrage of mindless communications. The end result of too many e-mails from a single person or organization is the tuning out of all of them. We get hit with far too many communication messages on a daily basis, so we're looking for ways to reduce the number on which we need to focus. Better to spend time on creating useful messages, sent occasionally, rather than mindless reminders, sent repetitively.

WIIFM (Technology-Version) WIIFM—What's In It For Me—from the perspective of your customer. Why would they want to read your e-mails? If all you are doing is sending information about the conference, it will look just like a continuous hard sell. Since this is a marketing medium (as well as one that can finalize the sale), use the technology to create a dialogue of important information for your customer. Give them educational information. Inform them of useful tools to help them become better at their job. Oh yes, you can also tell them about your conference's benefits, but that information is better received in an environment of trust than one of constant sales.

Keep It Simple Don't write your novel in every e-mail. Over the past generation, where we have become accustomed to sound bites, we must understand that people don't have time to read lengthy pieces (you can always give access to that, but allow them to venture down that path). Keep your messages easy to read, and as short as possible. And, if you're providing any links, make sure that they work.

Room Design Software

Another level of more efficient communications is how the planners share information with the facility to ensure that their wants are translated into the actions of the facility. Conference resumes create a very effective flow chart of what has to happen, and at what time (as a side note, use of a standard database, such as Access in the MS Office Suite, is very good at helping create a professional-looking resume).

Certain aspects of your event (themed parties, banquets, or just unique setups) are not as efficiently communicated by the written work. In these cases, planners use CAD (computer-aided design) room design software to enhance the communications.

Our industry has many versions of this type of software. They tend to be simple to use, but can greatly range in price. Some work better for meetings, others focus on special events. Two products that provide this capability include Meeting Matrix (http://www.meetingmatrix.com) and Vivien (http://www.cast-soft.com).

The latest in room design enhancements is the 3D room tour. Once you create your room setup, a click of a button transforms it into a virtual 3D tour, with the room setup precisely as you diagrammed. In some cases, the hotel can enhance that by providing the actual room images (carpeting, windows, lighting, sconces) as part of the 3D walkthrough. In this case, you may not even be sure if the image is real or virtual.

Selling the Show Floor

Another way technology is enhancing the event communications and marketing is by assisting the trade show manager in selling the show floor. Traditional exhibit sales were focused on a document called the Exhibit Prospectus, along with a generic layout of the show floor.

By posting the show floor diagram on the Web, and using its interactivity, trade show managers can now offer potential buyers a better look at where they might want their booth. Advantages of this include updated layouts (as the show floor diagram is frequently modified when exhibitors buy space), as well as helping buyers locate a floor space that is either near or far from their competitors (depending on their approach). The use of colors to represent booths can help differentiate which ones are available, and the ones where premium costs apply.

3-D view of exhibition booth.
Courtesy of Maxfx, Dreamstime LLC—
Royalty Free.

Almost every trade show now uses some kind of virtual enhancement to the trade show floor selling process. These sites also include a downloadable version of the Exhibit Prospectus, as well as other information of use for the exhibitor.

Virtual trade shows are further discussed in the "Webinars and Virtual Events" section, including a discussion on how the actual event can be an online experience for the attendee and exhibitor.

Online Registration

A few years ago, when discussing event technology, the topic of online registration would dominate the conversation. One of the first critical benefits of the technology to the MEEC industry, the ability to register for the event online, truly enhanced the marketing and communication of the event organizers.

Currently, the industry needs to look at online registration as a relatively mature technology, which most planners who need to use it do. It is interesting to note that all meetings still do not use online registration. Many meetings, especially internal meetings where attendance is mandatory, do not wish to incur the expense of establishing a professional online registration presence, preferring to use more traditional, or even e-mail approaches to handling meeting registration.

With this said, there are still a number of issues that confront planners when establishing the online registration process. The largest one for many planners is the integration of data. If we conceptually agree that even in the best of circumstances, 100% of the attendees will not use an online service, then the planners' challenge is to make sure that when they integrate the data, there are no inaccuracies or duplication of records. Ensuring that the online service can properly export into whichever tool you are using to maintain the remaining records (such as Excel) is a critical question to ask when considering companies to use.

Another issue that is raised by organizations using online services is in the added, unexpected expenses. One particular area of concern is in the creation of additional reports. The planner has two approaches to offset this issue. One is understanding all of the reports they might require, and having this discussion negotiated into the package to purchase the service. The other, more technology-savvy approach is to learn how to use the report writing feature. Many online registration services use the product Crystal Reports to generate reports for the client.

Regarding online resources that can perform the online registration service, there are too many to mention. Research using an industry portal such as Corbin Ball (http://www.corbinball.com) and his industry favorites will give the user a plethora of options from which to choose.

Desktop Applications

While there are dozens of industry specific software packages on the market, the clear leader in our industry is still the basic MS Office Suite. With Word, Excel, Access, and PowerPoint, the meeting professional has the tools on his/her desktop to manage all components of any event.

While not a true desktop application, we can't discuss Office without mentioning that these tools are migrating to the Web. With the release of Office 2010, Microsoft is offering online access to these applications. In all likelihood, this is due to the huge success of the free Google Docs (www.docs.google.com), providing the user word processing and spreadsheet capabilities through their Google account. Most important, these tools allow for real-time sharing of documents (negotiating a contract in real time, or discussing convention specs).

However, this general package does not fill every need. Many planners, especially in organizations with noncentralized meeting departments, need tools that allow information to be shared across the organization. The industry has a number of tools that foster better information centralization.

At the core of this need to centralize information is the ability for organizations to get a handle on the amount of purchasing leverage they have. The individual planning a small meeting within a large organization is at a disadvantage in terms of negotiation, unless they can combine their hotel room contracting with others within the organization. This is where third-party software tools can have a significant advantage over the MS Suite. While more expensive, they frequently provide exceptional cross-organization value by allowing organizations to bundle their purchasing needs.

The Convention Industry Council, the organization that manages the Certified Meeting Professional (CMP) examination, has been at the forefront of establishing **APEX–Accepted Practices Exchange**—for our industry. The essential concept of APEX is to make the industry more efficient by creating a set of standards that all parties within the industry would accept. (A great link to learn more about APEX is found at the Convention Industry Web site http://www.conventionindustry.org/apex/apex.htm).

As it relates to technology, the APEX Technology Advisory Council has created APEX Office Ready for Meeting and Event Planning. It is a series of templates throughout Word, Excel, and PowerPoint that help the users manage their information utilizing the standardization, which is the core of the APEX initiative.

DURING THE EVENT

You've created the ideal Web site. The social networks are in place and active. You efficiently communicated and marketed to your prospective attendees and exhibitors. You established an ongoing dialogue with your constituents using the various Web 2.0 technologies. Is your technology usage finished? Of course not.

Even before you go on-site with the meeting, you need to be considering how you want technology to support your goals and objectives at the conference. From your setup work to awareness of the devices that can complement your (and your attendees') goals, technology is playing an enormous role in creating a successful conference experience for all of the event's shareholders—planners, exhibitors, and attendees.

Setting Up Your Infrastructure

The meeting professional understands the importance of negotiations with hotels. From rates, dates, and space to every other aspect of the event, the planners, armed with knowledge and information about their event and the destination, can have a productive give and take with the hotel, to create a win–win event.

However, many planners, fearful about or unaware of the technologies, leave out any discussion of the technology during this part of the planning process. And, this can be a very expensive omission. The technology-savvy planner, however, understands enough about the technologies that support their event that they know what the need to plan for (even negotiate) during the initial stages of planning.

Planners need to think about issues of bandwidth. They also need to think about how they will use the Internet and other technologies to support their goals. In addition, the technology-savvy planners will think about how their attendees will want to use technology to enhance their meeting experience. While Jane Planner may not be able to implement all of these technologies, she can identify which ones are most critical (and useful) to successfully implement everyone's goals, thereby allowing the technology to play a spectacular supporting role in the success of the conference.

Bandwidth

Bandwidth is the amount of information that can pass through a communications line. The more bandwidth, the more information (number of e-mails, hits to a social networking site) can occur simultaneously. It is a shame that many hotels and convention centers do not provide adequate bandwidth to the planner for their needs (not to mention overcharge for it).

How much bandwidth is needed? Here is where the planners may need help, and it can come from their own IT folks. But only if they understand and plan for their on-site needs. Here is a partial list of tasks where the planner needs to use bandwidth (and understand how much) at the event:

- Registration networking (for the planner)
- Internet Cafes (including e-mail access)
- HQ office and press room bandwidth for office communications
- Speaker Internet access for presentations
- Live Web-conferencing (streaming audio and video) for sessions

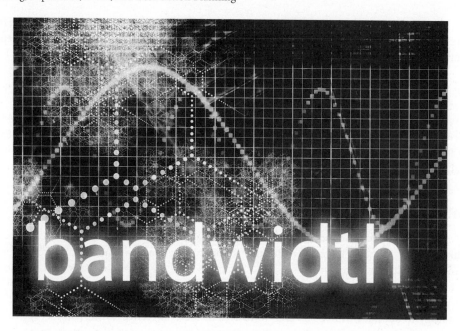

Bandwidth. *Courtesy of Kentoh, Dreamstime LLC—Royalty Free.*

So how much bandwidth will you need? That depends on the answers to those (and other) questions. Having that dialogue with your IT staff (or a third-party organization with whom you contract to support your on-site technology setup) before the contract is signed will enable you to ensure that the facility can meet your needs, and allow you to negotiate costs to a more reasonable level.

Wired vs. Wireless

Most attendees will want to access their e-mail wherever they go in the hotel. With the proliferation of **3G mobile phones** (such as the iPhone, Google Phone, and Blackberry), the attendee can typically get that on their mobile device. But, can you assume all of your attendees have these devices (Which is not a safe assumption)? Or, is the meeting space below ground (thus lacking a strong signal) . . . or even in an international destination, where the attendee might not be able to use their devices.

A facility that allows for the attendees' computer to pick up a wireless signal, whether it is in their guest room or in the public space, is still an important service to provide. Guest rooms can also provide wired access. If you have ever connected to a wireless network, you know that it is not always a panacea. Wireless network signals are not always as strong as you need them to be. Many of them have the tendency to drop out (always at the most inopportune moment). Even in guest rooms, the strength of the wireless signal is not always sufficient to allow the guest to adequately check e-mail, let alone browse the Web.

The wireless standard is an engineering specification named **80211**. This spec, adopted in the late 1990s, defines how a wireless interface between clients and access points is constructed. However, there are a number of flavors of 80211. Each one provides a different amount of potential bandwidth to the user: Talk to your IT department about the limitation of 80211b, 80211g, and the latest 80211n standards.

If you ask many speakers who require high-speed access for the success of their presentation, they will respond by stating that they prefer hard wired (an Ethernet cable attached to their computer, as opposed to going wireless). As our industry progresses to create a more seamless broadband experience, wireless may (and should) become the standard. However, a good planner will at least have a hard wired backup in case the wireless signal is not an adequate solution.

Digital Recording and Streaming Media

The General Session is a critical part of any annual meeting or conference. The marketing success of many conferences depends on the quality (and often name recognition) of the keynotes, who establish the tone of a conference.

However, there are many people who cannot attend, who would like to watch/hear the talk, either in real time, or on an archived basis. The organization can extend its keynotes (as well as other meeting components) to those who cannot attend by digitally recording the event, and streaming it over the Internet (frequently referred to as webcasting), or creating podcasting content to share or sell.

If you have never done this at a meeting, be aware that a lot of extra coordination and support is required, especially with video content. You'll need to have cameras (and video/audio engineers) in the session to ensure that the recorded material is of good quality. You'll need a company to digitize the video into a format that can be electronically distributed. You will need to determine whether the event should be streamed live (always a more risky proposition) or archived. And, will people have free access to it, or will the organization charge a fee for people to virtually attend?

An excellent resource for the planner foraying into this initially is on the Web site of MAP Digital (http://www.mapdigital.com). Their Explore MetaMeetings section provides an excellent overview of how this type of company can assist the planners in their approach to offering an integrated technology infrastructure at their event.

While learning about the technical side, the planners must also understand a great deal about their audience, and what they might want to view online. Age and demographics certainly play a role in whether an entire session should be digitized, or if a highlights approach is best for their group. The adage "Know Your Group" applies to all aspects of meeting planning, even the technological side.

To VoIP or Not to VoIP?

Many folks recognize VoIP by another name, digital telephone. **VoIP** (Voice over Internet Protocol) is the more accurate term used for your high-speed Internet connection to make and receive phone calls. This model may ultimately replace traditional telephones, due to its significantly cheaper calling costs. In fact, many Fortune 500 companies, as well as a number of hotels, have switched their telephone infrastructure to a VoIP system.

How it affects the planner at the event is in numerous ways. Leading the approach is whether the hotel/facility has changed over to a VoIP system. If so, decreases in charges may (depending on how the facility cares to share that savings) be realized.

Planners can also choose to establish VoIP as their main approach in making phone calls while at the event. Anywhere there is a strong broadband signal is a place where VoIP service can work. The planner must be aware that the service is not fully mature, and numerous VoIP customers have indicated that the service does occasionally cut out a call (if the high-speed signal fails, so does the phone service using VoIP).

Some mobile phone manufacturers have begun to package VoIP software (Skype, http://www.skype.com is one of the leading consumer VoIP products) with their phones. So, planners and suppliers down the road may need to do nothing more than use their mobile phone to access the VoIP service.

NFC and RFID

These two acronyms are at the core of many of the interactive technologies available onsite at conferences. **NFC** stands for Near Field Communications, which is a short-range, high-frequency wireless technology, allowing for information exchange between certain devices. **RFID** stands for Radio Frequency Identification, and are the tags (readers) that can be used to access these signals. We are very used to RFID tags, as any of us living in a city with tolls from bridges or tunnels can obtain RFID tags (known by a variety of names, including EZPass, SmartPass, and others) to quickly pay these fees. They also can be used to inventory products in a company's warehouse, enabling workers to better track their products. RFIDs and NFC are finding a use in our industry as well, mainly in use in **interactive nametags**.

Interactive Nametags and Networking Devices

Perhaps the most widely used RFID is occurring in nametags. Either attached to a slim piece of paper behind your badge, or as part of a slightly larger wearable nametag device, the RFID-based

RFID Nametage. *Photo by George G. Fenich, Ph.D.*

service offers better networking and interactivity between conference attendees, as well as between attendees and vendors.

One of the top RFID devices in the industry is made by nTag (purchased in 2009 to Alliance Tech) (www.ntag.com), whose wearable badge/device allows attendees to identify things of interest to them. When the attendee approaches another attendee wearing the badge (who has also identified interests), the two badges communicate with one another, with the digital display showing commonality between the attendees.

Another industry tool is SpotMe (www.spotme.com). While not a hanging nametag, these devices support the nametag and on-site networking through a handheld device. A unique feature of their service is the radar functionality, where the attendee can choose to "spot" or locate an attendee he/she wishes to see. When they come within 30 meters, the device will indicate that they are in the area.

In addition to enhancing live networking, RFID devices frequently contain program contents, surveys, instant messaging capabilities, and other interactive tools for the attendee to utilize while at the event. The badge is now their communication device, and program (as well as nametag) for the duration of the event.

If this isn't enough, the interactive, RFID-driven nametag, has two more meeting-specific uses:

CEU Tracking Many organizations need to track attendance at each breakout session, in order to provide CEUs (continuing education units) for the attendee (in many industries, these units are critical to maintain certification required for employment). The RFID-based tag, coupled with readers in each room, can automatically track attendance, so that proper CEUs can be awarded. Medical and scientific meetings are conferences where a significant value of attending is to allow the individual to obtain the required CEUs.

Interactive Message Centers In the older days, conference message centers consisted of a phone (and a hired attendant to take messages), along with a cork board and push pins. Today's RFID-based system can provide an electronic board that, as you walk past the board, will display your name, and indicate whether you have any messages waiting. This is a far cry from cork board and push pins.

When thinking about the networking advantages of RFID devices, don't forget about the pre-event attendee networking options discussed earlier in the chapter. Today's attendee, when supported by a technology-savvy meeting professional, can truly take advantage of the enormous benefits of conference networking by using these systems. Tomorrow, perhaps these services will be completely integrated into your own mobile device.

Lead Retrieval Systems

For many years, trade shows and exhibits have used **Lead Retrieval Systems** to help capture customer information. The process begins with the meeting organizer asking questions during the registration process that will help identify information of importance to the exhibitor. These questions often include the attendees purchasing responsibility, and nature of products and services in which they may have interest.

The information is coded into a badge, though it needn't be an RFID. From the 1990s through today, many groups still use a simple bar coding on the badge (or even a credit card-based system) that can contain this information.

When the attendee enters the trade show floor, and interacts with an exhibitor, the exhibit staff members can ask to swipe the badge with their lead retrieval device (typically, these are rented to the exhibitor for the duration of the show by a vendor who is supporting the meeting). Once swiped, this information now resides in their handheld lead retrieval device. At day's end, the exhibitors can download this information to their spreadsheet or database, and have customized thank you notes e-mailed to the attendee before their work for the day is complete (not to mention excellent information about their prospective clients).

The planner's job in this process is to identify and select a system or service that can support the lead retrieval process. Since exhibitors require this level of information to determine whether exhibiting at a function will potentially help their business, lead retrieval systems are primarily used for trade shows. However, these systems have also been used to help facilitate attendee surveying using automated kiosks around the event.

Also available to the planner is what is known as a reverse lead retrieval system. Instead of the exhibitor scanning the planner's badge, the planner uses a handheld device to scan information positioned in the both of the exhibitor. When utilized, it is frequently for much larger shows.

Bar Code on Name Badge. Photo by George G. Fenich, Ph.D.

Name Badge Reader. *Photo by George G. Fenich, Ph.D.*

Audience Response Systems and Speaker Interaction

If you've ever watched certain audience participation game shows, you've seen the host poll the audience to determine their opinion about a question. The audience is outfitted with small key-pads that allow them to answer questions quickly, and have their data tallied immediately. This is the essence of the **Audience Response System** (ARS).

Historically, ARS systems have been expensive propositions for the planner to implement, but today's technologies have made it a more affordable, and in today's two-way communication lifestyle, a more necessary part of many meetings. One such service is Poll Everywhere (www.polleverywhere.com), which uses SMS (texting), in addition to Web and Twitter voting that interfaces with a real-time Web-based poll. The audience members responds, and the data are instantaneously updated and posted for all to see.

Another product that has simplified the ARS process is Turning Point (www.turningtechnologies.com), which allows for real-time poll integration into your PowerPoint. In addition to using handsets, their latest product also supports certain mobile device-specific responding.

Twitter is also now being used to help facilitate interactivity during a session, whether it's for the purpose of providing an audience chat discussion, or used as a way to send messages and questions directly to a speaker. SMS (through texting of questions to a session moderator) is another way that these technologies have created a better real-time connection between a speaker and his/her audience.

This technology allows the meeting organizer and speaker to gain instant information (demographic or otherwise) about attendees, and can be used to highly customize content and direction of educational sessions.

Attendee Blogs and Tweets

We discussed blogging earlier as a function of the pre-event marketing. A few years ago, blogging was starting to pick up steam as a tool for event attendees to communicate with non-attendees about what was happening at the conference. However, with the phenomenon known as microblogging (more familiarly referred to by the name of its best known product, Twitter) now used by more than 30 million people, it's Twitter that has become the attendee tool of choice for many groups to communicate during an event.

The meeting professionals' responsibility, if they wish to facilitate attendee blogging, is to provide wireless broadband connectivity in any/all of the meeting rooms and prefunction space. Although this can run a significant cost, the establishment of this wireless environment allows the attendees to enter sessions and utilize their computers. However, Twittering, with its finite message size (140 characters) and access from any mobile device that has a browser, has become the standard in real-time attendee communications at an event.

Some groups and speakers do not like this, as it can be a distraction to a speaker, which can be said for much of the integration of the social media technology within the event. In some cases, Twittering during a session, especially when the audience is displeased, can help to incite an unsatisfied audience into one that can affect the actual event. Still, it is a technology that is not going away, and with the proliferation of Web 2.0 tools, planners are best off learning and harnessing how Twitter can be used to support the meeting objectives.

The most important Twitter tool for event planners to know is the hashtag, which is the number/pound symbol (#). In the world of Twitter, the hashtag establishes and feeds a threaded conversation that everyone can view and join in. Some events establish a single hashtag for their event, sending out information before and during the event through Twitter, while providing attendees an opportunity to also be a part of the dialogue. With larger, more tech-savvy groups, some events have multiple hashtags, allowing for more focused dialogues to occur.

Twitter is also being used in our industry outside of the actual event, to engage the community in industry dialogue. One of the best ones is the Event Professionals tag (#eventprofs), which holds weekly online tweet-ups, each week focusing on one or two topics of interest to the community.

Mobile Technologies and Mashups

Mobile technologies are redefining how information flows within our (and all) industries. Most people who attend conferences have a mobile device that is capable of surfing the Web, and running applications of services that just a few years ago were the sole domain of a PC/Mac-based desktop or laptop. Because of this, event organizers and suppliers need to think about how best to use these tools to help them connect with their audience.

Smart Phones (3G and 4G)

Today's mobile phone is nearly (and likely soon will be) an adequate replacement for a desktop or laptop computer. While the issues of keyboard size and viewing image still need to be improved, the ability of mobile devices to do anything a computer can do is upon us. Once the domain of voice-only communication, **3G phones** (defined as the third generation of mobile devices, phones that carry both voice and data) allow for high-speed data transmission, including full motion video and streaming content audio and video streaming, among others.

Because of the proliferation of these phones as mobile computers, planners have been developing applications for events. As far back as ten years ago, when 3G was just concept and PDAs (Personal Digital Assistants, such as the Palm Pilot) ruled the mobile landscape, event professionals were looking into how these devices could be a conduit for information before and during an event.

Imagine sending the conference program to the attendee's smart phone prior to (or upon arrival) at the event, or having a customized schedule, along with trade show floor, viewable as the attendee traverses the event. How about sending last-minute notifications to all event attendees? All of these functions are very doable today, and are so because of the proliferation of the 3G phone.

If you combine those tasks with a reality browser, such as Layar, discussed earlier, the 3G phone could create an augmented reality for event goers that provides more and more useful information for them, enhancing the value of their attending the event.

Hotels are also hotly going after this market. A number of chains are swiftly adopting mobile strategies for communicating with planners and guests. Apps such as Hotel Evolution (www.runtriz.com) are offering the hotel guest access to all hotel services directly from their mobile device. In fact, many hotels are starting to reconsider their need to actually place a telephone in the guest room . . . and some properties have already removed them.

I-Phone. *Photo by George G. Fenich, Ph.D.*

On the horizon are **4G phones**. These fourth-generation devices, while not yet specifically defined, will continue to see greatly increased network speed that will continue to take the mobile device beyond what computer-based connectivity could do only a few years ago.

Mashups

What may be the next revolutionary change we see won't at all be revolutionary, but evolutionary. A mashup, by definition, is the combination of the functionality of two services to create a third hybrid tool that serves a specific need. An example (and one of the first) of a mashup is the Web site "Housing Map" (www.housingmaps.com). Somebody combined (mashed) together the visual interface of Google Maps with the housing information found on Craig's List. What was created was a site that allowed integrated viewing by the user of the information from both services.

The next iteration of tech discoveries in our industry will likely come from this area. The real estate industry is using **mashups** to provide greater data and house/neighborhood visualizations for home buyers. How mashups will impact our industry is yet to be significantly realized. What it should do is bring together planners and their IT departments or vendors to try and create applications that further support the functionality of meetings.

POST-CONFERENCE TECHNOLOGY APPLICATIONS

Technology has clearly served a great purpose in the marketing and running of the meeting. However, it continues to be a useful tool once the meeting is completed. From the postconference evaluation process to the digital highlights (which weave into the marketing for the next conference), there is more to review regarding technology applications in our industry.

Evaluations and Surveys

Many organizers have moved the meeting evaluation process from a paper-based process on site (it can be digitized as well) to a postconference, online approach. While there is much debate over whether postconference evaluations provide the best accuracy of information, along with whether the post-event approach offers the best quantity of completed evaluations, its success cannot be ignored.

Regardless of one's position, it is a system in use by many planners. In fact, Web-based tools such as Zoomerang (www.zoomerang.com) have become increasingly popular for this process. The Web-based services not only distribute the evaluations, but also tally them and provide the planner with easy-to-read analysis of the questions they posed to the attendees. In fact, many integrated online solutions for meeting professionals include event survey functionality.

This process should not be limited to conference evaluations. Any meeting professional who is involved in the programming process understands that learning about the needs of his or her audience is one of the best tools to identify program elements that create greater value for the attendee. The online survey, independent of the conference evaluation, can be of significant support to that process.

Marketing the Media

The essence of postconference technology is to extend the event past the traditional time borders. A conference is no longer bound to a Monday to Thursday time frame. It can begin with attendee networking months prior to the opening session, by using tools such as pre-event networking. After the conference, the planner can provide content to those who didn't attend (or even those who wish to view it again).

As the planners makes arrangements to video and stream activities at their conference, the wheels are placed in motion to consider how they will deliver this information. Issues of cost and delivery are a significant part of the conversation. Regarding cost, will the planners charge for virtual attendance? Will they provide complimentary video clips of the event on their Web site (either to enhance purchasing or help the marketing of future events)?

As for delivery, especially in a live environment, the planner needs to make certain that they have the servers and technology (including bandwidth) available so that whoever wishes to log on and view the event can do so without the signal degrading or breaking up.

The planners' best marketing tool is the success of their previous event. The digitization and distribution of this content is then an absolutely critical tool for not only generating revenue from this year's event, but continuing to attract attendees in future years.

VIRTUAL GATHERINGS

As we discuss the event-based technology, we need to also focus on the purely virtual meeting. Many smaller meetings, where stakeholders cannot afford (in terms of either time or money) to travel to attend, can be run virtually. The generic term "webinar" seems to have become the standard term used to describe the online services that allow audio, data, and sometimes streaming content to be delivered over the Internet. In addition, virtual gatherings can include virtual worlds, such as Second Life, as well as virtual trade shows.

Webinars

The creation of a successful **webinar** is very different than a live event. All day live events are rarely successful (who's going to sit at their desk all day to actively view a meeting?). Short burst training (sometimes as short as 15-20 minutes) can be as, if not more, effective than more standard session durations of sixty to ninety minutes. The speaker, who is getting no visual or audio cues from the audience, must be able to keep the audience engaged. Q&A tends to be relegated to a specified time frame following the session.

There are many webinar providers that a planner can use. One such service is ReadyTalk (www.readytalk.com). The planners should make certain that the service they use is priced properly for their needs. Additional questions include how the service handles the audio (VoIP or teleconferencing), the maximum capacity of the virtual event, whether the service provides interactive tools such as chat and polling, and how easy it is for the event organizers and speaker to switch the view from the platform being used to their desktop, so they can showcase their applications and browser.

Second Life. *Courtesy of Walex101, Dreamstime LLC—Royalty Free.*

A more expensive, yet far more interactive approach comes from Cisco, whose TelePresence videoconferencing provides face-to-face communications between the attendees. With HD and top-quality audio, events or meetings held using this service can seem to tear down the walls between real and virtual events.

Second Life

Second Life is a 3D virtual community, where people use representations of themselves, called Avatars, to navigate and explore. It is a free service to join, but commerce is readily available, with over $300,000,000 in money transacted for people to create and buy Second Life elements (designing infrastructure, buying land, etc.).

You may think of this as strange or weird, but consider the story told earlier about Starwood's Aloft property being built in Second Life well before they ever broke ground for Virtualis (www.virtualiscenter.com), the first and most comprehensive convention center in Second Life. It is created by Dan Parks, who also designed the Meetings Community (MeCo) mansion in Second Life.

While virtual worlds may not be the first place you think about for holding your next meeting, the numbers indicate the steady growth in their use over the past few years, and it may not be long before your organization considers a Second Life event to augment its actual conference. Clearly, planners need to be aware of developments in virtual worlds as another way their planning may develop down the road.

Virtual Trade Shows

Second Life is not the only service that can offer virtual events. A number of providers are now making virtual trade shows a reality. At its most basic, a virtual trade show can be an online trade show floor plan, with hypertext links to the sites of the exhibitors for the attendees to visit.

However, a virtual trade show can also be a virtual experience in itself, with the attendee virtually walking through the event and clicking on information (or in some cases, actually chatting with sales reps). In addition to what's available in Second Life, Digitell's VirtualU (www.virtualbeginnings.com) offers another option for planners to create virtual trade show experiences.

While some people fear that these virtual events will replace face-to-face ones, it is pretty clear that for the foreseeable future, these services work best as an adjunct to actual events, or used when a face-to-face event isn't possible to hold. Whichever format is used, the main benefit of a virtual trade show of this style is that it greatly extends the trade show from the two to three days of live exhibits to potentially a year round buying and selling marketplace.

FUTURE TRENDS

Corbin Ball recently listed the top ten trends in technology for the MEEC industry. They are:

10. Mobile phones are morphing into advanced mobile meetings technology platforms.
9. Social networking technology finds numerous meeting applications.
8. Microblogging (Twitter) is proving particularly well suited for events.
7. Social review sites are moving to meetings.
6. Strategic meetings management program (SMMP) options are increasing.
5. More video to promote and improve the meeting experience.
4. Audience response technology gets cheaper and more diversified.
3. Low-cost, two-way, mobile lead retrieval options for meetings and trade shows attendees are emerging.
2. Telepresence is finally gaining a foothold at hotels for virtual meetings.
1. Despite the economic downturn and the increased use of virtual meetings technology, face-to-face meetings and trade shows remain viable.

For a complete discussion of these trends visit http://www.corbinball.com/articles_ technology/index.cfm?fuseaction=cor_av&artID=7321

Summary

Today's technology-savvy meeting professional has an arsenal of tools at their disposal to enhance their organization's event, both from the focal point of the attendee and from the organization. Social media has become an enormous focal point for many event planners to integrate into their event marketing and management. Since time, money, and objectives don't require every technology being integrated, the true role of the planner today is to identify and determine those tools that add the greatest value to their meetings, while continuing to learn about other technologies that could also impact their organization. Technology is also used in the "green movement" (see Chapter 13 on green meetings).

Key Words and Terms

For definitions, see GLOSSARY, or http://glossary.conventionindustry.org.

3G Phones	Mashups	Room Design Software	VoIP
4G Phones	NFC	RSS	Web 2.0
APEX	Online Meetings	Second Life	Webinars
Audience Response Systems	Podcasting	Social Media	80211
Blogging	Portal	Twitter	
Interactive Nametags	RFID	Virtual Tours	
Lead Retrieval Systems	RFP	Virtual Trade Shows	

Review and Discussion Questions

1. How can technology impact site selection?
2. List three new technologies that support meeting networking.
3. What are the seven types of Web-based gatherings?
4. How is third-party software used, and what is its advantage?
5. Why has the Web become so important to meeting planners and suppliers?
6. What are the five facets of the e-marketing strategy of the technology-savvy meeting professional?
7. In addition to enhancing live networking, RFID nametags frequently contain what other interactive tools?
8. What is the major benefit of attendee blogging during a session?
9. List four types of e-conferencing and discuss each.
10. What are some of the benefits of using online evaluations?
11. What is the main benefit of a virtual trade show?
12. What is green technology?

About the Chapter Contributors

James Spellos is the president of a company called MeetingU. He is a consultant and frequent speaker on technology issues in the MEEC industry.

Contributors to previous editions
Dennis Rudd, Ed.D. of Robert Morris College
Kathleen Taylor Brown, Robert Morris College

Green Meetings and Social Responsibility

The skyline of Vancouver Canada with the Vancouver Convention Center in the foreground. The center is a green facility including the grass on its roof.   *Courtesy of Maford, Dreamstime LLC—Royalty Free.*

Chapter Objectives

After reading this chapter, the learner will be able to:

- Understand the definition of "green meetings"
- Understand the meaning of "social responsibility"
- Be able to describe best practices in green meetings
- Understand where there are opportunities for meetings and events to be more environmentally sensitive
- Understand the costs of "being green"
- Be able to define and discuss "greenwashing"

INTRODUCTION TO GREEN MEETINGS

The **Green Movement**, as it was initially referred to, was first started in the 1960s with environmentalists advocating the sustainable management of resources and the protection of the natural environment through changes in public policy and individual behavior. Throughout history, the movement has attempted to incorporate itself into religion, ecology, health, and human services. However, it wasn't until 2005 and the arrival of Hurricane Katrina that the world started truly paying attention to the potential catastrophic effects of global warming and the wastefulness that was taking place all over the world. And it was even more recently that meeting professionals began to fully consider the importance of environmentally friendly events. As more

Tidbit

"[Green meetings are] not a fad," says Amy Spatrisano, principal of Portland, Ore. – based Meeting Strategies Worldwide.

planners strive to minimize their events' environmental impacts, suppliers are also working to make their products and services more earth-friendly.

The movement toward green meetings within the industry is impacting all areas of meeting planning. Meeting planners are actively learning the ins and outs of executing green meetings, and meeting suppliers are jumping on board accordingly. Meeting planners, clients, customers, venues, exhibitors, contractors and suppliers are actively taking part in the green movement. When meeting planners begin planning more eco-friendly meetings, the ripple effect has an impact on all parties involved.

Definition of a **green meeting**: A common expression meaning environmentally responsible.

WHY GO GREEN—THE BOTTOM LINE

In an industry as hectic as the meetings and events industry where every detail is important, it is easy to understand why planners, suppliers, vendors, and facility managers want to streamline wherever possible. So why should industry professionals take on the extra challenge of going green?

The answer boils down to a few important points:

Economic

It makes good business sense to go green, and companies that choose to do so are reporting higher gross margins, higher return on sales, higher return on assets, and a stronger cash flow than their less sustainable competitors. Once a company has made the commitment to go green within its own organization, it is easier to follow the same guidelines for meetings and events that will ultimately lead to a better return on investment. Although there are some upfront costs associated with going green, the end result is generally a significant savings.

Taking small steps to go green can make an enormous difference in a company's bottom line, as well as in the environment. Simply switching from bottled water to pitchers of water for attendees saved Oracle $1.5 million dollars at its OpenWorld 2008 event in San Francisco. Reusing name badge holders saved another group over $500 in just one year. In addition to the monetary savings to these groups, the amount of waste deposited into a landfill was dramatically reduced, just by making these small changes.

Another example of environmental responsibility is to reduce the amount of printed materials associated with a meeting or event. Take advantage of technology to market the event and encourage attendees to access important information via the Web instead of printing and mailing materials to them. For example at the 2010 Professional Convention Management Association's Annual Conference in Dallas, Texas, on demand printing was available for attendees prior to each session. Participants had the option of printing session materials on-the-spot or downloading them from the Web site at a later date. In doing this, planners reduce waste and as well as the cost of printing and mailing.

Going Green Globally

A recent column in *Successful Meetings* (November 2009) reported that the United Nations was promoting virtual events as Green. It went on to say that their International Telecommunications Union (ITU) was calling on the U.N. to include information and communication technologies in its efforts to fight global warming.

Increasingly, companies are looking at sustainability, both personal and company-wide, as a galvanizing force to get their employees to become more engaged in their work

Sustainability arguably provides one of the most engaging topics for a theme of an employee engagement program. People are curious about it, and it is quite utilitarian (i.e., it has something for everyone). Sustainability encompasses people's health (healthy food, clean drinking water, etc.), the health of the environment (clean air, clean water, healthy ecosystems providing ecological services like keeping disease at bay), societal issues (safe public parks, walkable communities, connecting with our neighbors, getting people together and away from the TV), and economic sustainability (people's paychecks, business success, etc.). It's so ubiquitous, in fact, that it lends itself well to improving employee satisfaction, morale, productivity, and retention. And just as importantly for the entrepreneur or manager, it also has terrific potential for contributing to the bottom line of the company.
http://greenbusinessvillage.com/2010/02/12/

Social

While the concept of **social responsibility** is not necessarily a new one, the idea that businesses should contribute to the welfare of their communities both locally and globally is one of the trends of the millennium. Everyone wants to feel like he or she is making a difference. Employees who are satisfied with their organization's commitment to social and environmental responsibility are likely to be more positive, happier, and more productive than those working for less socially responsible employers. Businesses that recognize the importance of social responsibility often have employees who tend to be more satisfied with their jobs. According to an article on green business practices, the HR department at Patagonia reports more than 900 applicants for every job opening is directly related to their environmental record and workplace learning sustainability program. In addition, companies such as the Vancouver-based Vancity Credit Union, Interface, Inc., in Atlanta, and the Australian and New Zealand Banking Group all report an increase in retention and engagement (of employees) as a result of their environmental efforts. By that same token, the ability of the organization to attract employees with the same commitment increases as well.

How does this work? Employees who work in organizations that support green efforts could be healthier due to working in an office that is naturally lighted or better ventilated for energy savings. They may be encouraged to take the stairs or ride their bike to work, obviously contributing to their personal health. In addition to obvious health reasons, employees like to be a part of something that is good overall. According to a recent survey, 92% Americans are interested in an increased use of solar power. If you are working for a company that is using solar power, you are likely to feel that you are participating in making a positive contribution. Encouraging employees to become participants in green efforts often means encouraging them to live a healthier and more active lifestyle, thus leading to happier and more productive individuals in the workforce.

Meeting and event attendees are also positively impacted by sustainable efforts and enthusiastically participate in reduce, reuse, and recycle programs. One industry expert reminds us that most attendees participate in environmentally responsible efforts on a daily basis at home and consider it a non-issue to continue to act responsibly when attending events. Some organizations encourage attendees to become actively involved in a project while at the event, which also shows improvement in attendee satisfaction.

Perhaps answering the question of "why go green?" includes more than a single bottom line could report. Some experts consider the "triple bottom line" as a more accurate measure of a company's accomplishments and a better answer to the question. Considering the **triple bottom line** of people, planet, and profit expands the concept of success to include ecological and social accomplishments in addition to financial accomplishments of an organization. Research suggests that many forward thinking organizations, associations, and companies are applying the triple bottom line concept as they measure success and answer to stakeholders.

GMIC Helps Clean the World
by Katherine Manfredi and Danielle Adams

Each day thousands of bars of partially used soaps and toiletries are discarded in hotel rooms. Each day 9,000 children die from acute respiratory and diarrheal disease. Pneumonia and diarrheal disease are the top two killers of children under five. Simple hand-washing can reduce those 3.5 million annual deaths by up to 60%. A small but effective group came out in Orlando to help Clean the World by recycling soap and partially used toiletries. As a pre-conference CSR event to the 2nd Annual Green Lodging and Hospitality Conference, the GMIC Florida/Caribbean chapter-in-formation hosted eager participants at the Clean the World warehouse.

Helping sanitize and repackage soaps and toiletries for delivery to those in need, everyone learned the brief history of CTW and the importance of their mission before rolling up their sleeves to rotate through the five stations—toiletry recovery as well as soap surface cleaning, dipping, sanitation, and wrapping. That last step in the soap recycling process was so gratifying, knowing that the next time that bar of soap would be touched would be when it was put into the hands of those who could not afford so much as a bar of soap.

In less than 90 minutes, a small group of volunteers under the guidance of the CTW staff:

- surfaced cleaned 70 lbs of soap
- sanitized 390 lbs or 3,000 bars of soap
- wrapped 140 lbs of soap
- recovered 100 lbs of amenity bottles.

This event was such a great match for GMIC and the hospitality conference attendees. In addition to the reasons why recycling hotel toiletries makes "green" sense, the activity was a good match with the attendees given that the conference and activity were of the same industry and intersected with that organization's goals. This **CSR** (Corporate Social Responsibility) activity resonated with the hospitality industry attendees not only because it is "green" and provided help to children that tug on heartstrings, but also because it was rooted in the hospitality industry. CSR is most powerful when strategic. Strategic CSR occurs at that point of intersection between an organization (or meeting), society, and the environment—where the needs of the organization or meeting intersect with the needs of the environment and society. This activity was taking daily discards from the hospitality industry (soap and other amenities) that otherwise go to landfill, and "recycling" them to improve—and potentially save—the lives of others while reducing damage to the environment. This program utilized an everyday component of the lodging and hospitality industry, greened the environment by diverting waste from landfill, and repurposed that "waste" to the immense benefit of children in need. By selecting a CSR activity that was directly related to the industry and also met environmental goals and the needs of society, there was an increase in the relevance and power of that activity.

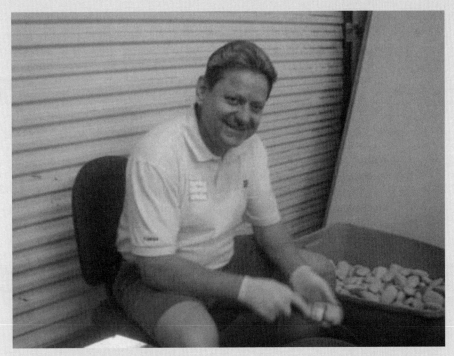

Surface cleaning is one of the initial steps in preparing the reclaimed bars of soap for "recycling" to those in need. Paul Steen cheerfully prepped his share of the 70 lbs of soap surfaced cleaned by volunteers during the Dec 8th GMIC event. *Photo courtesy of GMIC*

(Continued)

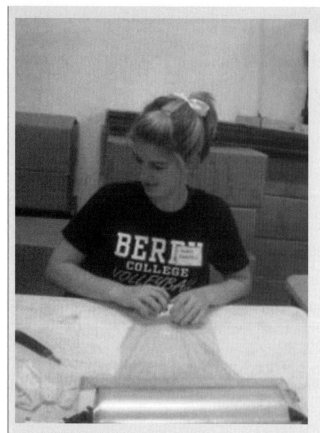

From budget to luxury hotels come bars of "hope" in all shapes and sizes. At one of the workstations, bars of soap are dipped in a special solution as part of the sanitization process. Once completely sanitized and dry, the soap is wrapped for transit. Alexa Sparrell gladly wrapped some of the 140 lbs of soap that night, knowing the next time those bars changed hands would be when received by a child in need.   *Photo courtesy of GMIC*

As one of the final sanitization steps, soap to be steamed is loaded. Over 3,000 bars of soap—or 390 lbs—were sanitized by the GMIC volunteers at the 90-minute Clean the World event.
Photo courtesy of GMIC

Not only are our landfills saved from some of the contamination and overburden from these discards, but these leftover bars of soap become little bars of hope. Eager faces greet Clean the World each time they arrive in Haiti or any of the other third-world countries they service. Education and soap can help save lives. Visit www.CleanTheWorld.org for information about how recycling soap saves lives and what you can do to get involved as a hotel, or individually! Also go to http://www.youtube.com/user/CleantheWorld2009#p/u/6/GyELD_769Mk to see video.

GREEN MEETING INDUSTRY COUNCIL
WEB SITE:www.greenmeetings.info

Meaningful Meetings

- When you book your business meeting, The Ritz-Carlton will donate 10% of the total guest room revenue equally between a charity of your choice and The Ritz-Carlton Community Footprints Fund. Some examples of which are:
  - Working side-by-side with members of **Habitat for Humanity** to transform a building site into a home for displaced residents and to impact the physical and social landscape of New Orleans
  - Harvesting organic crops at the renowned **The Chef's Garden** for donation to a local food bank (Cleveland)

Corporate Social Responsibility: The Emerging Opportunity

More than three-quarters of EMEA meeting planners (76%) report that corporate social responsibility (CSR) will be a focus for their organizations in 2010, along with 63% in the United States and 60% in Canada. Nearly three-quarters of corporate planners (73.1%) and 48.4% of association planners say CSR will be on their organizations' radars over the next year.

Among suppliers, CSR is a focus for 67% of respondents in EMEA and 61% in North America.

FutureWatch 2010 revealed small differences in the way planner and supplier organizations take action on CSR.

Table 13-1 CSR Effort, Planners' Organizations

	Overall		Canada		EMEA		US	
	2010	**2009**	**2010**	**2009**	**2010**	**2009**	**2010**	**2009**
No organizational CSR efforts	21%	19%	25%	16%	13%	12%	21%	20%
Unsure of organizational CSR efforts	15%	18%	15%	14%	11%	8%	16%	20%
Organization does address CSR	64%	6%	60%	71%	76%	80%	63%	61%

CSR Effort, Planners' Organizations

	Overall		Association		Corporate	
	2010	**2009**	**2010**	**2009**	**2010**	**2009**
No organizational CSR efforts	21%	19%	30%	27%	16%	15%
Unsure of organizational CSR efforts	15%	18%	21%	25%	11%	15%
Organization does address CSR	64%	63%	48%	43%	73%	70%

CSR Effort, Suppliers' Organizations

	Overall		Canada		EMEA		US	
	2010	**2009**	**2010**	**2009**	**2010**	**2009**	**2010**	**2009**
No organizational CSR efforts	20%	18%	11%	13%	23%	18%	21%	18%
Unsure of organizational CSR efforts	17%	21%	14%	16%	9%	11%	18%	23%
Organization does address CSR	64%	61%	61%	71%	67%	71%	61%	59%

Organizations' CSR Solutions, Planners and Suppliers

	Planners	Suppliers
We have a group(s) or committee(s) who guide us in our efforts	19%	22%
Our leadership requires that we understand and attempt to demonstrate CSR	18%	22%
We have a department dedicated to CSR	15%	11%
One or more people in our organization have been assigned to oversee efforts for us all	13%	20%
One or more people in our organization have taken personal responsibility for CSR	13%	15%
Various departments have people who are dedicated to CSR	12%	12%
We discuss CSR, but only occasionally mandate any related activities or behaviors	8%	5%
CSR is very loosely or poorly managed in our organization	5%	4%
Other	1%	4%

Source: FutureWatch 2010. Used with permission of Meeting Professionals International.

OPPORTUNITIES TO GO GREEN

According to recent studies, more than half of all meeting professionals are considering environmental practices as they plan their conferences. No longer it is possible to limit your considerations to sleeping rooms. At all major events held by Meeting Planners International (MPI), the board of directors purposefully considers the eight areas of "green meetings" as defined by the Convention Industry Council. These include: destination selection, transportation, venues, accommodation, food and beverage, communications, on-site operations, and expositions.

Planning a green meeting used to be thought of as difficult and expensive, when in reality, it is simply paying attention to the decisions that you make regarding your company policies and then applying them to your planning practices. The more it is done, the easier it will become. Here are some simple steps to making your next meeting green:

• *Create Standards:* Establish environmental standards within your business. Get buy-in from your organization's management and clientele. Share your standards with suppliers, vendors, and participants. Be sure to explain what you expect from them as it relates to your new standards.

- *Use Technology:* Take advantage of technology to reduce your need for paper. With easy-to-use Web site platforms, electronic registration vehicles, and e-mail, there is virtually no need to produce printed materials. To cut down on travel costs, utilize podcasting, webinars, and video streaming. In doing so, you may find an increase in your attendance numbers because you are making it easier for more people to attend.

- *Choose a Local Destination:* Choose a destination close to where your participants live to reduce the distance that must be traveled to attend. Be sure to choose a venue or hotel that is close to the airport and that is within walking distance of each other. Research public transportation options in your host city and consider venues or hotels close by.

- *Reduce, Reuse, and Recycle:* Add proper recycling bins to your event supplies list, and train your staff in the proper ways to recycle. Ask the venue to provide visible and accessible recycling services for paper, metal, plastic, and glass. Speak with the banquet manager about composting options or give-away programs and also the option of using real china for meals. If this is not possible, choose disposable plates made from renewable resources that will biodegrade in a landfill. Collect name badge holders and lanyards for use the next year.

- *Volume Up:* Encourage food and beverage providers to serve sugar, creamer, and other condiments in bulk dispensers. Find hotels that use dispensers for shampoo and lotions. Request that water stations not offer bottled water, but pitchers of water or water coolers. Give attendees a water bottle for their personal use throughout the meeting.

- *Eat Local:* Speak with the banquet manager about using local fruits and vegetables that are in season. Include more vegetarian meals, as they require less carbon energy to prepare. Obtain an accurate headcount prior to finalizing the amount of food to order to avoid waste.

- *Decorate with Nature:* Use local flowers and plants to decorate your tables and leave them in pots so that you can use them as gifts or prizes. This ensures that they are not wasted once the meeting is over.

- *Use Paper Wisely:* If you must print materials, use chlorine-free, recycled paper, and vegetable based inks. Print on both sides of the paper and only print materials for a participant if requested.

- *Save Energy:* Look for venues and hotels that have an energy efficient policy in place. Coordinate with the venue to ensure that lights, audiovisual equipment, and air-conditioning in meeting spaces will be turned off when not in use. Remind attendees to conserve energy in the guest rooms by turning off lights when they leave and not leaving electronics plugged in and powered on unnecessarily.

- *Inform Everyone:* Tell participants, speakers, suppliers, vendors, and the media about your efforts and your expectations from them as event partners. Communication is the key in

Decorating with nature.   *Photo by George G. Fenich, Ph.D.*

A New Convention Center

The city of Pittsburgh constructed a new convention center that tripled the size of its exhibit space from the previous building. It is the David L. Lawrence Convention Center. The facility became fully operational in 2003. Architect Rafael Vinoly, who was inspired by the suspension bridges that connect the city to its neighbors, was the lead project designer. He imitated this by designing an upward swooping roofline that flows with the bridges. The structural plans received input from civic leaders in the fields of hospitality, planning, architecture, and economic development as well as input from the local arts.

This $331 million center is an outstanding example of form and function. Merged within the cultural district and business district allows a perfect fit for diversity. Visitors will find points of interest that are appealing while attending functions within the convention center. The Lawrence Convention Center boasts the following:

- Prefunction area facing Allegheny River
- 330,000 square feet of exhibit space
- 250,000 square feet of column-free exhibit space
- 80,000 square feet in secondary hall
- 34,000 square-foot ballroom
- 53 meeting rooms and two 175-seat lecture halls, totaling nearly 90,000 square feet
- 12,000 square-foot main kitchen
- 37 highly accessible loading docks
- 750 parking spaces
- 3,000 committable hotel rooms in downtown business district
- New adjoining hotel in development
- State-of-the-art teleconference and telecommunications capabilities
- Internet access throughout
- Pedestrian walkway to river and riverfront trail

Green Technology

Not only does the David L. Lawrence Convention Center boast state-of-the art technology, but it also can claim that it is the first environmentally smart convention center in the United States. The goal of the design team was to receive a gold rating under the U.S. Green Building Rating System. The center estimated that 30% to 50% could be obtained in energy savings.

Water for the convention center is taken from an underwater aquifer that exists under the city. An aquifer is a formation of permeable material that yields a sufficient amount of water to wells and springs. This water is used to reduce the energy consumption for heating and cooling. All the plants and landscape around the center are native. There is no need for water sprinklers around the facility, thus conserving water.

Energy conservation is helped by the design of the sloped roof by pulling up cool breezes off the water, creating the first naturally ventilated exhibit hall of its size in the United States. Natural lighting is used throughout the building, and blackout shades are available to darken rooms or to control temperatures.

The convention center is using materials in the building that emit fewer toxins; 25% of the building was constructed with recycled material, and local materials were used in order to cut down transportation costs.

This was a new direction for convention centers, and Pittsburgh took the helm and ran with it—the superior technology that the center was wired with, to a new green technology that was just on the horizon, to the award-winning service that the Greater Pittsburgh Convention and Visitor Bureau team has had for years.

Buildings that bear the Green standard are at the forefront of an innovative way of constructing new buildings. The issue of the environment has helped the world to see that not only a more environmentally friendly building can be achieved but also a much more efficient and cost-effective building can be constructed.

The David Lawrence Convention Center in Pittsburgh, PA. *Photo by George G. Fenich, Ph.D.*

The David Lawrence Convention Center has translucent ceiling to allow natural light to enter the building. *Photo by George G. Fenich, Ph.D.*

encouraging and securing active participation from all involved parties. For example, in the speaker contract, make the green expectations very clear so that speakers do not arrive with printed handouts when electronic versions of the handouts are expected.

- *Sources:* priorLIFE.com will recycle your meeting banners into wallets, tote bags, laptop sleeves, coolers, and more! Give these unique products away or sell them to add to your bottom line.

GREENWASHING

Definition

The term **greenwashing** refers to any misrepresentation by a company that leads the consumer to believe that its policies and products are environmentally responsible, when its claims are false, misleading, or cannot be verified. Greenwashing is also used to identify the practice of companies spending more money on the campaign to notify customers of their environmentally friendly efforts, than the efforts themselves. Another term, **green sheen**, has also been used in a similar way. This term refers to companies that are making a concerted effort to show that they are adopting green practices regardless of whether their claims are true.

The actual practice of greenwashing began in the mid 1960s when companies were eager to be seen as part of the environmental movement that was taking shape. Companies were promoting themselves in line with this green movement; and when false claims began to be made through these advertising efforts, a Madison Avenue advertising executive named Jerry Mander coined the phrase "ecopornography."

As these practices continued to evolve, they eventually became known as greenwashing, a term that was first used in an essay written by environmentalist, Jay Westerveld in 1968. His essay reviewed the practice of placing a card on the pillow in each hotel room explaining that the hotel encourages reuse of guest towels for environmental responsibility. Upon closer examination of this practice, Westerveld surmised that, in most cases, the hotels were not actually making any efforts to be environmentally responsible and that the main reason for the practice was to increase profits.

Today, as consumers become more and more aware of environmentally sound practices, companies are responding by incorporating these green efforts into their business standards. As these companies compete for consumers, many become too eager to tout their green campaigns, achievement, or standards. As awareness grows, it is becoming more difficult for even the consumer to distinguish between those companies that are actually implementing green practices and those who are greenwashing.

Identifying

The meeting industry continues to respond to this challenge in many ways. One of the first steps was to identify greenwashing. In December of 2007, the TerraChoice Environmental Marketing Consulting Company became known for a study in which the "Six Sins of Greenwashing" were identified. Through a later study, an additional "sin" was added. Here is a list of the "sins" with an example to illustrate each point

- *Sin of the Hidden Trade-Off:* Providing an organic product that requires shipping instead of an equally beneficial local product.
- *Sin of No Proof:* Stating that eco-friendly cleaners are being used but not being able to produce evidence of these claims when asked.
- *Sin of Vagueness:* Using terms that are not particularly clear, such as a zero-waste conference.
- *Sin of Irrelevance:* Using or referencing environmental efforts or products that do not make sense (such as a water-conserving light bulb.)
- *Sin of Fibbing:* Stating that the property or product has a specific certification when it does not, or there is no such certification in existence.
- *Sin of the Lesser of Two Evils:* Claiming eco-friendly statements about products or services that are by nature, not eco-friendly. Using "environmentally friendly pesticides" or planning a "carbon neutral conference" where no emissions were actually reduced.
- *Sin of Worshipping False Labels:* Claiming a third-party endorsement through the use of words or images when no such endorsement exists. Using a label, for example, that by design implies that the product is eco-friendly, when it is not.

Preventing

Now that we have some idea of how to identify greenwashing, how do we prevent it within our conferences, meetings, and events?

First, meeting planners must be aware, knowledgeable, and not afraid to ask questions. As this area of the industry continues to evolve, it is the responsibility of all of us to stay on top of current trends, regulations, and questions regarding this topic. Meeting planners must take responsibility for understanding what is being said and ensuring that the terms being used are credible and make sense. Just because something is "natural" or "organic," for example, does not mean that it is healthy.

Understanding the criteria for certifications and labels is also important. A meeting planner now has to have a greater understanding of how the location became certified and what is included within the certification. Again, the responsibility falls upon the meeting planner to investigate.

A back-of-the-house tour should be part of the due-diligence process of the meeting planner and can be very helpful in validating (or not validating) the green claims being stated by any given company. Greenwashing can be spotted on these types of tours if one is aware and observant. If a claim was made by the participating venue, for example, that recycling opportunities were readily available, and will be made available for all attendees, evidence of this should be apparent during the back-of-the-house tour. You should be able to observe where the recycled material is stored and the process that takes place once it is removed from the event space. If the venue has made claims that local produce is used for all meals, evidence of this could be apparent during this tour as well. Boxes from local companies may be observed, or you may have an opportunity to speak with those working in the kitchen area. These tours provide opportunities for the venue contact to validate their claims, and/or often prompt questions by the meeting planner that validates or contradicts the claim. Lastly, planners must practice being green within their departments and companies so that they can be an advocate and lead by example. While there are numerous checklists available that can be used to assist meeting planners with planning a green meeting, the checklist included in this chapter is a good place to start. Once a planner is aware of the obstacles greenwashing can present, it is easier to identify those areas of concern and proceed in a positive manner with the planning of a green meeting.

GREEN MEETING STANDARDS

The hospitality industry is moving quickly toward the very real possibility of green meetings becoming the norm of the future. Evidence that corroborates this theory lies in the number of green guidelines and certifications that are currently available, or in the development stages. With new guidelines in place to set an industry standard in green practices, greenwashing will soon become much more difficult for companies to get away with and much easier for meeting planners to identify. As greenwashing becomes less of an issue within the industry, meeting planners will have the ability to ask the right questions with more confidence that the answers they receive will be within their expectations. Greenwashing may never disappear completely, but once industry standards are in place, the threat is reduced.

These green meeting standards will help identify, unify, and contain these efforts. While there are numerous certifications available, the Convention Industry Council along with the ASTM (originally known as the American Society for Testing and Materials) has been working diligently to create standards that can be used throughout the industry. In fact, as this book goes to press, their work continues.

ASTM/APEX Green Meeting Standards

According to Karen Kotowski, chief operating officer of the Convention Industry Council, the Convention Industry Council (CIC)'s Accepted Practices Exchange (**APEX**) Panel on Green Meetings and Events is in the final stages of the development of standards for sustainable meetings and events. The standards will be the only ASTM-certified standards for green meetings. The final standards are expected to be completed in early 2010.

The standards cover nine individual topic areas: accommodations, audiovisual, communication, exhibits, food and beverage, on-site office, destinations, meeting venue, and transportation. ASTM International is an American National Standards Institute (ANSI)-accredited standards developing organization. Although the APEX process has always followed the voluntary consensus model mandated by ASTM and ANSI, APEX elected to take the extra step in

Logo courtesy of GMIC

partnering with ASTM in order to create standards that were accepted by both the meetings industry and those outside the industry such as the federal government. The ASTM/APEX Green Meeting and Event Standards will be voluntary. However, voluntary standards developed in this manner are often cited in laws, regulations, and codes, giving them even greater credibility.

Hundreds of APEX volunteers from the meetings industry, government, international organizations, and nongovernment organizations (NGOs) have devoted countless hours of discussion and refinement as the first step in solidifying green meeting practices. The APEX panel has worked cooperatively with the Environment Protection Agency as well as other sustainable hospitality industry organizations such as Green Meetings Industry Council and Green Seal that were also stakeholders in this process.

For updated information on these standards, go to the Convention Industry Council Web site at www.conventionindustry.org or call them at 571-527-3116.

Industry Certifications

Preceding these standards, there have been numerous (eco-friendly) certifications within the industry that are currently recognized. The Green Meeting Guide offers a fairly inclusive list:

A. Accommodations
- The Hotel Association of Canada's (HAC) Green Key Eco-Rating Program
- Audubon GreenLeaf Eco-Rating Program
- Green Hotel Association
- Coalition for Environmentally Responsible Economics (CERES) Green Hotel Initiative
- Green Globe 21
- National Geographic Geotourism Award
- Ecotel Certification
- International Tourism Partnership
- Leadership in Energy & Environmental Design (LEED)
- Building Owners and Managers Association (BOMA) of Canada
- Energy Star Qualified Buildings
- Acknowledged by their national tourism association's environmental awards scheme.

B. Catering/Food & Beverage
- Marine Stewardship Council (MSC)
- Fair Trade Certified
- USDA Certified Organic
- Conseil des Appellations Agrolimentaires du Québec

C. Décor/Trade Show Rentals
- The Sierra Eco Label
- VeriFlora™
- The Flower Label Program (FLP)
- Rainforest Alliance Certification

D. Event Logistics
- EcoLogo Program
- Audubon GreenLeaf™ Eco-Rating Program
- Green-e Program
- Gold Standard

E. Printing/Promotional/Gifts
- Forest Stewardship Council (FSC)
- EcoLogo Program
- The Programme for the Endorsement of Forest Certification Schemes (PEFC)
- The Sustainable Forestry Initiative(r) Program (SFI)
- American Tree Farm System (ATFS)
- Member of Waterless Printing Association
- Rainforest Alliance
- Green Seal

F. Transportation/Tours
- Green Globe 21 (GG21) Sustainable Travel & Tourism Certification
- International Ecotourism Standard (IES)

- Blue Flag
- Green Seal
- Tourism Industry Association of Canada Code of Ethics & Guidelines for Sustainable Tourism
- World Wildlife Fund's (WWF) Membership Travel Program
- Transport Canada's ecoAUTO Rebate Program
- International Tourism Partnership

G. Venues
- The Hotel Association of Canada's (HAC) Green Key Eco-Rating Program
- Leadership in Energy & Environmental Design (LEED)
- Building Owners & Managers Association (BOMA)
- Audubon Green Leaf(tm) Eco-Rating Program
- BS 8901:2007
- Green Hotels Association
- Green Globe 21
- National Geographic Geotourism Award
- Ecotel Certification
- Acknowledged by their national tourism association's environmental awards scheme.

In addition to the certifications that suppliers, vendors, and venues can earn, meeting planners themselves can earn a certification in green meetings. The **Certification in Green Meetings & Events** (CGME) is designed to assist meeting professionals with all stages of the meeting planning process in a way that promotes social and environmental responsibility. This certification is not required in order to plan green meetings and events, but it does offer credibility to the planner and ensures the client that the planner is well-versed with regard to green practices.

While not all of the meeting industry certifications are noted here, the list of these certifications continues to grow. From a meeting planner's perspective, it is important to gain a thorough understanding of what is required for each certification that is claimed. They all have individualized requirements, but the overall goal is to bring a level of quality to the ever-evolving practice of incorporating eco-friendly applications. Due diligence on the part of the meeting planner will ensure that there is no misrepresentation to the attendees of the meeting and will also help guarantee that the green goals for the meeting will be met.

Vancouver Convention Centre

The Vancouver Convention Centre is the perfect example of how, with an open mind and forward thinking, positive changes can be made when updating a meeting venue. With the construction of the new Centre, a strong commitment to economic, environmental, and social responsibility has become the norm with planners, suppliers, and attendees. Hosting more than 350 events per year, the Vancouver Convention Centre remains dedicated to maintaining an outstanding environmental program and continues to work closely with clients to ensure sustainability in all events.

Stats:

Recycling: An average of 180,000 kilograms of materials is recycled annually—nearly half of the total volume of waste generated.

Food & Beverage: The 'scratch' kitchen uses fresh local ingredients without additives, avoids disposable utensils and dishes, and donates leftover food to local charities.

Green Design:

- A six-acre green roof, the largest non-industrial green roof in North America, with 400,000 native plants and grasses, as well as hives for 60,000 bees, providing natural habitat to birds, insects, and small mammals.
- Seawater pump system for heating and cooling that takes advantage of the constant temperature of adjacent seawater
- An underwater habitat skirt or artificial reef that is part of the centre's foundation is providing new habitat for barna-

(*continued*)

The skyline of Vancouver with a good view of the "living roof" of the Vancouver Convention Center. *Courtesy of Mhryciw, Dreamstime LLC—Royalty Free.*

cles, mussels, seaweed, starfish, crabs, and various fish species.
- Shoreline and marine habitat restoration
- On-site black water treatment and de-salinization systems that are projected to cut potable water use 60% to 70%
- Radiant floor cooling
- 400,000 square feet of walkways, bike-ways, public open space, and plazas
- Energy efficient fixtures
- Advanced energy management systems
- Natural ventilation in many of the public and pre-function spaces to support healthy indoor air quality.

- Extensive day lighting through an ultra clear structural glass system surrounding the building.
- Local materials are used throughout, in-cluding 100,000 square feet of walls and ceilings that are clad in Douglas fir and Hemlock wood harvested from Vancouver Island and the Sunshine Coast.

Statistics and other information compliments of the Vancouver Convention Centre.

EVALUATING EFFORTS

Evaluating the return on investment is crucial to the efforts of going green. ROI not only refers to the financial impact of a green meeting but also the success of the efforts put forth to achieve sustainability. It is important for meeting planners and companies to set clear goals in the beginning so that it is possible to measure the success or failure of an event. Fortunately, because of the growing interest in conducting green meetings, several tools have been created to help in the evaluation process.

Carbon Footprint Calculator

The **Carbon Footprint Calculator** allows planners to easily see which destination sites have the least amount of carbon emissions generated by air travel based on points of origin. A planner can enter the number of attendees that are coming from each region and select potential destinations for the event. Once the site has been selected and the resulting carbon footprint calculated, planners can communicate this information to attendees so that they can make an informed decision about participating. Planners can also offer options for attendees to offset carbon emissions through various programs such as planting trees.

City Scorecard

The Scorecard ranks cities according to environmental programs that are administered by the local convention and visitors' bureau, convention center, and hotels offered in the city's conference package. With this instrument is it easy to quickly see the top "green cities" and know that their efforts have been verified by a third party, MeetGreen, and been found valid.

For an example of how data can be collected and measured, consider the Grand Carolina Resort and Spa. The resort was chosen to host the 1,000 delegates over six days. While it was not particularly "green" at the outset, management responded to the client's greening requirements by altering standard operating procedures and implementing capital improvements, such as installing solar panels. Delegates joined in the effort by reducing their own consumption while on site.

For the duration of the event, data were collected each day on utility usage and waste generation, and reported the following morning at general sessions. Total consumption was compared with the average of a similar convention held the previous year. The results were impressive: Total electricity consumption had been reduced by 21%, water use by 48%, and solid waste by 34%. The greening measures were estimated to save the resort over $1 million per year.

As the need for measurable outcomes continues to grow and companies look for ROI on green strategies, the ability to measure sustainability factors will become increasingly important. Look for new and more sophisticated tools that track carbon, energy, and water footprints, BS 8901, and overall conference achievements. Newer tools will work hand-in-hand with established tools such as paper savings calculators and the MeetGreen Calculator.

GOING GREEN VERSUS SUSTAINABILITY

While sometimes used interchangeably, the terms Going Green and Sustainability have different meanings.

Going Green is "a phrase referring to individual action that a person (or company) can consciously take to curb harmful effects on the environment through consumer habits, behavior, and lifestyle." The term **Green** is usually product or service specific; and while taking the current state of the environment into consideration, it is not usually associated with the overall impact of future generations.

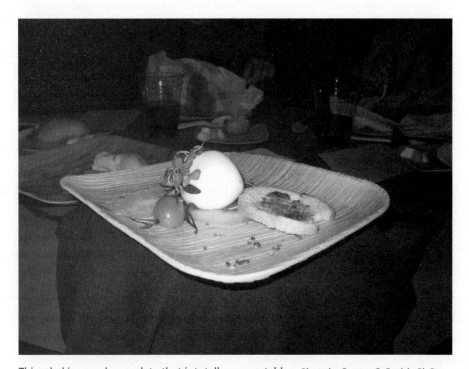

This salad is served on a plate that is totally compostable. *Photo by George G. Fenich, Ph.D.*

Sustainability is a more encompassing term that includes implementing and executing a plan to save resources while improving performance. (1) This term suggests that the impact that a company has on the environment, society, and the economy has been taken into consideration. Sustainability is doing business in a way that meets current consumer demands, while not impacting the ability for future generations to meet their demands. (2) *Green* can be considered as a part of, or a bi-product of, sustainability.

Fad or Here to Stay? The industry of green meetings is quickly growing and all indicators point to these practices eventually becoming the norm within the meeting industry. With large green meetings taking place and the ripple effect continuing to impact all involved, many companies are changing the way they do business with positive results. As more and more associations and corporations make demands for green efforts, suppliers will respond and those that can't will not compete.

"It's a buyer's market, and the buyers appear to want green," reports Tyler Davidson, editorial director, Meetings Media. "There was a sizeable jump in the number of meeting planners who are planning or expect to plan a green meeting, led by 51 percent of independents [a 16 percent jump over the last survey] and followed by 46.8 percent of corporates [a 10.5 percent jump over the last survey], and 44.4 percent both of association planners and government planners."

In a 2009 TripAdvisor survey, over a third of respondents said they would visit an eco-friendly hotel or resort in 2009. Also, 32% of respondents said they would be more environmentally aware with their travel decisions than they have in the past. The data indicate that we will continue to see an increase in green efforts by clients and customers. Meeting planners are being challenged by their clients, and they in turn are challenging their vendors as they plan and execute meetings. The end result is green meetings, a better environment, happier employees, happier attendees, and an overall contribution to the state of our world.

FUTURE TRENDS

- Green meetings and social responsibility are the future of MEEC.
- Green meetings and social responsibility will be incorporated into increasing numbers of events.
- Many national governments are likely to demand that meetings and events they organize and sponsor incorporate "green elements" and that these elements are measurable.
- There will be increasing "accountability" and requirement that planners "prove" their meetings and events are green.
- There is increased focus on cost versus benefits of "going green." Being able to document and calculate the true cost of going green versus the true benefits is crucial.

Summary

This chapter dealt with the most recent developments in the MEEC industry: green meetings and social responsibility. These are not "fads"; they are facts of life in the twenty-first century.

The challenge is how to incorporate green elements along with social responsibility into meetings and events.

Key Words and Terms

For definitions, see GLOSSARY, or http://glossary.conventionindustry.org

APEX	Green Meeting	Greenwashing	Sustainability
Carbon Footprint Calculator	Green Movement	Recycling	Triple Bottom Line
CSR	Green Sheen	Social Responsibility	

Review and Discussion Questions

1. Discuss the economic advantages and disadvantages of a meeting going green.
2. How does a meeting manager evaluate green efforts?
3. Explain the difference between the terms "going green" and "sustainability" and give examples for each that support your answer.

4. How can greenwashing be regulated within the industry and handled by a meeting planner?

References

Harding, Dan. http://eco-officegals.com/2010/01/10/guest-post-a-green-office-is-a-happy-office/

Spatrisano, Amy and Wilson, Nancy J. (2007). *Simple steps to green meetings and events: The professional's guide to saving money and the earth.* Meeting Strategies Worldwide.

Davidson, Tyler. (2008). *2008 Meetings market trends survey.* Meetings South. http://www.meetingsfocus.com/Magazines/ArticleDetails/tabid/136/ArticleID/9722/Default.aspx

Green Meetings Industry Council. (2009). *GMIC helps Clean the World.* http://www.greenmeetings.info/GMIC_News?mode=PostView&bmi=258546. Accessed December 18, 2009.

Meetings Net. Strategic Meetings Management Special Report, *The Bottom Line,* July 1, 2009. http://meetingsnet.com/checklistshowto/checklist/0701-going-green-savings/

"Social Responsibility Boosts Employee Engagement," Management Issues May 2007. http://www.management-issues.com/2007/5/9/research/social-responsibility-boosts-employee-engagement.asp. Accessed February 13, 2010.

"Volunteaming," Ritz Carlton Web site http://www.ritzcarlton.com/en/Meetings/SocialResponsibility.htm. Accessed February 13, 2010.

Kilkenny, Shannon. *The Complete Guide to Successful Event Planning.* HotelsMag.com

"Our Responsibility," *MPI: Committed to improving our world.* http://www.mpiweb.org/AboutMPI/CSR.aspx. Accessed February 13, 2010.

Ecomii, "Greenwashing," http://www.ecomii.com/ecopedia/greenwashing. Accessed December 13, 2009.

Greenwashing Fact Sheet. March 22, 2001. http://www.corpwatch.org/article.php?id=242. Accessed November 14, 2009.

What is Greenwashing? http//www.greenecocommunities.com/News/What-is-greenwashing.html. Accessed December 13, 2009.

Lodging Magazine. "The Real Deal," http://www.lodgingmagazine.com/ME2/dirmod.asp?sid=&nm=&type=Publishing&mod=Publications%3A%3AArticle&mid=8F3A7027421841978F18BE895F87F791&tier=4&id=FD212DB2AA944808BF5CE6519B2BCC06. Accessed November 9, 2009.

McKinley, Shawna. "Coming Clean about Greenwash," http://www.meetgreen.com/files/docs/DailyPlanIt08Jul.html. Accessed November 19, 2009.

McKinley, Shawna. "Six Sins of Greenwashing," http://greendestinations.blogspot.com/2007/12/six-sins-of-greenwashing.html. Accessed November 19, 2009.

EcoMarketer, "The Seventh Lesson of the Sixth Sin," Issue 6 2008, http://www.terrachoice.com/Home/EcoMarketer/Issues/05_2008_Seventh_Lesson. Accessed December 14, 2009.

Wilson, Nancy J. "What is Greenwashing? Don't let the truth-stretchers pull the wool over your eyes," www.meetingsfocus.com. Accessed November 12, 2009.

Wilson, Nancy J. "Selling Green Meetings to YOUR Stakeholders," http://greenmeetings.travelportland.com/greenmeet101/sellingGreenMeetings.html.

Kotowski, Karen. Chief Operating Officer of the Convention Industry Council, e-mail dated December 14, 2009.

Neenah Paper. "Environmental Calculator," http://www.neenahpaper.com/ECOPaperCalculator/index.asp?ft=Home. Accessed January 21, 2010.

XeroxSustainability Calculator. http://www.consulting.xerox.com/flash/thoughtleaders/suscalc/xeroxCalc.html. Accessed January 24, 2010.

EPA Victoria, Ecological Footprint Calculator. http://www.epa.vic.gov.au/ecologicalfootprint/calculators/event/introduction.asp. Accessed January 21, 2010.

Meet Green. "Best Places to MeetGreen," www.bestplacestomeetgreen.com. Accessed January 21, 2010.

Meet Green. "MeetGreen® Calculator", www.meetgreen.com. Accessed January 21, 2010.

Blue Green Meetings, "More Success Stories," http://www.bluegreenmeetings.org/MoreSuccessStories.htm. Accessed January 21, 2010.

Meeting Strategies Worldwide, "State of the 2009 Sustainable Meeting Industry," https://www.meetgreen.com/files/docs/MSWW_ 2009.SustainableMeetingIndustry.pdf. Accessed January 21, 2010.

Meetings Net. (July, 2007) "Carbon Neutral Events," http://meetingsnet.com/green_meetings/meetings_meeting_clean/. Accessed January 21, 2010.

Green Meeting Guide. "Recognized Certifications," http://www.greenmeetingguide.com/recognized-certifications.asp. Accessed December 14, 2009.

AGME. "Certification in Green Meetings and Events (CGME™)," http://www.agmeinc.org/index.php?option=com_content&task=view&id=11&Itemid=29. Accessed December 14, 2009.

Green CIO. "What's the Difference Between Green and Sustainability?" http://blog.gcio.org/2009/06/whats-the-difference-between-green-and-sustainability.html. Accessed June 15, 2009.

"Green versus Sustainable Public Procurement," http://ec.europa.eu/environment/gpp/green_vs_sustainable.htm. Accessed February 7, 2009.

LOHAS Online: Lifestyles of Health and Sustainability, LOHAS Glossary, http://www.lohas.com/glossary.html#g. Accessed December 1, 2009.

Sustainability and Securing Talent. http://green-business-practices.suite101.com/article.cfm/. Accessed February 15, 2010.

"What Is Employee Engagement and How Can Your Company Use It to Increase Sales," http://greenbusinessvillage.com/2010/02/12/. Accessed February 15, 2010.

About the Chapter Contributors

Nancy Bailey is the president of Carolina Event Consultants, a South Carolina-based event and meeting planning firm. She has been working in the event planning industry for more than ten years offering professional planning advice and services to corporations, associations, and not-for-profit organizations. Nancye graduated with a BA in public relations and a minor in hotel, restaurant, and tourism management from the University of South Carolina.

Carole Sox currently teaches at the University of South Carolina within the School of Hotel, Restaurant and Tourism Management. She started her career at the National Gallery of Art in Washington, D.C., and was employed there for approximately ten years. She then worked for a national company in the Marketing and Communications Departments where she managed the local, re-gional, and national meetings for the corporation. Carole has also worked for several for-profit universities. She earned her BS at St. Mary's College of Maryland and her MSM at Southern Wesleyan University.

Dr. Sandy Strick, a graduate of Purdue University, has been on the faculty of the School of Hotel, Restaurant and Tourism at the University of South Carolina for over twenty years. She teaches Meeting Management both at the graduate and undergraduate levels, Wine and Spirits, and Multicultural Human Resources. Dr. Strick is the coauthor of *Meetings and Events and Introduction to the Industry,* one of the first textbooks in the discipline of meetings' management. She is a Certified Hospitality Educator and Director of Graduate Studies.

APPENDIX

GREEN MEETING CHECKLIST

The following can be used as a practical guide in determining where and how your meeting or event is achieving a higher green standard.

Communications and Marketing

Paper Reduction

- Minimize paper usage by encouraging participants to register online
- Give preference to electronic documentation over paper or use double-sided copying and printing
- Provide materials via PDA download or online where possible
- When printing, use recycled stock or Forest Stewardship Council (FSC)-certified stock
- Format any distribution materials to minimize the amount of printed paper
- Use a digital registration bag when possible
- Collect name badge holders for recycling
- Inform staff, attendees, and stakeholders of event environmental practices
- Work with event staff to evaluate past events of a similar scope and size to forecast the amount of materials and handouts Needed

Selecting Recyclable & Recycled Materials

- Use recycled, high (100%) post-consumer content paper where possible
- Use FSC-certified paper
- Print materials on an Energy Star certified printer and used vegetable-based-inks
- Limit the use of paper that is difficult to recycle, such as glossy paper, goldenrod, and florescent paper

Promotional Materials

- Distribute advertising, promotion, and registration materials electronically
- Request that all banners and signs are reusable and made from recycled content
- Give preference to mailing labels that use water-based adhesives
- Sent event confirmations electronically or mail only when requested

- Limit the number of event program books available on-hand, encouraging participants to access the event program online

Onsite Event Materials

- Print any event collateral locally rather than shipping it to the event
- Reuse plastic name badge holders/lanyards and consider holding a deposit to encourage participants to return the items
- Request digital signage over paper signage
- Computerize registration process at the opening of the event
- Transmit handouts, brochures, and session notes electronically after the event via e-mail and post to Web site
- Encourage exchange of electronic event materials via USB drives
- Use dry erase boards instead of paper flip charts
- Provide pens and notepads only if requested by participants and use pens and notepads made with recycled content when requested
- Ensure that an event sponsors subscribe to the environmental guidelines for promotional materials

Sponsor and Guest Materials

- Encourage speakers/guests to provide electronic copies of handouts and post the materials to the event/organization Web site
- When unavoidable, request that speakers/guests subscribe to the environmental guidelines for any promotional materials must be printed

Food and Beverage

General

- Confirm the guaranteed number of event participants in order to eliminate excessive food waste

Elimination of Disposable Service Ware

- Give preference to reusable glassware and dishware over disposable
- Encourage participants to use mugs in a coffee stations and water coolers instead of disposable cups
- Use bio-degradable disposable if using disposables is unavoidable
- Replace plastic/wooden stir sticks with reusable spoons
- Use cloth napkins and table cloths

- Eliminate additional wasteful usage of glassware/dishware by encouraging participants to drink out of can/bottle

Food Service

- Source locally grown organic ingredients and in-season vegetables from local farmers
- Use fairly traded products (particularly fair trade, shade grown, organic coffee, tea, chocolate, and cocoa)
- Avoid bottled water by requesting water be served from jugs
- Consider giving attendees a reusable water bottle or mug for use throughout the event
- Avoid excess and throw-away packing by encouraging suppliers to use re-usable containers
- Ensure food and beverage packaging is recyclable
- Give preference to condiments, ingredients and beverages purchased in bulk
- Request that all food and beverage condiments are served in bulk containers rather than individual packets
- Avoid using garnishes or use only edible garnishes
- Arrange the donation of leftover untouched prepared food to local shelters and/or food kitchens
- Offer vegetarian meal selections (vegetables require less energy input than meat selections)
- Serve only seafood that was harvested in a responsible manner (farmed vs. fished, management of operation)

Alcoholic Beverages

- Feature locally sourced alcoholic beverages
- Give preference to reusable ceramic or wood-corked coasters over disposable coasters
- Replace disposable drink napkins with cloth napkin or compostable alternatives
- Request alcoholic beverages only from producers whose packaging and containers can be easily recycled
- Ensure that all bottles and cans are property recycled

Food Composting

- Verify that kitchen waste and prepared food that has been touched is composted
- Ensure that leftover untouched prepared food is not composted and instead consumed as staff meals or donated to local food banks, missions, or charities

Contracts and Suppliers

- Clearly outline and communicate the event's sustainability guidelines to all contractors and suppliers
- Include all the food and beverage sustainability guidelines in supplier contracts

Event Production
Recycling Initiatives

- Place recycling containers in various easy-to-access areas with adequate signage
- Arrange for recycling areas to be staffed with advisors that can guide recycling efforts and address any questions/concerns
- Provide small trash bins at reception areas only if requested and provide no trash bins if the event objective is zero-waste
- Give participants advance notice of the general recycling programs at the event via e-mail or post the information on the event's Web site
- Communicate recycling waste prevention initiatives to event participants at the opening/general sessions and periodically remind participants of the initiatives at intermissions

Recycling Signage

- Display clear signage indicating the type of recyclable material each container accepts, differentiating from cans, bottles, paper, organics, etc.
- Request digital signage if available or use paper with recycled content
- If paper signage is used, follow the same guidelines outlined in Communications & Marketing

Design and Decor

- Request centerpieces and decorations that organic, such as flowers, or that can be reused for future events
- If organic centerpieces are used, encourage participants to take the items with them, thereby eliminating waste
- Request that any other design features or décor items use materials that are both recycled and recyclable

Food Service Suppliers

- Request that reusable containers that are used to transport any items/materials to and from the event
- Create a no waste policy that places the responsibility of disposing any garbage on the suppliers and/or vendors
- Consider charging a fee for excessive waste left at the event

Cleaning Services

- Ensure that housekeeping staff uses only non-toxic, eco-friendly cleaning solutions such as Certified Green Seal products
- Request that housekeeping staff replace paper cleaning towels with reusable cloth towels

Energy and Electricity

- Purchase green power (or offset power consumption) during the event and notify participants of the renewably-sourced electricity
- Make a request to the event facility manager to see the thermostat in the venue to minimal, but comfortable temperature in order to decrease energy consumption
- Take advantage of naturally lit meeting and exhibit space

Event Staff

- Communicate the event's sustainability guidelines to staff prior to the beginning of the event
- Ensure that the staff is effectively trained on appropriate environmental behavior such as sorting recyclables, minimizing waste, and composting organic waste
- Create a green committee comprised of stakeholders from various parties to oversee the event and monitor the event's sustainability guidelines
- Develop a reward program that encourages responsible behavior from event participants, staff, and committee members

Exhibits and Exhibitors
Reducing Packaging for Giveaways

- Request that all exhibitors not over-package any giveaways. Hold exhibitors responsible for discarding/recycling the packaging
- Encourage exhibitors to select giveaways made of recyclable materials or reusable items
- Consider sourcing eco-SWAG (souvenirs, wearable, and gifts)

Exhibitor Promotional Materials

- Extend environmental guidelines for communications and marketing materials to the promotional materials and exhibitors

(continued)

- Communicate the expected number of participants to exhibitors in order to minimize any additional waste
- Encourage exhibitors to bring smaller quantities of promotional materials and require that exhibitors offer access to electronic materials on their Web site as an alternative

Packaging Materials

- Encourage exhibitors to reuse any boxes or packing that was used on arrival at the event venue
- Enforce a pack-in/pack-out policy or zero-waste criteria to ensure exhibitors leave with everything that was brought to the event
- Discourage exhibitors from using any external chemical substances on-site

Event Closing Protocol

- Develop check-out procedures that require exhibitors to interact with event staff prior to departure, ensuring their area is clean and waste-free
- Enforce fines for exhibitors that leave discarded materials, trash, carpet, or anything that accompanied them to the event

Recycled-Content in Display Booths and Exhibits

- Encourage exhibitors to use recycled content in the fabrication and assembly of display booths/exhibits
- Encourage exhibitors to use booths/exhibits that can be reused for future events

Reward Green Exhibitors

- Reward exhibitors with a "Green Exhibitor Award" at the end of the event, recognizing the exhibitor in front of all participant

Accommodations

General

- Identify any accommodation providers that are certified by an eco-rating program, such as the Green Key
- Highlight any accommodation providers that subscribe to a specific industry environmental code of practice
- Request in-house environmental policies/guidelines of potential accommodation providers and consider eliminating any accommodation providers whose environmental policies/guidelines do not support the event's sustainability goals
- Schedule a site visit with accommodation providers to verify on-site environmental practices
- Request that the accommodation provider dedicate a channel at the hotel that contains specific information about the event as well as any important updates
- Request that hotels change linens and towels every other day unless specifically requested by the guest

Accommodation Location

- Give preference to hotels within walking distance of the event venue, thereby eliminating the need for transportation and
- Allowing participants to walk from the hotel and back
- If transportation is unavoidable, consider bundling accommodation and transportation by operating a shuttle from the hotel to the event venue and back

Cooperation from Event Participants

- Ask event participants to reuse the linen at their hotels rather than use the laundry service everyday
- Remind participants to turn off lights, television, and air conditioners or heaters when leaving their hotel room for an extended period of time

Transportation

General

- Allow Web-conferencing abilities for participants that cannot physically travel to the event
- Establish an idle-free zone around the event venue

Low-Impact Air Travel

- Notify event participants of the various airlines that allow passengers to offset their emissions

Emissions Offsets

- Partner with local offset companies and request them to setup a display booth/exhibit at the event and sell offsets directly to participant
- Work with offset companies to offer emissions offsets at a discount rate if purchased in bulk
- Ask a representative from a local offset company to deliver a brief presentation on the importance of offsetting emissions
- Offer reduced attendance fees to event participants that purchase emissions offsets

Shuttle to/from Hotel

- Encourage all participants to travel together to or from the event
- Work with accommodation providers to develop a schedule of pick-up and drop-off times

Zero Emission Alternatives

- Partner with local bicycle vendors to arrange bicycle rentals that give participants the option to ride between the hotel and event and explore the city
- Establish appropriate bicycle storage areas with the facility manager

Mass-Transit Passes

- For hotels located across town or outside of walking distance, provide participants a bus or mass transit pass and directions on how to travel between the hotel and event
- Include the cost of a transit pass in the overall fee of attending the event, for delegates who must use transportation to reach the event

Hybrid Vehicle Rentals

- For participants who require a private vehicle, partner with car rental companies that offer hybrid vehicles
- Request that hybrid models are on reservation and ready for pick-up before the event
- Work with parking operators to allocate a certain amount of parking stalls for participants that arrive to the event in a hybrid vehicle

Hybrid Taxis

- Use taxi companies that have a large hybrid fleet and encourage participants to specifically request hybrid taxis
- Notify taxi companies of the event prior to the start date and communicate the event's sustainability guidelines

Car-Pooling

- Encourage car-pooling by dedicating a section of either the event's Web site or the organization's Web site that permits local participants and car rental users to make arrangements
- Work with parking operators to allocate a certain amount of parking stalls for participants that car-pool to the event

Information Technology

Web site and Online Content

• Request that the event venue or client organization create a section of its Web site that contains event materials accessible only by participants or request that the event provides a link on its Web site to the organization's Web site

• Notify and periodically remind participants of the Web site and its content

Equipment

• Encourage laptop usage over desktop computers, as laptops typically use less energy than desktops

• Use liquid crystal display (LCD) monitors instead of cathode ray tube (CRT) monitors

• Activate sleep mode on any equipment used in the event's production, including projectors, computers in the registration area, and personal computers of participants

• If purchasing any equipment for the event, give preference to Energy Star products that use less energy

Recycled Components

• Request that recycled print cartridges are used when printing event-related materials

• Request that recycled print cartridges contain vegetable-based inks

• Recycle any electronic waste, such as print cartridges, that is left behind at the end of the event

RESOURCES:	USFI, Visitseattle.org, Vancouver Convention Centre, Green Hotels Association, PCMA
TERMS: **FSC**	FSC is a nonprofit organization that sets certain high standards to make sure that forestry is practiced in an environmentally responsible and socially beneficial manner. If a product, often a piece of wood outdoor furniture, is labeled as "FSC Certified," it means that the wood used in the piece and the manufacturer that made it met the requirements of the FSC.
ENERGY STAR	Energy Star is a U.S. government program created in 1992 by the U.S. Environmental Protection Agency in an attempt to reduce energy consumption and greenhouse gas emission by power plants. What began originally as a voluntary labeling program has grown in to one of the largest efforts worldwide to promote energy efficient consumer products.
SWAG	Souvenir, wearable, and gifts typically found at tradeshows or other promotional events
GREEN POWER	Energy produced from renewable or non-polluting and non-hazardous technologies such as air turbines (windmills), geothermal power plants, solar-cells.
FAIR TRADE PRODUCTS	For a product to carry either the International Fair-trade Certification Mark or the Fair Trade Certified Mark, it must come from FLO-CERT (the inspection and certification body for labeled Fair-trade), inspected and certified producer organizations.
	The crops must be grown and harvested in accordance with the international Fair-trade standards set by FLO International.
	The supply chair must also have been monitored by FLO-CERT, to ensure the integrity of labeled products.
CERTIFIED GREEN SEAL	A product is eligible for green seal certification when it has passed rigorous testing and evaluation using a life-cycle approach, which means they evaluate a product or service beginning with material extraction, continuing with manufacturing and use, and ending with recycling and disposal.

CHAPTER 14

International Aspects in MEEC

Chapter Outline

MEEC organizers must be prepared to work with diverse people and cuisines.
Courtesy of Scott Cunningham, Merrill Education

Chapter Objectives

This chapter provides the reader with an understanding of the following:

- How trade fairs exhibitions and conferences vary around the world
- The status of the trade fair industry in different regions
- The terminology and protocol differences among various countries
- Aspects to consider before committing to an international trade fair or conference

INTRODUCTION

The growth of international communications and travel has brought about phenomenal changes in how the world does business. Twenty-five years ago, only the largest companies were considered "international." Today, there are few large companies that do not have an international presence.

Consequently, the meetings, expositions, events, and conventions (MEEC) industries have expanded internationally. In this chapter, we look at how the international scope of MEEC has evolved and how it differs in various parts of the world.

The 69th UFI (Union of International Fairs) Congress in Munich, Germany, announced some incredible statistics about the international **trade fair** industry. Dr. Hermann Kresse, AUMA CEO, announced that the economic impact of trade fairs in Germany was 23 billion Euros, and employment reached 250,000 full-time jobs in the exhibition industry. "The report shows that the overall Asian exhibitions market grew over 12% in 2005 in terms of actual space sold by organisers. Exhibition sales topped 10 million square metres in the year according to the UFI/BSG research. China remains

"Day ticket from CeBIT 2010 in Hannover, Germany.   *Courtesy of Wolandmaster, Dreamstime LLC—Royalty Free.*

the top market with almost 40% of space sales in the region, followed by Japan in second place and South Korea in third." Regardless of the location, the purposes of international meetings and exhibitions remain the same—communication, learning, networking, and marketing.

HOW MEEC VARIES AROUND THE GLOBE

Despite similarities of purpose, cultural and business influences have created different models for meetings and exhibitions in various parts of the world. In this section, the types of meetings and exhibitions held in different regions of the world are surveyed, with a discussion of how they differ in scope and operation, and what areas of the world are embracing trade fairs as a primary method of marketing. Included at the end of this chapter is a compilation of international trade fair organizations with their corresponding Web addresses.

Report from CeBIT 2009

CeBIT 2009 got off to a powerful start and ended on a successful note, boosting optimism in the world ICT industry. A majority of the 4,300 companies from 69 countries drew fresh optimism from being at CeBIT. A huge number of exhibitors and visitors are leaving Hannover with a renewed sense of buoyancy as well as bulging order books and a solid foundation for new business. The show lived up to their expectations.

More than 400,000 visitors—a drop of just under 20% on the previous year's figure—came to CeBIT 2009 to generate new business.

A marked increase in the trade visitor ratio however meant its expectations were often exceeded. Companies that came well-prepared reported a jump in significant business leads of more than 20%. This CeBIT has been a good investment for exhibitors and visitors alike, delivering real benefits to everyone.

The percentage of visitors from abroad remained steady at 20%. A decrease in attendance from Asia was offset by increased attendance from the Americas and the Middle East. (http://www.cebit.de/show_report).

The Grassmarket has been a focal point in the Old Town for 500 years and a trading place since the beginning of the city of Edinburgh, Scotland.   *Courtesy of Omnia, Getty Images Inc.—Hulton Archive Photos*

Europe

The trade fair industry's roots are in Europe. During the Middle Ages, the concept began with farmers and craftsmen bringing their products and wares to the town center to link with their customer base. Although the world wars of the twentieth century devastated European industry, today Europe is the focal point of international trade fairs and exhibitions.

There are two primary reasons for this. First is location—Europe has always been the crossroads of the world. International hub airports in Frankfurt, London, Amsterdam, Paris, and Rome enable visitors and cargo to easily arrive from all parts of the world. In addition, a superlative network of rail transportation within Europe enables many cities to be within a day's transportation from one another. The second reason for the growth of trade fairs is Europe's industrial base. With reconstruction help from the United States, Europe was able to recover its manufacturing and distribution base within a few decades of World War II. With the help of their governments, European industrial centers develop trade fair facilities that are unrivaled in other parts of the world.

The Largest Exhibition Venue

Hannover, Germany, is the model for government and private industry working together to create a successful trade fair venue with an unparalleled economic impact on a region. Managed by Hannover Messe A.G., Hannover Fair, the world's largest exhibition venue, consists of over 5 million square feet of indoor exhibit space and 1 million square feet of covered outdoor space, restaurants, warehouses, and meeting facilities. More important, the regional government and the management company have worked together to establish excellent transportation and lodging facilities. Local companies have also contributed to making this facility the best in the world.

Hannover Fair

Hannover Fair 2009 opened—April 20, 2009

On Sunday, 19th April, German President Horst Köhler opened the 2009 Hannover Messe, one of the world's premier technology shows. From 20 to 24 April, 6,150 exhibitors from a total of 61 nations presented their products at an impressive 224,800 square meters of exhibition space in Hannover.

Exhibitors showcased products and innovations from the fields of industrial automation, motive power engineering, energy, industrial subcontracting, and R&D. For added value, the rich arrays of exhibits were complemented by a great many forums, conferences, seminars, and workshops.

Apart from Germany, Hannover Messe's biggest exhibitor contingents came from Italy, which has about 500 exhibitors. While 480 exhibitors came from China, this year's partner country South Korea sees 210 exhibitors participating. India, which was the partner country at the 2006 Hannover Fair, participated with 129 exhibitors for this year. Turkey had 180, Taiwan 127, Switzerland 125, France 113, North America 95, Spain 85, and the Netherlands 84. (http://www.german-info.com/press_shownews.php?pid=1015)

Germany is usually thought of as the center of industry and trade fairs in Europe. Trade fairs and exhibitions are a $10.5 billion business in Germany alone. Over 165,000 exhibitors participate in 133 international events each year. Over 40% of trade fair exhibitors in Germany are from countries not in the European Union. Four of Europe's top five trade fair facilities are located in Germany (Hannover, Frankfurt/Main, Cologne, and Dusseldorf). In addition, five of the world's top international trade fairs and exhibitions are held in Germany:

- Hannover Fair—Industrial; over 7,000 exhibitors
- CeBIT—Information technology; over 8,000 exhibitors
- Domotex—Flooring; over 3,000 exhibitors
- Frankfurt Book Fair—Over 4,000 exhibitors
- Biotechnology—Over 3,000 exhibitors

Italy is another center of international trade fair activity. Milan is the fashion trade fair center of the world and attracts buyers from around the world for its almost constant fashion-related trade fairs. Rome hopes to rival Hannover and Dusseldorf for industrial trade fairs. Many trade fairs and exhibitions in Italy are sponsored by the strong network of world trade centers in cities across the country.

The nations of the United Kingdom hosted over 1,800 exhibitions, attracting 17.3 million visitors to over 450 venues. Top exhibitions included:

- Birmingham Spring Fair
- World Travel Market (London)
- Furniture Show (Birmingham)
- Birmingham Fall Fair
- Security Solutions (Birmingham)

The Benelux nations also have a strong trade fair program. Excellent facilities exist in Amsterdam, Rotterdam, Brussels, and at Schipol Airport. New Congress facilities in Paris are attracting new trade fairs as well. Again, world trade centers in these cities are the focal point of the promotion and operation of trade fairs.

Perhaps the greatest growth of trade fairs in Europe is occurring in the countries of Eastern Europe. New facilities are opening in Zagreb, Belgrade, Warsaw, and most recently Moscow.

It is anticipated that the growth of the European Union, its common currency of the Euro, and the removal of trade barriers and tariffs will only make the European trade fair and exhibition industry continue to grow.

The many halls in the Moscow Trade Center are identified by color with this being the red hall.
Courtesy of B2d, Dreamstime LLC—Royalty Free.

Travel and Tourism Trade Fair in Moscow

Great Success for Otdykh LEISURE 2008

The 14th International Trade Fair for Tourism **Otdykh LEISURE** took place **23–26 September 2008** in **IEC Crocus Expo**. The exhibition was again a great success with 1,095 exhibiting companies including **75 tourism boards from 112 countries and regions** of the world.

Traditionally held within **MATIW—Moscow Autumn Travel Industry Week**, Otdykh LEISURE 2008 welcomed a record number of Russian and international key players who exhibited at the most global tourism event in Russia and the CIS.

What is MATIW?

The Moscow Autumn Travel Industry Week (MATIW) is the main autumn event for Russia's tourism market, attracting an ever greater number of its direct participants and visitors from year-to-year. This year, the largest international exhibition center in Russia, Crocus Expo, which has at its disposal the most modern equipment and developed infrastructure, once again was the venue for the exhibitions. Holding Moscow Travel Industry Week at the Crocus Expo IEC allowed the provision of a high level of service for exhibitors and visitors.

MATIW 2008 figures:

Exhibition space, 23,000 sqm

Number of Exhibitors, 1395

Countries and regions presented, 129

Number of Trade Visitors, 71,150

Countries represented in 2008

Abu Dhabi Andorra Argentina Australia Austria Barbados Belarus Brazil Bulgaria Cambodia Chile China Croatia Cuba Cyprus Czech Republic Dominican Republic Dubai Ecuador Egypt Finland France Fujairah Germany Ghana Great Britain Greece Hungary India Indonesia Israel Italy Jordan Kenya Korea Laos Latvia Lithuania Malaysia Maldives Malta Mauritius Mexico Monaco Montenegro Morocco Myanmar Nepal New Zealand Norway Oman Peru Philippines Poland Portugal Ras al Khaimah Romania Russia Saint - Barthelemy Seychelles Sharjah Singapore Slovakia South Africa Spain Sri Lanka Switzerland Tanzania Thailand Tunisia Turkey Uganda Ukraine USA Uzbekistan Venezuela Vietnam Zimbabwe

September—best date for Russian tourism professionals

September is a period of intense work for tour business professionals, the establishment of new business contacts, and determination of pricing for the autumn and winter season. **This is the best exhibition date for all exotic, long haul, winter sun and traditional winter sun, and winter travel destinations.** The Moscow Autumn Travel Industry Week affords a splendid opportunity to reflect the overall picture of the tourism market's modern condition and become a point for the intersection of the business interests of tour industry specialists.

While spring exhibition events are focused on summer sun destinations, mainly in Europe, Otdykh LEISURE in September is well recognized as a must attend event for all winter—sun, long haul, and exotic destinations, as well as all winter travel destinations, including ski resorts, spa vacations, and city breaks.

Otdykh LEISURE 2008—the Opening

The show was officially opened by a record number of high level and VIP guests, including Mr. Yarochkin, Head of the Federal Agency for Tourism of Russia, Mr. Joan Mesquida, Spain's State Secretary for Tourism, Mr. Amr el Zabi - Head of the Egyptian tourism board, Mr. Juli Minoves Triquell – the Minister of Economic Development, Tourism, Culture and Universities of the Principality of Andorra, H.H. Sheik Abdullah al Hossani - The Sultanate of Oman's Ambassador to the Russian Federation, Mr. Phineas Alburo - The Philippines Deputy Minister for Tourism and many others.

Easier to get to

A new road to IEC Crocus Expo and recently opened metro station (Strogino) was highly appreciated by visitors and exhibitors as their way to the exhibition was easy and took less time than ever before. Easy approach, free car parking for 12 000 car, modern pavilions and well developed infrastructure definitely make Crocus Expo Moscow's best exhibition venue.

Comprehensive program for tourism professionals

The 3 first days of the show were extremely busy and offered a unique combination of educational sessions, countries presentations, seminars and networking events.

Latin America Day was held on 24 September and was one of the highlights of the exhibition, sponsored by Natalie Tours and held with support and cooperation of EMBRATUR – the Brazilian tourism board, Venezuela Ministry of Tourism, the Dominican Republic Ministry of Tourism, Argentinean Embassy in Moscow, Cuba Ministry of Tourism, companies Caribbean Club, TourExpress, Journey Travel Company Peru, Travel Mark Argentina, Tours Brasil. Country presentations, national dance performances, round tables etc were held during the whole day,

and in the evening a Latin American Party was organized for the Russian travel agencies.

MIBEXPO Russia Conference

The 4th International MIBEXPO Conference was again perceived as a highlight of the event, where delegates had a unique chance to meet International and Russian experts during the two conference days. The conference was moderated by Mr. Jury Sarapkin, Vice president of the Business Travel Agencies Association of Russia (BTAA). Renowned speakers contributed to the success of MIBEXPO and offered seminars, master classes and round tables to the delegates. The excellent international speakers were Michel Neijmann (Head of International Affairs, AIM Group), Richard Lewis (Chairman, Richard Lewis Communications), Ian Epps (Director of Partnership Relations, ITP), Tasso Pappas (Representative of The Society of Incentive and Travel Executives, SITE) and Kristina T'Seyen (Deputy Director, DMAI).

SPA and Heath Conference

The 4th International Conference for health tourism, (Spa & Health) was held on 24th September. This event was again part of the outstanding parallel program and it constituted an excellent platform for specialists to learn more about global trends in spa technologies and the wellness industry. The Spa Conference offered the possibility to communicate personally with spa industry experts from all over the world and to receive first-hand information about the opportunities of the worldwide health tourism market.

Renowned international and Russian speakers provided a very good insight into their business and discussed basic as well as current topics concerning health tourism, such as quality standards, strategies for spa and health resorts, training of employees and spa in general. The international speakers were Adrian Egger (Schletterer Wellness & Spa Design, Senior Consultant International Project Development, Austria); Kurt von Storch (European Spas Associations ESPA); Constantine Constantinides (HealthCare Cybernetics, Greece); and Laslo Zopcsak (International Wellness Institute – Europe Wellness Education Center, Hungary).

Otdykh LEISURE 2008 FIGURES:

Exhibition area 19,000 sqm

Number of Exhibitors 1095

International 604

Russian 491

Countries and regions presented 112

Trade Visitors 62,250

Source: http://www.tourismexpo.ru/en/

Asia

The growth of trade fairs and exhibitions in Asia has been phenomenal over the past fifteen years. New facilities and government promotions have taken the industry from its infancy to world class in little more than a decade. Primarily, Asian trade fairs focus on high technology, consumer electronics, and food. However, all types of manufacturing and service industries are well represented. Asian trade fairs and exhibitions are either sponsored by trade organizations, such as the world trade centers, or individual governments.

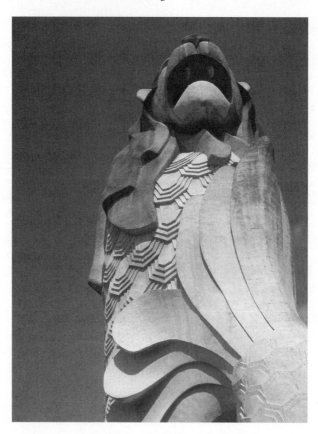

The Merlion is the symbol of Singapore. It is half fish and half lion. *Photo by George G. Fenich, Ph.D.*

Taiwan and Singapore have been the backbone of Asian trade fairs and exhibitions. Taiwan has excellent facilities and routinely sponsors trade fairs in the semiconductor, consumer electronics, and food industries. Taiwan is also the world's leader in exhibiting at trade fairs and exhibitions in North America and Europe.

Singapore is a major "destination" city and consequently attracts many visitors to its textile, fashion, food, and electronics trade fairs. It has multiple facilities all linked to world-class shopping and entertainment complexes. Singapore is also attractive because it provides excellent transportation facilities with a world-class airport serving every continent, and every facility or attraction in the city is generally within walking distance or a short taxi ride from each other. The government of Singapore is very active in promoting exhibitions. The Singapore Trade Development Board is the lead agency for marketing Singapore as an international exhibition city. It provides financial and marketing support for trade fairs organized by both Singaporean and international organizers. It also chairs the Exhibition Management Services Council, a public/private partnership of government agencies, industry associations, chambers of commerce, and exhibition companies.

China, as it opens up to international trade, is expanding the number and quality of its trade fairs and exhibitions. Major new facilities have been built in Hong Kong, Shanghai, and Beijing. The Shanghai International Exhibition Corporation facility covers over 1.5 million square feet. Recent trade fairs have focused on consumer goods, food, and electronics. In Hong Kong, there are more than thirty fair organizers belonging to the Hong Kong Exhibition and Convention Organizers' and Suppliers Association. These include for-profit companies, associations, and government agencies.

China

The section that follows in China was contributed by Dr. Wang Chunlei, associate professor and the Chair of Event Management Department, Shanghai Institute of Tourism, Shanghai Normal University.

The phrase "Convention & Exhibition"... in Chinese was put forward in the late 1980s in China. If we input the Chinese characters of "Convention & Exhibition" in Google, we can get various words such as "meeting industry," "exhibition industry," "Convention & Exhibition industry," or "Convention & Exhibition tourism industry." In other words, the professionals and the scholars in China have different opinions on the range of convention and exhibition industries. But just like many other countries, "event" is becoming a more and more popular term in China. Accordingly, event management has gradually got the common recognition and acceptance by industrial practitioners as an independent science.

With annual GDP growth rates of nearly 8% in recent years and continued economic reform, China has become one of the world's largest markets for the sale of raw materials and products. Economic prosperity, coupled with the liberalization of the regulatory regime as part of China's World Trade Organization (WTO), and entry commitments have been the greatest stimuli to the rapid and sustainable development of the Chinese convention and exhibition industries. At the same time, incentive travel, festivals, and special events are becoming more and more popular with local governments.

CONVENTION AND EXHIBITION INDUSTRIES   In 1978, only six international conventions and exhibitions were held in China, and it held and took part in twenty-one exhibitions abroad. The first exhibition company, Shanghai International Exhibition Company (SIEC), was established in 1985. Today, the quantities and scales of exhibitions in China have been increased by hundred folds and penetrated into all fields of the national economy; as a consequence, each industry had its own international professional exhibitions. By the end of 2007, there were a total of 220 large and medium exhibition centers, and the indoor exhibition floor space was over 3 million square meters. In 2008, the formal exhibitions held in China exceeded 3,000, and the direct revenues reached 14 billion Yuan (2 billion USD). The revenues of the related industries were about 130 billion Yuan (18.6 billion USD), realizing excellent economic and social benefits.

Five convention and exhibition economic belts, the Yangzi River Delta, Zhujiang Delta, Bohai Bay Area, and Northeast and Central China, have been formed in the mainland, and many trade shows have reached as far west as Chengdu, Sichuan Province; Chongqing city; and Xi'an, Shaanxi Province. As far as the scales and impacts of exhibition projects go, Beijing, Shanghai, and Guangzhou have been the most important three cities of Chinese convention and exhibition industries, with the market shares accounting for 10% to 20% in the whole country. As one form of economic concentration, some cities have grown into regional centers, such as Dalian, Shenzhen, Chengdu, Hangzhou, Nanjing, Ningbo, Suzhou, Qingdao, Xiamen, Xi'an, Wuhan, Nanning, Kunming, and Chongqing.

Generally speaking, there are five essential reasons that can explain the current malaise of China's convention and exhibition industries: poor industry positioning in many cities, government involvement in industry management, weak domestic exhibition enterprises, lack of international competitiveness, and outdated professional education and training. For example, to date the only existing national convention and exhibition associations are the China Convention and Exhibition Society (CCES) and China Association for Exhibition Centers (CAEC), but CCES is mainly concerned with research while most members of CAEC are convention centers. And different government departments are designated to oversee an exhibition that corresponds with its industry and level. That is to say, if a trade show organizer plans to launch an exhibition in Shanghai, it must receive approval from the relevant municipal government departments mainly according to the exhibition's theme, the scope of exhibitors or attendees (international or domestic), and the qualification of the organizer.

However, it's a good fact that Chinese convention and exhibition industries are enduring great changes in all-round fields. For example, many Chinese cities began to realize the importance of meetings, which could contribute to the balanced development of the convention industry and the exhibition industry. Furthermore, to further optimize the market order, related governmental departments are organizing officials and experts from different fields to draft laws and regulations on convention and exhibition industries, with the hope that free competition can be carried out for capital at home and abroad in a fair environment, finally realizing the optimized collocation of convention and exhibition resources through competition and cooperation.

FESTIVAL AND SPECIAL EVENTS (FSE)   With the rapid development of the national economy and the improvement of living standards in China, festivals and special events with various themes are welcomed by more and more local governments, and especially the tourism industry.

Generally speaking, the Chinese FSE industry shows different attributes: The content of events is colorful, including entertainment, sports, and trade shows; the industries of culture, tourism, sports, and manufacturing have been integrated together; there are public service and private products in most festivals and special events. The most important fact is that culture and arts are becoming much more important when developing festivals or special events in China.

But there are also prominent short-sighted phenomenons that lead to low efficiency in the operation of events. In Germany, France, the United States, Hong Kong, and other areas where festivals and special events are prosperous, the industrial administration mainly depends on self-discipline and self-discipline norms. Generally, the government intervenes into the infrastructure, industrial policy formulation, and assistance in attracting visitors for local hallmark festivals (especially international events). However, currently different levels of Chinese government play the roles of both referee and sportsman during the development of FSE. It is a common practice that a lot of festivals and special events are hosted or subcontracted by these governments.

In addition, in a broad sense, many Chinese city governments still manage FSE in a classification-and-level oriented manner. It means that the government dismisses its macro-administration and gives its authorities to departments such as commerce, domestic trade, science and technology, culture, and trade promotion committees. This kind of administration system could easily lead to political issues. And under the pattern of cross administration, the government is far from bringing out its strength in adjusting and controlling that should be segmented into statistics, planning, making policy, or regulations.

INCENTIVE TRAVEL   Incentive travel is a new kind of business in the Chinese tourism industry, but with a huge potential market. With more and more Chinese organizations and companies making use of incentive travel, a lot of traditional travel agencies in China began to change their business model or offer new services.

At the same time, there came forth some professional trade shows, the most famous two of which are China Incentive Business Travel & Meetings Exhibition (CIBTM) and Incentive Travel & Convention, Meeting IT & CM China. The first international exhibition in China dedicated to the business travel, incentives, and conferences, CIBTM, was launched in 2005 and has become the driving force behind the professional incentive travel industry across China and Asia. CIBTM offers exhibitors much more than just a show, but the opportunity to meet qualified buyers with an interest in different business travel products and services.

Currently, organizations in China using incentive travel as a kind of management tool are mainly foreign companies such as Amway, HP, IBM, Samsung, and Microsoft. Most domestic companies don't recognize the real effects of incentive travel, but only regard it as one part of welfare offered for employees or customers. Accordingly, Chinese travel services, especially those with strength and experience, ought to develop and offer suitable products to the professional clients.

Furthermore, with plenty of tourism resources, competitive prices, and good tourism image, China is expected to become one of the most popular incentive travel destinations in the world. On the other hand, with its rapid economic prosperity, China is also becoming one of the key incentive travel markets. And many countries such as Australia, the Netherlands, and Egypt are enhancing marketing to trade customers and residents in China.

Korea

Thailand is a major center for clothing and textile trade shows. Excellent transportation facilities in Bangkok make it easy for visitors to arrive from around the world.

The Coex Center in Seoul has over 400,000 sq. meters. It is one stop shopping—with exhibition space, hotels, entertainment, shopping, and the city airport terminal. It is one example of the future of convention centers: One stop shopping. Click on http://www.coex.co.kr/eng/intro/overview.asp for more detailed information.

Other countries nurturing trade fair programs with government promotion include Vietnam, Malaysia, and India. In these countries, the facilities are usually owned and operated by the government, and promotional activities are sponsored by various government agencies. Vietnam has taken a strong position in clothing and food trade fairs, while India is at the forefront of Asian information technology and software shows.

Africa

The section that follows on Africa was contributed by Uwe P. Hermann who holds a masters degree in tourism and hospitality management and is a lecturer and researcher in the Department of Tourism Management, Tshwane University of Technology, Pretoria, South Africa. His research interests focus primarily on responsible/sustainable tourism and events in Southern Africa.

Two main centers for MEEC exist in Africa, Egypt, and the Republic of South Africa. The MEEC industry in Africa has seen significant growth over the past few decades, particularly in South Africa. Since the early 1990s, South Africa has become an increasingly important player not only on the continent but worldwide. Presently South Africa enjoys just over 1% market share of the global business tourism industry. The International Congress and Convention Association currently ranks South Africa in thirty-first position worldwide as a meeting destination, while the Union of International Associations ranks South Africa as the twenty-eight position as a top meetings destination in the world. In the African context, however the country is far ahead, hosting 23% of all business tourism meetings on the continent. Cape Town is the most popular urban meeting destination in Africa with approximately 10% of all meetings in Africa being hosted in the city.

Traditionally, the MEEC industry in South Africa is concentrated around hotel venues and game lodges but considerable development has taken place in the creation of large multipurpose conference and exhibition facilities. In South Africa, three cities dominate the MEEC industry, namely Cape Town, Durban, and Johannesburg. All three of these cities have invested in the creation of major international convention centers, which now form a main part of each city's marketing campaigns. These three cities have also embarked on large-scale investment of support infrastructure, such as accommodation, technology, and transport. To support the development of MEEC in South Africa, the Tourism Grading Council of South Africa launched a star grading system for meetings and exhibition venues; this initiative is considered a world first.

Large numbers of domestic trade fairs and conventions dominate the South African industry, predominantly around Johannesburg, although South Africa as a destination for trade fairs is growing rapidly. Currently, there are over 1,000 conference and exhibition venues in the country. The six major venues in South Africa include:

- Cape Town International Convention Centre
- Durban International Convention Centre
- Gallagher Estate (Johannesburg)
- Johannesburg Expo Centre
- Sandton International Convention Centre (Johannesburg)
- Tshwane Events Centre (Pretoria Showgrounds)

The Johannesburg Expo Centre is the largest exhibition space on the continent. The three venues in Johannesburg have a combined exhibition space of 100,000 m² (1,076 391 sq ft). The demand for exhibition space in Cape Town currently exceeds supply. Upcoming cities in the MEEC industry in South Africa include Bloemfontein, Port Elizabeth, and Pretoria.

Cairo in Egypt is dominated by the Cairo International Fairground with 57,000 m² (613,542 sq ft) of exhibition space, which is the largest exhibition space in North Africa. Other venues with significance may also be found in Botswana, Nigeria, Senegal, Uganda, and Zimbabwe. Exhibition space in the rest of Africa is relatively scarce.

For the first time in history, the World Cup (soccer) was held in Africa in 2010. *Courtesy of Gladcov, Dreamstime LLC—Royalty Free.*

The South African Tourism INDABA is an annual event that has been held in Durban since 1997. This is one of the largest tourism marketing events on the African continent that showcases a variety of tourism products and attracts international visitors and media from across the globe. In 2008 this exhibition attracted 13,200 visitors and hosted 1,761 exhibitors from over 100 countries. In that year the event contributed an estimated R260 MIL (US$35 million) toward the economy of the kwazulu natal province.

The major problems facing the development and hosting of MEEC in Africa include the low-income threshold of the population, low levels of professionalism, the general poor standing of the continent compared to other parts of the world, and the relative high costs of travel, especially to South Africa.

References:

www.ufi.org

www.saaci.co.za

www.exsa.co.za

Middle East

Trade fairs and exhibitions in the Middle East are concentrated in Dubai and Abu Dhabi in the United Arab Emirates. This concentration is the result of excellent government promotion, new facilities, and ease of travel access. Both Dubai and Abu Dhabi have international airports with service to every continent. This "crossroads" concept, as well as the fact that exhibition facilities are located at or near the international airports, is emphasized heavily in promotional materials. For example, both Dubai and Abu Dhabi strongly promote the duty-free zones near their airports and the extensive duty-free shopping available at their facilities. In addition, the regional market for consumer goods is very strong and puts the focus of trade fairs on items like furniture, automobiles, and consumer electronics.

Latin America

The huge population base of Latin America makes it well suited for trade fairs and exhibitions. Until recently, most of the Latin American trade fairs and exhibitions have been regional. However, new facilities and promotional efforts have set the stage for a growth in international exhibitions. New facilities in Sao Paulo, Brazil; Santiago, Chile; and Mexico City are the hubs for this activity. The Feria International de Santiago contains over 1 million square feet of covered exhibition space and almost the same amount of open-air space. The Las Americas Exhibition Center in Mexico City provides the latest in technology to support exhibitors and attendees. In addition, the center is built within an entertainment complex that includes a horse racing track, restaurants, hotels, and a shopping center.

OWNERSHIP, SPONSORSHIP, AND MANAGEMENT MODELS

In the United States, many trade shows are adjuncts to association meetings and are owned by the association. Others are sponsored by private, entrepreneurial companies and operated on a for-profit basis. Ownership and management are usually accomplished by two companies working toward the success of the show. Other service companies support the industry by helping both the trade show management company and exhibitors.

This model is not typically followed for international trade fairs and exhibitions. In other countries, associations do not play a major role in the organization and sponsorship of trade fairs. Often governments, in collaboration with organizing companies, plan and operate the trade fairs. For example, the government of China plays a major role in the sponsorship of most trade fairs held in Beijing, Hong Kong, and Shanghai.

Professional Congress Organizer (PCO)

In the United States, organizers and sponsors of MEEC events will typically work with a DMO (CVB) and / or a DMC or third-party planning consultant. Outside the United States, there is an alternative, the PCO. The PCO represents the client in dealing with the DMO, DMC, hotel, restaurant, transportation company, and other suppliers. The PCO will negotiate with vendors on behalf of the client. PCOs tend to charge a flat fee rather than the sliding scale or per-person basis found at DMCs. PCOs also tend to be more familiar with international issues like customs, taxation, and government regulations. The PCO may even handle financial transactions, letters of credit and foreign bank accounts. PCOs have their own association called the International Association of Professional Congress Organizers (IAPCO). See http://www.iapco.org/ (Source: Wright (2005). *The meeting spectrum: An advanced guide for meeting professionals.* Amherst, MA:HRD Press.)

WORLD TRADE CENTERS ASSOCIATION

The **World Trade Centers Association** was created in 1970 as a not-for-profit, apolitical organization to promote the concept of world trade centers worldwide and to encourage reciprocal programs between all of its members. Today, there are more than 300 world trade centers in 100 countries servicing more than 750,000 international businesses (see http://world.wtca.org.)

The purpose of a world trade center is to bring together businesses and government agencies involved in international trade. Most world trade centers provide business services to their member companies, such as support and meeting facilities, videoconferencing, secretarial services, and translation capabilities. Many also conduct group trade missions to help businesses explore new markets.

Many world trade centers have also found the benefits of trade fairs and exhibitions appealing to their member companies. Thus, most world trade centers have built exhibition centers as part of their facilities. Throughout the year, the center sponsors trade fairs and events that showcase its members' products.

World trade centers also sponsor trade meetings and educational events open to businesses in their area and internationally.

INTERNATIONAL MEEC CONSIDERATIONS

Lessons to Be Learned

It is important for trade fair, event, and exhibition managers to learn the reasons for success in different aspects of the international marketplace. For example, North American trade show managers can learn from their European colleagues in three areas:

- *Excellence of Infrastructure:* Few American facilities rival those of Germany. In addition, public transportation systems in Europe provide excellent support of trade fairs and exhibitions. We have already discussed the case of Hannover, Germany, earlier in this chapter. Other European cities are following their model, including Dusseldorf, Berlin, Cologne, and Rome. Berlin has invested heavily in infrastructure to support its facilities.
- *Logistics:* International trade fair organizers are, by necessity, experts in logistics. Because the lifeblood of many international shows is the international exhibitor, many have specialized departments devoted to helping exhibitors overcome obstacles for exhibiting in their countries. Shipping and storage procedures are simplified and expedited by these agencies to help make exhibiting in their countries as easy as possible.
- *Support Organizations:* In America, many trade shows are sponsored and organized by associations. Even though they may be very successful, trade shows are often a secondary mission of associations. In other parts of the world, trade fairs and exhibitions are sponsored and organized by trade promotion organizations, such as the world trade centers or government agencies.

By the same token, many international trade fairs can learn from how North Americans conduct trade shows. For example, although the typical trade show staff in America can use additional boothmanship training, this is a dire need in most other countries. What American exhibitors consider "sins," such as leaving a booth unattended, is commonplace in other countries. The lesson here: When in Rome, do as the Romans do. Many exhibitors in Europe set up private meetings with clients and potential clients as a way of targeting their message. This is becoming more popular in America, but has been in use in Europe for many years.

Methods of Exhibiting

There are a number of differences between exhibiting at an American trade show and at an international trade fair or exhibition. These differences need to be a part of the basic research before initiating an international trade fair program.

Typically, companies have choices in how they will exhibit at an international trade fair or exhibition. The U.S. government sponsors U.S. pavilions at many trade fairs, and a U.S. company can work through the government to be part of the U.S. exhibit. If a company does decide to be a part of the exhibit, the U.S. Department of Commerce can provide significant help.

Another option is to exhibit under the auspices of another company that is organizing a pavilion. Similar to U.S. government sponsorship, a private company may be the main interface, and contractual arrangements are made with it. Companies should fully investigate this type of situation to ensure that the organizing company is reputable and has experience in the host country and with the desired trade fair.

Joint ventures can also be formed between companies, particularly when one has experience exhibiting at a certain trade fair. In this case, it is important that companies be sure that their products or services do not compete with each other. This type of arrangement works best when the two companies' products complement each other, and it is an excellent way for a company to enter the international trade fair marketplace and gain valuable experience.

"Going it alone" is another option for companies entering the international trade fair arena. Many large companies choose this route because they have the budget and staff to support the complexities of international exhibiting. Smaller companies must ensure that they have a clear understanding of all the requirements, costs, and scheduling before committing to this route. For example, smaller companies must factor in all the personnel time and costs involved in verifying that all tasks are completed. Assuming that the preparation time for an international trade show is the same as that for a domestic trade show can be a very costly mistake.

Terminology

In many parts of the world, an exhibit is not called an exhibit—or even a booth. Rather, it is called a **stand**. And this is only the beginning of the differences in terminology. Depending on where the trade fair is being held and who is managing it, participating companies must be familiar with those differences.

For example, in Germany the following terms must be understood:

- **Ausstellung:** Consumer show
- **Congress:** Meeting or convention
- **Gesellschaft:** Company or society
- **GMBH:** Limited liability company
- **Messe:** Trade fair
- **Messegelande:** Fair site
- **PLC:** Public limited company
- **Trade Exhibition:** Trade show

Contractual and Procedural Issues

In addition to terminology differences, contractual and procedural differences abound. Labor rules in the United States are very different from those in Europe or Asia. In Asia, there are few unions and no jurisdictional issues. Exhibitors have much more freedom in what they can do within their exhibit. In Europe, although there are unions, they are much more flexible than many in the United States.

Companies should not assume that setup or logistical contracts read the same as those in their home country. Substantial differences exist from country to country and from trade fair to trade fair. Companies should read each contract closely and adhere to all the requirements. If something is not understood, it should be brought to the attention of show management immediately.

Customs Clearance

Exhibition organizers at international shows provide access to experienced international freight forwarders, who also act as custom brokers, to ensure that everything is in order and arrives on time. The freight forwarders are knowledgeable about the custom regulations for the host country and take action to ensure that exhibitors know of every requirement and deadline.

Typically, goods can be temporarily imported to an international show site without having to pay duties or taxes, using either a **carnet** or a **trade fair bond**. A carnet can be very complicated to obtain, and a hefty bond must often be established. However, most trade fair venues offer trade fair bonds, which are simple to arrange. Again, the international freight forwarders are the point of contact for trade fair bonds. Be sure to inquire about host country rules on giveaways and promotional

First International Trade Show

At one point before joining the academe, Dr. George G. Fenich had the job of running all the marketing and trade shows for a company. The first international show in which the company participated was held in Innsbruck, Austria. The equipment to be displayed was airfreighted well in advance of the trade show, and the written material and brochures were sent later but with ample time to clear customs. Dr. Fenich sent one of his technical representatives to man the booth. On arrival, the tech rep frantically called Dr. Fenich. Although the crate was delivered to the booth and appeared in good order, when the container was opened it was found that a critical high-tech component was missing, and in its place was a box of inexpensive nails. Some time during shipment, probably while waiting to clear customs, thieves had opened the box and stolen the equipment. They replaced it with the box of nails so that the weight of the container would remain the same and not draw suspicion. There was no time to get another piece of high-tech equipment to Austria before the show closed.

On another occasion, the tech rep arrived at a trade show the day before it was to open only to find that the written materials and brochures had been lost. He called back the company and asked that a new set of brochures be sent "overnight express" to be there in time for the opening of the show. The problem was that, while the shipment could get there overnight, it would take three or four days to clear customs, and the trade show would have ended.

materials. In some countries, a duty is charged when the value is above a certain limit; in others, a duty is not charged for materials used for this purpose.

Freight forwarders are also cognizant of the estimated time for materials to clear customs, and they factor these times into the schedules that they provide to exhibitors. Companies fully adhere to these schedules to ensure that their materials arrive on time. Countries vary widely in the amount of time to clear customs, so be very aware of the differences if you are exhibiting in more than one country. Do not assume that because it takes only one day to clear customs in Paris or Frankfurt that it will be the same in Dubai or Taipei.

Protocol

It is the responsibility of the company trade fair manager to research the business customs of the host country and the individual trade fair. Staff should then be thoroughly trained on these differences before departing for the trade fair. Always remember that what is acceptable in one country or at one trade fair may very well be offensive in the next country or at another trade fair. Although English is normally the "official" language of international trade fairs, it is not safe to assume that all attendees or other exhibitors speak English. The wise company will ensure that at least some of the staff is bilingual, particularly in the host country's language.

Exhibit staff members will be greeting people from many countries to their international exhibit. It is imperative that they be familiar with the appropriate greetings for different cultures and forms of address. Although most visitors will not be offended if protocol is not strictly followed, it does give visitors a positive impression if their cultural standards are observed. It is also important for visitors to be aware of negative gestures for various cultures. What is a normal gesture in one culture may be extremely offensive in another. Gift giving and invitations are other areas that require research and training before embarking on an international trade fair program. Staff should also be aware of other cultural factors concerning dining and traveling in the host country. If spouses are traveling to the host country, they should be given briefings on the host country and its cultural expectations as well.

Examples

- In Indonesia, greetings are stately and formal. Do not rush. Hurried introductions (which commonly occur in trade fair settings) show a lack of respect.
- In the Netherlands, always avoid giving an impression of superiority. Egalitarianism is a central tenet of Dutch society. Everyone in a Dutch company, from the boss to menial laborers, is considered valuable and worthy of respect.
- When interacting with French visitors to an exhibit, never use first names until you are told to do so.
- Germans generally take a long time to establish a close business relationship and may appear cold in the beginning. This will change with time.

- Be very careful regarding what your exhibit staff wears. What is the customary business dress for the host country? What colors should not be worn? For example, avoid wearing yellow in Singapore; it is the color worn at funerals.
- At a business meeting in Saudi Arabia, coffee is often served toward the end of the meeting as an indication that the meeting is about to end.
- Also, in most Arabic countries, the left hand is considered dirty, so you should never eat or accept anything with this hand. Be sure when giving gifts or promotional materials that you do so with the right hand.
- When giving away gifts in Switzerland, avoid giving away knives—it is considered bad luck.
- If a Japanese person gives you a gift, do not throw away the wrapping or tear it up. It is considered part of the gift.
- Aside from handshakes, there is no public contact between the sexes in many countries. Do not kiss or hug a person of the opposite sex in public—even if it is your spouse. On the other hand, in some countries contact is permitted between people of the same sex. Men may hold hands with men and even walk with arms around each other; this is interpreted as nothing but friendship.
- Westerners frequently find Arabic names confusing. The best solution is to request the names of anyone you meet, speak to, or correspond with. Find out their full names (for correspondence) as well as how they are to be addressed in person.
- Understand the hierarchies of doing business within a foreign country. For example, the managing director in England equates to the CEO in an American firm.
- Keep in mind that the English do not consider themselves European. This is vital when discussing issues regarding the European Union.
- In many European countries, employees get four or five weeks of summer vacation. Many countries virtually shut down for the month of August.
- Eye contact among the French is frequent and intense—often this is intimidating to U.S. visitors.
- When negotiating in China, always give many alternatives so that the Chinese negotiators have room to negate several options with dignity. Also, always keep the same negotiating team throughout the process.
- The traditional Chinese greeting is a bow. When bowing to a superior, you should bow more deeply and allow him or her to rise first.
- In many Asian countries, it is not appreciated to pat people on the shoulder or initiate any physical contact.
- When negotiating in Italy, a dramatic change in demands at the last minute is often a technique to unsettle the other side. Be patient—just when it appears impossible, the situation will clear itself.
- In Japan, the host will always treat when you are taken out. Allow your host to order for you. Be enthusiastic while eating and show great thanks afterwards.
- In Japan, business cards are presented after a bow or handshake. Present your card, using both hands, with the Japanese side facing your colleague, in such a manner that it can be read immediately. Handle cards very carefully, and do not put them in your pocket or wallet. Never write on a person's business card in his or her presence.
- Age and rank are very important in Korea, so it is usually easiest to establish a relationship with a businessperson of your own age.
- The Swedes tend to be very serious, and humor is not part of the business environment.
- Hospitality is very important in Taiwan. Expect to be invited out every night after hours. This will entail visiting local nightspots and clubs, and may go until the wee hours of the morning.
- Avoid pouring wine at a social occasion in Argentina. There are several complex taboos associated with wine pouring that a foreigner can unknowingly violate. For example, pouring with the left hand, a common practice in the United States, is a major insult in Argentina.
- In the United States, the hand gesture where the thumb and forefinger are forming a circle with the other three fingers raised is considered the "OK" sign.
  - In Brazil, it is considered a vulgar or obscene gesture.
  - In Greece and Russia, it is considered impolite.
  - In Japan, it signifies money.
  - In southern France, it means zero or worthless.

Japanese persons exchanging business cards. Stock Boston

- In the United States, waving the hand back-and-forth is a means of saying hello.
  - In Greece, it is called the *moutza* and is a serious insult: The closer the hand is to the face of the other, the more threatening it is.
  - In Peru, waving the whole hand back-and-forth can signal "no."
- In most of the world, making a fist with the thumb raised means "OK."
  - In Australia, it is a rude gesture.

These are simply a few of the cultural issues that foreign businesspeople must face. Before traveling to any country, it is wise to consult as many sources as possible to learn the appropriate business and social behaviors for the culture. Take the time to learn the appropriate behavior in the host country and the greeting expectations for potential visitors to the trade fair.

The following are some Web sites that deal with international protocol:

- http://www.ediplomat.com/
- http://www.state.gov/s/cpr
- http://www.cia.gov/cia/publications/factbook/
- http://www.executiveplanet.com/
- http://www.usapa.army.mil/pdffiles/p600_60.pdf

The following are aspects of international trade fairs that are different from U.S. trade shows. Keep in mind that these are generalizations and do not apply to all situations.

- Hospitality events are generally held on the exhibit floor, with many companies providing food and beverages as a matter of course in their exhibit.
- Height restrictions may be nonexistent. Many large exhibits may be two or three levels.
- Rules on smoking in the exhibit hall may not exist, and many exhibitors and attendees may smoke in the exhibits.
- Some trade fair organizing companies may not offer "lead retrieval" systems that U.S. companies are accustomed to. It is always wise for a company to bring its own method of capturing leads.
- International trade fairs are often longer in duration than U.S. trade shows and often are open on weekends as well. Although in Europe the show may run from 9 AM to 6 PM, in Brazil or other Latin American countries it is common for trade fairs to open at 2 PM and run until 10 or 11 PM at night.
- Be aware that most of the world outside the United States is metric. Voltages may differ, and exhibitors may need plug-in adaptors or transformers. The video format may be different, so the VHS videotapes you had carry to the show may be worthless if the television only accepts PAL format.

Determining Whether to Participate

Because exhibiting at an international trade fair or exhibition is a significant investment, it is important that companies seriously consider if this move makes good business sense. First, consider the following top-level questions:

- Would international trade fair exhibiting support our business objectives?
- Who is our international audience that can be reached through a trade fair program?
- What trade fairs or exhibitions are available in our industry?
- What is the audience profile for each potential trade fair or exhibition?
- Do we have a system in place to determine our return on investment?

If these questions support a company's decision to initiate an international trade fair program, the following questions help analyze the situation before making a final decision:

- What are the costs associated with exhibiting at each potential trade fair or exhibition? Companies must be sure to calculate the costs for travel, shipping, translated materials, and other items that are not a normal part of domestic exhibiting.
- What are the cultural consequences of exhibiting at each potential trade fair or exhibition? Investigate how the fair operates, what cultural rules may apply, and provide training for all staff who will participate.
- Does the company have the personnel resources to support adding international trade fairs to its marketing mix? International trade fairs are often longer than domestic trade shows and therefore may require more staff.
- What type of participation is best for the company? Explore the options that are available—U.S. Pavilion, joint venture, or going it alone.
- Have all the requirements for each trade fair been identified and analyzed? Every trade fair is different, and an exhibiting company must be clear on all requirements before committing funds and resources.
- Does senior management support an international trade fair program? An international trade fair or exhibition is a serious investment—one that should require commitment from the highest levels of company management.
- Are the logistic requirements fully understood? Although trade fair management companies generally provide detailed instructions to exhibitors, it is imperative that key people in the company understand all the requirements, especially deadlines, for shipping materials.

Other Considerations

- Visas may be required for entry and exit.
- Items that Americans take for granted may have to be declared upon entry to a country. For example, brochures and written materials must be declared and taxes paid on them
- Many international destinations require payment of departure taxes.
- Most countries require that payment be made to ensure that goods exhibited at a trade show are exported and not sold within the country. A freight handling company can arrange a bond as security.
- Not only is the language in a foreign country likely to be different but so is the electrical current (120 V in the United States compared to 220 V elsewhere), recording media and playback mechanisms, television/VCR monitor protocols, and measurement (which will be in meters, not feet/inches).
- AND many more! When in doubt, ask.

TRADE FAIR CERTIFICATION

The **U.S. Department of Commerce** has developed a program to promote exports of U.S. products and services abroad. The **Trade Fair Certification Program** endorses independent and association show organizers who manage and organize overseas events. The certification helps trade fairs attract more exhibitors, provides additional support and value-added services for exhibitors, and promotes the event through a variety of publications and sources. Requirements for Department of Commerce Trade Fair Certification include the following:

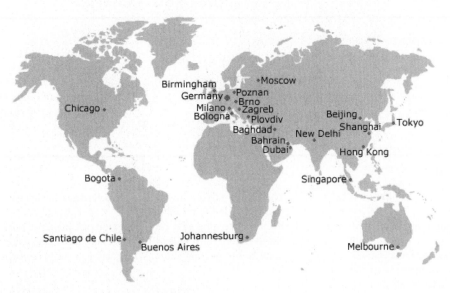

FIGURE 14.1 Trade Fair Certification.

Source: http://www.ustrade.gov/website/website.nsf/webbysubj/tradeevents_trade_fair_certification

- Must have either a U.S. Pavilion or commitment to attract at least ten U.S. exhibiting companies.
- Must have a U.S. office or agent.
- Must have exhibited before.

FUTURE TRENDS

- Rapid expansion of the MEEC industry will occur in developing countries such as those in Africa or the Middle East. The FIFA World Cup (football or soccer depending upon your location) was being held in South Africa in the summer of 2010. This is the first time this event was held in the African continent.
- Rapid expansion of the MEEC industry is also occurring in China. Facilities continue to be built or expanded. Some, such as the "birds nest" stadium built for the 2009 Beijing Olympics, have unique architectural features.
- As MEEC planners reach out to increasingly international audiences, technology will be used more and more to promote events and to put forth "virtual" aspects of those events.
- Environmental factors such as the economy or natural disasters will cause ripple effects well beyond local boundaries.
- As proud as many nationalities are of their "native" language, English is increasingly the common language of the MEEC industry.

Summary

The growth of international trade fairs and exhibitions has been phenomenal over the past fifteen years. Europe, the historical home of trade fairs, continues to strengthen its hold on the world's largest trade fairs and those with the most significant economic impact. Asia has made great strides by building state-of-the-art facilities and promoting its efforts throughout the world. The Middle East, Africa, and Latin America all have strong efforts under way to capture a larger piece of the international trade fair and exhibition market.

Worldwide communications, easy travel access, and open markets have been a boon to the international trade fair and exhibition industry. Few large companies can afford not to be in the international marketplace today. What was once the playground of only the world's largest companies is now a necessity for most companies of any size. Trade fairs and exhibitions are the easiest method for these companies to enter the marketplace and meet their potential customers.

Exhibiting at international trade fairs is not easy. Cultural and business differences present a new set of challenges for the exhibitor, along with more complex logistics and travel procedures. Companies must seriously analyze all factors before committing to an international trade fair program.

Key Words and Terms

For definitions, see GLOSSARY, or http://glossary.conventionindustry.org

Ausstellung	GMBH	Trade exhibition	World Trade Centers Association
Carnet	Messe	Trade fair	U.S. Department of Commerce
Congress	Messegelande	Trade fair bond	Trade Fair Certification
Gesellschaft	PLC	Stand	Program

Review and Discussion Questions

1. List some ways that international trade fairs may differ from U.S. trade shows.
2. What are two reasons for Europe's strength in the international trade fair industry?
3. What is the purpose of the World Trade Centers Association?
4. What are some of the complexities that a company must consider before exhibiting at an international trade fair or exhibition?
5. What options does a company have for participating in an international trade fair or exhibition?
6. Before proceeding with your exhibition or conference outside of North America, list at least five pieces of knowledge you will require before moving ahead. Where will you get the information from?

Internet Sites

Address (URL)	Description
http://www.aeo.org.uk	Association of Exhibition Organisers (U.K.)
http://www.ufinet.org	Union des Foires Internationales
http://www.auma-fairs.com	Association of German Trade Fair Industry
http://www.caem.ca	Canadian Association of Exhibition Management
http://www.fairlink.se	Scandinavian Trade Fair Council
http://www.exhibitions.org.hk	Hong Kong Exhibition and Convention Organisers and Suppliers Association
http://www.inter-expo.com	Association
http://www.saceos.org.sg	Singapore Association of Convention Organisers and Suppliers Association
http://www.thaitradeshow.org	Thailand Tradeshow Organization
http://www.ccpit.org	China Council for Promotion of International Trade
http://dcoem.com	China events
http://emeca.com	European Major Exhibition Centres Association
http://www.fil.be	Association des Expositions, Foires et Salon Wallonie
http://www.exobel.be	Federation Belge des Activites de l'Expos
http://www.febelux.be	Federation des Foires et Salons de Belgiq du Grand-Duche de Luxembourg
http://www.ffme.org	Federation Francaise des Metiers de l'Exposition
http://www.francecongres.org	France-Congres
http://www.foiresaloncongres.com	Foires Salons et Congres de France
http://www.fama.de	Fachverband Messen und Ausstellungen
http://www.famab.de	FAMAB Design-Exhibition-Event
http://www.fme-net.de	Forum Marketing-Eventagenturen
http://www.gcb.de	German Convention Bureau
http://www.idfa.de	Interessengemeinschaft Deutscher Fachmesse Ausstellungsstadte
http://www.assoexpo.com	Associazione Promozione Mostre
http://www.aefi.it	Associazione Enti Fieristici Italiani
http://www.federlegno.it	Associazione Nazionale Aziende Allestrici Fieristici Mostre
http://www.feram.org	Feram I&CT
http://www.eaaoffice.org	European Arenas Association
http://www.esah.nl	Exhibition Services Association Holland
http://www.fbtn.nl	Branchevereniging voor Beurzen & Evenemen

http://www.nlcongress.nl	Netherlands Convention Bureau
http://www.nvbo.nl	Netherlandse Vereniging van Beursoorganisato
http://www.afe.es	Associacion de Ferias Espanolas
http://www.osec.ch	Schweizerische Zentrale Fur Handelsforderung
http://www.myswitzerland.com	Switzerland Convention & Incentive Bureau
http://www.expo-event.ch	Swiss Expo & Event Makers
http://www.messenschweiz.ch	Vereinigung Messen Schweiz
http://www.beca.org.uk	British Exhibition Contractors Association
http://www.exhibitionvenues.com	Exhibition Venues Association
http://www.primary.uk.com/naa	National Arena Association
http://www.efct.com	European Federation of Conference Towns
http://www.esae.org	European Society of Association Executives
http://www.ettfa.org	European Tourism Trade Fair Association
http://www.evvc.org	Europaischer Verband der Veranstaltungs
http://www.xmeurope.com	Associated European Exhibition Organization
http://www.afida.com	Asociacion de Ferias Internacionales de Am
http://www.aipc.org	Association Internationale des Palais de Congres
http://www.bie-paris.org	Bureau International des Expositions
http://www.cope.org.uk	Confederation of Organisers of Packaging Expositions
http://www.iaam.org	International Association of Assembly Managers
http://www.iacvb.org	International Association of Convention and Visitor Bureaus
http://www.iapco.org	International Association of Professional Congress Organizers
http://www.icc.org	International Chamber of Commerce
http://www.icca.nl	International Congress and Convention Association
http://www.iela.org	International Exhibition Logistics Associates
http://www.iesaj.org	International Exhibit System Association
http://www.ifesnet.org	International Federation of Exhibition Services
http://www.uia.org	Union des Associations Internationales
http://www.venue.org	World Council for Venue Management
http://www.wtca.org	World Trade Centers Association

About the Chapter Contributors

Sandy Biback, CMP, CMM, has been involved in the designing and implementing of business events/conferences/tradeshows for over thirty years. Biback currently teaches Meetings and Conventions at the University of Nevada–Las Vegas; George Brown College, Toronto, as well as courses in Sponsorship Design and Risk Management at Centennial College in Toronto. She is a member of Professional Convention Management, Association (PCMA) and Canadian Society of Professional Event Planners (CanSPEP).

The contributor to previous editions was **Ben McDonald,** Vice-President of BenchMark Learning, Inc.

Putting It All Together

Chapter Outline

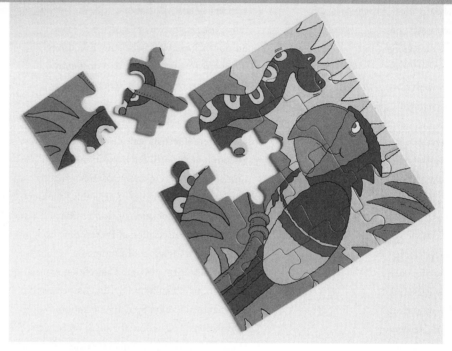

MEEC events are like puzzles—eventually they must be put together. *Courtesy of Dorling Kindersly Media Library*

Chapter Objectives

This chapter provides the reader with an understanding of the following:

- Key tasks in creating a citywide meeting
- Method to create a statement of conference objectives
- Ways to identify budget expenses and income sources
- Timetable for implementation of different meeting planning tasks
- Process of conducting a site inspection
- Assessment of success of the meeting

INTRODUCTION

Many books contain a concluding chapter that repeats and summarizes the elements of the earlier chapters. In this textbook, a fictitious case study of a citywide convention serves the same purpose. The goal of this case study is to bring together all the previous chapters. Throughout this text, you have read about the tasks associated with meeting planning. Through this case study, you will learn more about topics from the previous chapters and how they apply to a citywide annual conference for 3,000 attendees. The objective of this case study is to help you understand the various tasks a planner must complete in order for a meeting, exposition, event, or convention to be successful. In addition, this case study will help you understand the complexities of the budget and timetable, as well as the many people with whom a planner must communicate.

This case study uses a three-year planning timetable for one citywide conference. The meeting planning cycle is continuous, and it is important to understand that two of the key skills a planner must possess are the abilities to organize and to multitask. Planners typically work on three to five meetings or events simultaneously, each in different stages of development.

As you review the budget portion of the case study, it is important to understand that many variables, including the time of year the meeting is held, the planner's ability to negotiate, the value of the business to the facility, and the trade-offs, will affect the budget. This budget is broad and was created to highlight the many details the planner must consider.

THE ASSOCIATION

As a meeting or event planner, it is important to understand your audience—the attendees of the event. For association meeting planners, this is critical as they market the conference to association members and to potential members. The meeting planner must also communicate information about his or her association members to suppliers for the convention. The better a supplier understands the audience of the meeting planner, the better the supplier can serve them. For example, if a hotel knows that the majority of the people attending a meeting are women, the hotel might add products that women use, such as hand cream or shower caps, to the room amenities.

The American Small Animal Association (ASAA) is an example of a typical association in the United States. The ASAA is an 8,000-member nonprofit association whose members are veterinarians from throughout the United States who specialize in care for small animals. The ASAA was founded ten years ago by a group of veterinarians who saw the need to update research and to network with other veterinarians specializing in small animal care. Over 60% of the organization's membership operates independently owned veterinary clinics; the remainder of the association members are suppliers to the veterinary industry. The suppliers include pharmaceutical companies, prescription food companies, and product suppliers. Although the number of women members is increasing, 70% of the members are male; 60% Caucasian; 30% African American; and 10% a mix of Latino, Asian, and Native American. It is important to know the makeup of the organization so that the event can meet its wants and needs. The planner or organizer must ask two questions: Who is the group? Why are its members here?

Logo for the (fictitious) American Small Animal Association.

An executive committee and a board of directors operate the ASAA, while the executive director and seven committee members oversee the day-to-day operations of the association. Members of the board of directors are elected from seven established regions and serve two-year terms. All board elections take place during the annual meeting and are announced during the final night.

Sue Rodriguez is the director of meetings for the ASAA and is a full-time employee. Sue is one of the five full-time employees and is responsible for coordinating the seven regional meetings and the annual conference; she reports directly to the executive director. Planning for the annual conference begins three years in advance of the meeting date. For the past five years, attendance at the annual conference has increased 5% per year; and last year, 37% of the membership attended the meeting. This increase is attributed to the success of the trade show portion of the conference that was added five years ago.

Goals

To begin preparation for the annual conference, Sue reviews past annual conference evaluations from attendees and members of the board of directors. The board of directors wanted to save money by cutting down on the cost related to networking activities, but the members indicated how important it is to have time to meet other professionals from around the country. The board also would like to see the money collected from this conference increased by 10% because other than membership dues, the annual conference is the largest revenue source for the association. Last year, the ASAA created the Small Animal Preventive Disease Certificate (SAPDC). During the annual convention, veterinarians earn five continuing education units (CEUs) and learn about the preventive medicines that can be used to save the lives of small animals.

To help focus her thoughts, Sue reads the ASAA mission statement: The mission of ASAA is to provide an educational forum for members to exchange ideas and develop ways to ensure the health of small animals. This mission is accomplished by providing quality education for its members, offering assistance to new veterinarian clinics, and providing a forum for members to meet and to assist each other with emerging technologies.

To help Sue measure **return on investment (ROI)**, she creates operational and educational objectives. The operational objective for this conference is to increase meeting profits by 5% over last year's conference. Sue works with the program committee to create the educational objective for this meeting, which is to increase the number of attendees enrolled in SAPDC classes by 10% and to provide additional networking opportunities. Sue hopes to meet these objectives by offering a four-day conference focused on education and networking that will result in an increase of conference profits by 5%.

Budget

To create the budget (see Tables 15-1 and 15-2), Sue reviews the past meeting budgets. For her expenses, she includes the cost of marketing materials, the convention center, host hotel, decorator, audiovisual equipment, speakers, entertainment, and staff. In addition, Sue must consider operational objectives for the meeting. To locate income sources, Sue looks at past meeting **sponsors** and exhibitors.

The hotel budget will include meeting room rental, food and beverage, staff sleeping rooms, and service charges and gratuities. In creating the budget, Sue knows that she will have some negotiation opportunities based on the ASAA sleeping and meeting room usage ratios. The better that the ASAA's use of meeting rooms to sleeping rooms will match the hotel's ideal sleeping room to meeting room ratio, the better the rate that can be negotiated. To assist in managing the hotel blocks, Sue uses a housing bureau and includes that cost in the hotel expense item.

The convention center expenses will include the cost of space for meeting rooms, exhibit hall, electricity, Internet connection, garbage pickup, security, and staffing for coffee and food stations. To maximize dollars, Sue plans the majority of her educational events at the convention center. This not only enables her to use the daily rate for the rooms at the convention center but also is a selling point for the exhibitors who want attendees near the trade show.

Sue will need to identify an **exposition service contractor (ESC)** to provide decorations and to set up the trade show. She will also need to assess audiovisual needs for both the hotel and convention center. The ESC will provide staging for the reception, general session, trade show,

Table 15-1 Budget Income

Budget		Income	Registration
			3,000 attendees
Members			1,680 attendees
	early (at 60% = 1,008 people)	$600 p/p	$604,800
	late (at 40% = 672 people)	$800 p/p	$537,600
Nonmembers			
	early (at 50% = 300 people)	$700 p/p	$210,000
	late (at 50% = 300 people)	$900 p/p	$270,000
Student	(at 5% = 120 people)	$100 p/p	$12,000
Speakers	(100 people)	$300 p/p	$30,000
Exhibitors		Included in exhibit fee	
Registration Total			**$1,664,400**
SAPDC	(500 people)	$100 p/p	$50,000
Exhibitors	(500 exhibitors)	$3,000 p/exhibit	$1,500,000
Sponsors			$120,000
Extended Learning			$10,000
Other			$5,000
Total Income			**$3,349,400**
Expenses			$1,881,438
Net Income			**$1,467,962**

Table 15-2 Budget Expenses

Budget	Expenses
Convention Center	$350,000
Host Hotel	$212,643
Decorations	$102,245
Signage	$80,000
Audiovisual Equipment	$125,000
Webcasting	$60,000
Pressroom	$50,000
Transportation	$18,250
Off-Site Venue	$50,000
Golf Event	$150,000
Marketing Committee	$185,000
Program Committee	$10,000
Speakers	$52,000
Entertainment	$17,000
Security	$180,000
Insurance	$100,000
Special Services	$5,000
News Delivery	$30,000
Temporary Staff	$67,200
Tote Bags	$30,000
Site Visits	$2,100
Other	$5,000
Total Expenses	**$1,881,438**

and awards night, and the **audiovisual (AV) company** will provide sound and light. In order to provide an accurate quote, the ESC must be given information on carpeting requests, number of trade show booths, estimated freight use, and types of staging needed for the opening session, general session, and awards dinner. The AV company will need to know the sound and lighting needs for each venue and the type of production for the general session, opening reception, and awards dinner. The general session will be sent via webcast to members who are unable to attend, so Sue lists this as a separate expense (see Table 15-2).

To budget transportation, Sue looks at past budgets to determine how many attendees used the shuttle service for airport transfers, but she knows this expense will vary greatly depending on the existing transportation options in a given city. At this point, she includes full shuttle service for each day of the conference, VIP transportation, and transportation to the off-site events and the golf tournament. In addition to ground transportation, Sue's transportation budget includes air transportation for staff and VIPs as well as freight shipping. Of the transportation items budgeted, freight shipping is the least expensive; due to the large shipping volume of exhibitors, the ASAA is charged a minimum for association shipping needs. The budget for the off-site golf tournament will vary depending on the conference location. To include these items, Sue uses the amount from the last meeting and increases the cost by 5%.

Reviewing the budget history is also a good starting place when Sue allocates funds for marketing. With a minimum of five marketing pieces being created, this can become very expensive; however, with the increased use of the Internet, more money is being spent on Web development rather than large marketing brochures.

Of the speakers for the ASAA, 75% are members presenting research papers. To encourage members to make presentations, the ASAA offers presenters a 50% discount on the early registration fee. The majority of the money allocated for speakers actually is used for a keynote speaker and entertainment. To locate the keynote speaker and entertainment, Sue uses a speaker's bureau; the speaker's bureau's fee is included in this expense item.

In order to have a smooth meeting, Sue will need to hire temporary staff. This budget item includes the cost for registration personnel, staff for on-site assembly of attendee packets, room monitors, and staff to distribute evaluations and carry out other duties. Sue will need to bring in temporary staff one day prior to the meeting for training and will pay staff for their time.

Security is an ongoing expense that the ASAA must include in its budget. Because the ASAA is increasing its involvement in new research for small animals and this new research is both confidential and controversial, more security will be needed.

Insurance is another increasing expense. Sue includes insurance to cover attrition and loss of revenue due to acts of God, terrorism, and liability. The $100,000 budgeted represents 5% of the cost to host this meeting.

To cover expenses for attendees with special needs, Sue includes a special services item in the budget, which will be used for members who identify themselves as needing translators, written material to be published in Braille, sign language interpreters, special accommodations for Seeing Eye dogs, and so on. For example, Sue knows that one of her key sponsors is legally blind and has a Seeing Eye dog. To accommodate him, Sue makes sure that water and dog food are available. Five of the ASAA members are hearing impaired, so for these members, Sue arranges for sign language interpreters to be on site to escort them throughout the conference.

When Sue creates the budgets, she contacts city officials where the meeting will be held. As a nonprofit organization, the ASAA is exempt from most city and state taxes, but she must file the documents to ensure the exemption. Furthermore, Sue will need to bring forms proving that the ASAA is a not-for-profit organization; the forms will also be filed with suppliers.

Sue includes some expenses in the budget even though she knows that these expenses will be picked up by sponsors. Each year, Sue has no problem finding a company to sponsor tote bags given to all attendees, the on-site newspaper, transportation, the meal for the opening reception, and the entertainment for the VIP dinner. It is important that Sue includes these items in the budget to document these expenses.

To allow for unexpected expenses, Sue creates an "Other" expense category, which is used to cover additional expenses that do not occur every year or that are not planned for. For example, if the cost of stamps increases, this contingency would be covered.

Sammy Busby, a member of People for the Ethical Treatment of Animals, was arrested during protests at the National Institutes of Health in Bethesda, Maryland. Several people were arrested while demonstrating against the use of animals for experimentation as part of the World Laboratory Animal Liberation Day.   *Courtesy of Marcy Nighswander, AP Wide World Photos*

Income

The income (see Table 15-1) will offset the expenses for the meeting. Estimated expenses for this meeting are $1,881,438. To reach the financial objectives and make a profit, Sue must not only pay all expenses but also build in a profit.

In determining the income, Sue starts with income generated from the registration fees. She first takes the expected attendance of 3,000 and subtracts 500 exhibitors whose registration fee is included in the exhibitor fee and then subtracts the 100 speakers who will pay a reduced registration. The ASAA has three registration fee categories: members, nonmembers, and students. Convention history shows that 70% are members, 25% nonmembers, and 5% students. In order to reduce attrition fees, Sue creates an early registration fee and a late fee for members and nonmembers. Typically, 60% of the members and 50% of the nonmembers will register early. Sue estimates that if registration alone will cover expenses, she must charge $629 per person. With this in mind, Sue's registration fee structure is $600 for an early member, $700 for an early nonmember, $800 for a late member, and $900 for a late nonmember. Students only pay $100, thus encouraging them to join when they are employed in the field. Sue estimates her registration income to be $1,664,400.

Following the income generated from registration fees, the exhibitors are the largest single source of income for the ASAA. It will cost the ASAA approximately $10 per square foot for the convention space, ESC, and audiovisual equipment. The ASAA will sell this trade show space for $30 per square foot. History shows a steady 10% increase in exhibitors per year; at the last conference, about 450 companies ordered booths. Sue estimates exhibitor income for this year to be $1,500,000 (500 exhibitors spending $3,000 each for a ten-foot by ten-foot booth).

Other sources of income that Sue will include in the budget are rebates generated from hotel rooms, the transportation company, and the ESC. Rather than accept commissions for these items, the ASAA negotiates a rebate per room night that becomes an income stream. There is a small amount of money raised by the sale of extended learning products, including DVDs, CDs, books, and audiotapes.

Income from the SAPDC is $100 per person, in addition to the registration. Last year, the ASAA charged $200 per person—the cost is low to encourage attendees to take classes toward certification.

REQUEST FOR PROPOSAL (RFP)

Once the meeting objectives are laid out and a budget determined, Sue creates a **request for proposal (RFP)**. In creating the RFP, Sue wants to include accurate information to help hotels and cities submit good proposals. She includes meeting specifications on the ASAA and explains that the RFP is sent three years prior to the annual conference date. Sue collects proposals and reviews them with Dave Rogers, executive director, and Elizabeth Rice, a board member serving as the convention chair. Sue, Dave, and Elizabeth will choose two cities to visit in order to conduct an initial site inspection. After the initial site inspections to all selected cities are complete, a decision will be made, and Sue and Dave will conduct a second site inspection to the chosen city to begin contract negotiations. In order to avoid any bias, the ASAA will pick up the cost of the site inspection with the understanding that when a city is selected; the host city will rebate the cost of the site inspection.

The RFP will include a list of cities under consideration and the preferred dates. Although the dates may vary between the months of March and April, the days of the week must be Thursday to Sunday. The annual conference is held around the country, primarily in large cities near places where members of the board of directors reside.

Sue's RFP includes a detailed grid of her meeting room needs. She includes special requests; for example, her classroom sets require two chairs per six-foot table and a water station set in the back of the room. She also includes a food and beverage summary that notes special dietary needs of attendees. Her meeting room grid includes the event, number of attendees, and room set.

The ASAA prefers to use no more than five hotels in a given city. A grid is created requesting the number of suites, single rooms, and double rooms that the ASAA anticipates using at each hotel. In considering a city, Sue looks for downtown hotel properties that offer a wide range of room prices, but the hotels need to be in close proximity to each other. The host hotel must be willing to block a minimum of 900 rooms; in addition to the sleeping room block, the host hotel will be the site of the opening night reception and breakout rooms for special-interest groups.

A detailed history, in the form of a grid of the last three years, is included in the RFP. The history grid shows the peak room nights, meeting room block, sleeping room block, pickup for the host hotel and the room block, and pickup at each of the nonhost hotels. She also includes a food and beverage section showing reported use. The ASAA reports a 10% increase in meeting attendees per year over the last two years and has an attrition rate of only 2%.

The final portion of the RFP is a two-page questionnaire for the hotel to complete and submit with the proposal. Questions include comp room policy, deposit policy, definition of "sold out," attrition policy, master accounts, split folios, shuttle service availability, tax rate, nonprofit tax policy, gratuity distribution, Internet connection, phone charges, and fitness facilities. Sue also includes questions about how the hotel handles "in conjunction withs" (ICWs) and exhibitor room blocks and whether the hotel will work to create priority housing for members over non-members. Sue found that this form provides a quick way for her to compare hotels.

The RFP is sent to the destination marketing organization (DMO) **convention and visitors bureau (CVB)** for distribution to appropriate hotels. Included in the RFP is a questionnaire for the DMO to complete. The questionnaire includes questions regarding state, local, and hotel room taxes as well as holidays, union contracts, special venues, DMO services, and citywide events or holidays that take place during the ASAA meeting dates.

FIRST SITE INSPECTION

Sue, Dave, and Elizabeth have reviewed the proposals and identified two cities with available dates to host the ASAA citywide: Chicago and Dallas. Sue calls the DMOs in those cities to arrange to spend three days in each city and explains to them that the team plans to conduct a detailed site inspection to look for hotels, off-site venues, and golf courses. She sends the site inspection form that the team will use to evaluate the city and properties, explaining that the team will stay at the hotels under consideration as host properties and will conduct short tours of nonhost hotels under consideration. For the nonhost properties, the team only needs to meet with the hotel sales contact, see a standard room, and tour the outlets.

Day One

Mark Tester, vice president of sales, Chicago CVB, meets Sue, Dave, and Elizabeth at Chicago's O'Hare airport. On arrival, Mark gives a driving tour of downtown, passing by all the hotels under consideration. They have lunch at the Chicago Museum of Art, where they are joined by Kesha Evans, owner of Windy City, a **destination management company (DMC)**. Kesha explains the various services she can provide, including transportation and arrangements for off-site events, spouse tours, and private dining. Tom Delaney, catering manager at the Chicago Museum of Art, introduces himself and takes the group on a tour of the private function areas of the museum and recommends the best area for an off-site event. He gives Sue a sales packet with sample menus and pricing.

After lunch, Mark takes the inspection team to the Hyatt Regency McCormick Place to meet with its sales manager, Bob Taylor, and its general manager, Larry Rose. They tour the property, looking at sleeping rooms, suites, singles, and doubles as well as the meeting rooms and ballrooms for possible locations for the opening reception, special-interest group meetings, and available outlets. After the tour, they meet in one of the conference rooms to discuss available dates and rates.

Then Sue, Dave, and Elizabeth meet at 6 PM in the hotel restaurant for dinner. During dinner, they make observations, noting how the guests are treated, what the quality of the food is, the time food is served, and whether the wait staff are attentive. They order different entrées to sample the many types of food their attendees might order if they stay at this hotel. After dinner, Sue walks the meeting space, looking into the meeting rooms to see how the rooms are set.

Day Two

At 8:30 AM, Mark meets the team members who have already eaten breakfast and checked out of the hotel. Mark has arranged for a 9:00 AM meeting with Randy Moses, senior sales manager of McCormick Place Convention Center. Randy gives a tour of the facility, taking time to show them what he sees as the best locations for their functions, loading docks, and shuttle drop-off and pickup, as well as the areas where sponsored items such as banners are allowed. Sue asks about available dates, food and beverage concession hours, taxes, union rules, and contract renewal dates. Randy provides this information and discusses the security and the medical and emergency procedure guidelines. Both Mark and Randy explain to Sue, Dave, and Elizabeth how the CVB and convention center work as a team to help market the Chicago meeting to attendees. They discuss marketing options, including premailers and on-site promotions the year prior to coming to the host city.

For lunch, Mark takes the group to the Golden Princess, a luxury yacht owned by ABC Charters, a company that provides dinner tours of Lake Michigan. Rich Cunningham, general manager of ABC Charters, meets with them. Today, they are having a special lunch for meeting planners to sample the menu and enjoy a mini-charter experience. The president of Chicago DMC Services, Deborah Adams, explains her services and has photos showing other off-site locations Sue may want to consider.

The afternoon is spent making contacts and touring the hotels under consideration. Mark arranges thirty-minute tours of each nonhost hotel and explains to the hotel sales contact that they only want to see sleeping rooms and restaurant areas.

By 4 PM, Sue, Dave, and Elizabeth are ready to check into the Hyatt Regency Chicago, the second hotel under consideration as the headquarters hotel. Rachel Monroe introduces herself as the association sales manager and begins the tour. She is excited about a new ballroom that was recently added and explains how the ballroom could be used for the opening reception. After the tour, Richard Moore, the general manager, joins the group to look at available dates and rates.

Sue, Dave, and Elizabeth take an hour break and meet in the restaurant for dinner. During dinner, they review all notes from the past two days. After dinner, Sue takes her tour of the meeting rooms.

Day Three

The team checks out early and waits in the hotel lobby. They notice a line forming as people check out of the hotel. They take mental notes, observing how long the checkout time is and how courteous the employees are at the front desk and bell stand. Mark arrives at the hotel and takes the group to the first stop, Harborside International Golf Center, a four-star course only twelve miles from downtown Chicago. The group meets with the special events manager of the Harborside to discuss the optional golf outing that is part of the ASAA event. The tournament is held Thursday afternoon, prior to the opening reception. Mark takes the group to one more golf course and on two more hotel site inspections before they depart for the airport.

Sue, Dave, and Elizabeth thank Mark for his time and inform him that they will be touring Dallas next month and plan to make a decision in two months. After the Dallas site inspection, the ASAA will make its decision and will contact the bureau regarding that decision.

One month later, Sue, Dave, and Elizabeth go to Dallas for another three-day site inspection. Patty Towell, the sales manager of the Dallas CVB, arranges for the group to meet with staff from the hotels, the convention center, and the off-site locations.

After both site inspections conclude, the inspection team reviews their notes. Due to the conflict of dates with other industry meetings, they decide to meet on St. Patrick's Day. In evaluating Chicago, they are concerned about room availability, the renewal dates for some union contracts, and the fact that the cost to hold the meeting in Chicago is 25% more than in Dallas. This increase in cost might be offset by the number of attendees who prefer to meet in Chicago over Dallas, but this meeting will attract more attendees seeking the SAPDC—thus location will not be as much of an issue. Dallas is selected for the annual conference. Sue calls Mark from the Chicago CVB, expresses their concerns, and explains why Dallas was selected. Sue reminds Mark that they have not held a meeting in Chicago in five years and would like to look there again in the future.

SECOND SITE INSPECTION

Day One

Sue sends Patty Towell, at the Dallas CVB, a letter of intent to hold the conference in Dallas and contacts her to help arrange a second site inspection. This second site inspection will include only Sue and Dave and will be for three days. The goal is to finalize nonhost properties, select off-site venues and a golf course, select the DMC and transportation company, and begin contract negotiations. When Sue and Dave arrive in Dallas, they rent a car and take a self-guided tour of the city. They check in at the Hyatt Regency Downtown, the location of the headquarters hotel for the meeting.

At the Hyatt Regency in downtown Dallas, Sue and Dave meet with Nancy Simonieg, the senior sales manager, and Rizwan Naqvi, CMP, LES, the **convention services manager (CSM)**. Once the contract is signed, Sue will work with the CSM for the remainder of the meeting. During this meeting, Sue and Nancy will begin negotiations for sleeping rooms, meeting rooms, shuttle service, and so on.

After the meeting with the hotel staff, Sue meets Sonja Miller, sales manager of the Dallas Convention Center; Erika Bondy, CMP, senior event coordinator; and Bill Baker, director of catering. Once the contract is signed, Sue will work with Erika on all her meeting details and with Bill on meeting food and beverage requirements. Today, Sue begins negotiating rates with the Dallas Convention Center; at the meeting, she will review her needs and see what is the best win–win situation for her attendees and the convention center.

Sue and Dave have lunch at the Dallas Museum of Art and meet with the catering sales manager, Cindy Hartman, to review rates for having the VIP dinner in the restaurant. Carolyn Petty, president of EMC (a DMC), joins Sue and Dave for lunch to discuss what the DMC can provide for the ASAA meeting, including gift baskets and general transportation needs.

In the afternoon, Patty has arranged for Sue to meet with two of the nonhost hotels under consideration in the city for sleeping room space; at each hotel, Sue meets the sales manager to negotiate the rates and amenities. For dinner, Patty takes Sue and Dave to a small Mexican restaurant that is a favorite of the locals. At dinner, Patty discusses the services the bureau can assist with, including registration personnel, marketing, slides, leads for suppliers, transportation, Internet services, and on-site brochures. She will staff a promotional booth at the meeting prior to the one in Dallas.

Day Two

The morning is spent touring and reestablishing contact with the remainder of hotels that will provide sleeping rooms. Sue and Dave have lunch at the Dallas World Aquarium because they are looking for a fun site for the VIP meeting; they meet with Jose Lopez, sales manager, for a tour and a discussion of possible dining options. Although this is an option, it might be too casual for the group. Jose brings a portfolio with pictures of events held at the aquarium, and Sue's concerns dissipate.

In the afternoon, Sue and Dave tour two golf courses. For each course, Sue makes contacts, has the event sales manager take them on a nine-hole tour, and begins discussing rates. Sue pays attention to where the group might meet before and after the tournament to determine if there is an area where the group might meet as they finish playing golf.

Her evening is free to review her notes. Sue will catch up on e-mails missed during her day of meetings and will carefully look at all the brochures she is given. She really likes the idea of having the VIP dinner in an unusual location.

Day Three

Sue and Dave begin the day meeting the ESC contact, Jack Boyd, account executive for the Freeman Companies, and Darren Temple, vice president of sales, AVW TELAV Audio Visual Solutions, an AV company that is part of the Freeman Companies. Jack, Darren, Dave, and Sue meet first at the Dallas Convention Center and then at the Hyatt Hotel to discuss ESC and audio-visual equipment needs. They tour each venue, discussing specific staging, setup, and other needs for each event. Sue realizes the impact that the ESC and the AV company have in making a meeting successful. Sue takes the time to review all meeting details. For example, since this is a medical meeting and attendees will receive CEUs for poster session presentations, the poster session must be set up at least four feet from any exhibitor. Once all the details of each venue are known, the ESC and the AV company can provide an accurate estimate of expenses. When all the details are wrapped up, Sue and Dave catch their flight home.

MARKETING COMMITTEE

ASAA has both an in-house marketing department and an outside advertising agency, and they work together to create the marketing pieces for the annual conference. After Sue returns home from the second site inspection, she meets with George Day, the ASAA director of marketing, and Julie Love, the account manager for Idea Maker, Inc., an advertising company. Sue discusses the convention location and the meeting objectives and also explains how important promoting the new SAPDC is for this conference.

After two weeks, Sue meets with George and Julie again. Julie brings theme ideas and visuals for the marketing pieces. After reviewing several themes, "Power of Prevention" is selected. The visual will be the skyline of Dallas with the Hyatt Regency Hotel ball of lights brightly shining on the downtown area, with the ball of lights representing the power and the light shining on the city showing its power.

After reviewing the success of past marketing pieces, it is decided that four marketing tools will be used. A four-color postcard-size mailer will be developed as a teaser and mailed to all past conference attendees and targeted to potential members; this teaser will also be used as an advertisement that will be placed in industry newsletters and magazines. The second piece will be a magazine-style brochure to be sent to all association members. This brochure will include a convention agenda giving dates, times, and speakers; a program-at-a-glance grid; current sponsors; and convention and housing registration forms. Idea Maker, Inc., designs Web pages and maintains ASAA's e-mail newsletter. The third marketing approach will be a Web page that will serve as an electronic brochure, allowing people to register for the meeting and make hotel reservations online. The final approach is the e-newsletter that will feature convention information and will include testimonials from people who have earned their SAPDC.

In creating the meeting program to be given to attendees on check-in, Sue meets with George and Dave to discuss content of the program. Dave is concerned that attendees will take the wrong class because they will not understand the level of instruction. George assures Dave that each session will be color-coded to provide easy identification of the education level and that this color-coded scheme will be repeated in the program. Among topics discussed are the size of sponsors' ads and the amount of copy for educational event descriptions. All agree that to support the objective, the SAPDC should receive a full-page description in the front of the program.

During each conference, a new board of directors is introduced, awards are given, and important announcements must be made. Sue, George, and Dave meet to discuss the types of presentations that will be made and the scripts that George and his team will write. Sue is responsible for arranging rehearsal time for each presentation.

The marketing committee is responsible for creating press releases that will be sent to professional publications. For each conference, a new piece of research is featured, and the marketing committee works to promote this research to the public.

CREATION OF THE PROGRAM

When Sue returns from the Dallas site inspection, she meets with the program committee to begin creating the educational content of the meeting. Serving on the program committee is Doug Walker, board member and chair of the SAPDC; Dan Dearing, chairman of the board of directors of the Program Committee for the Power of Prevention annual convention; and his appointed committee members Liz Stewart and Mark Collins, along with Donna Smith, ASAA administrative assistant. These five people and Sue will work together to create the content of the meeting.

Sue begins the meeting by giving each committee member a notebook with responsibilities of the committee members, past convention notes, and the meeting theme, the "Power of Prevention." Sue wants to make sure that the committee members understand the objective of the meeting: to increase the number of member attendees taking the SAPDC by 10% by offering a four-day conference that is focused on education that will increase meeting profits by 5%.

The committee agrees to follow the same meeting agenda as in the past: opening reception, general session, awards dinner, and poster session (which runs at the same time as the trade show). The conference will include an ASAA VIP dinner, a golf tournament, and a total of 120 ninety-minute education sessions in two days. The one change in the schedule is to add 2 four-hour segments for the SAPDC class. The committee will locate speakers for SAPDC classes and all breakout sessions. ASAA members will present 100 of the 120 educational sessions. To help the program committee, a separate committee—called the paper review committee—is created that will issue the call for papers, grade and evaluate papers, and inform the program committee of its final selection for presentations and poster session. Sue will use a speaker's bureau for the opening reception, general session, awards dinner, ASAA VIP dinner, and all entertainment.

Sue reviews the time line with the committee. The paper review committee will begin the call for papers one year prior to the meeting; six months prior, the paper review committee will provide the program committee with the final selection, and the program committee will make initial contact with presenters and speakers. The committee will recommend speakers for all sessions. Once speakers and backup speakers have been identified, Sue will send out invitation letters, in which she will ask the speaker to sign a commitment sheet and will require the speaker to provide an abstract of the presentation and his or her biography.

The committee will be responsible for contacting all the speakers and following up with those not responding. There will also be a point person for all speaker questions. Once speakers have been selected, Sue's role is to collect information, assign time slots, and correspond with the speakers, including letters of acceptance and a reminder letter.

One key feature in the conference is the exhibitors. Jill Kochan, ASAA staff, is the ASAA trade show manager for the conference. Jill is responsible for all communications with the exhibitors and the ESC as they set up the trade show. Jill will work closely with Sue to communicate exhibitor needs and will meet with the ESC to create specifications for the exhibitor prospectus.

PARTNERSHIPS

As Sue prepares for this meeting, she knows the importance of her meeting partners. Throughout the conference, Sue depends on many companies to provide excellent service and to create a memorable experience for the ASAA members. She reviews her contact list, looking at the many companies she will partner with for the upcoming conference.

Although most housing bureaus can provide a complete housing package, including hotel selection, negotiation, and contract, Sue prefers to work with the housing bureau after she has selected the hotels. Once the selections have been made, the housing bureau will manage the hotel room block. The housing bureau will create a web link for attendees to book rooms online and a paper form for attendees to complete and fax. Once an attendee selects a hotel, the housing bureau will send a confirmation letter. One of the best aspects about Sue's partnership with the housing bureau is room block management: Rather than call all the hotels being used, Sue calls the housing bureau for monthly, weekly, and daily rooming reports as needed and depends on the housing bureau to manage the exhibitor room block.

Sue likes to partner with a local DMC for the annual conference. For this conference, Sue uses the DMC for arranging the airport transfers, VIP transportation, and shuttle service from hotels to the convention center. The DMC made all logistical arrangements for the VIP dinner, which allowed Sue to concentrate on VIP invitations and content of the event. Sue also appreciates the fact that a DMC normally has access to many motor coach suppliers because transportation is always an area of concern for Sue. Once, in Washington, D.C., Sue contracted with a motor coach company, and one of the motor coaches broke down with all her attendees in it. The company had no back-up motor coaches, so her attendees waited almost an hour to be rescued and taken to the event.

For key speakers and entertainment, Sue uses a speaker's bureau because she does not have the time to research the many speakers and entertainers who could speak to ASAA members. The speaker's bureau will make recommendations on the best speakers and entertainers; and once Sue makes her selection, the speaker's bureau will handle all arrangements. It will ensure that the speakers are at the meeting on time; and if something happens, the speaker's bureau can quickly arrange for a backup speaker.

Sue selects an online registration company to help with the many attendees who prefer this registration method. The designated registration company will accept registrations electronically, automatically send attendees a confirmation letter, and store the registrations for easy retrieval to create name badges at the meeting site.

Sponsors are important partners for the ASAA conference. Sue will work with all the sponsors to ensure that they receive exposure to members in exchange for their financial and/or in-kind support. Sue realizes that without annual conference sponsors, the ASAA would not reach its financial objectives for the convention.

The ASAA has always included meeting security for attendees' safety and exhibitor products, but for this conference Sue will increase security. An animal rights association contacted the ASAA and plans to protest a new test being conducted on laboratory rats. Sue realized that she must allow this group to protest, but she wants to ensure that they protest peacefully and do not disturb meeting attendees.

Key partners in making the conference a success are the ESC providing the decorations and the AV company supplying the electronic equipment. Sue considers the ESC as the partner that brings the theme to life, so the decorations must wow attendees visually. Sue recognizes the important role the ESC plays in keeping the exhibitors happy in addition to pleasing the conference attendees. This is important to the ASAA, as the exhibitors generate 44% of the revenue for the conference.

Sue loves to work with the AV company because this partner is crucial for every meeting event. Without proper projection and sound, the attendees would not be able to learn. Sue works closely with its staff during the meeting. One burned-out light bulb or malfunctioning microphone can ruin a breakout session.

In selecting an ESC and an AV company, Sue chooses the Freeman Companies. Unlike other ESCs and AV companies, the Freeman Companies offers both ESC and AV supplier services under one company. This makes communications run more smoothly. In addition, the organizational structure of the Freeman Companies allows Sue to have one contact from sales to service of the meeting.

In order to keep things running efficiently at the conference, Sue hires temporary staff and builds a partnership early with these people. They will be part of the team and will represent the ASAA during the conference.

Contracts

Sue has a contract for each convention partner and every service provider. Each contract specifies the exact services that are expected and the penalties if the expectations are not met. Early in Sue's career, she worked with an association that signed a contract that did not include a realistic attrition clause. The association did not meet its room block and paid the hotel over $10,000 for unused

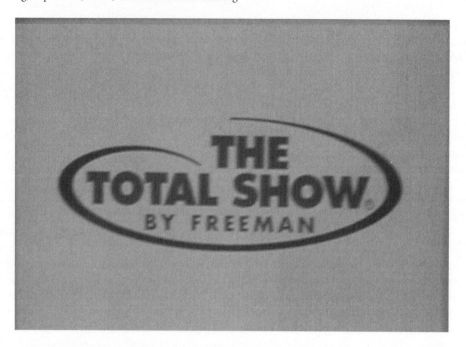

"The Total Show" is a promotional concept used by the Freeman Companies.   *Photo by George G. Fenich, Ph.D.*

rooms. At least one year out, Sue reviews each contract carefully. Before the meeting begins, Sue will have contracts finalized with the host hotel, housing bureau, airlines, off-site venue, golf course, speaker's bureau, security, AV company, DMC, ESC, and many others.

ONE-YEAR TO SIX-MONTH COUNTDOWN

Sue looks at her **meeting time line** and realizes that she is eighteen months away from the Power of Prevention annual conference. She takes out her meeting resume and reviews all contracts. She meets with George and Julie from the marketing committee to look at the blue line of the marketing pieces and the first draft of the program. The blue line, or "proof" as it is also called, is the final copy that will be reviewed before the marketing piece is printed. If Sue and her team miss an educational session or a grammatical error, then that is the way it will be printed. If the mistake is important enough, the marketing piece will be reprinted and the expenses added to the cost of the conference.

She arranges a meeting with Doug and Dan from the program committee to select the speakers for the convention. On selection, Sue mails out the acceptance letter to the speakers; in her letter, Sue requests that the speaker confirm his or her commitment by sending a speaker biography, presentation abstract, and audiovisual needs form. Sue makes a point to contact the speaker's bureau to check the status of the motivational speaker and entertainment. She requests that all electronic equipment needs are identified one year prior to the meeting. By doing this, Sue is able to have a more accurate budget item for the equipment and can spot any potential fire hazards associated with its usage.

Sue secures ten sponsors for the meeting, including Small Vets Pluss, a company that supplies the vaccines for small animals, for the tote bags; Houver Pharmaceutical, a small-animal antibiotic producer, for transportation; LabSmlab, a provider of medical instruments used in animal surgery, for the opening night reception; Mix-a-vet, developer of special food for small animals, to sponsor the newspaper; and Smalco, a pet store featuring small-animal products. Small Vets Pluss will cosponsor the VIP entertainment and the awards dinner. Sue will contact each sponsor to confirm the commitment and sign the contract. In her conversation, Sue reminds sponsors that she needs to have them return a form with the exact spelling of their company name and the design of their signage or logo.

The trade show floor plan for the Dallas conference was created and approved fourteen months prior to the Dallas meeting. Exhibit space for the Power of Prevention conference was sold on site at the ASAA conference prior to Dallas—the ASAA has an 87% exhibitor retention. Nine months out, the ESC updates the floor plan and mails exhibitor packets to potential exhibitors.

In addition to the trade show, Sue works with the ESC in finalizing the setup for the opening reception, general session, and awards dinner. She determines where the media center and the registration area will be located. Sue depends on the ESC to recommend the best location to place sponsor banners and signage. Most convention centers have strict rules regarding banner and signage placement, and ESCs that work with convention centers frequently know the rules and have great ideas on how sponsors can be recognized.

SIX MONTHS TO DAY OF THE MEETING

Fast forward to the six-month countdown for the Power of Prevention conference. The marketing committee writes and sends press releases. If timed correctly, the press releases will be published within a month of when the convention ads are scheduled to run.

Early registration forms begin to arrive within weeks after being sent. In reviewing the registration forms, Sue notices that three of the attendees indicated that they have mobility disabilities and will need special accommodations. In compliance with the Americans with Disabilities Act (ADA), Sue will work with all meeting partners to ensure that these attendees are able to fully participate in the conference. She needs to arrange for handicapped rooms and notes that the meeting rooms will need to be set with aisles to accommodate these attendees.

Sue receives the menus from the hotel catering manager and selects the meals. She makes a special note informing catering that she will require five special meals for attendees with dietary needs.

She contacts the host hotel and convention center to get the names of the meeting rooms that will be used for the Power of Prevention conference. It is important for Sue to get the name of the location of the meeting rooms so that this information can be added to the convention program. Hotels and convention centers rarely want to give this information out early, as they do not want to commit to a particular meeting room that might be sold to another planner, so good communication and flexibility are important.

Sue works with the DMC to review the menu and with the ESC for the VIP dinner at the Dallas World Aquarium. The DMC located a florist that will create floral arrangements that look like coral reefs on the sea bottom. The entire event is designed to make attendees feel like they are underwater.

Sue contacts Larry Grant, the event organizer at Tennison Golf Course, to finalize tournament rules. It looks like this will be a great year for this event—ten people are already registered for this event. Sue gives Larry the names and handicaps.

During this time, Sue will also contact the DMC to finalize shuttle routes to all events, enabling her to begin ordering signage for transportation. Sue learns each year how even highly educated people get lost at meetings—it baffles her that veterinarians cannot read the location material in their program. Sue must clearly list all the events, their locations, and the shuttle service times. Signage is very important in the total conference experience.

Month Five

Five months prior to the meeting, Sue sends out reminders to all speakers, and she works with the marketing committee to finalize and send the marketing brochure and the e-mail announcement. After some quiet time to proofread the meeting program, she creates a detailed work schedule for staff, temporary employees, and volunteers. Sue orders meeting name badges and meeting supplies and then calls the security company to review her needs.

Months Four And Three

During the fourth and third months prior to the meeting, Sue monitors registration on a weekly basis. At the third month, Sue reviews registration and makes adjustments to her room block (she negotiated this option in her hotel contract as a way to control attrition).

Sue looks at her initial room block and compares it with current hotel registrations. Convention history shows that 60% of the people register early, indicating that in a perfect world, the host property would have 600 rooms reserved and the remaining properties would have 300 each. In looking at the actual hotel registrations, Sue notices that all rooms have been filled at the Fairmont, but she is unable to get additional rooms so will need to close reservations for the

Hotel	Hyatt Regency Downtown Dallas	Fairmont	Wyndham Anatole	W Hotel	Holiday Inn
Initial Room Block	1,000	500	500	500	500
90-Day Room Block Review	700	500	300	300	100
Room Block Adjustment	Over—will add + 50 rooms	No change	On schedule	On schedule	Under—will remove 200 rooms
New Room Block	1,050	500	500	500	300

Table 15-3 ASAA Hotel Room Blocks

Fairmont. The Wyndham and W Hotel are right on schedule and will require no changes. The Holiday Inn is 200 rooms less than what it should be; Sue reduces the block by 40% and is now obligated for 300 rooms rather than 500. She has the opposite problem with the Hyatt Regency, the host hotel—the host property is 100 rooms over what she expects, so she conservatively increases the block by 5% and is obligated for 1,050 rooms.

In addition to the room block adjustments, she has received calls from the convention center to move the location of meeting rooms and calls from speakers needing to cancel. These changes affect the information in the program, so it must be revised. She sees this as a time of many changes, but these changes are all part of Sue's job. The work she did a year ago is paying off. A speaker cancels, so she contacts the program committee to see who they have planned as a backup.

Month Two

At two months out, Sue arranges another trip to Dallas. Patty, CSM of the Dallas CVB, arranges for Sue to meet with all the key contacts to make the Power of Prevention conference a success. Rizwan, the CSM at the Hyatt Hotel Downtown, meets with Sue to conduct a property walk-through, and he will introduce Sue to the catering manager to review the menu, the accounts receivable contract to explain the bill review process, the front desk manager to confirm pre-key guests and the check-in and check-out process, and the director of security and medical staff to review emergency procedures. The CSM explains that he is the hotel contact and will assist Sue in providing information needed from the hotel, from room pickup to bill review. Rizwan and Sue will work closely together.

At the Dallas Convention Center, Sue will meet with Erika Bondy, senior event coordinator, to conduct a walk-through and invites the ESC and the AV contacts to join her. By doing this, Sue has many eyes looking for potential problems that might occur. She will also spend time with the catering manager to review the menu for lunch and awards dinner.

Sue meets with the DMC representative to walk through hotel transportation routes and finalize menus, decorations, and entertainment for the VIP dinner at the Dallas World Aquarium. Sue then meets with the event coordinator at the Tennison Golf Course to update the player list and review pairings.

When Sue returns from Dallas, she makes final changes to the program and sends it to the printer. She also ships material to the convention site; works with the marketing committee on the final scripts; and reviews her staging guide that has all her contacts, the time line, contracts, menus, and notes for her to review.

Month One

One month prior to the meeting, Sue continues weekly monitoring of the registrations and sends reminder letters to all the speakers. She works with the advertising firm to approve press releases to announce research findings that will be presented at the Power of Prevention conference; she also works with the staff to finalize work schedules, marketing, scripts, and rehearsal times. Sue will create a checklist and pack her convention material. She is a good planner and has thought about backup plans for her activities; for example, if the golf tournament is rained out, the group will spend the morning on a sports tour of Dallas.

Sue likens the month before the meeting to a tennis match. Emergencies—which feel like five to ten tennis balls coming across the net at her at the same time—can hit her, so Sue knows she must be ready with her racket in hand to successfully hit those balls back over the net and be ready for the next barrage of balls.

Premeeting Activities

Three days prior to the meeting, Sue and her staff arrive in Dallas to set up the meeting headquarters. She is happy to see that all her convention material arrived safely. Sue meets all contacts to finalize meeting plans and arranges a walk-through of the host hotel and the convention center with her staff, temporary employees, and volunteers. The host hotel arranges a pre-con meeting where everyone working on the meeting will get together and review the meeting resume for any changes or concerns.

Sue monitors the setup of all meeting events and conducts on-site troubleshooting. Something always needs to be changed; it might be a sponsor sign with an error that needs to be redone by calling the ESC or a more complicated situation like the space for the registration being too small. This is a time of constant problem solving.

Sue joins George and the marketing staff as they rehearse for the general session, set up the pressroom, and conduct a press conference. George takes time to review the press list with Sue because she needs to know the names of press attendees to ensure that when they arrive, someone from the ASAA staff can quickly assist them. Good publicity can ensure the success of future conferences.

Meeting Day Activities

The meeting begins, and Sue is busy working with the staff to ensure all meeting rooms are set up properly and that all speaker materials and evaluations are ready. Her role is to work behind the scenes to make the attendees' experience perfect. She is the first one to arrive on site and will be the last person to leave. The day is filled with questions that she must clarify or problems that need to be solved. This is the time that excites Sue—the time when she sees all her hard work become a reality. She uses the contacts she made to quickly solve problems. For example, the equipment in one of the rooms is not working, so she calls the AV company and the problem is quickly solved. At the beginning of each day, Sue meets with the hotel CSM and the accounts receivable department to conduct a bill review. She also checks with the housing bureau to follow up on a comparison of the ASAA registration with the in-house guest list to ensure that ASAA attendees are properly coded to the ASAA block, which helps with future event accommodations.

A special ASAA exhibitor headquarters office opens at the convention center. Jill, the ASAA's trade show manager, will remain in this office to handle any problems that might occur during the trade show and to accept exhibitor bookings for next year's ASAA conference.

AFTER THE MEETING

Immediate Postmeeting Activities

A tired Sue sips coffee and takes a moment to review the successes and the areas of opportunity of the Power of Prevention conference. Before leaving Dallas, Sue will facilitate a post-con meeting to evaluate this year's conference, where people who attended the pre-con meeting will be present to discuss the conference and answer questions: What were the problems? What could be done to improve this situation for future conventions? She will work with the hotel and vendors to reconcile registration numbers, review all pickups, and estimate ancillary business.

Planning a convention is a team event. Sue takes time to thank all speakers, sponsors, committee members, and facilitators for helping with the conference—she also rewards her staff by giving them a free day in Dallas to relax.

Two-Month Postmeeting Activities

After the statistics and evaluations have been reviewed, Sue begins her report to the executive director and to the board of directors regarding conference ROI. It is important after each conference that an evaluation is conducted. In creating this conference, Sue and her team set the convention objectives: to increase the number of attendees taking the SAPDC by 10% by offering a four-day conference that is focused on education and networking that will increase conference profits by 5%. What is the point of having a convention if the success is not measured? Part of the meeting planner's job is to demonstrate how a convention or meeting helps achieve organizational goals. By establishing objectives and reviewing ROI, a planner can show his or her role in supporting company objectives and the bottom line.

Sue is excited about the Power of Prevention convention. The industry press gave excellent premeeting coverage, with over $50,000 tracked as nonpaid advertising. Sue believes this third-party endorsement definitely increased attendance. The meeting objectives were met: 500 people took the classes for SAPDC (a 10% increase from the 454 who took SAPDC classes last year), and meeting profits grew from $1,393,297.60 to $1,462,962.50 (a 5% increase).

Sue finishes her report and takes a call from the Orlando Convention Center, the location for next year's annual conference. She is twelve months away from the conference and is receiving the names of the meeting rooms that will be used ... and the meeting cycle continues.

Summary

In this chapter, you have learned about the process of creating a citywide meeting. This is a large task for one person and requires many partners to make the conference successful. Through this case study, you have been able to see a day in the life of a meeting planner on a site inspection and have looked at the many tasks leading up to the conference. The chapter began with creating conference objectives and budgets, and it ended with evaluating ROI to determine the success of the meeting.

Key Words and Terms

For definitions, see the Glossary, or http://glossary.convention industry.org.

Audiovisual (AV) company	Destination management company (DMC)	Request for proposal (RFP)
Convention services manager (CSM)	Exposition services contractor (ESC)	Return on investment (ROI)
Convention and visitor bureau (CVB)	Meeting time line	Sponsor

Review and Discussion Questions

1. Who is the group in this chapter? Why are they here?
2. Where else has the group met?
3. What are the steps Sue goes through to plan this meeting?
4. Whom does Sue work with on her staff?
5. Whom does Sue work with in the city where the meeting is being held? Which suppliers or vendors?
6. What does Sue do after the meeting is over?

About the Chapter Contributors

M. T. Hickman, CTP, CMP, is the head of the Travel, Exposition, and Meeting Management program at Richland College in Dallas, Texas. She began her career at the Irving, Texas, CVB, where she worked in many departments, including tourism sales, convention sales, and special events. Over the years, she has worked as director of marketing for the National Business Association and as a proposal writer for WorldTravel Partners. She is active in the meeting and exposition planning associations, including MPI, PCMA, and IAEM.

Other Chapter Contributors

Erika Bondy, CMP, Senior Event Coordinator, Dallas Convention Center

David Gisler, Director of Sales and Training, Total Show University, Freeman Companies

Dana Nickerson-Rhoden, CMP, CMM, Manager of Scientific and Corporate Meetings, American Heart Association

Nancy Simonieg, Senior Sales Manager, Hyatt Hotel Downtown Dallas

Patty Towell, Sales Manager, Dallas Convention and Visitor Bureau

APPENDIX

This appendix includes a detailed example of a Site Selection Sample Request for proposal (RFP). It is used with permission of the originator, Joan L. Eisenstodt.

FORMS FOR USE IN REQUESTING A PROPOSAL AND ON-SITE SELECTION

The sections that follow provide a number of forms, or frameworks, that are used by meeting professionals. Studying and reviewing these documents will help provide the reader with a better understanding of the myriad of details that a meeting professional must deal with.

Site Selection—Sample Request for Proposal (RFP)(v. 18b)

Group or Meeting Sponsor: Full name of organization (acronym in parentheses)

Contact Information: Name(s) including alternate contacts, title(s), address(es), communication numbers (phones, fax, e-mail, tdd/tty), and contact times and time zones

Organization: Provide brief organizational description—structure, mission, purpose.

The Meeting: Provide brief description—purpose, goals and objectives, general format, and audience profile.

History: Provide up to 2 years of meeting history—dates, attendance, hotel(s) used, rooms blocked and picked up, and range of rates.

Schedule for Future Meetings; Future Years for Meeting

Considerations for This Meeting:

    Destination(s) and site(s)

    Dates (acceptable and unacceptable)

    Rates

    Special requirements/information (transportation, attractions/restaurants, quirks)

References: Request for meetings of similar size, focus/scope, held in last 6 to 12 months

Proposals Due/Decision Process: Provide date by which proposal must be received and what collateral materials should be included. Describe decision process and date by which decision is expected.

Meeting Specifications:

Sleeping Room Block: Describe day-by-day, including early arrivals/late departures; bed and room types; suites.

Meeting Space: Provide day-by-day description of the program, including meeting/conference office space, speaker ready room, lounges, and times needed.

Exhibit/Display Space: For literature tables, other displays or exhibits and the times the space is needed. Include move-in and move-out times.

Site Selection
Request for Proposal
Organization Name
Attachment A

If you plan to submit a proposal, please keyboard all information and upload these forms to (*e-mail address*).

Property name _____ *City/State* _____

Property contact name/title/e-mail and phone _____

Year property built _____ Last building inspection and results _____

Number of floors _____ Total number of rooms _____ suites _____

Single/one-bedded rooms _____ Double/two-bedded rooms _____

Number of nonsmoking rooms _____ Number of disability-accessible rooms _____

Year of last guest room renovation _____ Year of last public space renovation _____

Scope of Planned Renovation and Schedule:

Type of property

      ☐ *meeting/convention*   ☐ *resort*   ☐ *full service*   ☐ *limited service*

Market tier: ☐ *luxury*   ☐ *upscale*   ☐ *moderate*

Property location: ☐ *suburban*   ☐ *downtown/city center*

Property ownership & management

Chain owned? (Y/N) _____ If no, name of owners. _____

Management Company _____

Franchise? (Y/N) _____

Owner's company is at least 51% owned, controlled, and operated by an American citizen minority? (Y/N) _____

Owner's company is at least 51% owned, controlled, and operated by an American citizen nonminority woman? (Y/N) _____

> ## Site Selection
> ## Request for Proposal
> *Organization Name*
> *Attachment A*

If you plan to submit a proposal, please keyboard all information and upload these forms to (*e-mail address*).

Property name _____ *City/State*_____

Property contact name/title/e-mail and phone _____

Rating

AAA Diamonds   *1*   *2*   *3*   *4*   *5*   not rated
Mobil Stars   *1*   *2*   *3*   *4*   *5*   not rated

Other rating(s) (specify) _____

Outlets

Name _____ Location _____ Hours _____
Full or Ltd. Service _____ Nonsmoking?_____

Transportation and Parking

Airport One
Name   _____ 3-Letter code _____
Distance from property _____ miles
         Minutes/rush hour _____ Minutes/nonrush hour_____
Complimentary shuttle (Y/N) _____
Estimated taxi charge (each way) _____
Alternate mode of transportation _____ Cost each way _____
Driving directions (attach)

Airport Two
Name   _____ 3-Letter code _____
Distance from property _____ miles
         Minutes/rush hour _____ Minutes/nonrush hour _____
Complimentary shuttle (Y/N) _____
Estimated taxi charge (each way) _____
Alternate mode of transportation _____ Cost each way _____
Driving Directions (attach)

Number of parking spaces at property _____ Charge for self-park _____
Charge for valet park _____
Identify facility's parking capacity for large trucks, semitrailers, etc.: _____

Taxes, service, and/or gratuity charges
The current rooms tax is ____% plus $____ occupancy tax.
    ' There is ___ is not ___ a ballot initiative in the next election to raise those taxes.
There is a ____ gratuity or a ____ service charge of _____% on group food and beverage.
    ' This is taxed at _____%.

> **Site Selection**
> **Request for Proposal**
> *Organization Name*
> *Attachment A*

If you plan to submit a proposal, please keyboard all information and upload these forms to (*e-mail address*).

Property name _____ *City/State* _____

Property contact name/title/e-mail and phone _____

Facilities/Services on Property (check all that apply)

☐ Cocktail lounge
☐ 24-hour room service OR
    ☐ Room service Start time _____ End time _____
☐ Safety deposit boxes/lobby area
☐ Express check in and out   ☐ Video review/check out
☐ Full business center   Hours _____ A.M. to _____ P.M.   Days of the week _____
☐ Gift/newsstand   Hours _____ A.M. to _____ P.M.   Days of the week: _____
☐ Full-service health club   Hours ___ A.M. to ____ P.M.   Days of the week: _____
☐ Laundry/valet service (circle applicable responses)

Circle one: On property or *Sent out*

    Circle service: 5 days/week   *6 days/week*   *7 days/week*   *overnight service*
☐ Shoe shine service
☐ Indoor pool   ☐ outdoor pool
☐ Airline desk(s)   (specify) _____, _____
☐ ATM (Current use fee is $ ____.____.)
☐ Car rental desk(s)   (specify) _____, _____
☐ Evening turndown service   ☐ All guests   ☐ VIPs only
☐ Golf course
☐ Tennis court(s)
☐ Racquetball courts
☐ Other (specify) _____

Guest Rooms

☐ In-room safe   ☐ No charge   ☐ Charge to use ($_____/day)
☐ Working desks with outlets above floor
☐ Voice mail   ☐ Personalized voice mail
☐ 2 line phones/all rooms   ☐ 2-line phones/concierge/specialized rooms only
☐ Data ports on all phones   ☐ Digital or analog phone lines
☐ Phone in bathroom   ☐ bathroom phone/concierge or specialty rooms only
☐ Access charge for local phone calls _____ Access charge for toll-free calls _____
☐ AM/FM radio   ☐ with cassette player   ☐ with CD player
☐ Color TV
☐ Remote control TV   ☐ Cable TV   ☐ Satellite TV
☐ All news cable channel   ☐ Weather channel
☐ Other special channels (specify) _____
☐ In-room movies on demand
☐ Closed-circuit television (CCTV)

> **Site Selection**
> **Request for Proposal**
> *Organization Name*
> *Attachment A*

If you plan to submit a proposal, please keyboard all information and upload these forms to (*e-mail address*).

Property name _____ *City/State* _____

Property contact name/title/e-mail and phone _____

Guest Rooms (cont.)

☐ In-room video players
☐ Iron/ironing board
☐ Mini-bar   ☐ Refrigerator on request
☐ Coffee/Tea maker   ☐ Daily complimentary coffee/tea
☐ Working desk/desk lamp
☐ Free **daily** paper delivered to room   ☐ Paper/**weekdays only**

Reservations and Check-in/out

☐ Reservations may be made through a toll-free number.
  ☐ That number is _____   ☐ Number is accessible throughout United States.
  ☐ A number that can be used for those residing in the state in which the reservations department is located:
  ☐ A reservation number for those outside the United States is ( ) _____.
  ☐ The TTY/TDD number is ( ) _____.
  ☐ The fax number for reservations is ( ) _____.
  ☐ Reservations may be made on line at http://www._____,
  ☐ or by email to _____.
☐ All rooms in a group's block are released to the toll-free number.
☐ The property has an in-house reservations department.
☐ The reservations department is located off-site.

Check-in time is _____. Check-out time is _____.

☐ The facility will audit the room reservations using a group's registration list.

<u>Site Selection</u>
<u>Request for Proposal</u>
Organization Name
Attachment A

If you plan to submit a proposal, please keyboard all information and upload these forms to (*e-mail address*).

Property name _____ *City/State* _____

Property contact name/title/e-mail and phone _____

<u>*Safety and Security (check all that apply)*</u>

☐ Smoke detectors in all guest rooms   Hardwired?   *Y/N* _____
☐ Smoke detectors in hallways   Hardwired?   *Y/N* _____
☐ Smoke detectors in public areas   Hardwired?   *Y/N* _____
☐ Audible smoke detectors   ☐ Visual alarms for people with hearing impairments
☐ Sprinklers in all guest rooms   Sprinklers in hallways
☐ Sprinklers in public areas
☐ Fire extinguishers in hallways
☐ Automatic fire doors
☐ Auto link to fire station
☐ Auto recall elevators
☐ Ventilated stairwells
☐ Emergency maps in guest rooms/hallways
☐ Emergency information in all guest rooms
☐ Emergency lighting
☐ Safety chain on door   ☐ Doors with viewports ("peep holes")
☐ Deadbolts on all guest room doors
☐ Restricted access to guest floors
☐ Property has AEDs (automatic external defibrillators)
    ☐ Staff has been trained to use defibrillators   *Per shift* ____
☐ Staff trained in CPR   CPR-trained staff *per shift* _____
☐ Staff trained in first aid   *Per shift* ____
☐ Secondary locks on guest room glass doors
☐ Room balconies accessible by adjoining rooms/balconies
☐ Primary guest room entrance accessible by interior corridor/atrium
☐ Guest room accessible by exterior entrance only
☐ Guest room windows open
☐ Uniformed security
☐ 24-hour security throughout facility   Number of staff ___
☐ Public address system
☐ Video surveillance in public areas/elevators
☐ Video surveillance at entrances
☐ Video surveillance in hallways
☐ Staff trained in issuance of duplicate keys/cards
☐ Emergency power source: _____
    ☐ SOPs for power outages _____

Food Safety:
Detail the frequency of inspection by county or city health inspectors and the results of the last three (3) inspections.

Site Selection
Request for Proposal
Organization Name
Attachment A

If you plan to submit a proposal, please keyboard all information and upload these forms to (*e-mail address*).

Property name _____ *City/State* _____

Property contact name/title/e-mail and phone _____

Emergency call response time (for fire, police, EMTs) in minutes to your property _____
Does property have an emergency evacuation plan? (Y/N) _____
   How often does property conduct emergency evacuation drills? _____
Nearest police station (blocks/miles) _____ Nearest hospital (blocks/miles) _____
Does facility comply with all country/state/local fire laws? (Y/N) _____

Please describe

—The actions your facility took beginning 9/11/01 for the safety and comfort of your guests:

—Any change of policies governing safety/security instituted or reinstituted since 9/11/01.

—The communication tree among your property and local/state/federal emergency management officials.

—Any policies in effect that govern "containment" of guests in the property for issues of bioterrorism? Inability to travel because of airport closures?

"Oversold/Underdeparted" ("Walk") Policies or Guidelines
☐ Property will arrange accommodations at comparable or superior property within 10 minutes of this property.
☐ Property will pay directly for one room night and tax at comparable property.
☐ Traveler will be provided with transportation.
☐ Traveler will be reimbursed for (number) _____ of phone calls to home and/or office.
☐ Other (specify) _____

<u>Site Selection</u>
<u>Request for Proposal</u>
Organization Name
Attachment A

If you plan to submit a proposal, please keyboard all information and upload these forms to (*e-mail address*).

Property name _____ *City/State* _____

Property contact name/title/e-mail and phone _____

Staff and Staffing
☐ Average length of employment at this property:
  Management staff _____ years   line staff _____ years
☐ Staff organized for the purpose of collective bargaining (List unions and staff positions, contract renewal dates on separate sheet.)

Policies and Miscellaneous Charges
☐ Credit cards are charged when reservation is made.
  ☐ If charged, is it for _____ first night _____ last night _____ all nights
☐ Guest may cancel guaranteed reservations without penalty/charge
    _____ to 4 P.M./day of arrival   _____ to 6 P.M./day of arrival   _____ 24 hours
    _____ 48 hours   _____ 72 hours   _____ other
☐ Guest substitutions are allowed, at any time, without penalty or charge to group and/or individual.
☐ Guest substitutions are not allowed without a charge to group and/or individual.
☐ Extended stays (based on availability) are allowed at no charge.
☐ Early checkouts incur a charge of $_____ if the front desk is not notified at check-in.
☐ The property charges $____/page for receipt of faxes.
☐ The property charges $___/page to send faxes.
☐ There is a charge of $_____ for receipt of packages.
☐ There is a charge of $_____ for property to send packages.
☐ There is a charge of $_____ to deliver packages to individual or group.

> ## Site Selection
> ## Request for Proposal
> *Organization Name*
> *Attachment A*

If you plan to submit a proposal, please keyboard all information and upload these forms to (*e-mail address*).

Property name _____ *City/State* _____

Property contact name/title/e-mail and phone _____

Policies and Miscellaneous Charges (cont.)

☐ Is a resort or hotel or other fee added to the room rate? Y/N _____

    ☐ If so, the current amount per room (or per guest) per night is $_____ which is/is not taxed.

       ☐ This covers:

    ○ Contractual issues that must be included in our contract are attached to this document.

Energy Issues

☐ The property does charge an energy surcharge of $_____ per room per night. This charge is or is not taxed. (Is ____ Is not ____) If taxed, it is at _____%.

☐ The power supply for the property is from _____.

☐ Describe the property's backup power source(s):

☐ Describe the property's emergency procedures for brownouts and blackouts:

☐ Describe the property's backup systems for water and phones:

☐ Define any charges for use of electrical outlets for meetings and/or in public space and/or in guestrooms:

Environmental Issues

○ Our property recycles the following materials:

      _____ paper   _____ plastic   _____metal/tin/aluminum

○ The method by which guests may recycle is:

○ We ask guests to advise us by use of a card if they want their towels and/or bed linens changed every day.

○ Other areas we protect the environment are:

Site Selection
Request for Proposal
Organization Name
Attachment A

If you plan to submit a proposal, please keyboard all information and upload these forms to (*e-mail address*).

Property name _____ *City/State* _____

Property contact name/title/e-mail and phone _____

Other Groups

During the group's preferred dates, the other events confirmed in the city, including conventions, festivals, other public and private events that are known to the bureau or the facility, are:

During the group's preferred dates, the other events confirmed in the facility are:

City/County Labor Issues

Note any groups organized for the purpose of collective bargaining in the city or county whose contract deadlines are 2 months on both side of preferred dates, and their history of labor actions:

Audio Visual Equipment

The in-house or recommended company is _____.

The facility has the ability to negotiate prices on behalf of the AV company. (Y/N) _____

A discount of _____% off list prices can be offered for AV equipment for the meeting.

The service charge is _____%. It is taxed at _____%. It is not taxed. _____

If an outside AV company is brought in by our organization, there is _____ is not _____ a fee.

   If there is a fee, it is _____.

Electricity Supply/Vendor

Electricity (for exhibits and meeting space) is provided to the facility by _____ in-house or _____ external vendor. (If external, specify _____.)

The facility has the ability to negotiate prices for meeting and exhibit electrical service.
   (Y/N) _____

Electricity is available to the outdoor portions of the facility (for outside exhibits).
   (Y/N) _____

A discount of _____% off list prices can be offered for meeting room and exhibit electricity for the meeting.

> ### Site Selection
> ### Request for Proposal
> *Organization Name*
> *Attachment A*

If you plan to submit a proposal, please keyboard all information and upload these forms to (*e-mail address*).

Property name _____ *City/State* _____

Property contact name/title/e-mail and phone _____

Operations and Technology

☐ *Our sales/convention services staff use* _____ *word processing software, version* _____.

☐ *Sales and convention services personnel use e-mail.* _____ *yes* _____ *no*
  E-mail addresses are:
    ☐ *Sales* _____
    ☐ *Convention/Catering services* _____
    ☐ *Reservations* _____

☐ *Sales and convention services have Web access.* ___ *yes* ___ *no*

☐ *Reservations is fully automated and can respond by e-mail.* ___ *yes* ___ *no*

☐ *Our Web site address is* _____.

☐ *Group/Meeting reservations can be made on line.*
    ☐ *If reservations may be made on line, please specify information that must be included in any published URLs and any restrictions and/or policies.*

```
┌─────────────────────────────────────────────────────────────────┐
│                 NATIONAL SALES RESPONSE FORM                      │
│                  (year/meeting) Site Selection                    │
│           Request for Proposal: (name of organization)            │
└─────────────────────────────────────────────────────────────────┘
```

Please complete and return this form <u>after</u> reading the RFP. To allow us to track proposals, please advise to which properties in which cities you will send the RFP. **Please upload this to** (*e-mail address*), **or fax this form to** (*name, fax number*) **to be received by** (*day, date, time/time zone*).

Please print or type in black:

Company _____

Contact name/title _____

Direct phone no. _____

Direct fax no. _____

E-mail address _____

The RFP is being sent to the following properties:

_____/City _____

_____/City _____

_____/City _____

_____/City _____

_____/City _____

_____/City _____

Comments:

CVB RESPONSE FORM
(Year/Meeting) Site Selection
Request for Proposal: (Organization/Meeting Name)

Please complete and return this form <u>after</u> reading the RFP. To allow us to track proposals, please advise to which properties you will send the RFP, keeping in mind that it should only be sent to properties not represented by the companies noted in the cover note and only to those that meet the criteria. If responses are received by properties that do not meet the criteria, or by vendors for whom we do not need services, we will reject the proposals.

Please upload this to (*e-mail address*)**, or fax this form to** (*name, fax number*) **by** (*day/date/time/time zone*)**.**

Please print or type in black:

CVB _____

Contact name/Title _____

Direct phone no. _____

Direct fax no. _____

E-mail address _____

The RFP is being sent to the following properties:

_____

_____

_____

_____

_____

_____

Comments:

Property RESPONSE FORM
(Year/Meeting) Site Selection
Request for Proposal: (Organization/Meeting)

Please complete and return this form <u>after</u> reading the RFP but before sending a proposal. There is no need to send a follow-up letter or e-mail, or to call once this form has been sent. **Please upload this to (***e-mail address***), or fax to (***organization/fax number***) to be received by (***day/date/time/time zone***).**

Full proposals and collateral are due by (day/date/time/time zone).

Please complete and return this information <u>whether or not</u> a proposal is being submitted. If completing by hand, please use black ink.

Property name/City _____

Contact name/Title _____

Direct phone no. (_____)_____

Direct fax no. (_____)_____

E-mail address _____

URL *http://www.* _____

Check/complete all applicable responses:

_____ **We will send proposal and collateral to be received by (***due date***).**

_____ **Dates noted on first option basis are being held for this group.**

_____ **Dates will *not* be held until a contract is signed.**

Dates available/First option   **Dates available/Second option**

_____   _____

_____   _____

_____   _____

_____   _____

_____ We regret we are *unable to send a proposal* for the following reason(s):

    _____ None of preferred dates available.

    _____ Meeting space and/or sleeping rooms not appropriate for meeting.

    _____ Unable to meet rate parameters.

    _____ Other (specify):

        _____

        _____

Comments:

GLOSSARY

Definitions are taken from the chapters or from http://glossary.conventionindustry.org.

80211: Engineering specification for the wireless standard. This defines how a wireless interface between clients and access points is constructed.

Accepted Practices Exchange (APEX): Initiative of the meetings, expositions, events, and conventions industry managed by the Convention Industry Council (CIC). APEX develops and manages the implementation of accepted practices (voluntary standards) for the industry.

Act of God: Extraordinary natural event such as extreme weather, flood, hurricane, tornado, earthquake, or similar natural disaster that cannot be reasonably foreseen or prevented and over which a contracting party has no reasonable control. It makes performance of the contract illegal, impracticable, or impossible; thus the parties have no legal responsibility to continue performance of the contract.

Action station: Place where chef prepares foods to order and serves them fresh to guests. Popular items for action stations include pasta, grilled meat or shrimp, carved meats, sushi, crepes, omelets, flaming desserts, Caesar salad, etc. *Also called* performance stations or exhibition cooking.

Agenda: List, outline, or plan of items to be done or considered at an event or during a specific time block and may include a time schedule.

Amenity: Complimentary item in sleeping rooms such as writing supplies, bathrobes, fruit baskets, shower caps, shampoo, and shoe shine mitts provided by the facility for guests.

American service: Serving style where guests are seated and served food that has been preportioned and plated in the kitchen.

American Society of Association Executives (ASAE): Membership organization and voice of the association profession. Founded in 1920, ASAE now has more than 22,000 association CEOs, staff professionals, industry partners, and consultant members.

American Society of Composers, Authors, and Publishers (ASCAP): Membership organization that represents individuals who hold the copyrights to music written in the United States and that grants licensing agreements for the performance of that music.

Americans with Disabilities Act (ADA): U.S. legislation passed in 1992 requiring public buildings (offices, hotels, restaurants, etc.) to make adjustments meeting minimum standards to make their facilities accessible to individuals with physical disabilities.

Amphitheater: Outdoor facility with a flat performance area surrounded by rising rows of seats or a grassy slope that allows the audience to view the performance. The seating area is usually a semicircular shape or adapted to the surrounding landscape.

Ancillary activity: Event-related support services within a facility that generate revenue.

Annual meeting: Meeting that takes place once a year.

APEX Initiative: Industry-wide task force formed to begin a codification of definitions and standardized practices, policies, procedures, and terminology.

Arena: Facility featuring a large, flat main floor surrounded by fixed seats in a sloping oval or modified oval shape, much steeper than the typical theater. Some are arranged in two or more tiers. Sight lines are nearly always designed for events the size of a hockey floor, circus, ice show, or basketball court.

Association: Organized group of individuals and/or companies that band together to accomplish a common purpose, usually to provide for the needs of its members. It is usually a nonprofit organization.

Association professional liability (APL): Policy that protects the organization and its officers, directors, staff, and volunteers against personal liability arising from their official actions. This type of policy is broader than a traditional directors and officers (D&O) liability policy in that it covers the organization as an entity as well as individuals.

Attrition: Difference between the actual number of sleeping rooms picked up (or food and beverage covers or revenue projections) and the number or formula agreed to in the terms of the facility's contract. Usually, there is an allowable shortfall before damages are assessed.

Audience response system (ARS): System in which the audience is outfitted with small keypads that allow them to answer questions quickly and have their data tallied immediately.

Audiovisual (AV) company: Supplier of technical staff and audiovisual equipment (e.g., projectors, screens, sound systems, video, and staging).

Ausstellung: German term for consumer show.

Awards ceremony: Event (usually formal) to honor outstanding performance.

Bandwidth: Amount of information that can pass through a communications line. As it relates to the Web, bandwidth comes in two basic flavors: dial-up and high speed.

Banquet Event Order (BEO): Form most often used by hotels to provide details to personnel concerned with a specific food and beverage function or event room setup.

Banquet French service: Serving style where platters of food are composed in the kitchen. Each food item is then served from the guests' left by the server from platters to individual plates. Any course can be "Frenched" by having the dressing put on the salad or having sauce added to an entrée or dessert after it has been placed in front of the guest.

Blogging: Online diary that is posted to the Web.

Bluetooth: Telecommunications standard that allows mobile devices to communicate a short distance with each other. Most devices are capable of utilizing Bluetooth at a distance of no more than thirty feet.

Board meeting: Meeting of the board of directors of an organization that is usually small in size.

Boardroom: Room set permanently with a fixed table and suitable seating.

Boardroom setup: Seating arrangement in which rectangle- or oval-shaped tables are set up with chairs on both sides and ends. It is often confused with hollow square setup.

Bonding: Purchase, for a premium, of a guarantee of protection for a supplier or a customer. In the hospitality industry, certain bonding programs are mandatory.

Break-even point: Figure calculated by the CIC manual as the total fixed cost divided by the contribution margin (the registration fee minus the variable cost).

Break-out room: Small function room set up for a group within an event as opposed to a plenary or general session.

Break-out session: Small-group session, panel, workshop, or presentation offered concurrently within the event, formed to focus on specific subjects. The event is separate from the general session but is held within the event format. The sessions can be arranged by basic, intermediate, and advanced levels or divided by interest areas or industry segments.

Broadcast Music, Inc. (BMI): Music licensing organization that represents individuals who hold the copyrights to music written in the United States. It grants licensing agreements for the performance of music.

Buffet: Assortment of foods offered on a table and self-served.

Butler service: (1) Style of service that offers a variety of both hot and cold hors d'oeuvres on platters to guests at receptions. (2) Style of table service where guests serve themselves from platters presented by the server. (3) Specialized in-room service offered by a hotel.

Call brand: Brand of liquor, distinguished from the house brands, selected by a customer according to personal preference. It is usually of a higher quality than house brands.

Carnet: Customs document permitting the holder to carry or send merchandise temporarily into certain foreign countries (for display, demonstration, or similar purposes) without paying duties or posting bonds. *Also called* trade show bond.

Cart French service: Style of service that involves use of serving pieces (usually silver); heating and garnishing of food tableside by a captain; and serving of food on a heated plate, which is then served to the guest by a server. Plated entrées are usually served from the right, bread and butter and salad from the left, and beverages from the right. All are removed from the right.

Catered event: Event that generally has one host and one bill. Most attendees eat the same meal.

Center for Exhibition Industry Research (CEIR): Member of the Convention Industry Council (CIC).

Certified meeting professional (CMP): The foremost certification program of today's meetings, conventions, and exhibitions industry. The CMP program recognizes individuals who have achieved the industry's highest standard of professionalism.

Citywide event: Event that requires the use of a convention center or event complex as well as multiple hotels in the host city.

Clear span tent: Tent that has a strong roof structure so that it is possible to hang lighting from the beams by using special clamps.

Community infrastructure: Those facilities and companies in a locale that support the MEEC industry.

Complete meeting package (CMP): All-inclusive plan offered by conference centers that includes lodging, all food and beverage, and support services, including audiovisual equipment, room rental, etc.

Comprehensive general liability (CGL): Policy that is the commercial equivalent of a homeowner's policy. It protects the organization against personal injury claims and loss (including theft) or damage to the insured's property as well as the property of others. Although these policies are designed to cover "all risks," they frequently have exclusions, and it is important to carefully review what is not covered as well as what is included within the policy's scope.

Concessionaire: Person or company that operates the concessions.

Concessions: All-inclusive plan offered by conference centers that includes lodging, all meals, and support services.

Concurrent session: One of multiple sessions scheduled at the same time. Programs on different themes or subjects are offered simultaneously.

Conference: (1) Participatory meeting designed for discussion, fact-finding, problem solving, and consultation. (2) Event used by any organization to meet and exchange views, convey a message, open a debate, or give publicity to some area of opinion on a specific issue. No tradition, continuity, or periodicity is required to convene a conference. Although not generally limited in time, conferences are usually of short duration with specific objectives and are on a smaller scale than congresses.

Conference center: Facility that provides a dedicated environment for events, especially small events. It may be certified by the International Association of Conference Centers (IACC).

Congress: (1) Regular coming together of large groups of individuals, generally to discuss a particular subject. A congress will often last several days and have several simultaneous sessions. The length of time between congresses is usually established in advance of the implementation stage and can be either pluriannual or annual. Most international or world congresses are of the former type, while national congresses are more frequently held annually. (2) Meeting of an association of delegates or representatives from constituent organizations. (3) European term for convention. *See* Conference and Convention.

Consideration: Cause, motive, price, or impelling influence that induces a contracting party to enter a contract.

Continuing education unit (CEU): Requirement of many professional groups by which members must certify participation in formal educational programs designed to maintain their level of ability beyond their original certification date. CEUs are nonacademic credit. One CEU is awarded for each ten contact hours in an accredited program.

Continuing medical education (CME): Requirement for doctors to retain their medical license. They must take a certain amount of CME courses to keep current with innovations in health care.

Contract: Agreement between two or more parties that creates in each party a duty to do or not do something and a right to performance of the other's duty or a remedy for the breach of the other's duty.

Convention: Event where the primary activity of the attendees is to attend educational sessions, participate in meetings/discussions, socialize, or attend other organized events. There is a secondary exhibit component.

Convention and visitor bureau (CVB): Not-for-profit organization charged with representing a specific destination and helping the long-term development of communities through a travel and tourism strategy. CVBs are usually membership organizations bringing together businesses that rely on tourism and events for revenue. For visitors, CVBs are like a key to the city. As an unbiased resource, CVBs can serve as a broker or an official point of contact for convention and event planners, tour operators, and visitors; they assist planners with event preparation and encourage business travelers and visitors alike to visit local historic, cultural, and recreational sites.

Convention Industry Council (CIC): Federation of national and international organizations representing individuals, firms, or properties involved in the meetings, conventions, exhibitions, and travel and tourism industries. Formerly the Convention Liaison Council.

Convention services manager (CSM): Person whose job is to oversee and arrange every aspect of an event. The CSM can be an employee or hired ad hoc to plan, organize, implement, and control meetings, conventions, and other events.

Copyright: Federal law that allows for the ownership of intellectual property (writings, art, music). Copy-written material cannot be used without the owner's permission or the payment of royalty fees.

Corkage: Charge placed on beer, liquor, and wine brought into the facility but purchased elsewhere. The charge sometimes includes glassware, ice, and mixers.

Corporate meeting: Gathering of employees or representatives of a commercial organization. Usually, attendance is required and travel, room, and most meal expenses are paid for by the organization.

Corporation: A group of people who obtain a charter granting them (as a body) legal power, rights, privileges, and liabilities of an individual but distinct from those individuals making up the group.

Cutoff date: Designated date when the facility will release a block of sleeping rooms to the general public. The date is typically three to four weeks before the event.

Dates, rates, and space: Words that begin the maxim "Dates, rates, and space–You can only have two," which is used by hoteliers to sum up meeting negotiations. The meaning is that the planner can get the dates and meeting space he or she wants for a meeting but may have to give on the rate.

Destination: City, area, or country that can be marketed to groups or individuals as a place to visit or hold an event.

Destination management company (DMC): Professional services company possessing extensive local knowledge, expertise, and resources and specializing in the design and implementation of events, activities, tours, transportation, and program logistics. Depending on the company and the staff specialists in the company, a DMC offers, but is not limited to, the following: creative proposals for special events within the meeting; guest tours; VIP amenities and transportation; shuttle services; staffing within convention centers and hotels; team building, golf outings, and other activities; entertainment, including sound and lighting; décor and theme development; ancillary meetings for management professionals; and advance meetings and on-site registration services and housing.

Destination Marketing Association International (DMAI): World's largest resource for official destination marketing organizations (DMOs) dedicated to improving the effectiveness of DMOs in more than twenty-five countries. DMAI provides members with educational resources, networking opportunities, and marketing benefits worldwide.

Destination marketing organization (DMO): *See* CVB.

Destinations showcase: Fast-paced and productive one-day exhibition and conference sponsored by the International Association of Convention and Visitor Bureaus (IACVB) where qualified meeting professionals attend valuable education sessions, network with industry leaders and peers, and explore a full range of destinations from throughout the world.

DMAI online RFP: Service provided by the DMAI where the meeting professional can visit and select the cities he or she is interested in and either fill out the RFP form provided or attach an already prepared RFP. Go to http://www.destinationmarketing.org for more information.

Drayage: Delivery of exhibit materials from the dock to an assigned exhibit space, removal of empty crates, return of crates at the end of the event for recrating, and delivery of materials back to the dock for carrier loading.

Early bird rate: Lowered rate offered as an incentive for attendees to send in registration before a pre-definite date. *Also called* early bird discount.

Education session: Time period during which information or instruction is presented.

English service: Style of service where guests are seated and large serving platters and bowls of food are placed on the dining table by the servers. Guests pass the food around the table.

Exclusive: Agreement that limits who may provide specific products or services under certain conditions to only one party. A general service contractor, for instance, may have an exclusive in a particular facility, meaning that no other contractor is allowed to provide the same services or products in that facility.

Exclusive contract: Contract between a facility and a service provider designating that provider as the only provider of specific services or products in that facility.

Exclusive service: Service that is provided only by the official service contractor.

Exhibit hall: Area within a facility where the exhibition is located.

Exhibition: (1) Event at which products and services are displayed. The primary activity of attendees is visiting exhibits on the show floor. These events focus primarily on business-to-business (B2B) relationships. (2) Display of products or promotional materials for the purposes of public relations, sales, and/or marketing.

Exhibition management company (EMC): Company or individual who designs and/or builds exhibits. The EMC may also provide other services.

Exhibition service contractor (ESC): Organizer or promoter of an exhibition responsible for rental of space as well as financial control and management of the exhibition. Sometimes an agent can act in this capacity.

Exhibitor-appointed contractor (EAC): Company other than the designated "official" contractor providing a service to an exhibitor. EACs are a subset of service contractors that work for the exhibiting company and travel throughout the country setting up and dismantling their booths rather than working from one city or location.

Exhibitor service manual: Manual or kit, usually developed by the service contractor for an event, containing general event information, labor/service order forms, rules and regulations, and other information pertinent to an exhibitor's participation in an exhibition.

Expenditure Impact Study (ExPact): Study that updates the International Association of Convention and Visitor Bureaus (IACVB) delegate, exhibitor, and event organizer spending information for meetings, conventions, and trade shows. Additionally, ExPact provides an estimate for the economic impact that this industry has on the United States and Canada. Formerly known as the Convention Expenditure and Impact Study.

Exposition: (1) Event at which products and services are displayed. The primary activity of attendees is visiting exhibits on the show floor. These events focus primarily on business-to-business (B2B) relationships. (2) Display of products or promotional material for the purposes of public relations, sales, and/or marketing.

Exposition management company (EMC): Company that is in the business of owning and managing trade shows and expositions. EMCs both develop and produce shows that profit their companies as well as produce events for a sponsoring corporation, association, or government client.

Exposition service contractor (ESC): *See* General Service Contractor (GSC).

Fair: (1) Enterprise principally devoted to the exhibition of products of agriculture or industry. Typically, fairs also provide entertainment activities such as rides, games, and food concessions. (2) Exhibition of products or services in a specific area of activity held with the objective of promoting business.

Fam trip: Familiarization trips. Method of promoting a destination or particular facility to a meeting planner. Fam trips are a no- or low-cost trip for planners to personally review sites for their suitability for a meeting. These trips may be arranged by a local community or by a hotel directly.

Festival: A special celebration usually involving a community.

Field staff: Staff that are responsible for handling the installation and dismantling of freight, drayage, carpentry, electrical equipment, and plumbing and the oversight of iron workers, riggers, and maintenance crews.

First-tier city: City that is notoriously expensive based on the average year-round cost for one night—single room, corporate rate, plus three meals per day, and taxes—at a first-class hotel. *See* Second-tier City.

Fixed costs: Expenses incurred regardless of the number of attendees.

Force majeure: Event (e.g., war, labor strike, extreme weather, or other disruptive circumstances) or effect that cannot be reasonably anticipated or controlled. *Also called* fortuitous event. *See* Act of God.

Frame tent: Tent that is set up on the grass. It is one of the simplest of all meeting venues and requires little advance planning beyond making sure the tent rental people can get set up in time. *Also called* open-sided tent.

Function: (1) Organized occasion that contributes to a larger event. (2) Activity or role assigned to an event planner (or other industry professional).

General service contractor (GSC): Organization hired by the show manager to handle the general duties necessary to produce the show on site, providing a wide range of services. *Also called* official show contractor. *See* Exposition Service Contractor (ESC).

General session: Meeting open to all those in attendance at a event. *See* Plenary Session.

Gesellschaft: German term for company or society.

GMBH: German term for a limited liability company.

Greenwashing: refers to any misrepresentation by a company that leads the consumer to believe that its policies and products are environmentally responsible, when its claims are false, misleading, or cannot be verified. Greenwashing is also used to identify the practice of companies spending more money on the campaign to notify customers of their environmentally friendly efforts, than the efforts themselves

Guarantee: Amount of food that the planner has instructed the facility to prepare and that will be paid for.

Hard data: *See* Quantitative Data.

History: Record of an event over time.

Hotel: A type of accommodation where one pays for the service.

House brand: Brand of wine or distilled spirits selected by a hotel or restaurant as its standard when no specific brand is specified. *Also called* well brand.

Housing bureau: Third-party outsourced company that handles all hotel arrangements for a fee (that may be paid by the local convention and visitor bureau).

IACVB Resource Center: Online center that is a new and developing industry resource and that houses valuable information for CVB professionals. As the center continues to grow, a wealth of resources, such as sample bureau operations documents and bureau research statistics, will be provided. The IACVB Resource Center will also strive to act as a referral source for other industry-related information.

Incentive event: Reward event intended to showcase persons who meet or exceed sales or production goals. *Also called* incentive program.

Incentive trip: Travel reward given by companies to employees to stimulate productivity.

Indirect costs: Costs that are listed as overhead or administrative line items in a program budget. These are organizational expenses not directly related to the meeting, such as staff salaries, overhead, or equipment repair.

In-line exhibit: Exhibit space with exhibit booths on either side and back.

Interactive name tag: RFID either attached to a slim piece of paper behind a badge or made part of a slightly larger wearable name tag device. The RFID-based service offers better networking and interactivity between conference attendees as well as between attendees and vendors.

International Association of Conference Centers (IACC): Association in which member facilities must meet a list of over thirty criteria to be considered an approved conference center.

International Association of Convention and Visitor Bureaus (IACVB): Member of the Convention Industry Council (CIC). Now DMAI.

Island booth: Booth/stand space with aisles on all four sides.

Keynote address: Session that opens or highlights the show, meeting, or event.

Lead retrieval system: Process used to capture customer information. The process begins with the meeting organizer asking questions during the registration process that will identify information of importance to the exhibitor.

Level: (1) Level of audio volume. Level refers to the power magnitude in either electrical watt or acoustic watts but is often incorrectly used to denote voltage. (2) The relative depth of knowledge of attendees.

Local event: Event, such as a graduation ceremony or a local festival, that draws its audience primarily from the local market. Typically 80% of attendees reside within a 50-mile (80-km) radius of the event site. Local audiences typically do not require overnight accommodations.

Loss leader: Item offered by a retailer at cost or less than cost to attract customers. *Also called* price leader.

Material handling: Services performed by general service contractor (GSC) that include delivery of exhibit materials from the dock to assigned space, removal of empty crates, return of crates at the end of the event for recrating, and delivery of materials back to the dock for carrier loading. It is a two-way charge, incoming and outgoing. *See* Drayage.

MEEC: Meetings, expositions, events, and conventions.

Meeting: Event where the primary activity of the attendees is to attend educational sessions, participate in meetings/discussions, socialize, or attend other organized events. There is no exhibit component to this event.

Meeting event order (MEO): Specifications for each function that is part of the overall meeting or event.

Meeting event specification guide: Document used by a planner to communicate specific requirements for a function. It includes a general overview of the event, a timetable outlining all functions that compose the overall event, and specifications for each function that is part of the overall event.

Meeting Industry Network (MINT): Online information network tracking historical and future site/booking information. MINT is provided by the International Association of Convention and Visitor Bureaus (IACVB) to its members. Formerly the Convention Industry Network (CINET).

Meeting professional: Person whose job is to oversee and arrange every aspect of an event. This person can be an employee or hired ad hoc by large companies, professional associations, or trade associations to plan, organize, implement, and control meetings, conventions, and other events.

Meeting Professionals International (MPI): Member organization of the Convention Industry Council (CIC).

Meeting time line: Schedule that includes each task to be accomplished. It is the core of the program plan.

Messe: German term for trade fair.

Messegelande: German term for fair site.

Multilevel exhibit: System often used by large companies to expand their exhibit space without taking up more floor space. The upper floor may be used for special purposes, such as meeting areas, private demonstration areas, or hospitality stations.

Needs analysis: Planning tool used to determine the client's needs and expectations for a meeting.

Negotiation: Process by which a meeting planner and a hotel representative (or other supplier) reach an agreement on the terms and conditions that will govern their relationship before, during, and after a meeting, convention, exposition, or event.

Network: (1) Two or more computers or peripherals that are linked together for the purpose of sharing data. (2) Two or more people gathering in an informal setting.

Nonprofit association: Association whose members may not benefit financially from its net proceeds.

Not-for-profit: Organization that exists with the intention of providing a service for its members.

OfficialTravelGuide.com: Official Web site of the International Association of Convention and Visitor Bureaus (IACVB) that links consumers and meeting professionals directly to the CVBs and tourist boards. On this site, there is official information for 1,000+ destinations, including information on hotels, conference centers, convention centers, attractions, and activities.

Off-premises catering: Foods that are usually prepared in a central kitchen and transported for service to an off-site location.

Online meeting: Web-based service where participants meet virtually, using tools such as shared desktops, PowerPoint presentations, IM/chatting, and voice conferencing.

On-premises catering: Meals that are catered on site during an event.

Opening ceremony: Formal general session at the beginning of a congress or convention.

Operations and production: Performance of the practical work of operating a program. It usually involves the in-house control and handling of all phases of the services, both with suppliers and with clients.

Outlet: Restaurant, lounge, or retail store within a facility.

Outsourcing: Hiring of an outside firm or individual to perform a task instead of using in-house staff or subcontracting of a task or responsibility to a third party.

Parol evidence: Evidence of an oral agreement that can be used in limited instances, especially where the plain meaning of words in the written document may be in doubt. A court will generally construe a contract most strongly against the party that prepared the written document; if there is a conflict between printed and handwritten words or phrases, the latter will prevail.

Peninsula booth: Exhibit with aisles on three sides.

Per diem rate: Rate paid per day. Some event attendees, such as government employees, have a limited amount of money (a daily allowance) they can spend per day on food, lodging, and other expenses.

Permit: License required by many local governments to use parks or even private property for special events. The police, the fire department, and (in many places) the building code officer must be notified when a permit is desired.

Personal digital assistant (PDA): Mobile communications device that provides individuals with most of their critical needs, such as calendars and contacts, in a handheld device.

PLC: German term for public limited company.

Plenary session: General assembly for all participants.

Podcasting: Method of distributing multimedia files, such as audio or video programs, for playback on mobile devices and personal computers.

Pole tent: A temporary fabric-covered shelter that is supported by one or more poles in the middle of the area.

Portal: An electronic access point.

Postconvention meeting: Meeting held after an event to address any billing discrepancies, service failures, and other problems or to praise facility staff for a job well done.

Poster session: (1) Display of reports and papers, usually scientific, accompanied by authors or researchers. (2) Session dedicated to the discussion of the posters shown inside the meeting area. When this discussion is not held in a special session, it can take place directly between the person presenting the poster and interested delegate(s).

Preconvention session: Meeting at the primary facility at which an event will take place just prior to the event beginning. Attendees generally include the primary event organizer and/or representatives of the final adjustments as needed. *Also called* pre-con meeting.

Prefunction space: Area adjacent to the main event location often used for receptions prior to a meal or coffee breaks during an event.

Premium brand: Higher-quality, higher-priced spirits (hard liquor).

Preregistration: Process of registering attendees weeks or months in advance of an event. This benefits the planner in several ways.

Presenter contract: Contract for the person explaining a given topic in an informational session.

Preset service: Style of service that puts plated foods on banquet tables prior to seating guests.

Profile: Detailed information about a traveler and/or a company kept on file by a travel management company.

Program: Schedule of events that gives details of times and places.

Promotional mix model: Mix that includes four elements: advertising, sales promotion, publicity and/or public relations, and personal selling. However, this author views direct marketing as well as interactive media as additional major elements in a promotional mix model.

Proposal: (1) Plan put forth for consideration or acceptance. (2) Communication sent by a supplier to a potential customer detailing the supplier's offerings and prices.

Public show: Exhibition that is open to the public, usually requiring an entrance fee. The attendees are basically defined by their interests and geographic proximity to the show location.

Qualitative data: Descriptive information that is a record of what is observed, presented in narrative by the respondent. *Also called* soft data.

Quantitative data: Information that is represented numerically, that can be assigned ranks or scores, and that can be used to determine averages and frequencies. *Also called* hard data.

Rack rate: Facility's standard preestablished guest room rates.

Radio frequency identification device (RFID): Tag attached to a product or device that emits a short-distance signal that allows the user to accurately track information.

Really simple syndication (RSS): Tool by which a Web site creates or gathers a feed of information about a specific topic and publishes it as an RSS feed. This information is updated continuously.

Request for proposal (RFP): Document that stipulates what services the organization wants from an outside contractor and requests a bid to perform such services.

Return on investment (ROI): Net profit divided by net worth. This financial ratio indicates the degree of profitability.

Risk management: Recognition of and plan for the possibility of injury, damage, or loss as well as the means to prevent it or provide insurance.

Room block: Number of rooms guaranteed by the event planner. These rooms are subtracted from the hotel inventory as attendees make reservations.

Room design software: Computer-aided design (CAD) that is applicable to room design. This software is used to enhance communications between the venue, the meeting planner, and the client.

Room list: Listing that is compiled as attendees reserve rooms with their organization and then given to the hotel. In the case of a small high-profile event, the room list includes the type of room and special requests.

Room setup: Physical arrangement of a room, including the layout of tables, chairs, and other furniture.

Roundtable session: Group of experts who meet on an equal basis to review and discuss specialized professional matters, either in closed session or (more frequently) before an audience.

Russian service: Style of service where foods are cooked tableside on a rechaud (portable cooking stove) that is on a gueridon (tableside cart with wheels). Servers place the food on platters and then pass the platters at tableside. Guests help themselves from the platters.

Sales and marketing: Process of identifying human wants and needs and developing a plan to meet those wants and needs. It encompasses everything involved with convincing an attendee to come to the event and also refers to providing information to support the exhibit sales function.

Schedule: Listing of times and locations for all functions related to an event. This information should be included in the specifications guide for an event.

Schedule of events: Timetable that outlines all functions that compose the overall meeting or event.

Seasonality: Period of time when the demand for a certain supplier's product or service is usually high, low, or neither. For example, winter in Florida is high season, while summer is low season.

Second-tier city: Destination city that is often more affordable than major cities. It is more likely to negotiate the best prices for accommodations and services. *See* First-tier City.

Service contractor: Outside company used by clients to provide specific products or services (e.g., pipe and drape, exhibitor manuals, floor plans, dance floors, or flags).

Shoulder: Beginning and ending days of a room block when fewer rooms are contracted.

Shoulder season: Period when the demand for a supplier's product or service is neither high nor low.

Showcase: Event to preview/highlight someone or something.

Signing authority: Person from the sponsoring organization who has the authority to make additions or changes to what has been ordered.

Site inspection: In-person on-site review and evaluation of a venue or location for an event. *See* Fam Trip.

Site selection: Process of deciding the physical location for the event, the type of facility to use, the transportation options, and many other meeting components.

SMART: Acronym for the critical components of a well-written objective: Specific, Measurable, Achievable, Relevant, Time.

Smart phone: 3G phone that supports not only voice but high-speed data transmission. This allows the smart phone to be used for services such as Web browsing, e-mail access, and audio/video streaming.

SMERF: Acronym for certain categories of meeting market segments: Social, Military, Educational, Religious, and Fraternal.

Social event: (1) Event with the purpose of facilitating pleasant companionship among attendees or (2) life cycle celebration (e.g., wedding, bar/bat mitzvah, anniversary, birthday).

Soft data: *See* Qualitative Data.

Speaker bureau: Professional talent broker who can help find the perfect speaker to match the event objectives as well as the budget.

Speaker guidelines: (1) Instructions regarding the specific expectations for a speaker at an event. Usually outlined is the required format for presentations, AV request procedures, travel and accommodations instructions, etc. (2) Instructions regarding the required format to be used for the written preparation of a speech.

Speaker ready room: Area set aside for speakers to meet, relax, test audiovisual equipment, or prepare prior to or between speeches. *Also called* ready room and try-out room.

Special event: One-time event staged for the purpose of celebration; unique activity.

Specialty service contractor: Supplier that deals with a specific area of show production or event service, such as photography, furniture rental, audiovisual equipment, or floral decoration.

Specification Guide: Spec Guide. The industry preferred term for a comprehensive document that outlines the complete requirements and instructions for an event. This document is typically authored by the event planner and is shared with all appropriate vendors as a vehicle to communicate the expectations of services for a project. *Sometimes called* Staging Guide, Resume, Bible.

Sponsor: (1) Person or company underwriting all or part of the costs of an event. Sponsors may or may not participate in any of the profit from the event. (2) Individual who assumes all or part of the financial responsibility for an event or commercial sponsor that provides financial backing for an aspect of an event and in return receives visibility, advertising, or other remuneration in lieu of cash.

Sporting event: Event where athletes compete and spectators view the athletic activities and ceremonies.

Stadium: Facility that is usually designed for baseball or football as a primary function and that may be domed or open. It is sometimes difficult to distinguish a stadium from a large arena.

Stand: European term for booth or exhibit. *See* Standard Booth.

Standard booth: One or more standard units of exhibit space. In the United States, a standard unit is generally known to be a 10-foot by 10-foot space (one standard booth/stand unit equals 100 square feet). However, if an exhibitor purchases multiple units side by side or back to back, the combined space is also still referred to as a booth or a stand. It is a specific area assigned by management to an exhibitor under contractual agreement. *See* Stand.

Theater: Facility with fixed seats, usually on a sloped floor, with sight lines focused on a permanent stage. Typically, a stage box is located behind the proscenium, which contains the performance area and the fly loft.

Theme party: Event at which all foods, beverages, decorations, and entertainment relate to a single theme.

Track: Separation of programming into specific genres, such as computer skills, professional development, marketing, personal growth, legal issues, certification courses, and financial issues.

Trade exhibition: *See* Trade Show.

Trade fair: International term for an exhibition.

Trade Fair Certification Program: Program developed by the U.S. Department of Commerce to promote exports of U.S. products and services abroad. The Trade Fair Certification Program endorses independent and association show organizers who manage and organize overseas events. The certification helps trade fairs attract more exhibitors, provides additional support and value-added services for exhibitors, and promotes the event through a variety of publications and sources.

Trade show: Exhibition of products and/or services held for members of a common or related industry that is not open to the general public.

Trade show bond: Method used so that goods can be temporarily imported to an international show site without having to pay duties or taxes. *See* Carnet.

Variable costs: Expenses that vary based on the number of attendees.

Venue: (1) Site or destination of meeting, event, or show. (2) Location of a performance, such as a hall, a ballroom, or an auditorium.

Videoconference: Conference that uses video (and typically audio) to send content to and from facilities. Traditionally, videoconferencing is not Web-based; it uses production facilities to both upload and download the information.

VIP services: Services provided to a very important person who has a special function at the event (speaker, dignitary, etc.) and who should be treated with special care and attention.

Virtual tour: Technology tool that is ideal for remote site inspections but that can also be used in tandem with a traditional site visit (perhaps used with a laptop or personal computer), where a planner can call up alternate room setups and capacity information at a single click.

Virtual trade show: Attendee-based trade show that is an online experience where the individual can "walk the floor" and "visit booths" without leaving his or her home or office. Varying styles of interactivity and graphics are used in this approach.

Voice over Internet protocol (VoIP): Digital telephone that is used with a high-speed Internet connection to make and receive phone calls.

Webcasting: Streaming audio and video, using the Web as the delivery tool to deliver content to individuals.

Web conferencing: Catch-all term to describe the various types of e-learning options available to the planner and attendee.

Well brand: Brand of wine or distilled spirits selected by a hotel or restaurant as its standard when no specific brand is specified. *Also called* house brand.

Workshop: (1) Meeting of several persons for intensive discussion. The workshop concept has been developed to compensate for diverging views in a particular discipline or on a particular subject. (2) Informal and public session of free discussion organized to take place between formal plenary sessions or commissions of a congress or of a conference, either on a subject chosen by the participants themselves or on a special problem suggested by the organizers. (3) Training session in which participants, often through exercises, develop skills and knowledge in a given field.

World Trade Centers Association: Association created in 1970 as an apolitical not-for-profit organization to promote the concept of world trade centers worldwide and to encourage reciprocal programs among all of its members. Today, there are more than 300 world trade centers in 91 countries servicing more than 750,000 international businesses.

Yield management: Computer program that uses variable pricing models to maximize the return on a fixed (perishable) inventory, such as hotel rooms, based on supply-and-demand theory.

INDEX